RAILROADS AND AMERICAN ECONOMIC GROWTH:

Essays in Econometric History

RAILROADS AND AMERICAN ECONOMIC GROWTH:

Essays in Econometric History

BY

Robert William Fogel

THE JOHNS HOPKINS PRESS, BALTIMORE AND LONDON

The Johns Hopkins Press, Baltimore, Maryland 21218
The Johns Hopkins Press Ltd., London

ISBN-0-8018-0201-6 (clothbound edition)
ISBN-0-8018-1148-1 (paperback edition)

Originally published, 1964
Second printing, 1970
Johns Hopkins Paperbacks edition, 1970

TO MY SONS

MICHAEL AND STEVEN

Preface and Acknowledgments

The pages that follow contain a critical evaluation of the proposition that railroads were indispensable to American economic growth during the nineteenth century. The analysis is, for the most part, based on the accepted narrative of the American transportation system. However, certain limited but crucial aspects of the narrative are re-examined with the aid of the analytical and quantitative techniques of modern economics.

Particular emphasis is placed on measuring the incremental contribution of railroads to the level of national output. Chapters II and III estimate the amount by which the production possibilities of the nation would have been reduced if agricultural commodities could not have been shipped by railroads. In this connection an attempt is made to establish boundaries beyond which commercial production would have ceased. The possibility that alternative forms of transportation could have been extended and the potential impact of such extensions on the social loss that would have been occasioned by the absence of the railroad are also considered.

The first problem in evaluating the increment in manufacturing output directly attributable to the construction and maintenance of railroads is the absence of aggregated data on the railroads' consumption of various goods. The extent of the research involved in reconstructing the missing information precluded the attempt to go on to the more basic question of incremental effects. However, even when consideration is limited to gross consumption, the findings of Chapters IV and V reveal that the impact of railroads on the rise of manufacturing during the antebellum era was more limited than is usually presumed.

Many conspicuous social and political aspects of railroads are not discussed in this volume. The omission does not imply the view that such matters are uninteresting or irrelevant to an understanding of American economic growth. Rather, they are too important to be treated casually; and they are too complex to be treated adequately within the confines of a study that focuses on a specifically defined set of economic problems.

While most historians will agree that the subject matter of the volume is drawn from their domain, some will reject the methodology as alien to the spirit and purpose of their discipline. But if history is to attempt to reveal what actually happened in the past, then the methodology employed below cannot be dismissed. For this methodology yields results which contradict prevailing assumptions on a series of major issues.

I do not mean to suggest that the highly detailed, explicitly theoretical, and quantitative type of analysis presented herein is the only useful type of economic history. In the exploration of large and complex historical phenomena, impressionistic surveys are extremely valuable. The essays in this volume could not have been written without the enormous pre-existing literature on railroads, much of which is loosely constructed.

It is, of course, impossible to challenge simultaneously the whole body of accepted knowledge of a phenomenon as many-sided as the nexus between railroads and economic growth. The most that can be done at any point is to determine the consistency between a limited set of statements and the remaining body of the accepted historical evidence. Hence the validity of the conclusions presented below cannot be absolute. Nevertheless, to the extent that these conclusions are the consequence of corrections in unwarranted assumptions, they represent an advance in existing knowledge and are a demonstration of the applicability of scientific methods to the study of history.

During the more than five years of work on the essays, I have incurred a long list of obligations. None are greater than those I owe to my supervisors, Simon Kuznets and G. Herberton Evans, Jr. This study was prompted by one of Professor Kuznets' lectures on economic growth. To footnote all the particular ideas that were suggested in private discussions with him, by his classroom lectures, or in his writings is not feasible. If readers familiar with the work of Professor Kuznets detect methodological as well as substantive similarities, it is because I have consciously tried to emulate that blend of the empirical and the deductive which is the hallmark of his studies. Dean Evans was unstinting in extending moral and material support to my work. The discussions I had with him, especially those that took place during my first year of research, helped me in discriminating between the primary and the secondary in the topic I had chosen.

During my residence at Johns Hopkins I profited from Professor Fritz Machlup's lectures on "Methodology" and "The Theory of Relative Incomes"; these heightened my appreciation of the applicability and power of formal economic theory in the study of history. As in the case of my monograph on the Union Pacific, Professors James K. Kindahl and Edwin S. Mills gave generously of their time in discussions which helped to clarify the theoretical implications of various quantifying techniques.

I am particularly indebted to my colleague and friend Richard N. Rosett of the University of Rochester. In addition to the benefits I derived from stimulating discussions with him on theoretical and statistical problems, I gained from the valuable suggestions he made while reading virtually every draft of every chapter. Professor Rosett also programmed two important computations.

I was first introduced to the important developmental issues connected with railroads by Carter Goodrich. Professor Goodrich read most of the chapters of this study and made many helpful suggestions.

Criticisms made by Albert Fishlow enabled me to improve the arguments of Chapters IV and V. My research on the iron industry was facilitated by Peter Temin who generously made his findings on this industry available to me. Douglass C. North and William N. Parker provided both general and specific criticisms of a late draft of the study. Professor Parker's editing of the original essay that forms the basis of Chapter II was more than stylistic; he discovered certain errors in my earlier estimates.

Others who have read drafts, brought errors to my attention, or provided me with opportunities for discussion include Lewis W. Beck, Yoram Barzel, James P. Baughman, James Cairnes, Thomas C. Cochran, Alfred Conrad, Willson H. Coates, John H. Dales, Paul David, David Donald, Alexander Eckstein, Stanley Engerman, Everett M. Hafner, Muriel E. Hidy, Ralph W. Hidy, Paul W. Gates, Harry Grubert, Ronald W. Jones, Lionel W. McKenzie, Walter Oi, Rudolph Penner, Ruth Rasch, Jack Richardson, Hugh Rose, Lester Telser, Hirofumi Uzawa, Glydon Van Deusen, William Whitney, Jeffry Williamson, Peter Winch, and Edward Zabel. If this list were extended many-fold, it would still be incomplete.

Mr. Samir Dasgupta was my principal research assistant for three years. He aided in the computation of most of the tables and charts in Chapters III, IV, and V and prepared all of the final drawings. Mr. R. K. Koshal conducted most of the detailed and difficult research required to locate the proposed canals shown in Figure 3.5. He prepared the original profiles of the canals as well as the map in Appendix A. Enid M. Fogel, Akihiro Amano, A. Anastasopoulos, K. S. Chhatwal, Blair Currie, Emmanuel Drandakis, Steven Frazer, Clell Harral, Constantine S. Kalman, Nobuo Minabe, and Edwin Schulman aided me as research assistants during various phases of the study.

Martina Gold, Jane Munk, and Alan Feiveson efficiently programmed most of the larger computations in Chapters III, IV, and V. Donald

G. Adam ably edited drafts of the first, fourth, fifth, and sixth chapters.

I also benefited from the aid I received from John R. Russell, Director of the Library at the University of Rochester; Margaret E. Lough, Head of the Social Sciences Library at Johns Hopkins University; Morris Rieger, Archivist-in-charge of the Labor and Transportation Branch at the National Archives; John Hansley of the Civilian Records Branch in the Federal Record Center at Alexandria; and Arch C. Gerlach, Chief of the Map Division of the Library of Congress.

Marian W. Duncan, Rosemary K. Currie, Alma C. Saraydar, Marguerite Gross, Mildred Verblaw, and members of the secretarial pool of the College of Arts and Sciences under the direction of Marian A. McClintock at the University of Rochester typed the many early drafts. The final draft was typed by Carolyn Johannsen and Delores Gardner.

The research on which this volume is based was made possible by fellowships and grants from the Department of Economics at Johns Hopkins University, the Social Science Research Council, The Ford Faculty Fund of the Department of Economics at the University of Rochester, the Faculty Grants-in-Aid Program of the College of Arts and Science at the University of Rochester, and the Ford Foundation Research Professorship of the University of Chicago. The Department of Economics at the University of Rochester provided me with research assistants, programmers, and computing time.

I am grateful to the *Journal of Economic History* for their permission to reprint, in somewhat altered form, the major portion of my essay, "A Quantitative Approach to the Study of Railroads in American Economic Growth: A Report of Some Preliminary Findings," *The Journal of Economic History,* XXII, No. 2 (June, 1962), 163–97. Rand McNally and Company generously gave their permission for the reproduction of the map used as the base of Figure 3.4.

ROBERT W. FOGEL

Chicago, Illinois

Contents

Preface and Acknowledgments vii

I. THE ISSUES 1
   The Evolution of the "Axiom of Indispensability" 1
   The Supply of Alternative Opportunities 10

II. THE INTERREGIONAL DISTRIBUTION OF AGRICULTURAL
    PRODUCTS 17
    The Geographical Pattern of Production and Distribution 17
    The Conceptual Basis of the Test 19
    The Data Problem 29
    A Preliminary Estimate of the Social Saving 37

III. THE INTRAREGIONAL DISTRIBUTION OF AGRICULTURAL
     PRODUCTS 49
     The Estimation of the Social Saving 52
     The Data Problem 58
     Preliminary α and β Estimates 73
     *The Possibility of Technological Adaptation to a Non-Rail
     Situation* 91

IV. RAILROADS AND THE "TAKE-OFF" THESIS: THE AMERICAN
    CASE 111
    Structural Change During the "Take-off" 114
    Railroads and the Leading Sectors Thesis 129

V. THE POSITION OF RAILS IN THE MARKET FOR AMERICAN
   IRON, 1840–60: A RECONSTRUCTION 147
   *The Index of the Position of Rails in the Market
   for American Iron* 149
   The Domestic Production of Pig Iron 151
   The Production and Consumption of Rails 166
   Rails and the Domestic Consumption of Iron 190

VI. SUMMARY AND INTERPRETATION 207
    The Primary Effect of Railroads 208
    The Derived Effects 224
    Implications for the Theory of Economic Growth 234
    *Measurement and Theory in the Study of Economic
    History* 237

Appendix A. An Extended System of Internal Navigation in 1890 250
Appendix B. Some Material Supplementary to the Chapter
                on Rails 254
Selected Bibliography 263
Index 287

List of Tables

TABLE   PAGE

2.1 Shipments of Corn and Wheat from Primary Markets, 1890 31
2.2 Estimated Requirements of Secondary Markets 34
2.3 A Comparison of the Estimates of the Local Consumption
     Deficits of Wheat for Two Trading Areas 35
2.4 Estimate of the Average Actual Rate 39
2.5 First Approximation of the Social Saving 42
2.6 Estimated Cost of Insurance 43
3.1 Tonnage Entering into Intraregional Transportation, 1870
     and 1890 58
3.2 Preliminary α Estimate of the Intraregional Social Saving in
     the North Atlantic Division 60
3.3 Per Capita Consumption of Butter by Regions 62
3.4 Butter Shipped Out of County 63
3.5 Amount by Which $\bar{Z}^i$ Understates Z^i in the North Atlantic
     Region 65
3.6 Agricultural Products Shipped from Counties, 1890 76
3.7 Loss in National Product due to Decrease in the Supply of
     Land 82
3.8 First Approximation of the β Estimate 86
3.9 First Approximation of the α Estimate 87
3.10 Preliminary α and β Estimates 92
3.11 Proposed Canals 94
3.12 Loss in National Product due to Decrease in Land Supply
     after Construction of Proposed Canals 99
3.13 α and β Estimates Adjusted to Take Account of the Pos-
     sibility of Extending Internal Navigation 100
3.14 α and β Estimates Adjusted to Reflect Both the Extension of
     Internal Navigation and a Reduction in Wagon Rates 110
4.1 The Percentage Distribution of Income in Current Prices by
     Nine Sectors—Martin's Data 116

TABLE   PAGE

4.2   The Percentage Distribution of Income in Current Prices by
      Three Sectors—Martin's Data 117
4.3   Percentage Distribution of Income Originating in Commodity
      Production—Martin's Current Price Data 117
4.4   Percentage Distribution of Value Added in Commodity
      Production—Gallman's Current Price Data 118
4.5   Percentage Distribution of Value Added in Commodity
      Production—Gallman's Constant Dollar Series 119
4.6   Absolute Increases in Manufacturing's Share of Value Added
      in Commodity Production—Gallman's Constant Dollar
      Series 121
4.7   Cotton Spindles in Operation in Twelve States, 1820 and 1831 123
4.8   The Consumption of Domestic Iron by Railroads, 1840–60.. 132
4.9   The Consumption of Lumber by Railroads, 1840–60 138
4.10 Value Added in 1859 by Industries Supplying Transportation
      Equipment for Steam Railroads 140
4.11 An Estimate of the Proportion of Value Added in the Pro-
      duction of Machinery Attributable to Railroads, 1859 142
4.12 Value Added in Manufacturing Attributable to Railroad Con-
      sumption of Manufactured Goods, 1859 145
5.1   Production of Pig Iron as Estimated by Grosvenor and Carey 154
5.2   Capacity of Blast Furnaces in Pennsylvania at Year End ... 154
5.3   Prices of British and American Pig Iron 161
5.4   Estimated Production of Pig Iron in Pennsylvania, 1845–47 162
5.5   The Relative Position of Pennsylvania in the National Output
      of Pig Iron 164
5.6   The Revised Estimates of Pig Iron Production 166
5.7   The Distribution of the Wear of Iron Rails 172
5.8   The Estimated Consumption of Rails, 1830–69 174
5.9   Average Weight of Rails on Main Track in 1840 and 1869.. 179
5.10 Average Weight of Rails Laid on Main Track by Years,
      1830–40 181
5.11 Estimated Average Weight of Rails Laid on Track, 1830–69 182
5.12 The Inventory Cycle in Rails 183
5.13 Rails Scrapped, 1840–69 189
5.14 The Production and Consumption of Crude Iron, 1840–60... 192
5.15 Pig Iron and the Production of Rails, 1840–60 194

TABLE   PAGE

5.16 Crude Iron Used in the Production and Consumption of Rails, 1840–60 196

5.17 A Comparison of Indexes I_2, I_4, I_5, and I_6 200

6.1 The Social Saving in the Interregional Distribution of Agricultural Commodities 211

6.2 Preliminary α Estimate 214

6.3 Loss in National Product due to the Decrease in the Supply of Land (By Regions) 217

6.4 Preliminary β Estimate 217

B2.1 A Value Index (I_1) of the Position of Rails in the Market for Iron, 1856 256

List of Charts

CHARTS   PAGE

5.1 The Production of Pig Iron, 1840–1860 167

5.2 The Values of M_t When Estimated From Poor's Data, Shuman's Data and the Average of the Two Series 170

5.3 The Effect of Changes in the Form and Parameters of the Model of Rail Wear on M_t 173

5.4 Estimated Quantities of Rails Used for New Construction and Replacements 175

5.5 A Comparison between M_t and the A.I.S.A. Data 177

5.6 A Comparison between M_t and the A.I.S.A. Data Adjusted for Changes in the Average Weight of Rails 185

5.7 The Inventory Cycle in Rails 186

5.8 Rails Scrapped, 1840–1869 190

5.9 The Production of Pig Iron and the Consumption of Crude Iron 191

5.10 Rail Consumption, Crude Iron Used for the Domestic Production of Rails, and Net Consumption of Domestic Pig Iron Directly Attributable to Rails 197

5.11 A Comparison of Indexes I_2, I_4, I_5, and I_6 198

List of Figures

FIGURES   PAGE

3.4 Area of Feasible Commercial Agriculture 81

FIGURES   PAGE

3.5   Proposed Canals 93
3.6   Profiles of Proposed Canals in Michigan, Indiana, Illinois,
      Wisconsin, Minnesota, and Iowa 101
3.7   Profiles of Proposed Canals in Minnesota, Iowa, North
      Dakota, and South Dakota 102
3.8   Profiles of Proposed Canals in Iowa, Missouri, Nebraska,
      and Kansas 103
3.9   Profiles of Proposed Canals in Missouri, Kansas, and Texas 104
3.10 Canals in New York 105

A.1   An Extended System of
      Internal Navigation in 1890 .... (following) 250

CHAPTER I

The Issues

In history as anywhere else in empirical science, the explanation of a phenomenon consists in subsuming it under general empirical laws; and the criterion of its soundness is not whether it appeals to our imagination, whether it is presented in suggestive analogies, or is otherwise made to appear plausible—all this may occur in pseudo-explanations as well—but exclusively whether it rests on empirically well confirmed assumptions concerning initial conditions and general laws.—CARL G. HEMPEL

The prevailing interpretation of the influence of railroads on American economic growth during the nineteenth century is still dominated by hypotheses spawned during that era. This long rule has been facilitated by three features of recent historiography: first, the acceptance of certain propositions propounded during the Gilded Age as obvious truths that did not require critical examination; second, a tendency to analyze issues connected with the construction and operation of railroads within the conceptual framework established during the post-Civil War debates on railroad policy; and third, a failure to exploit the quantitative techniques and theoretical tools of modern economics. Escape from the confines of the past is never easy; it has been particularly difficult in this case. The evidence that must be re-examined is vast, and the economic significance of railroads is intricately intertwined with a host of social and political issues. Under these circumstances the re-evaluation of the nineteenth century conception of the place of railroads in American economic development must be a process rather than a single act. Such a process has in fact been under way for some time. However, the required revisions are much more extensive than has been generally recognized.

THE EVOLUTION OF THE "AXIOM OF INDISPENSABILITY"

The railroad was not born with the distinction attributed to it by later generations. Far from being viewed as essential to economic de-

1

velopment, the first railroads were widely regarded as having only limited commercial application. Extreme skeptics argued that railroads were too crude to insure regular service, that the sparks thrown off by belching engines would set fire to buildings and fields, and that speeds of 20 or 30 miles an hour could be "fatal to wagons, road and loading, as well as to human life." More sober critics questioned the ability of railroads to provide low cost transportation, especially for heavy freight. Benjamin Wright, a superintendent of construction on the Erie Canal and adviser to the New York Legislature on the Erie railroad, placed "a railroad between a good turnpike and a canal" in transportation efficiency. Even railroad executives appear to have had, at least initially, a limited conception of the role of railroads. Most of the first enterprises expected to make their profit largely by carrying passengers, by serving small localities, and by serving as feeders to waterways. The prevailing opinion of the thirties appears to have been expressed in a report presented to the New York Legislature by three engineers. "We are . . . led to the conclusion," they wrote, "that in regard to the cost of construction and maintenance and also in reference to the expense of conveyance at moderate velocities, canals are clearly the most advantageous means of communication. On the other hand, where high velocities are required, as for the conveyance of passengers, and under some circumstances of competition, for light goods of great value, in proportion to their weight, the preference would be given to a railroad."[1]

By the mid-forties most of the early doubts about railroads were quelled. Some four thousand miles of track had been built in the East and South and iron rails were pushing past the Appalachian barrier into the states of the Old Northwest. Considerable advances had been made in railroad technology. Engines were larger, more powerful, and less prone to breakdowns. These and other developments made it possible for trains to pass through mountainous regions as well as over level terrain. Railroad advocates no longer argued the feasibility of railroads. Although waterways still carried the great bulk of the nation's freight, far-sighted innovators now declared that the "iron horse" had superseded the waterway in inland transportation and proposed vast projects for covering the nation with railroads. J. W. Scott, editor of the *Toledo Blade,* was one of these prophets. "The railroad," he proclaimed, "has become the great instrument of land commerce and trade." But railroads were not being built rapidly enough. "No nation," he asserted, "can

[1] The three quotations are cited on pages 10, 37, and 42 respectively of Thurman William Van Metre, *Early Opposition to Steam Railroads* (New York, 1924).

maintain its position among the foremost in civilization" without fully exploiting this new means of transportation. He, therefore, called on Congress to finance the construction of six great trunk lines: two running north and south—along the Atlantic seaboard and from the Great Lakes to New Orleans; four leading from the Atlantic seaboard to the West—along routes which today roughly parallel the New York Central, the Pennsylvania, the Chesapeake and Ohio, and the Southern railroads. Such a system of trunk lines, said Scott, would transform the nation:

> To commercial exchanges through the interior, it would give an activity beyond anything witnessed heretofore in inland trade. A face of gladness would animate every department of toil, and new motives be held out to activity in enterprise. Social as well as commercial intercourse of the people of distant States, would break down local prejudices and annihilate sectional misunderstandings. The wages of labor would be improved, and the profits of capital increased beyond the whole cost of these works. . . . As long as the hills stand, or the valleys disclose their beauty, so long will these works bear evidence to posterity of the energy and spirit of those who erected them.[2]

Congress did not adopt the specific program called for by Scott. But it did turn in the direction suggested by such prophets. Between 1850 and 1872 the federal government gave an empire of land to promoters who promised to build railroads across the sparsely settled territory of the West. While Congress dispensed over 100,000,000 acres of the public domain, state and local governments provided an additional $280,-000,000 in cash or credit (about 30 per cent of the total capitalization of railroads) in the decades preceding the Civil War.[3] Spurred by such inducements the railroad network expanded swiftly. The legacy left to the Gilded Age included a system of track over 35,000 miles long—almost half the world's total.[4]

In 1867 the *North American Review* surveyed the effects wrought by railroads and found that they were stupendous. "With perhaps two exceptions," it said, the railroad was "the most tremendous and far-

---

[2] J. W. Scott, "A National System of Railways," *Merchants' Magazine and Commercial Review*, XVII (December, 1847), 564–71.

[3] Carter Goodrich, *Government Promotion of American Canals and Railroads, 1800-1890* (New York, 1959), pp. 268–70.

[4] U.S. Bureau of the Census, *Historical Statistics of the United States, Colonial Times to 1957* (Washington, D. C., 1960), p. 427; hereafter referred to as *Historical Statistics* (1960).

reaching engine of social revolution which has ever either blessed or cursed the earth." It was this innovation that "made our century different from all others—a century of greater growth, of more rapid development." The railroad, the distinguished journal held, had peopled the "wilds of America" and turned "the very Arabs of civilization" into "substantial communities." It made the nation cosmopolitan; removed the old distinctions between classes, changing both dress and manners; "abolished" the Mississippi River; crushed the southern rebellion; made "the grass grow in the once busy streets of small commercial centers, like Nantucket, Salem, and Charleston"; robbed "New Orleans of that monopoly of wealth which the Mississippi River once promised to pour into her lap"; and simultaneously turned New York into "an overgrown monster." The "iron arms" of the railroad, the *Review* concluded, "have been stretched out in every direction; nothing has escaped their reach, and the most firmly established institutions of man have proved under their touch as plastic as clay."[5]

Thus by the opening of the Gilded Age the railroad had already won a strong claim to the title of indispensability. During the next three decades the concept of the railroad as the chief agent of economic and social transformation became an integral part of popular thought. The further extension of the railroad network—to 181,000 miles in 1895—made what was an imposing industry at the close of the Civil War even more monumental.[6] Companies engaged in competing forms of transportation were vanquished one after the other as the railroad technology advanced. The size, speed, and pulling power of locomotives increased; the substitution of steel for iron rails permitted larger and heavier loads. At the same time the rail network, which had been a discontinuous conglomeration of segments with track gauges varying from 3 to 6 feet, was rationalized into an integrated system with a uniform gauge of 4 feet, 8½ inches. As a result of these and other changes the average cost of commodity transportation by railroad dropped more than 50 per cent during the Gilded Age—from 1.925 cents per ton-mile in 1867 to 0.839 cents in 1895.[7] By 1890 railroads had achieved almost complete domination of intercity freight shipments. The magnitude of the railroad victory over its chief competitor—waterways—is summarized by two ratios: in

[5] "The Railroad System," *North American Review*, CIV (1867), 476–511.

[6] *Historical Statistics* (1960), p. 429.

[7] H. T. Newcomb, *Changes in the Rates of Charge for Railway and Other Transportation Services*, U.S. Department of Agriculture, Division of Statistics, Bull. No. 15, revised, 1901, p. 14; hereafter referred to as *Changes in Rates*.

1851-52 boats carried six times as much freight as railroads; in 1889-90 railroads carried five times as much freight as boats.[8]

To the men of the Gilded Age the primacy of the railroad in the promotion of American economic growth became an indisputable fact. Among the most obvious of the many effects assigned to the railroad was the rapid growth of the internal market. Available statistical data, particularly those bearing on the development of states west of the Alleghanies, appeared to give unambiguous support to this attribution. States such as Indiana, Illinois, Michigan, and Ohio experienced a marked increase in population, construction, and manufacturing following the completion of rail lines across their territories. And these states together with Minnesota, Nebraska, Iowa, Wisconsin, and Kansas replaced New York and Pennsylvania as the granary of the nation. Common sense also supported the attribution. "If produce cannot be carried," said an observer in 1866, "it can only find local markets. If it only finds local markets, prices must abate. If prices abate the stimulus to cultivation is lost. . . . The prosperity of the West, the value of its produce, the value of its land, and the extent of land cultivated—all depend, therefore, upon increased facilities for the conveyance of produce; and these facilities railroads must afford."[9]

Economic theory also appeared to support the attribution. Richard T. Ely, a distinguished economist of the era, deduced "a universal dependency on the railway" from the proposition that productivity depended on the division of labor. For a "primary condition" for the "widespread, far-reaching division of labor" that characterized their epoch, said Ely, was "the improved means of communication and transportation which the inventions and discoveries of our century have placed at our disposal."[10] Sidney Dillon gave vivid expression to the dominant opinion at the close of the Gilded Age when he wrote:

> The growth of the United States west of the Alleghanies during the past fifty years is due not so much to free institutions, or climate,

---

[8] There was double counting in the data on which these ratios are based. U.S. Congress, Senate, *Andrews Report,* Exec. Doc. No. 112, 32nd Cong., 1st Sess., pp. 903-6; U.S. Bureau of the Census, *Eleventh Census of the United States: 1890, Report on the Transportation Business,* Part I, pp. 452, 548, 640; Part II, pp. 9, 10, 163, 308, 384, 436, 479; the second citation will hereafter be referred to as *Census of Transportation, 1890.*

[9] Sir S. Morton Peto, *Resources and Prospects of America* (New York and Philadelphia, 1866), p. 281.

[10] Richard T. Ely, "Social Studies; I. The Nature of the Railway Problem," *Harper's Magazine,* Vol. 73 (1886), p. 252.

or the fertility of the soil, as to railways. If . . . railways had not
been invented, the freedom and natural advantages of our Western
States would have beckoned to human immigration and industry in
vain. Civilization would have crept slowly on, in a toilsome march
over the immense spaces that lie between the Appalachian ranges
and the Pacific Ocean; and what we now style the Great West
would be, except in the valley of the Mississippi, an unknown and
unproductive wilderness.[11]

The dominant role of railroads in determining the course of economic
growth also appeared to be inherent in the great power that railroads
exercised over the commercial destinies of individual firms and groups
of firms. The investigations of railroad rate practices by a special committee of the New York State Assembly (the Hepburn Committee) in
1879 did much to develop public consciousness of the rate-making power.
The proceedings revealed a pattern of special contracts with favored
shippers at rates below those rates generally charged. The most publi-
cized example of the practice was the Standard Oil case. The Pennsylvania Railroad entered into a contract with the Rockefeller organization
under which it agreed to maintain the business of Standard Oil "against
injury or loss by competition" by raising the rates charged to other
refiners "as far as it legally may, for such times and to such extent as
may be necessary to overcome such competition."[12] The Standard Oil
Company, said Ely, received "$10,000,000 in eighteen months in rebates.
If it had done business at what would have been cost for others, it would
still have had that enormous sum as profit. . . . It is a matter of course
that its competitors were ruined."[13]

Few rebates were as large as those granted to Standard Oil. But few
had to be. In the shipment of such commodities "as wheat, coal and
flour," noted William Larrabee, Governor of Iowa, "a small advantage
in rates is sufficient to enable the favored shipper to 'freeze out' all competitors."[14] According to the Hepburn Committee, a concession on railroad rates equal to less than 4 per cent of the market price of wheat
enabled two firms to control the grain trade of the largest secondary

[11] Sidney Dillon, "The West and the Railroads," *North American Review,*
CLII (1891), 443.
[12] State of New York, Legislature, Assembly, *Proceedings of the Special Committee on Railroads* (8 vols.; Albany, 1879), Vol. 6, p. 41; hereafter referred to
as the Hepburn Committee.
[13] Richard T. Ely, "Social Studies; II. The Economic Evils in American Railway Methods," *Harper's Magazine,* Vol. 73 (1886), p. 455.
[14] William Larrabee, *The Railroad Question* (Chicago, 1893), p. 141.

market in the nation—New York City—during the winter of 1877.[15]
"The railway charge is so important an element in the prices of every
commodity carried from a distance in the United States . . . ," declared
Simon Sterne, counsel for the New York Board of Trade, "that it is
within the power of our railway magnates to become partners in every
special line of occupation, and it is this power to destroy and to build up
which no community can allow to roam and exercise itself unchecked,
which must be restrained, curbed and rendered subservient to the general
public weal through the instrumentality of wise legislation rigidly
enforced."[16]

In the course of the bitter battles over government control, the indispensability of railroads to American economic growth was elevated to
the status of an axiomatic truth. Critics and defenders of railroad
management argued about the appropriate basis for setting rates, the
size of a fair profit, the necessity of various types of discrimination, the
effectiveness of competition, and the wisdom of private pools, but they
rarely debated the indispensability of railroads. Quite the contrary, the
invocation of the "axiom of indispensability" was usually the first step
in the argument of every disputant. "By the aid of the railway," said an
advocate of strong government action, "the wilderness has been made
productive, countless farms brought within the reach of the great markets, mines opened, mills, factories, and forges built, villages, towns, and
cities brought into existence, and populous States carried to a higher
development than would have been possible in centuries without such
aids." This great power, he argued, made railroads "public trusts."
Managers of railroads, however, had violated the trust placed in their
care by using "watery fiction, to extort from railway users the enormous
sum of $1,592,280,471" in 15 years. It was therefore the duty of legisla-
tures "to formulate such statutes as will protect user and investor, both
of whom are at the mercy of a small body of men who can and do make
and mar the fortunes of individuals, cities, and States, without let or
hinderance."[17] Opponents of government control found the axiom
equally useful in opposing government action. "Let us imagine for a
moment," the president of one of the nation's leading railroad complexes
suggested, "that all the railways in the United States were at once an-
nihilated. Such a catastrophe is not, in itself, inconceivable; the imagina-

---

[15] Hepburn Committee, *Proceedings,* Vol. 6, p. 57.
[16] *Ibid.,* Vol. 4, p. 3971.
[17] C. Wood Davis, "The Farmer, the Investor, and the Railway," *The Arena,*
Vol. 3 (1891), pp. 291–313.

tion *can* grasp it; but no imagination can picture the infinite sufferings that would at once result to every man, woman, and child in the entire country. Now, every step taken to impede or cripple the business and progress of our railways," he concluded, "is a step towards just such a catastrophe, and therefore of a destructive tendency."[18]

While many distinguished treatises have been written on railroad history and related topics in recent decades, it is no slight to the importance of these works to point out that their central focus has not usually been analysis of the effects of railroads on economic growth. Most studies of railroad history tend to subordinate the interaction between the railroads and the growth process to more limited issues— to tracing the origin of the railroad "idea," to the early difficulties in winning popular support, to descriptions of the spread and integration of the network, to the study of railroad entrepreneurship, to the anatomy of railroad finance and organization, to the examination of railroad land policies, and to narratives of such technological changes as the increase in the capacity of locomotives and cars, the standardization of track and the introduction of the air brake. The effect of these events on the growth of the economy as a whole, if not taken for granted, is usually noted in brief sections that tend to stress the relationship between the particular subject matter of the study and the emergence of the railroad as a decisive agent of social and economic transformation.

Some scholars have departed from this implicit tendency to accept the axiom of indispensability. A case in point is Kent T. Healy's pithy critique of the proposition that railroads were responsible for the development of the trans-Appalachian West. Despite its slowness and uncertainty, water transportation rather than railroad, said Healy, brought about the "astonishing redistribution of population and economic activity" of the ante-bellum era. While only a "negligible proportion" of the population lived west of the Appalachians in 1790, "50 years later, before a single railroad had penetrated that area from the coast, some 40 per cent of the nation's people lived west of New York, Pennsylvania, and the coastal states of the South. The center of population had moved during these years from a point 25 miles east of Baltimore to a spot almost on a line with the western border of Pennsylvania." Railroads, concluded Healy, might in theory "have led to the establishment of important dry-land intermediate centers, but the practice of quoting lower rates for centers served by water than were quoted for dry-land points placed definite restrictions on any such development."[19]

A more recent, and perhaps more far-reaching, criticism of the tendency to exaggerate the developmental impact of the railroad has been made by Carter Goodrich. "Although the early canals were soon supplemented and later overshadowed by the railroads," said Goodrich, "it must not be forgotten that the initial reduction in costs provided by canal transport, as compared with wagon haulage, was more drastic than any subsequent differential between railroads and canals. The effect of this reduction was decisive for the opening of substantial trade between the east and west."[20]

But caveats such as these are the exception rather than the rule. They have not been frequent or detailed enough to match the impact of the axiom of indispensability on current thought. As a consequence the echoes of the Gilded Age still reverberate in text books on economic history. In his encyclopedic *Economic History of the United States,* Chester Wright declared that "few things have done more to change the economic organization" of the nation than the railroad. "Its revolutionizing effects," he continued, "can scarcely be exaggerated."[21] In a more recent text, Gilbert C. Fite and Jim E. Reese state that railroads at the close of the nineteenth century had "the power of life and death over the economy. Access to railroads or even differences in freight rates determined the growth or decline of whole cities."[22] Herman E. Krooss refers to railroads as "the principal single determinant of the levels of investment, national income, and employment in the nineteenth century."[23] And August C. Bolino writes: "Besides stimulating investment and creating a demand for goods and factors, the railroad also provided a transportation service which was essential to the development of capitalism in America."[24]

[19] Kent T. Healy, "American Transportation Before the War Between the States," *The Growth of the American Economy,* ed. Harold F. Williamson (New York, 1944), pp. 187–88.

[20] Carter Goodrich, *et al., Canals and American Economic Development* (New York, 1961), p. 249.

[21] Chester W. Wright, *Economic History of the United States* (1st ed.; New York, 1941), p. 343; cf. (2nd ed.; 1949), p. 279.

[22] Gilbert C. Fite and Jim E. Reese, *An Economic History of the United States* (Cambridge, Mass., 1959), p. 325.

[23] Herman E. Krooss, *American Economic Development* (Englewood Cliffs, N. J., 1959), p. 439.

[24] August C. Bolino, *The Development of the American Economy* (Columbus, Ohio, 1961), p. 173.

THE SUPPLY OF ALTERNATIVE OPPORTUNITIES

If the axiom of indispensability merely asserted that railroads were an efficient form of producing transportation services, there would be no reason to question it. Railroads were and are capable of carrying many different types of commodities in varying quantities over a wide range of circumstances at a very low cost. The evidence on this point is beyond dispute.[25] But the axiom of indispensability is not primarily a description of the performance characteristics of a particular innovation. The crucial aspect of the axiom is not what it says about the railroad; it is what it says about all things other than the railroad. The crucial aspect is the implicit assertion that the economy of the nineteenth century lacked an effective alternative to the railroad and was incapable of producing one.

Evaluation of the axiom of indispensability thus requires not only an examination of what the railroad did but also an examination of what substitutes for the railroad could have done. Railroads warrant the title of indispensability only if it can be shown that their incremental contribution over the next best alternative directly or indirectly accounted for a large part of the output of the American economy during the nineteenth century. Yet the historical evidence used to buttress the axiom is limited almost exclusively to descriptions of what the railroads did. There are few systematic inquiries into the ability of competing forms of transportation to have duplicated effects ascribed to railroads. As a consequence the range and potentiality of the supply of alternative opportunities are virtually unknown. The conclusion that the developmental potential of substitutes for railroads was very low therefore rests on a series of questionable assumptions rather than on demonstrated facts.

An interesting case in point is the notion that railroads made a unique contribution to the creation of a psychological atmosphere favoring economic growth by building lines across sparsely settled territories. Although the evidence demonstrating that the eruption of a boom psychology followed in the wake of such enterprises is considerable, no evidence has been supplied which demonstrates that the absence of the

---

[25] Even this point can be exaggerated. Not every farm had a railroad siding. Despite all of its technological sophistication, the railroad was less efficient than the wagon in very short movements of goods and persons in areas of low population density. Nor was the railroad more efficient than the boat in movements of bulky goods of low value over very long distances well endowed with natural waterways.

railroad would have deprived the nation of this desirable mental disposition. And it is doubtful that such evidence can be supplied. For if the boom psychology was a response to the opportunity to profit from unexpected changes in the value of land and other assets, it was not a unique consequence of railroads. The same favorable mental disposition could have been created by the construction of a new canal or the introduction of any new mode of transportation that unexpectedly and drastically reduced the cost of transportation in a given area.

If not all of the important effects of railroad were unique, neither were all of its unique effects important. An economy that relied exclusively on water and wagon transportation probably would not have given rise to block signals, air brakes, or the compound rail. Nor would it have required the services of track walkers, switchmen, and pullman porters. Still it would be difficult to argue that each of these unique, mechanical, and occupational appurtenances had a major effect on the efficient operation of the railroad, let alone on the efficient operation of the entire economy.

Even the demonstration that railroads produced effects that were both unique and important does not automatically sustain the axiom of indispensability. One must be able to show also that those aspects of economic life uniquely and importantly affected by railroads had a bearing on the level of aggregate output. It does not, for example, follow that because railroads were able to crush firms and cities by denying them access to railroad services, the absence of the railroad system would have represented a crushing blow to the economy as a whole. To reason in this way is to fall victim to the fallacy of composition. The presence of the fallacy is demonstrated by the following example. In 1890 Kansas City merchants sold large quantities of wheat in New York City. If success in this operation required a profit of 6 per cent on the sale price, the average profit of the merchants would have been $1.98 per ton.[26] Suppose now that railroads denied their facilities to one of the merchants and that the next most favorable form of transportation involved a 50 per cent increase in shipping charges. Such an occurrence would have been a catastrophe for the merchant involved. A rise in shipping costs of the stipulated magnitude would have transformed the mer-

---

[26] The average New York price of spring wheat was $33.03 per ton in July, 1890. U.S. Congress, Senate, *Wholesale Prices, Wages and Transportation,* Report of the Committee on Finance, Rept. No. 1394, Part 2, 52nd Cong., 2nd Sess., p. 63; hereafter referred to as *Aldrich Report.*

chant's normal profit into a 7 per cent loss.[27] However, the total freight revenue of all railroads in 1890 was $714,000,000.[28] Consequently, if in the absence of railroads there were a 50 per cent increase in the cost of shipping all those goods that were actually carried by railroads in 1890, the reduction in the production potential of the economy would have been only $357,000,000 or about 3 per cent of gross national product.

While the absence of railroads would in this illustrative case have left the economy worse off than it actually was, the reduction in transportation efficiency is hardly enough to justify the characterization of "indispensable." Given the historical stability of the aggregate saving and capital-output ratios, the hypothetical example implies that an increase in transportation costs sufficient, when *discriminatorily applied,* to ruin individual firms would have retarded the development of the economy by just one year—that is, reduced the economy's production potential to the level that prevailed in 1889. The great power of railroads over the destiny of individual firms or groups of firms does not necessarily imply a similar influence over the economy as a whole. The former existed because of the sensitivity of profits to relatively small changes in cost conditions; the latter depends on the ratio of the aggregate of such changes in costs to total national product.

The preceding argument is based on a hypothetical case and is not intended to prove that railroads were inessential to economic growth. But it does illustrate the difficulty involved in attempts to infer the incremental contributions of railroads to the overall performance of the economy from the evidence assembled by committees which investigated nineteenth-century railroad practices. While these investigations provided convincing demonstrations of the power of railroads to redistribute wealth and income among both individuals and regions, large equity effects do not necessarily imply large changes in the productive efficiency of the economy. The Rochester miller whose business was ruined by the low through rates granted to Milwaukee millers may have believed that his personal loss in income was also a loss to society. However, the loss in national income, if it existed, was the amount by which the gain to Westerners fell short of the loss to Easterners. Whether this difference was positive, zero, or negative is still to be determined. The issue can only be settled empirically. There is no basis for making such a determi-

---

[27] The rail rate on the shipment of wheat from Kansas City to New York was $8.72 per ton in the summer of 1890. Fifty per cent of this figure is $4.36 or 2.2 times the hypothetical profit. *Ibid.,* Part 1, pp. 516, 517, 551.

[28] *Historical Statistics* (1960), p. 431.

nation on a priori grounds even in situations where one of the consequences of rate discrimination was the establishment of industrial monopolies. For it is entirely feasible that, as Joseph Schumpeter argued, the reductions in cost due to large scale operations more than compensated for any misallocations of resources due to monopolistic practices.

It is also erroneous to leap from data that demonstrate the victory of railroads over waterways in the competition for freight to the conclusion that the development of the railroad network (particularly the trunk lines) was a prerequisite for the rapid continuous growth of the internal market. The only inference that can safely be drawn from such data is that railways were providing transportation services at a cheaper cost to the buyer than other conveyances. For if rail transportation was a perfect or nearly perfect substitute for waterways, all that was required for a large shift from waterways to railroads was a small price differential in favor of the latter. Whether the shift produced a significant increase in the width of the internal market depends not on the volume of goods transferred from one medium to the other but on the magnitude of the associated reduction in transportation costs. If the reduction in costs achieved by railroads was small, and if waterways could have supplied all or most of the service that railroads were providing without increasing unit charges, then the presence of railroads did not substantially widen the market and their absence would not have kept it substantially narrower. The conclusion that the railroad was a necessary condition for the widening of the market thus flows not from a body of observed data but from the unverified assumption that the cost per unit of transportation service was significantly less by rail than by water.

Still another foundation of the axiom of indispensability is the proposition that the quantity of manufactured goods used in the construction and maintenance of railroads was of decisive importance in the growth of the manufacturing industry during the nineteenth century. This theme, while enunciated by writers of the Gilded Age, has been put forth even more vigorously by modern scholars. W. W. Rostow, for example, argues that railroads triggered the American "take-off" into "self-sustained growth," and that the quantity of manufactured goods consumed by railroads "led on to the development of modern coal, iron and engineering industries."[29] However, the belief that railroads dominated the market for various manufactured products involves at least

[29] W. W. Rostow, *The Stages of Economic Growth* (Cambridge, Mass., 1960), p. 55.

three unverified assumptions. It assumes not only that the volume of goods purchased by the railroad was large relative to the total output of the supplying industries but also that purchases were directed toward the domestic rather than foreign markets. It assumes further that if there had been no railroad, the demand for manufactured goods by other forms of transportation, such as boats, would have been significantly smaller and its impact strategically different from the demand associated with railroads.

In evaluating the incremental contribution of railroads, consideration must also be given to the role that motor vehicles might have played. It may seem strange to include as a prominent element in the nineteenth century's supply of alternative opportunities an innovation so poorly developed that it provided only a trivial amount of transportation service —and that mainly during the last decade of the century. However, the observed pattern of economic growth is the consequence of a succession of choices, most of which are made on the basis of incomplete information. What appears to be optimal in the light of limited information may be shown to have been erroneous in the hindsight of fuller knowledge. The decisions which led society to invest billions of dollars in railroads between 1830 and 1890 while allocating only paltry sums to the perfection of motor vehicles may fall into this category.

Given the information generally available in 1830, the preference for railroads over the horseless carriage is quite understandable. Although carriages powered by steam engines were sufficiently perfected to be commercially successful in the absence of railroad competition, they were less efficient than the early railway.[30] The experience gained as the railroad system expanded revealed specific ways in which locomotives, cars, and track could be improved. With millions of dollars invested in new railroads annually, and with virtually each new extension of the system embodying some technological advance, the efficiency gap between the railroad and the horseless carriage became increasingly great—perhaps to the point that the latter no longer appeared to be a practical alternative. At any rate, it is interesting to note that the pace of experimentation on horseless carriages and wagons does not appear to have regained the peak attained in the twenties and thirties until half a century later. By that time it cost the Minnesota farmer as much to haul a ton of wheat 15 miles by wagon as it did to ship the same quantity 375 miles by rail. And the railroad network was too dense to reduce significantly the cost

[30] D. C. Field, "Mechanical Road-Vehicles," *A History of Technology*, eds. Charles Singer *et al.* (New York and London, 1958), V, 420–26.

of wagon haulage by further additions to the system. Thus motor vehicles were perfected and put into commercial production when the developmental potential of railroads had more or less run its course.

The axiom of indispensability proceeds on the implicit and unverified assumption that the success of railroads did not choke off the search for other solutions to the problem of overland transportation. This assumption is open to doubt. The crucial step in the perfection of motor vehicles appears to have been the substitution of the internal-combustion engine for the steam engine as the power source in horseless carriages. However, "not only the fundamental internal-combustion engine theory, but even that of the diesel engine" was published as early as 1824.[31] Consequently, one cannot foreclose the possibility that in the absence of railroads more capital and talent would have been devoted to the perfection of the horseless carriage, and that as a result the engineering knowledge and technical skills required to produce effective motor vehicles would have emerged decades sooner than it actually did.

The object of the preceding discussion has been to suggest that the evidence usually cited does not support the traditional interpretation of the imperative role of the railroad in American economic growth. This evidence fails to establish a causal relationship between the railroad and either the regional reorganization of trade, or the change in the structure of output, or the rise in per capita income, or the various other strategic changes that characterized the American economy of the last century. It does not even establish the weaker proposition that railroads were a necessary condition for these developments. Conclusions regarding causality and the establishment of the railroad as a necessary condition follow not from the traditional body of evidence but from implicit assumptions that have been introduced into the interpretation of the evidence.

It is always easier to point out the need to test a given set of assumptions than to propose a feasible method for testing them. The next chapter deals with the problems involved in evaluating one of the most common assumptions regarding the influence of the railroad on American economic development. The question to be considered is: Did the interregional distribution of agricultural products—a striking feature of the American economy of the nineteenth century—depend on the existence of the long-haul railroad? To answer the question I define and

---

[31] Orville Charles Cromer, "Internal-Combustion Engines," *Encyclopaedia Britannica* (Chicago, 1961), Vol. 12, p. 494; Field, "Mechanical Road-Vehicles," V, 426–34.

propose a method of measuring the "social saving" in interregional transportation attributable to the existence of the railroad. The discussion that follows is based chiefly on the consistency between the size of this "social saving" and the hypothesis that railroads were a necessary condition for interregional agricultural trade.

The third chapter investigates the social gain due to the availability of railroads in the intraregional or short-haul distribution of agricultural products. Since shipments from farms to primary markets involved the movement of a large set of products over thousands of routes, the analysis of the problem involves the utilization of sampling procedures. In the course of the chapter an attempt is made to demonstrate that the theory of rent can be used to establish boundaries beyond which the absence of railroads would have led to a cessation of commercial agricultural production.

The fourth chapter is concerned with the empirical justification for the extension of W. W. Rostow's stages-of-growth theory to the American case. Data are presented that bear on structural change in the economy during 1843-60, the period designated by Rostow as the American "take-off." The ensuing discussion deals with the significance of the indicated transformation and the extent to which it can be attributed to the quantity of manufactured goods required for the construction and maintenance of railroads.

The fifth chapter focuses on the problems involved in determining crucial magnitudes when only fragmentary data are available. The case in point is the share of the output of the iron industry consumed as rails during the ante-bellum era. An effort is made to develop a statistical model which incorporates the maximum number of data fragments in an empirically justifiable and logically consistent manner. This model is used to test the prevailing view that rails dominated the market for iron during the last two decades of the ante-bellum period.

CHAPTER II

The Interregional Distribution of Agricultural Products*

Is it legitimate for the historian to consider alternative possibilities to events which have happened? . . . To say that the thing happened the way it did, is not at all illuminating. We can understand the significance of what did happen only if we contrast it with what might have happened.—MORRIS RAPHAEL COHEN

THE GEOGRAPHICAL PATTERN OF PRODUCTION AND DISTRIBUTION

The massive change in the geographical pattern of agricultural output during the nineteenth century has been a leading theme of American historiography. The meager data at the start of the century strongly suggest that the main sections of the nation were agriculturally self-sufficient.[1] By 1890 the North Atlantic, South Atlantic, and South Central divisions, containing 25 states and 60 per cent of the nation's population had become deficit areas with respect to various agricultural commodities, particularly foodstuffs.[2] The greatest shortages were incurred in the North Atlantic region, which comprised the New England states, New York, New Jersey, and Pennsylvania. This division produced only 36 per cent of the wheat required to feed the local population, 45 per cent of the corn requirement, 33 per cent of the beef requirement,

---

* Permission granted to reprint Robert W. Fogel, "A Quantitative Approach to the Study of Railroads in American Economic Growth," *The Journal of Economic History*, XXII, No. 2 (June, 1962), 163–97.

[1] New England is the only notable departure from this pattern of complete, or virtually complete, agricultural self-sufficiency. The available evidence suggests that in New England the output of grain fell below local demand. But even here the deficiency appears to have been relatively small. Thomas Jefferson, writing in 1808, estimated that "90,000 persons in Massachusetts subsisted on imported flour." This implies that, although deficient, the state's output of wheat was large enough to meet the needs of 80 per cent of the population. And the Massachusetts deficit was offset, at least in part, by the surpluses of Vermont and New Hampshire. Percy Wells Bidwell and John I. Falconer, *History of Agriculture in the Northern United States, 1620-1860* (Washington, D. C., 1925), p. 236; *Historical Statistics* (1960), p. 13.

[2] U.S. Bureau of the Census, *Eleventh Census of the United States, Compendium,* Part I, p. 2; hereafter referred to as *Eleventh Census, Compendium.*

and 27 per cent of the pork requirement.[3] While the South produced a bigger share of its local needs, it too had to look outside of its borders for a major part of its food supply. The local supply of foodstuffs in the deficit regions appears even more inadequate when the product absorbed by the export market is added to domestic consumption. In the North Atlantic division, for example, the local supply of wheat shrinks from 36 per cent of the local requirement to 24 per cent of the combination of local consumption and exports.[4]

In contradistinction to the decline in the output of foodstuffs in the East and South, the North Central division of the country became a great agricultural surplus area. Virgin territory at the start of the century, the 12 states lying in this region were producing 71 per cent of the country's cereal grains by 1890 and were also the national center of cattle and swine production.[5] The magnitude of their surpluses is well illustrated by wheat. In the crop year 1890-91, the 12 states produced 440,-000,000 bushels. At 5 bushels per capita this was enough to feed 88,000,000 people—four times the number that actually inhabited the region.[6] Approximately two-thirds of the grain surplus of the North Central states was consumed in the East and South. Most of the rest was used to feed the nations of Europe and South America.

The process by which the agricultural surpluses of the Midwest were distributed can be divided into three stages. In the case of grain, the first stage was concentration of the surplus in the great primary markets of the Midwest; that is, in Chicago, Minneapolis, Duluth, Milwaukee, Peoria, Kansas City, St. Louis, Cincinnati, Toledo, and Detroit. Over 80 per cent of the grain that entered into interregional trade was shipped from the farms to these cities.[7] The second stage involved the shipment

[3] Estimated local requirements and supplies for the North Atlantic region (in thousands of tons) are:

	Wheat	Corn	Dressed Pork	Dressed Beef
Local requirement	2,507	4,956	297	381
Local supply	895	2,219	79	127
Deficit	1,612	2,737	218	254

The procedure followed in the construction of these estimates is discussed below, pp. 30–36.

[4] Wheat exports from ports in the North Atlantic region were approximately 1,260,000 tons. St. Louis Merchants' Exchange, *Annual Report, 1890*, p. 168.

[5] U.S. Congress, House, *Report of the Industrial Commission on the Distribution of Farm Products*, Doc. No. 494, 56th Cong., 2nd Sess., 1901, p. 37; hereafter referred to as *Industrial Commission, Distribution*.

[6] U.S.D.A., Bureau of Statistics, *Wheat Crops of the United States, 1866-1906*, Bull. 57, 1908, p. 18; hereafter referred to as *Wheat Crops*.

[7] See below pp. 29–31.

of the grain from the primary markets to some 90 secondary markets in the East and South.[8] Among the most important secondary markets were New York City, Baltimore, Boston, Philadelphia, New Orleans, Albany (N.Y.), Portland (Me.), Pittsburgh, Birmingham, and Savannah. The third stage involved the distribution of grain within the territory immediately surrounding the secondary markets and exportation abroad. The distributional pattern of meat products roughly paralleled that of grain. Perhaps the most important difference was that the first stage of the distributional process—the concentration of livestock in the primary markets—was dominated by only four cities: Chicago, St. Louis, Kansas City, and Omaha.

With this background it is possible to give more definite meaning to the rather vague term "interregional distribution." For the purposes of this chapter, "interregional distribution" is defined as the process of shipping commodities from the primary markets of the Midwest to the secondary markets of the East and South. For all other shipments, those from farms to primary markets and from secondary markets to the points immediately surrounding them, the term "intraregional distribution" is used. Similarly, the term "interregional railroad" is reserved for lines between primary and secondary markets and the term "intraregional railroad" is used for all other lines. This division between interregional and intraregional is useful in differentiating between the railroad's role as a long-distance mover of agricultural products and its other functions.[9] It also helps to clarify the hypothesis to be examined in this chapter. The hypothesis can now be stated as follows:

Railroad connections between the primary and secondary markets of the nation were a necessary condition for the system of agricultural production and distribution that characterized the American economy of the last half of the nineteenth century. Moreover, the absence of such railroad connections would have forced a regional pattern of agricultural production that would have significantly restricted the development of the American economy.

THE CONCEPTUAL BASIS OF THE TEST

In the year 1890, a certain bundle of agricultural commodities was shipped from the primary markets to the secondary markets. The shipment occurred in a certain pattern, that is, with certain tonnages moving

---

[8] See below pp. 30–36.
[9] The intraregional railroad is discussed in Chapter III below.

from each primary market city to each secondary market city. This pattern of shipments was carried out by some combination of rail, wagon, and water haulage at some definite cost. With enough data, one could determine both this cost and the alternative cost of shipping exactly the same bundle of goods from the primary to the secondary markets in exactly the same pattern without the railroad. The difference between these two amounts I call the social saving attributable to the railroad in the interregional distribution of agricultural products—or simply "the social saving." This difference is, in fact, larger than the true social saving would have been. Forcing the pattern of shipments in the non-rail situation to conform to the pattern that actually existed is equivalent to the imposition of a restraint on society's freedom to adjust to an alternative technological situation. If society had had to ship inter-regionally by water and wagon without the railroad, it could have shifted agricultural production from the Midwest to the East and South, and shifted some productive factors out of agriculture altogether. Further, the cities entering our set of secondary markets and the tonnages handled by each were surely influenced by conditions peculiar to rail transportation; in the absence of the railroad some different cities would have entered this set, and the relative importance of those remaining would have changed. Adjustments of this sort would have reduced the loss in national income occasioned by the absence of the railroad, but estimates of their effects lie beyond the limits of tools and data. I propose, therefore, to use the social saving, as defined, as the objective standard for testing the hypothesis stated above.[10]

With such a test, one cannot make definite statements about the rela-

[10] There are four possible ways of defining the "true" social saving:

1. The difference between the actual level of national income in 1890 and the level of national income that would have prevailed if the economy had made the most efficient possible adjustment to the absence of the interregional railroad.

2. The difference between the level of national income that would have prevailed in 1890 if the existing means of transportation had been used in the most efficient manner possible and the level of national income that would have prevailed if the economy had made the most efficient possible adjustment to the absence of the interregional railroad.

3. The difference between the level of national income that would have prevailed in 1890 if the existing means of transportation had been used in the most efficient manner possible and the level of national income that would have prevailed if the economy had made an inefficient adjustment to the absence of the interregional railroad.

4. The difference between the actual level of national income in 1890 and the level that would have prevailed if the economy had made an inefficient adjustment to the absence of the interregional railroad.

tionship between the social saving and the geographic structure of agricultural production except for extreme values of the social saving. If the calculation shows the saving to be zero, then obviously the absence of the interregional railroad would not have altered the existing productive pattern. On the other hand, if the social saving turns out to be very large, say on the order of magnitude of national income, it would be equally obvious that in the absence of the interregional railroad, all production of surpluses in the Midwest would have ceased. In this case either agricultural production in the East and South would have risen or the United States would have become an importer of agricultural commodities.

For small differences in the cost differential, there is very little that can be said about the change in the geographic structure of output. It is theoretically conceivable that even a social saving as small as one-fourth of 1 per cent of the national income would have ended all or most surplus production in the North Central states. But this limitation in the proposed index is not quite so serious as it might seem. For the central concern here is with the influence of the railroad on the course of American economic development. The crucial question is not whether the absence of the railroad would have left agricultural production in a different regional pattern, but whether such a pattern would have significantly restricted economic growth. From this point of view sharp regional shifts in production associated with very small values of the

---

For the purposes of this chapter, definitions (2) and (3) are irrelevant. The point at issue is not the most the railroad could have contributed to economic growth, but what it actually did contribute to economic growth. Definition (4) is indeterminate since there is no way of knowing how inefficient an adjustment might have been made to the absence of the interregional railroad. Hence, definition (1) is the "true social saving" to which the discussion in this chapter refers.

If it is assumed that institutional conditions would have been such as to create the same degree of inefficiency without the railroad as with it, it becomes possible to rank the definitions of the "true social saving" by size. The "true social saving" would be the largest under definition (3). Definitions (2) and (4) would yield social savings of equal size, but these would be less than the one implied by the third definition. The definition adopted in this chapter is the smallest "true social saving." The estimating procedure proposed below overstates all four definitions.

Finally, the treatment of the differential in transportation costs as a differential in levels of national income is based on the assumption that there would have been no obstacle to an adjustment to a non-rail situation. More specifically, it is based on the assumption that national income would have fallen only because more productive resources were required to provide a given amount of transportation service and that all productive resources not used for transportation would have remained fully employed. When treated in this manner, the social saving is a measure of the extent to which railroads increased the production potential of the economy (i.e., shifted the economy's production possibilities function).

social saving would be immaterial. They would have served to demonstrate that many geographic patterns of production were consistent with a given level of economic development; the geographic pattern of agricultural production could then be dismissed as a significant element in the growth of the American economy.

The social saving is calculated in my estimates for only one year, 1890. Yet the hypothesis to be tested refers to a period covering almost half a century. How sound an inference about the significance of the railroad's role with respect to agricultural development over almost half a century can be made on the basis of a single year's data? The answer depends on the relative efficiency of the railroad in 1890 as compared with earlier periods. If the railroad was relatively more efficient in 1890 than in any previous year, the social saving per unit of transportation in 1890 would have exceeded the saving per unit in all previous years. The available evidence suggests that this was indeed the case.[11] The four decades between 1850 and 1890 were ones of continuous advance in efficiency. The size, speed, and pulling capacity of the locomotive was steadily increased as was the weight of the load a freight car could carry. At the same time, scattered rail lines were integrated into an unbroken network, thus eliminating or reducing transshipment costs. Terminal facilities were expanded, and such important loading devices as the grain elevator were brought into general operation. But perhaps the most significant indication of the increase in the railroad's efficiency is the very considerable shift of heavy, low-value items away from water carriers. In 1852 boats and barges dominated the interregional transportation of these items, while in 1890 they were carried mainly by the railroad. Since the volume of agricultural commodities transported between regions also increased over the period in question, it seems apparent that the absolute social saving in 1890 exceeded in absolute amount the saving of previous years. While it is true that national income rose over the period, the amount of agricultural goods shipped interregionally appears to have risen just as rapidly. In the case of wheat, population and production figures suggest that local requirements in the deficit states were at least 1.1 million tons less in 1870 than they were in 1890. Export requirements were 1.8 million tons less. These

---

[11] See, for example, J. L. Ringwalt, *Development of Transportation Systems in the United States* (Philadelphia, 1888) ; Walter Arndt Lucas, ed., *100 Years of Steam Locomotives* (New York, 1957) ; *The American Railway: Its Construction, Development, Management, and Appliances* (New York, 1892) ; *History of the Baldwin Locomotive Works, 1830 to 1907* (Philadelphia, 1907).

figures indicate that the quantity shipped interregionally increased by 145 per cent over two decades—showing approximately the same rate of growth as real national income.[12] Thus, if it is shown that the social saving of 1890 was quite small relative to national income, the relationship would hold with equal force for the half century preceding 1890.

The problem posed here would be trivial if the wagon were the only alternative to the railroad in interregional transportation. By 1890 the average cost of railroad transportation was less than a cent per ton-mile. On the other hand, the cost of wagon transportation was in the neighborhood of 17 cents per ton-mile.[13] According to estimates presented below, approximately 7.7 million tons of corn and 5.0 million tons of wheat entered into interregional transportation.[14] Taking the differential between rail and wagon transportation at 16.5 cents per ton-mile, the social saving involved in moving these 12.7 million tons 1 mile would have been $2,100,000. Assuming that on the average the corn and wheat shipped interregionally traveled 1,000 miles, the total social saving would have been $2,100,000,000. Even this figure is low, since wagon rates did not reflect the cost involved in road construction and maintenance. If account were taken of these and other omitted charges, and if a similar calculation were performed for livestock, the figure for the social saving would probably increase by 50 per cent, to $3,000,000,000 or a quarter of gross national product in 1890.[15] This magnitude exceeds Gallman's 1889 estimate of gross income originating in agriculture.[16] Such a loss would have pushed the economy back a decade and probably cut the rate of investment by a quarter.[17] The calculation is very crude, of course, but there seems little doubt that the order of magnitude is correct.

The problem is not trivial because water transportation was a practical

---

[12] *Wheat Crops,* p. 7; *Historical Statistics* (1960), pp. 12, 13, 139; U.S.D.A., Bureau of Statistics, *Exports of Farm Products from the United States 1851–1908,* Bull. No. 75, 1910, pp. 44, 46; the second citation will hereafter be referred to as *Exports of Farm Products.*

[13] See the discussion of wagon rates in Chapter III below. Cf. U.S. Congress, House, *Report of the Industrial Commission on Agriculture and Agricultural Labor,* X, Doc. No. 179, 57th Cong., 1st Sess., 1901, pp. 690–91; hereafter referred to as *Industrial Commission, Agriculture.*

[14] See Table 2.2 below.

[15] *Historical Statistics* (1960), p. 139.

[16] Robert E. Gallman, "Commodity Output in the United States," Conference on Income and Wealth, *Trends in the American Economy in the Nineteenth Century* (Princeton, 1960), p. 47.

[17] This statement is based on the assumption of the relative constancy of the saving and capital-output ratios over the range of national income being considered here.

alternative to the railroad in interregional transportation. A glance at a map shows that all of the primary market cities were on navigable waterways. Duluth, Milwaukee, Chicago, Toledo, and Detroit were on the Great Lakes; Omaha and Kansas City were on the Missouri; Minneapolis and St. Louis were on the Mississippi; Cincinnati was on the Ohio; and Peoria was on the Illinois River, midway between the Mississippi and Lake Michigan. The lakes, inland rivers, canals, and coastal waters directly linked the primary market cities to most of the secondary market cities. Of the 43 most important secondary markets, 32 were located on navigable waters still in use in 1890. Seven were on waterways that had been forced into inactivity as a result of railroad competition, but which could have been used in the absence of the railroad. Only four cities were without direct water connection to the Midwest, and each of these was within a relatively short wagon haul of a major water artery.

The importance of a water route alternative lies in the fact that on a per ton-mile basis, water rates were lower than railroad rates. The all-rail rate on wheat from Chicago to New York, for example, was about 0.52 cents per ton-mile or nearly four times as much as the ton-mile rate by water.[18] This fact does not, of course, imply that the social cost or even the private cost on a given tonnage was less when shipped by water. Water routes were much more circuitous than rail routes. The time in transit was considerably greater. Loss of cargo was more frequent. Terminal charges were higher. These and other problems raised the cost of water transportation to a point where shipments between most primary and most secondary markets were cheaper by rail than by boat. What makes the problem interesting is that the amount by which water costs exceeded railroad costs is far from obvious. As has already been suggested, the massive switch from water to rail transportation by no means implies that the cost differential was large. Consider the hypothetical case of a Chicago wheat shipper who made a profit of 10 per cent on the Chicago price of wheat or 9 cents per bushel on a price of 90 cents. If the cost of shipment, all factors considered, were the same by both water and rail, the shipper would be indifferent as to which form he used. Suppose now that technological advances made it possible for the shipper to get his bushel to market for 2 cents less than before. How strong an inducement to switch from water to rail transportation would such a differential generate? By reducing his cost 2 cents per

[18] *Industrial Commission, Distribution,* p. 142; p. 38 below.

bushel, the shipper could increase his profit by 22 per cent. Clearly, the implication of this example is that a differential of 2 cents per bushel would have created a very strong pressure to shift all wheat that had been transported by water to railroads. Yet the social saving involved in such a shift would have been just $3,300,000—much too small an amount to justify the claim of the indispensability of the interregional railroad in American economic growth.[19]

Until now the discussion has been carried on as if all the agricultural commodities that entered into interregional trade were to be included in the estimate. In fact, the estimate will be based on only four commodities: wheat, corn, beef, and pork. These four accounted for 42 per cent of income originating in agriculture in 1889.[20] Neglect of the other products is not so serious as it first seems. What is important is not the share of wheat, corn, beef, and pork in total output, but their share in that part of output which entered interregional trade. Obviously, if none of the neglected 58 per cent of output moved interregionally, the restriction is of no real consequence. The most important of the omitted items is cotton, which represented 11 per cent of output.[21] But relatively little cotton entered interregional transportation as here defined, and a large part of the crop shipped interregionally was carried by water.[22] This is illustrated by the distribution of the 1898-99 crop. Of the output of this season, 79 per cent was shipped from southern farms to southern seaport cities, and from there carried by boat to Europe or to northern ports in the United States. Another 13 per cent was consumed in the South. Hence, at most only 8 per cent or 225,000 tons of cotton (i.e., 900,000 bales) could have entered into interregional rail transportation.[23] But 225,000 tons is only 1.8 per cent of the combined wheat-corn tonnage. The case of dairy products, which accounted for 12 per cent of total product, is similar.[24] There are three main dairy products: milk, butter, and cheese. Of these, milk was entirely an intraregional product. Census data on butter and cheese production in the Midwest indicate that the amount entering interregional trade was about

---

[19] The average wholesale price in Chicago of a bushel of wheat during 1890 was 87 cents. *Historical Statistics* (1960), p. 123.

[20] Gallman, "Commodity Output," pp. 46–48.

[21] *Ibid.*

[22] U.S. Congress, House, *Monthly Summary of Commerce and Finance,* Doc. 15, Part 7, 56th Cong., 1st Sess., 1900, pp. 2545–2636.

[23] *Industrial Commission, Distribution,* p. 174.

[24] Gallman, "Commodity Output," pp. 46–48.

166,000 tons or 1.3 per cent of the wheat-corn tonnage.[25] Again, while virtually all wool was transported from west to east, it was less than 1 per cent (closer to one-half of 1 per cent) of the wheat-corn tonnage. In short, neglected items probably do not account for more than 10 per cent of the goods that entered into interregional trade and would not justify the effort required to include them.

The most direct method of determining the social saving is to find the 1890 pattern of the shipments of the four commodities and then estimate both the actual cost of the pattern and the cost that would have obtained if the pattern were to have been executed with only boats and wagons. This method requires the following data: the amount of each commodity shipped from each primary market, the amounts received by each secondary market, the routes over which they were shipped, and the transportation costs by each medium. But not all of these data are available. The total volume of shipments from each of the primary markets can be determined, but not their destinations and routes. Looking at it from the other end, the receipts of the secondary markets can be estimated. But one cannot tell from which primary markets these goods were secured.

The impasse is, of course, only apparent. It is possible to bridge the gap in statistics because of a relatively new mathematical technique— linear programming—which permits one to arrive at the desired solution at a cheaper cost in terms of data requirements. It seems likely, incidentally, that in other cases as well as this one mathematical techniques of analysis can reduce the amount of information required to evaluate a given hypothesis.[26] This characteristic of mathematical technique is, by itself, a forceful argument for increasing efforts to apply mathematical analysis to historical problems. The linear programming problem is not solved here, but a short discussion will indicate its possibilities.

The actual method of analysis is quite simple. It involves a pair of linear programming models for each commodity. The procedure can be illustrated by considering the case of wheat. In 1890, a certain amount

[25] This estimate is based on data for 1899. U.S. Bureau of the Census, *Twelfth Census of the United States, Agriculture,* Part I, pp. clxxxii–clxxxiii; hereafter referred to as *Twelfth Census, Agriculture.*

It should be remembered that the East did not run the heavy deficits of dairy products that it did on grains and meats. New York and Pennsylvania were two of the three largest producers of dairy products. *Industrial Commission, Distribution,* pp. 268–69.

[26] Cf. Robert William Fogel, *The Union Pacific Railroad: A Case in Premature Enterprise* (Baltimore, 1960), especially pp. 81–85.

of wheat was shipped from the Midwest to the secondary markets. The first linear programming model will find the least cost of carrying the wheat from the primary to the secondary markets without imposing any restraint on the means of transportation that can be used—that is, allowing the shipments to be made in the cheapest manner, regardless of the transportation medium. The second model imposes the restriction that railroads cannot be used and then finds the least cost of shipping wheat from the primary to the secondary markets. Presumably these two least-cost figures will differ; but this difference will reflect only the absence of the railroad, since both the quantities shipped from each of the primary markets and the requirements of each of the secondary markets will be the same in both models. The difference between the two least-cost figures is the estimate of the social saving due to the use of the railroad in the interregional transportation of wheat.

What is the nature of this estimate? The desideratum is the "true" social saving—the difference between the actual 1890 level of national income and the level of national income that would have prevailed if the economy had made the most efficient possible adjustment to the absence of the interregional railroad. The cost differential obtained from the pair of linear programming models will exceed the true social saving. The linear programming differential would equal the true social saving only if the first model yielded the actual 1890 cost of the interregional transportation of wheat and if the second model took account of the most efficient adjustments that would have been made to the absence of the interregional railroad. However, the cost figure produced by the first model will be less than or equal to the actual 1890 cost, since the best the market could have done was to have found a least-cost (i.e., a linear programming) solution. Furthermore, the second model does not reflect the most efficient adjustment that could have been made to the absence of the railroad; it holds both the amounts shipped from the various primary markets and the requirements of the various secondary markets constant. Therefore, the estimate of the true social saving obtained by linear programming will have an upward bias.[27]

The water rates to be used in the second model must (with some exceptions) be those that actually prevailed in 1890. Even if water

---

[27] As pointed out in note 10, there are four ways of defining the "true" social saving. The estimate obtained by use of linear programming equals or exceeds all four definitions if it is assumed that in definitions (3) and (4) the deviation from efficiency would have been of the same degree in the case of waterways as it was in the case of railroads.

rates in 1890 equaled marginal costs, their use in the second model might still introduce a bias, since these rates applied to a tonnage which is less than the amount specified in the model. In other words, using the 1890 rates is equivalent to assuming that the marginal cost of water transportation was constant over the relevant range. This assumption probably accentuates the upward bias of my estimate. If all costs except those involved in the construction of canals and channels are considered variable, then it seems quite reasonable to assume that marginal costs were constant or declining. The basic operating unit in water transportation was the boat; and there is no reason to assume that the cost of producing or operating additional boats would have risen, unless bottlenecks developed along water routes. Most water routes were greatly underutilized in 1890 and would have been underutilized even if they had carried some relevant share of the additional interregional tonnage. The available data strongly suggest that, if anything, marginal costs would have declined over the range being considered since there were many maintenance and other operating costs (e.g., dredging, repairing locks, supplying water) that would have increased only slightly as the tonnage carried rose. Moreover, there may have been economies of scale in boat production. To the extent that these tendencies were operative, use of 1890 water rates will impart an upward bias to the estimate of the social saving.[28] Finally, it is important to note that the published 1890 rates did not reflect all of the costs involved in water transportation. In order to avoid introducing a downward bias into the calculations, it will be necessary to take account of such factors as spoilage, transit time, and the unavailability of water routes for five months

[28] Additivity hinges on the nature of marginal costs. If the marginal cost of water transportation was constant, there is no adding-up problem. If the marginal cost was declining, adding up the saving shown by the various pairs of linear programs will further accentuate the upward bias.

Preliminary calculations suggest that the Erie Canal was the only waterway on which a bottleneck might have arisen. In 1890 the Erie carried 3,200,000 tons. Capacity at the time was 10,000,000 tons. It is possible that without the railroad, the agricultural products shifted to the canal would have exceeded 7,000,000 tons, thus taxing the capacity of the Erie. On the other hand, it appears that the most the additional tonnage could have been was 10,000,000 tons. However, 13,000,000 tons was well below the capacity of the New York State Barge Canal. If the linear programming solution leads to shipments which exceed the capacity of the Erie, the cost figures of the Barge Canal, adequately adjusted for differences in the price level, etc., can be applied. The use of Barge Canal rates would further buttress the assumption of constant or declining marginal costs in water transportation.

out of the year. Methods of estimating these costs are discussed in the final section of the chapter.[29]

THE DATA PROBLEM

Use of linear programming would reduce, but not eliminate, the data problem. An enormous amount of information, some of which cannot be obtained directly, is needed. This section seeks to demonstrate how the necessary estimates can be derived from existing but largely neglected bodies of data. What is involved is the application of the estimating techniques usually reserved for the construction of national income accounts to a specific historical problem. It is important to emphasize that the results presented below are tentative; many obvious adjustments have not yet been made. Nevertheless, the figures on tonnages entering interregional trade are sufficiently close to the truth for the use to which they are put in the final section of this chapter. The problems encountered in translating a theoretically conceived estimate into an actual one can best be discussed by grouping them under four headings: shipments, requirements, railroad rates, and water rates.

The Shipments

Much has been written on the internal agricultural trade of the United States during the nineteenth century. In addition to Schmidt's series of

[29] As already noted, the estimate of the social saving in the interregional transportation of wheat, corn, pork, and beef requires a pair of linear programming models for each commodity. It might be thought that more than one pair of programs is required for each commodity. Wheat, for example, was carried East both as wheat and as flour. Pork was transported in even a wider variety of forms, including live swine, dressed pork, canned pork, mess pork, ham, bacon, etc. To the extent that each form of pork or wheat is considered a different product, one might be inclined to argue that a separate pair of models is required for each form. This costly complication can be avoided, if (in the case, say, of wheat) the ratio of wheat to flour demanded in each secondary market was roughly the same, by using information on the quantities of wheat and flour shipped from each primary market. Then, given the wheat equivalent of a given quantity of flour as well as the cost of shipping each form, there is obviously some transportation cost at which X ton-miles of flour can be converted into Y ton-miles of wheat. The assumption of a constancy in the ratio of wheat to flour shipments tends to introduce an upward bias in the estimate of social saving. If the relative transportation costs of flour and wheat were the same by both forms of transportation, no bias would be introduced. But the cost of shipping flour relative to the cost of shipping wheat was greater by water than by rail. Hence in the absence of the railroad more wheat and less flour would have been shipped. However, the conversion of flour into a grain equivalent is based on the proportions of each that were actually shipped in 1890.

articles in the *Iowa Journal of History and Politics* (1920–22), there are the studies in the *Census of Agriculture* for 1860 and 1880, the biennial reports on internal commerce issued by the Treasury Department between 1876 and 1891, the volume on the distribution of agricultural products compiled by the Industrial Commission of 1900, and a series of articles which appeared in the *Monthly Summary of Commerce and Finance* in 1900.[30] All of these studies examined the system of primary markets, and they provide a considerable amount of data on the relative importance of the various cities. Surprisingly enough, however, these sources—whether considered separately or together—fail to yield enough data to compile a complete schedule of the shipments of grains and provisions for any year during the nineteenth century. Schmidt comes the closest, giving a schedule of the receipts of grains by primary markets for the year 1890. While there is a relationship between receipts and shipments, Schmidt does not indicate how to convert one into the other. An even more difficult problem is the absence of a complete series on shipments of provisions.

Fortunately, the desired data were relatively easy to obtain. Figures on the shipments of each of the various commodities were culled from the reports of the produce exchanges, the boards of trade, or chambers of commerce of each of the primary market cities. These documents contain much highly reliable information. Except in the cases of Chicago, St. Louis, and New York, they have been badly neglected. Table 2.1 gives the preliminary figures on the shipments of corn and wheat from the primary markets.[31] The same sources contain the data needed to determine meat shipments.

The Requirements

The estimation of requirements of the secondary markets proved to be much more difficult than the shipments from the primary markets. The problem here was not merely the absence of a convenient series on the requirements of the various secondary markets; with the exception of such places as New York, Baltimore, and New Orleans, there was no

---

[30] The pattern of trade is summarized by Emory R. Johnson *et al., History of Foreign and Domestic Commerce of the United States* (Washington, 1915), Parts I and II.

[31] Table 2.1 includes only grain which was unloaded in the primary markets. Additional amounts were shipped through the primary markets without unloading. Obviously, these neglected amounts will eventually have to be included.

TABLE 2.1 SHIPMENTS OF CORN AND WHEAT FROM PRIMARY MARKETS, 1890
(thousands of tons)

Primary market	Wheat [1]	Corn [2]
Chicago	950	2,536
Minneapolis	1,322	53
Duluth-Superior	793	41
Milwaukee	516	7
Peoria	35	211
Kansas City	181	505
St. Louis	522	1,218
Cincinnati	181	70
Toledo	309	463
Detroit	125	32
Total	4,934	5,136

[1] Includes flour converted into wheat at the rate: 1 barrel of flour equals 0.1430 tons of wheat.

[2] Includes corn meal converted into corn at the rate: 1 barrel of corn meal equals 0.1262 tons of corn.

SOURCES: See discussion in text, pp. 29–30.

way of knowing which of the various cities of the East and South comprised the relevant secondary markets.

The first task, then, was to find some basis for dividing the deficit regions into marketing areas and for determining the cities which served as the distributing centers of the areas. The basic reference for making this division was a study of wholesale grocery territories carried out by the Department of Commerce in the 1920's.[32] This study divided the country into 183 trading areas. Each of the areas was composed of a group of counties served by a single city. The Boston trading area, for example, was determined by a survey of the wholesale firms situated in Boston and comprised the six counties immediately surrounding the city.

Since grain and provisions were wholesale grocery products, the Department of Commerce survey provided an appropriate framework for the estimates. That the territories it defined pertained to the economy of the 1920's is not a crucial consideration. The basic rail network, especially in the East, was well established by 1890 and remained stable over the ensuing three decades. In the 1920's truck had not yet altered existing geographical patterns of trade. They appear to have affected the size of the inventories carried by outlying retailers rather than the boundaries of the marketing areas. The impression that motor vehicles conformed to, rather than altered, pre-existing patterns is

[32] U.S. Bureau of Foreign and Domestic Commerce, *Atlas of Wholesale Grocery Territories,* Domestic Commerce Series, No. 7, 1927.

buttressed by a study of wholesale territories made in the late 1930's. The trading areas described by this survey were virtually identical with the earlier set.[33]

This demarcation of trading territories made it possible to devise a procedure for estimating the requirements of each territory by commodity. The area requirement for a given commodity was the difference between the area's total demand for the commodity (including exports) and the amount of the commodity supplied from within the area. Thus, to determine the requirements, estimates of both total demand and local supply were needed. The procedure for arriving at these estimates can be illustrated by considering the case of wheat.

The total demand for wheat in a given area consisted of two parts: the local demand and the export demand. The export demand was determined directly from export statistics provided by the Treasury Department; the local demand had to be estimated indirectly. The local demand for wheat was almost entirely for human consumption. For the country as a whole, about 10 per cent of the annual wheat crop was set aside for seed and about 2 per cent for animal feed.[34] However, the share of wheat demanded for seed in the deficit regions was considerably less than the national share since wheat production was quite small. This was especially true in New England, where wheat consumed as seed was only one-half of 1 per cent of the quantity consumed by humans. Similarly, the practice of feeding wheat to animals appears to have been practiced primarily in the areas of surplus production. Hence, the estimate of local demand was largely a matter of determining human consumption.

Total human consumption in a trading area was equal to per capita consumption multiplied by the population of the area. Statistics on area population were obtained from the 1890 census. The tentative estimate of average consumption by regions was calculated from a 1909 survey of urban workers conducted by the British Board of Trade.[35] Based

---

[33] U.S. Bureau of Foreign and Domestic Commerce, *Atlas of Wholesale Grocery Trading Areas,* Market Research Series, No. 19, 1938.

[34] U.S.D.A., *Yearbook of Agriculture,* 1923, p. 1140; *Wheat Crops,* p. 18.

[35] Great Britain, Board of Trade, *Cost of Living in American Towns* (London, 1911); reprinted as U.S. Senate, Doc. 22, 62nd Cong., 1st Sess. (ser. no. 6082).

The data needed to convert statistics on bread, cake, and macaroni consumption into a wheat equivalent were obtained from U.S.D.A., Office of Experimentation, *Bulletin,* Nos. 35 (1896) and 156 (1905); cf. *Farmers Bulletin,* Nos. 23 and 1450; William G. Panschar and Charles C. Slater, *Baking in America* (2 vols.; Evanston, 1956).

on these data, the estimated per capita consumption of wheat is 4.80 bushels per year in the North and 4.70 bushels per year in the South. These figures do not include an adjustment for urban-rural differences in wheat consumption. However, it does not seem likely that the adjustment, when it is made, will significantly alter the results. A 1913–14 survey indicated an average per capita wheat consumption of 5.08 bushels among 421 farm families in five North Atlantic states and an average per capita consumption of 5.13 bushels among 149 families in three southern states.[36]

The local supply of wheat in a trading area was the sum of the annual local production of wheat and the supply (positive or negative) out of local inventories. The Department of Agriculture has published estimates of the production of wheat in 1890 by states but not by counties. However, to determine local production in a trading area, county data

---

A convenient review of various budget and diet studies is contained in Faith M. Williams and Carle C. Zimmerman, *Studies of Family Living in the United States and other Countries*, U.S.D.A., Miscellaneous Publications, No. 223 (1935).

[36] W. C. Funk, *Value to Farm Families of Food, Fuel, and Use of House*, U.S.D.A. Bull. No. 410, 1916, pp. 5, 18. Funk's figures were in consumption per equivalent adult, with children 12 and under counted as one-half an adult. Funk's data were converted to a per capita basis on the assumption that the average proportion of persons 12 and under in all the families in his sample residing in a particular state was the same as that state's proportion of persons 12 and under in the rural population in 1910.

The finding that average wheat consumption in the South was about as large as in the North requires some explanation. The letters, journals, and diaries of noted travelers usually stressed the importance of corn in the southern diet. There is no necessary contradiction between the data culled from the budget studies and the commentaries of distinguished observers. Corn *was* the dominant breadstuff in the southern diet. During the period in question, Southerners probably consumed an annual average of about 6 bushels of corn per capita: the rest of the nation used about a bushel per person. One can easily see why travelers would stress the unique element of the southern diet, while passing over the fact that wheat was also consumed in sizable quantities. Historians have inferred that since the quantity of corn used was unusually large, the consumption of wheat must have been quite small. The budget studies suggest another interpretation: while some corn was substituted for wheat, even larger quantities were substituted for other commodities, especially dairy products. Average caloric intake in the South also appears to have been greater than in the North. Edith Hawley, *Economics of Food Consumption* (New York, 1932), p. 75.

A high rate of wheat consumption may have been characteristic of the South for the whole of the last half of the nineteenth century. Schmidt, in his series of studies on the grain trade, noted that the South imported an average of 10,000,000 bushels of wheat per year during the decade leading up to the Civil War. He estimated consumption of wheat for the year 1860 at 4.5 bushels per capita in the South and placed the national average at 5.5 bushels. Louis B. Schmidt, "The Internal Grain Trade of the United States 1850–1860," *Iowa Journal of History and Politics*, Vol. 18 (1920), pp. 101, 106.

were needed. The 1889 census production data by counties was multiplied by the 1890:1889 ratio of output for the state in which the particular county was located. Inventories of wheat were held by two main groups: wholesalers in the central cities of the trading areas and farmers. It was not possible to obtain data on changes in the inventories of wholesalers. However, reports on the inventories in the hands of farmers on March 1, 1890, and March 1, 1891, were published by the Department of Agriculture.[37] It was therefore possible to estimate the change in farmers' inventories which, as a factor in supply, was probably more significant than the change in wholesalers' inventories.

The estimate of the total wheat requirements of all the secondary markets in the deficit regions is given in Table 2.2. It is broken down into a local consumption deficit (obtained by subtracting local production and changes in farm inventories from my estimate of the local demand in each area) and foreign exports. The latter figure is based on the *Commerce and Navigation Reports* of the Treasury Department.

It is possible to test my procedure for estimating the local requirements of wheat. Data are available in reports of local boards of trade on the receipts and foreign exports of the five largest secondary markets. Abstracting from inventory fluctuations, the receipts minus foreign exports will be equal to the local consumption requirement, providing that no wheat is grown locally. This method of estimation cannot be used for three of these largest marketing areas (New York, Philadelphia, and Baltimore) since they grew considerable quantities of wheat, an undetermined amount of which was processed at merchant mills for local consumption and failed to enter into board of trade statistics.

TABLE 2.2. ESTIMATED REQUIREMENTS OF SECONDARY MARKETS
(thousands of tons)

	(1) Local consumption deficits	(2) Exports	(3) Total requirements (Col. 1 + Col. 2)
Wheat[1]	3,099	1,916	5,015
Corn[2]	5,415	2,320	7,735
Dressed pork	729	347	1,076
Dressed beef	701	304	1,005

[1] Includes flour converted into wheat at the rate: 1 barrel of flour equals 0.1430 tons of wheat.
[2] Includes corn meal converted into corn at the rate: 1 barrel of corn meal equals 0.1262 tons of corn.

SOURCES: See discussion in text, pp. 30–34.

[37] Baltimore Corn and Flour Exchange, *Annual Report, 1898, 1890*.

Only 441 bushels of wheat, however, were grown in the Boston trading area and 120 bushels in the New Orleans trading area, so virtually all the wheat demanded by these markets originated outside the trading areas and was recorded in commercial statistics. To eliminate inventory fluctuations a nine-year average (centered on 1890) of receipts minus exports was taken. As shown in Table 2.3, local requirements estimated in this way tend to support the basic estimating procedure. The figure on the New Orleans marketing region (with 64 per cent of the population living in rural areas) lends support to the finding that wheat consumption in the South was considerably higher than has been generally realized.[38]

The procedure followed in estimating corn requirements was similar to that used in the case of wheat. The most important difference was that human consumption represented only 8 per cent of the total demand for corn. Estimates of average animal consumption per head were obtained for each of the main categories of animals.[39] But these averages were available only on a national basis. To the extent that there were regional differences in animal consumption of corn, the estimates tend to overstate the requirements of some areas and understate the requirements of others.

In estimating the local demand for beef and pork, national per capita disappearance figures were first obtained, following the method of the Department of Agriculture. The national figures were transformed into regional per capita estimates by using weights taken from a 1901 budget study conducted by the Bureau of Labor. Supply was determined in

TABLE 2.3. A COMPARISON OF THE ESTIMATES OF THE LOCAL CONSUMPTION DEFICITS OF WHEAT FOR TWO TRADING AREAS (thousands of bushels)

	(1) Method one (local demand minus local supply)	(2) Method two (nine-year average of receipts minus exports)	(3) Column 1 as a per cent of Column 2
Boston	6,996	7,215	97
New Orleans	3,504	3,070	114

[38] Baltimore Corn and Flour Exchange, *Annual Report, 1890, 1894;* U.S. Census Office, *Eleventh Census of the United States, Population in the United States,* Part I, Tables 8 and 89 (hereafter referred to as *Eleventh Census, Population*); cf. note 36 in this chapter.

[39] These estimates are based on data for the years 1910–14. The relevant figures are: horses, 27.711 bushels; hogs, 16.568; dairy cattle, 5.112; other cattle, 2.460; sheep, 0.413; poultry, 0.671. U.S.D.A., *Consumption of Feed by Livestock, 1909–1956,* Production Research Report No. 21, (November, 1958), pp. 28–31, 80.

the manner described by Strauss and Bean.[40] Table 2.2 presents tentative estimates of the requirements of meat in the deficit areas. These figures will also have to be adjusted for urban-rural differences in consumption, but the adjustment will not significantly alter the aggregate meat requirement of the deficit areas. Funk's 1913–14 study indicated that average consumption of beef and pork in 570 northern and southern farm families was 157 pounds per equivalent adult. U.S.D.A. data indicate that for the population as a whole the corresponding 1913 figure was about 160 pounds per equivalent adult. However, since farm families ate considerably more pork than beef, the urban-rural adjustment will reduce the estimated amount of the aggregate beef deficit and increase the amount of the aggregate pork deficit in about the same proportions.[41]

The Railroad Rates

Standard sources such as the *Annual Reports* of the Interstate Commerce Commission, the Treasury Department reports on internal commerce, and the report of the Aldrich Committee, provide information on less than 10 per cent of the relevant interregional routes. Fortunately the tariffs filed with the I.C.C. under the Interstate Commerce Act of 1887 are available in a government warehouse near Washington. These files contain the published rates on all of the desired routes.

To the extent that rebating took place, published rates exceeded actual rates. State and Federal investigations produced voluminous reports and documents on the rebating problem. These contain data that can be used to adjust some of the published rates. Continuing research in archives may yield additional information. However, some procedure will have

[40] U.S.D.A., *Consumption of Food in the United States, 1909–1952,* Agricultural Handbook No. 52 (1953) ; U.S. Bureau of Labor, *Eighteenth Annual Report of the Commissioner of Labor, Cost of Living and Retail Food Prices* (1904) ; hereafter referred to as *Cost of Living* (1904). Frederick Strauss and Louis H. Bean, *Gross Farm Income and Indices of Farm Production and Prices in the United States 1869–1937,* U.S.D.A. Tech. Bull. No. 703 (1940).

[41] Funk, *Value to Farm Families,* pp. 5, 20; U.S.D.A., *Livestock and Meat Statistics,* Stat. Bull. No. 230 (July, 1958), pp. 283, 284; U.S.D.A., *Consumption of Food,* p. 197. Two adjustments were made to the U.S.D.A. data to make them comparable to Funk's: the per capita estimates were transformed to equivalent adult estimates on the assumption that the proportion of persons 12 years old and under was the same in 1913 as in 1910 (cf. note 36) ; edible offals were added to the U.S.D.A. figures on beef and pork since farm families generally consumed all parts of the animals they slaughtered. Carle C. Zimmerman, *Consumption and Standards of Living* (New York, 1936), pp. 81–82.

to be devised by which one can both check the reliability of the evidence in the public record and estimate rebates for which no direct evidence exists. One possible approach involves the use of published rates for a year like 1910 when rebating was rather generally eliminated. Abstracting from changes in the price level, the fall in average published rates between 1890 and 1910 is attributable to two factors: the elimination of rebating and the decline in actual rates.[42] Therefore, the differences between average published rates in 1890 and in 1910 (adjusted for changes in the price level) are the most that the average rebate could have been. By multiplying appropriate ratios of average 1910 rates to 1890 rates by the actual 1890 rates, one obtains an estimate of the least that average actual rates could have been in 1890.

The Water Rates

Water transportation was dominated by three main routes: the Great Lakes and Erie Canal route, the Mississippi route, and the intracoastal route. Every movement from a primary to a secondary market can be divided into movement along one or more of these lines plus an additional short movement along some other body of water. The rates on the main water highways are available in board of trade reports, tariffs filed with the I.C.C., and other documents. Thus only a small part of the charge to a shipper will have to be estimated. Moreover, possible deviations between published and actual water rates are less troublesome. To the extent that such deviations existed, the upward bias of the estimated social saving will be further accentuated.

A PRELIMINARY ESTIMATE OF THE SOCIAL SAVING

There is no reliable way to predict the outcome of the linear programming problems. In computations of this sort, surprises are common. Even if all the required data were compiled, it would be difficult to

---

[42] That actual rates declined between 1890 and 1910 is suggested by the fact that average freight revenue per ton-mile (adjusted for changes in the price level) declined by over a third (*Historical Statistics* [1960], p. 431). Of course, the decline in average revenue could have taken place even though actual rates were rising if there had been major changes in the composition of freight traffic. However, the available data suggest that the composition and pattern of traffic remained relatively stable during this period. Cf. data in *Census of Transportation* (1890), Part I and Interstate Commerce Commission, *Twenty-Fourth Annual Report on the Statistics of Railways in the United States for the Year Ending June 30, 1911* (Washington, 1913).

anticipate such results as the efficient patterns of trade in the rail and non-rail situations or the breakdown of the social saving by products, routes, and regions. However, a crude estimate of the *aggregate* social saving is possible. The calculation that follows involves guesses about average transit distances and average freight rates by both water and rail—averages that cannot reliably be calculated until the linear programming problems are solved. Despite its crudity, the calculation is useful for two reasons. First, it provides a convenient format for demonstrating the ways in which a number of costs—costs that have been considered unquantifiable—can be quantified. Second, it provides a rough idea of the magnitude of the aggregate social saving that one can expect to obtain from the models.

Comparative Rates, Tonnages, and Distance

The starting point of the calculation is the difference between the average ton-mile transportation rate by water and by rail. Various experts on transportation have pointed out that water rates were generally lower than railroad rates.[43] Thus, over the route from Chicago to New York, the average all-rail rate on wheat in 1890 was 0.523 cents per ton-mile, while the average all-water rate was 0.139 cents per ton-mile.[44] Casual examination of the available data suggests that these figures are approximately the same as those applying to all grains on this and other routes.[45] Hence, for the purposes of calculation it will be arbitrarily assumed that the New York to Chicago all-water rate per ton-mile on wheat equalled the average all-water rate (per ton-mile) on all grains over all the relevant routes. The assumption made on the all-rail rate is symmetric.

For the crude calculation of the social saving, the average national rate at which grain was actually transported in 1890 is needed. This actual rate must have been less than the all-rail rate. Not all grains shipped interregionally were carried exclusively by rail. Considerable quantities

---

[43] See, for example, Leland H. Jenks, "Railroads as an Economic Force in American Development," *Journal of Economic History*, IV (1944), 12–13; and Harold G. Moulton, *Waterways versus Railways* (Boston and New York, 1912), pp. 12–13, 33–38.

[44] *Industrial Commission, Distribution*, p. 142.

[45] See, for example, data in *Changes in Rates;* U.S. Congress, Senate, *Preliminary Report of the Inland Waterways Commission*, Doc. No. 326, 60th Cong., 1st Sess., 1908, pp. 205–9 (hereafter referred to as *Preliminary Report*) ; and Louisville and Nashville Railroad, *Southwestern Freight Tariff, No. 9* (November 16, 1890) ; hereafter referred to as *L and N, No. 9*.

were shipped by a combination of rail and water or completely by water. In contradistinction to the 0.523 cents all-rail rate per ton-mile on wheat transported from Chicago to New York, the lake-and-rail charge was 0.229 cents, and the lake-and-canal charge was 0.186 cents.[46] The average of these three rates, weighted by the quantities of grain shipped under each one, is 0.434 cents (see Table 2.4). This last figure will be taken as the "actual" national average rate on grains per ton-mile in 1890. In passing, it may be noted that the adjustment produced a figure which is less than a mill below the all-rail rate.

TABLE 2.4. ESTIMATE OF THE AVERAGE ACTUAL RATE

Type of transportation	(1) Rate per ton-mile (cents)	(2) Wheat and corn (millions of tons)	(3) Col. 1 × Col. 2 (cents)
1. All water	0.186	1.254	0.2332
2. Water and rail	0.229	2.423	0.5549
3. All rail	0.523	9.073	4.7452
4. Sum of columns		12.750	5.5333
5. Average actual rate in cents per ton-mile (sum of Col. 3 ÷ sum of Col. 2)			0.434

SOURCES AND NOTES:

Column 1. The three rates were determined by taking the Chicago to New York charges on wheat (including transshipment and insurance costs) and dividing each charge by the appropriate distance. *Industrial Commission, Distribution*, p. 142; George G. Tunnel, "The Division of the Flour and Grain Traffic from the Great Lakes to the Railroad," *Journal of Political Economy*, V (June, 1897), 345; U.S. Congress, Senate, *Select Committee on Transportation-Routes to the Seaboard*, Report No. 307, Part 1, 43rd Cong. 1st Sess., p. 17; below, Table 2.6.

Column 2. *Line 1* is the total amount of wheat (including the grain equivalent of flour) and corn shipped by canal from the lake ports of Buffalo, Oswego, and Tonawonda, plus the quantity of the same commodities shipped from St. Louis by river. The amount of flour shipped from St. Louis by boat was obtained by multiplying the proportion of flour shipped by river in 1898 by the total 1890 shipments of flour. *Line 2* is the amount of wheat (including the grain equivalent of flour) and corn received at the lake ports of Erie, Buffalo, Oswego, and Ogdensberg, minus the grain shipped from lake ports by canal. *Line 3* is the total quantity of wheat and corn shipped interregionally minus lines 1 and 2. Buffalo Merchants' Exchange, *Annual Report, 1891*, pp. 71, 106, 108, 109, 112; U.S. Congress, House, *Report on the Internal Commerce of the United States for the Year 1891*, Exec. Doc. No. 6, Part 2, 52d Cong., 1st Sess., XXVI; U.S. Bureau of Statistics (Treas. Depart.) *Monthly Summary of Commerce and Finance*, Vol. 7 (Jan., 1900), pp. 2006–7, 2009; *Aldrich Report*, Part I, p. 558; below, Table 2.6.

[46] The lake-and-canal rate differs from the all-water rate cited in the previous paragraph by 0.047 cents because the former includes transshipment and insurance charges. The lake-and-rail rate includes insurance but not transshipment costs, since the ex-lake rail rates included transshipping charges. Cf. with notes to Table 2.4.

In the case of meat and livestock products the calculation is based on the St. Louis to New Orleans rates on pork. The all-rail rate was 1.07 cents per ton-mile and the all-water rate was 0.45 cents.[47] Again, these rates are comparable to those that prevailed on other meat products shipped on this and other routes. Furthermore, since the quantity of meat shipped by water was a small part of the total interregional tonnage, no further adjustment need be made; that is, the all-rail rate on pork will be assumed to equal the actual average rate on all meat products.

The quantity of corn, wheat, pork, and beef shipped interregionally in 1890 was approximately equal to the net local deficit of the trading areas plus net exports.[48] Assuming that half of the meat products were shipped as livestock and half as dressed meat, the amount transported interregionally was 15,700,000 tons.[49]

Estimates of average distance are based on a sample of 30 routes (pairs of cities). The sample was randomly drawn from a population of 825 routes. The average rail distance in the sample was 926 miles and the average water distance was 1,574 miles.[50] Since only small amounts of meat were transported by water, 926 miles will be assumed to be the average distance over which meats were actually shipped in 1890. In the case of grains, an adjustment should be made for the tonnage that was carried partly or wholly by water. The adjusted figure, 1,044 miles, represents the estimate of the average distance over which grains were actually shipped in 1890.[51]

---

[47] The water rate is the highest that prevailed during the 1890 season of navigation. *Preliminary Report*, p. 343. The rail rate is taken from *L and N, No. 9*, 10.

[48] See Table 2.2 above.

[49] A breakdown of this figure is given in Table 2.6.

[50] The averages are simple arithmetic means. Water distances between the points in the sample are an average of 70 per cent longer than rail distances. This suggests a somewhat greater degree of circuity in water transportation than was indicated by the study of the Bureau of Railway Economics entitled *An Economic Survey of Inland Waterway Transportation in the United States* (Washington, 1930).

[51] The adjustment was made in the following manner:

Method	1 Distance (miles)	2 Tons of grain (millions)	3 Millions of ton- miles (Col. 1 × Col. 2)
1. All-rail	926	9.073	8,402
2. Water-and-rail	1,302	2.423	3,155
3. All-water	1,398	1.254	1,753
4. Totals		12.750	13,310
5. Average distance (sum of Col. 3 ÷ sum of Col. 2)			1,044

If rates and ton-miles were the only elements entering into the cost of transportation, it would have been cheaper to have shipped interregionally by water rather than by rail. As shown in Table 2.5, the social saving calculated on the basis of these elements is negative by about $38,000,000. This odd result is not difficult to explain. While the estimated actual cost of transportation includes virtually all relevant items, the estimated cost of water transportation does not. In calculating the cost of shipping without the railroad, one must account for six neglected items of cost not reflected in the first approximation. These are: cargo losses in transit, transshipment costs, wagon haulage from water points to secondary markets not on water routes, the cost resulting from the time lost when using a slow medium of transportation, the cost of being unable to use water routes for five months out of the year, and finally, capital costs not reflected in water rates.

When account is taken of the six neglected costs, the loss attributable to the railroad will be transformed into a saving. How big will the neglected costs have to be to produce a positive saving of 1 per cent of national income? In 1890 gross national product was about $12,000,-000,000, and 1 per cent of this amount is $120,000,000. Without the neglected costs, the interregional shipment of the four commodities would have been $38,000,000 cheaper by water than by rail. Consequently, in order to reach a social saving of 1 per cent of gross national product, the neglected costs will have to be approximately $158,000,000.

The Neglected Costs

The literature on the interregional transportation of agricultural products indicates that cargo losses were greater on water shipments than on rail shipments. Insurance rates can be used to estimate the cost of these water transit losses. Since the average value of a loss on a given shipment was approximately equal to the insurance charge on the shipment, the total value of cargo losses in the absence of the railroad would have been approximately equal to the average insurance charge on a water shipment multiplied by the total value of the goods transported interregionally. Moreover, since railroad rates included insurance, this figure would also represent the neglected cost of cargo losses. The desired calculation is shown in Table 2.6. The cost of insurance (cost of cargo losses) in the absence of the railroad would have been approximately $6,000,000. Subtracting this figure from $158,000,000, there is left $152,000,000 to cover the remaining costs.

TABLE 2.5. FIRST APPROXIMATION OF THE SOCIAL SAVING

Commodity	1 Quantity shipped (millions of tons)	2 Millions of ton-miles of water transportation (Col. 1 × 1,574 miles)	3 Water rate per ton-mile (dollars)	4 Cost of water transportation in millions of dollars (Col. 2 × Col. 3)	5 Average actual distance (miles)	6 Millions of ton-miles of actual transportation (Col.1 × Col. 5)	7 Actual rate per ton-mile dollars	8 Cost of actual transportation in millions of dollars (Col. 6 × Col. 7)	9 Social Saving in millions of dollars (Col. 4 − Col. 8)
Meats	3.000	4,722	.00451	21.296	926	2,778	.01071	29.752	− 8.456
Grains	12.750	20,069	.00139	27.896	1,044	13,311	.00434	57.770	−29.874
Totals	15.750	24,791		49.192		16,089		87.522	−38.330

SOURCES: See notes to Table 2.4, 2.6 and text, pp. 30–36.

TABLE 2.6. ESTIMATED COST OF INSURANCE

		1 Tons shipped inter- regionally	2 Price per ton	3 Value Col. 1 × Col. 2	4 Insurance rate as a proportion of value	5 Cost of insurance Col. 3 × Col. 4
1.	Cattle	949,000	$ 97	$ 92,100,000	.01	$ 921,000
2.	Dressed beef	503,000	138	69,400,000	.01	694,000
3.	Hogs	1,008,000	79	79,600,000	.01	796,000
4.	Dressed pork	538,000	110	59,200,000	.01	592,000
5.	Corn	7,735,000	13	100,600,000	.01	1,006,000
6.	Wheat	5,015,000	30	150,500,000	.01	1,505,000
7.	Totals	15,748,000		551,400,000		5,514,000

SOURCES AND NOTES:

Column 1. Estimates of tons shipped interregionally are based on the local net deficits of the secondary markets plus exports. In the case of meats, it was assumed that half the deficit was shipped as dressed meats and half as livestock. Dressed pork was converted into a live equivalent at the rate, one pound of dressed pork equals 1.874 pounds of live weight. The conversion rate for beef was one pound of dressed weight to 1.887 pounds of live weight. See pp. 30–36 above.

Column 2. The figures cited are the average Chicago wholesale prices except for dressed meats which are New York quotations. In the case of wheat and corn, the prices represent unweighted averages of the 12 average monthly prices with averages of missing months determined by linear interpolation. George K. Holmes, "Meat Situation in the United States," U.S.D.A., *Departmental Report*, No. 109, Pt. I, pp. 289–98; *Aldrich Report*, Pt. 2, p. 10; *Historical Statistics* (1960), p. 123.

Column 4. Insurance rates varied with the distance of a shipment and the route. In 1850 average insurance rates on the Mississippi and Ohio were about 1 per cent of the value of the cargo per thousand miles. In 1870 the rate on the Great Lakes was about the same. However, scattered data suggest that in subsequent years marine insurance rates fell sharply. By the 1890's insurance on the Lakes was 0.3 per cent per thousand miles. A decade later the rate on cargo from Pittsburgh to New Orleans was about 0.7 per cent per thousand miles while the intracoastal rate was about 0.1 per cent. In the absence of the railroad perhaps half of the tonnage would have been carried over the Lake or intracoastal routes. In view of the foregoing it seems reasonable to assume that in the absence of the railroad, the average insurance rate probably would not have exceeded the later Mississippi rate, i.e., 0.7 per cent per thousand miles or approximately one per cent for 1,574 miles. Louis C. Hunter, *Steamboats on the Western Rivers* (Cambridge, Mass., 1949), pp. 368–69; U.S. Congress, Senate, *Select Committee on Transportation-Routes to the Seaboard*, Report No. 307, Part 1, 43d Cong., 1st Sess., p. 17; George G. Tunell, "The Diversion of Flour and Grain from the Great Lakes to the Railroads," *Journal of Political Economy*, V (June, 1897), 345; *Preliminary Report*, pp. 332–33.

Transshipping costs were incurred whenever it became necessary to switch a cargo from one type of vessel to another. Grain shipped from Chicago to New York, for example, was transferred at Buffalo from lake steamers to canal barges. In the absence of the railroad there would probably have been an average of two transshipments on each ton carried from a primary to a secondary market. At a cost of 50 cents per ton per transshipment, transshipping charges on the grain and meat products in question would have been $16,000,000.[52] Subtracting this amount from $152,000,000 leaves a residual $136,000,000 to cover the remaining costs.

The two indirect costs of water transportation most frequently cited are the cost of the time lost in shipping by water and the cost of being unable to use water routes for about five months out of each year. Arguments based on the time factor and the limited season of navigation have been decisive in ruling out the possibility that water transportation could have been a good substitute for the railroad. Once invoked, these arguments are invincible, since the costs involved seem to be limited only by the intuition of the disputants. Without a means of quantifyng the cost of time and the cost of the limited season of navigation, the hypothesis posed in this paper cannot be tested.

The key to quantifying the cost of the time that would have been lost in water transportation is the nexus between time and inventories. If entrepreneurs could replace goods the instant they were sold, they would, *ceteris paribus,* carry zero inventories. Inventories are necessary to bridge the gap of the time required to deliver a commodity from its supply source to a given point. If, on the average, interregional shipments of agricultural commodities required a month more by water than by rail, it would have been possible to compensate for the time lost through an inventory increase in the secondary markets equal to one-twelfth of annual shipments. Hence the cost of the time lost in using water transportation was the 1890 cost of carrying such an additional inventory.[53]

---

[52] The cost of transshipping meat products appears to have been included in the water rate. U.S. Corporations Bureau, *Report of the Commissioner of Corporations on Transportation by Water in the United States,* Part III, *Water Terminals* (Washington, 1910), pp. 329–34; hereafter referred to as *Transportation by Water.*

[53] The assumption that boats took an average of a month longer than trains to provide the same transportation service introduces an upward bias into the estimate of the cost of time. The minimum time required by *express* freight trains on the run from New York to Chicago in 1896 was 75 hours, indicating an average speed of 12 miles per hour (Joint Traffic Association, *Proceedings of the Board of*

The problems inherent in the limited season of water transportation could also have been met by an increase in inventory. Since water routes were closed for five-twelfths of the year, I will assume that the absence of railroads would have increased the inventories of agricultural commodities held in secondary markets by five-twelfths of the annual interregional shipment. It should be noted that this assumption over-states the additional inventory requirement. Abstracting from risk considerations, the limited season of navigation would—at least with respect to grains—have had no effect on the inventory requirements of the nation, for, in any case, a crop once harvested was placed in inventory and drawn down throughout the year. A shorter transportation season would only have affected the way in which a fixed total inventory was divided between the Midwest and the secondary markets. Exclusive reliance on water routes would have increased the inventory total only if risk factors were operative. Under conditions of risk, the availability of a central depository reduces the size of the stock that must be held by a given set of cities. Nevertheless, the five-twelfths assumption will be adopted to simplify the computation.

The cost of the time lost in water transportation and the limited season of navigation would thus not have exceeded the cost incurred in carrying an inventory equal to one-half of the annual amount of agricultural products that were transported interregionally. As shown in Table 2.6, the Chicago wholesale value of the corn, wheat, beef, and pork shipped interregionally was about $550,000,000. Another $43,-000,000 should be added to approximate wholesale value at seaboard.[54] Hence, in the absence of the railroad, the limited season of navigation would have required an increase in the value of inventories of about $297,000,000. The cost of carrying such an additional inventory would have included the foregone opportunity of investing the same amount

Managers, 1896, p. 627). About the same period boats on the Great Lakes made the round trip from Duluth to Buffalo in nine days, indicating an average speed of over 9 miles per hour (Joseph E. Ransdell, "Legislative Program Congress Should Adopt for Improvement of American Waterways," *The Annals,* XXXI, 38). In 1912 the average speed of freight boats on rivers was about 7 miles per hour (U.S.D.A., Bulletin No. 74, p. 36). These facts suggest that the average time advantage of railroads in the interregional transportation of agricultural products was about a week. Some observers argued that in the transportation of bulk items boats actually provided quicker service than trains (Ransdell, "Legislative Program," p. 38).

[54] To the Chicago values shown in Table 2.6, $2.83 per ton was added for wheat, $2.59 for corn, $4.00 for cattle, and $5.00 for hogs. Dressed meats in Table 2.6 are quoted at the New York prices so no further adjustment was necessary. *Aldrich Report,* I, 518–19, 526.

elsewhere. If it is assumed that on the average capital earned 6 per cent in 1890, the alternative cost of the investment in additional inventory would have been about $18,000,000 per year. To this, one must add about $30,000,000 for storage charges.[55] Subtracting $48,000,000 from $136,000,000 leaves $88,000,000 to account for the two remaining costs.

Cities receiving approximately 10 per cent of the interregional shipments were not on water routes. Since they were an average of 90 miles from the nearest water point, the cost of wagon haulage (at 16.5 cents per ton-mile) would have been $23,000,000. Subtracting this amount from $88,000,000 leaves $65,000,000 to account for the last item—neglected capital charges.

Water rates failed to reflect capital costs to the extent that rivers and canals were improved or built by the government and financed out of taxes rather than tolls. If a complete statement of these uncompensated expenditures were available, one could easily estimate the neglected capital costs. Data exist on capital expenditures for water transportation, but much work remains to be done to develop a consistent and complete statement of uncompensated investment. Federal expenditures on river improvement over the years between 1802 and 1890 appear to have amounted to $111,000,000. Canals still in operation in 1890 were built at a cost of $155,000,000. In addition, there were abandoned canals which would have been in use in the absence of the interregional railroad. These were built at a cost of $27,000,000.[56] The total of the three items, $293,000,000, may either over- or understate the uncompensated capital involved in water transportation. Assuming that the various upward and downward biases, the omitted items and the double counting, cancel each other out, at an interest rate of 6 per cent the neglected capital costs would have been about $18,000,000—$47,000,000 short of

[55] The cost of elevating and storing grain in Buffalo from November 10 to the opening of navigation (about five months) was two cents per bushel or 0.4 cents per bushel per month (Buffalo Merchants' Exchange, *Annual Report,* 1890, pp. 88–89). At this rate storage charges on the six months of additional inventory of wheat and corn would have amounted to $5,300,000. In 1910 cold storage rates were $4.96 per ton per month on beef and $4.70 on pork (U.S.D.A., *Statistical Bulletin No. 93,* p. 44). At these rates, the additional storage charges on beef and pork would have been $31,000,000 in dollars of 1910 or $25,000,000 in dollars of 1890. However, cold storage would have been the most costly way of maintaining the additional inventory of meat. It would have been cheaper to store meat in the East by sending live animals to eastern feeders. In this case the cost of storage would have been essentially the cost of shipping more feed but smaller animals.

[56] *Preliminary Report,* pp. 180–81, 193–97, 202–3, 205–9; cf. U.S. Bureau of the Census, *Transportation by Water, 1906,* pp. 44–6.

the amount required to bring the social saving to 1 per cent of gross national product.[57]

Thus casual examination of the available data suggests that the social saving attributable to the railroad in the interregional transportation of agricultural products was about six-tenths of 1 per cent of national income.[58] The calculation is, of course, subject to considerable error; but there are grounds for having confidence in the result. Four of the estimates—those dealing with transshipment, wagon haulage, time lost, and the limited season of navigation—probably overstate the actual cost of water transportation. While the estimates of some of the other items may be too low, it does not seem likely that the errors are large enough to substantially alter the magnitude of the indicated social saving. Suppose, for example, that railroad rates on a ton-mile basis were not above water rates as has generally been assumed. If the initial water-rail rate differential had actually been zero on all commodities, the elimination of this error would increase the estimated social saving by only $56,-000,000. Indeed, if railroad rates are assumed to have been zero, the social saving would rise to only $161,000,000 or about 1.3 per cent of gross national product.

This chapter has focused on one aspect of the influence of the railroad on American economic development. A small aggregate social saving

[57] The preceding calculation may be summarized as follows:

First approximation of social saving	$-38,000,000
Neglected cargo losses	6,000,000
Transshipping costs	16,000,000
Additional inventory costs	48,000,000
Supplementary wagon haulage	23,000,000
Neglected capital costs	18,000,000
Total	$ 73,000,000

[58] How significant is a social saving of about 1 per cent of national income? This question cannot be answered without making further assumptions as to how the economy would have adjusted to the absence of the railroad. One consequence of the absence of the railroad would have been a rise in the seaboard prices of agricultural commodities. This could have had a significant effect on the U.S. balance of trade. Similarly, a shift from railroad to water and wagon transportation may have been a shift from a more to a less capital-intensive activity. Such a change might have aggravated market problems in the capital goods sector. On the other hand, it might have increased the demand for labor.

If one abstracts from these essentially Keynesian issues of insufficient demand and focuses on the economy's production possibilities, it is possible to interpret the social saving in a fairly simple way. Assuming that the marginal aggregate savings and capital-output ratios would have been what, in fact, they were when national income was 99 per cent of the 1890 level, the absence of the interregional railroad would have retarded the development of the economy by about three months.

in the interregional transportation of agricultural products would not prove that the railroad was unimportant in American development. Conclusions regarding the over-all impact of the railroad require, as Professor Kuznets has suggested, a thorough examination of all the avenues through which the most celebrated innovation of the nineteenth century may have exercised a strategic influence on economic growth. In this connection it is important to re-emphasize that the linear programming models referred to earlier in the chapter will do more than refine the crude estimate of the aggregate social saving. They will provide information on efficient patterns of agricultural distribution both in the rail and non-rail situations as well as breakdowns of the interregional social saving by regions and commodities. This type of information, supplemented by similar data on intraregional transportation, will facilitate a re-evaluation of such questions as the development significance of various commercial rivalries (e.g., the triumph of Chicago over St. Louis and Cincinnati), the determinants of the geographic pattern of urbanization, and the extent to which the railroad promoted a more efficient utilization of certain productive resources.

CHAPTER III

The Intraregional Distribution of Agricultural Products

Progress in science is thus possible because no single proposition in it is so certain that it can block the search for one better founded.—MORRIS RAPHAEL COHEN

Although in the minority, some of the critics of American transportation policies at the close of the Gilded Age argued that waterways were a good substitute for railroads in the long distance movement of agricultural products. They supported their contention with scattered bits of information drawn from a variety of sources. The 1890 report of the Chicago Board of Trade, for example, reveals that 43 per cent of the flour shipped out of that emporium, 58 per cent of the wheat, 63 per cent of the corn, 26 per cent of the oats, 30 per cent of the rye, and 20 per cent of the barley went by water. The statistics of shipments from Duluth, Milwaukee, and other important primary markets tell a similar story.[1] It was on the basis of such data that the Industrial Commission of 1900 concluded that water was the dominant transportation service in the movement of agricultural commodities from the Midwest to the East Coast. "Between Chicago or Duluth and Oswego," said the Commission, "lie a thousand miles of water, connecting the greatest consuming with the greatest producing section of farm products. These lake routes, plus the Erie Canal on the American side and the St. Lawrence River and its canals on the Canadian side, are the controlling factors, not only in determining the volume of movement in the North from West to East, but also the rate per unit at which that volume shall be distributed between producer and consumer."[2] The more fervent proponents of an expanded system of internal water transportation insisted that on long hauls internal waterways were not only competitive with, but actually superior to, railroads.[3]

[1] Chicago Board of Trade, *Thirty-Third Annual Report* (Chicago, 1891), p. 3.
[2] *Industrial Commission, Distribution*, p. 121.
[3] See, for example, Joseph E. Ransdell, "Legislative Program"; Missouri River Navigation Association, *Railways and Waterways* (Kansas City, Mo., 1930); Francis A. Collins, *Our Harbors and Inland Waters* (New York, 1924).

Yet even those who challenged the notion of the indispensability of the trunk lines accepted the necessity of interior railroads for American economic growth. They appear to have been impressed by the extent to which the iron horse pre-empted the movement of agricultural commodities between farms and primary markets. The 1890 figures on Chicago's grain receipts show that less than 2 per cent of all wheat entering that city arrived by lake or canal. The proportion of other grains carried to Chicago by water was of a similar order of magnitude.[4] Nor was this domination of the interior a development of the later part of the nineteenth century. Unlike the long-haul case, railroads linking farms to primary markets did not have to wait for a long series of technological improvements before they could compete effectively for the carriage of bulky, low value items. As George Rogers Taylor has pointed out, railroads built across Illinois and Wisconsin in the 1850's "had no trouble in getting all the business they could handle."[5] The first line running west from Chicago—the Galena and Chicago Union—fared so well on agricultural traffic that it was able to pay an average annual dividend of 16 per cent on its original capitalization during the first five years of its operation.[6]

However, facts such as these do not prove the proposition that the intraregional railroad was indispensable for the growth of the American economy. They merely demonstrate that the substitution of railroads for boats took place more rapidly within regions than between them. The higher time-rate of substitution does not even imply that intraregional railroads were more important than their long-haul counterparts. There are many possible relationships between this rate of change and the relative costs of rail and water transportation. One cannot leap from the facts cited above to conclusions about the developmental impact of the railroad without knowledge of both the price elasticity of substitution between the two services and the tonnage of goods carried from farms to primary markets.

On the other hand, one cannot assume that the inter- and intraregional problems are identical or that the social savings were equal. There is an important asymmetry in the two cases. Interregional transporta-

---

[4] Chicago Board of Trade, *Thirty-Third Annual Report,* p. 2.

[5] George Rogers Taylor, *The Transportation Revolution* (New York, 1950), p. 165.

[6] Paul Wallace Gates, *The Illinois Central Railroad and its Colonization Work* (Cambridge, Mass., 1934), pp. 85–86.

tion represents a movement between a relatively small number of points —11 great collection centers in the Midwest and 90 secondary markets in the East and South. Moreover many of the secondary markets fell on the same route. Five of the most important of these markets were located on the Erie Canal; another 13 were strung out along the Atlantic Coast. On the other hand, intraregional transportation required the connection of an enormous number of locations. Considering each farm as a shipping point, there were not 11 but 4,565,000 interior shipping locations in 1890; the number of primary markets receiving farm commodities was well over a hundred.[7] Clearly, not all of these points could have been connected by 26,000 miles of navigable streams, 4,000 miles of canals, the Great Lakes, and the coastal routes. These points were not even connected by the 167,000 miles of railroad track that laced the nation in 1890.[8] The movement of commodities from farms to primary markets was never accomplished exclusively by water or by rail. Rather it involved a mix of either wagon and water or wagon and train services. The size of the social saving attributable to interior railroads depends not only on the relative efficiency of the trains and boats but also on the amount of wagon transportation that had to be combined with each of these services.

This is the crux of the intraregional problem. If the evaluation of the impact of interior railroads merely involved an analysis of the effect of the substitution of rail for water transportation, there would be no reason to expect a large social saving. Considered in isolation, boats were a relatively efficient substitute for the iron horse. However, the absence of the railroad would not only have required greater utilization of water service but also greater utilization of wagon service. The average wagon haul from a farm to a rail shipping point in 1890 was about 10 miles. In the absence of a railroad the average wagon haul to a water shipping point might have been 30 or more miles. It is the additional mileage of very costly wagon transportation that would have been needed for the shipment of each ton of agricultural produce leaving the farm which suggests that the social saving attributable to interior railroads probably exceeded the social saving of the more celebrated trunk lines. Recognition of this point does not, of course, resolve the issue. The question persists: "By how much?"

[7] *Eleventh Census, Agriculture,* p. 74.
[8] *Preliminary Report,* pp. 35, 193–201; *Historical Statistics* (1960), p. 427.

THE ESTIMATION OF THE SOCIAL SAVING

The social saving attributable to the intraregional railroad will be estimated in two ways. The first measure (estimate α) utilizes the concept presented in the previous chapter. In 1890 a certain bundle of agricultural commodities was shipped from farms to primary markets. The bundle was shipped in a definite way at some definite but unknown total cost. Given the necessary data it is possible to determine both this cost and the alternative cost of shipping exactly the same bundle of goods from farms to primary markets in exactly the same pattern without the aid of railroads. The difference between these two total costs would then be a measure of the social saving attributable to the railroad in the intraregional transportation of agriculture products. In this case as in the interregional problem, the specified cost differential is an upper bound on the true social saving.[9]

Estimate α is less appropriate to the analysis of the short-haul than of the long-haul railroad. Since it contains an indefinite upward bias, the usefulness of estimate α depends on the size of the anticipated social saving. In the interregional case the social saving is so low that one need not be overly concerned with the extent of the bias. Given the larger social saving of interior railroads, the upward bias becomes a more important issue. It is therefore desirable to use an estimating procedure that reduces the exaggeration of the distances over which agricultural commodities would have been carried by wagon in the absence of the railroad. Estimate α is especially weak in this respect. For accepting the railroad pattern of shipments implies that, in the absence of the railroad, wagons would have carried certain agricultural commodities over distances in which wagon transportation costs exceeded the market value of the produce.

It is possible to reduce the upward bias in the estimate of the intraregional social saving by making use of available data on land values. Without the railroads, the high cost of wagon transportation would have limited commercial agricultural production to ranges of land lying within some unknown distance of navigable waterways. If the boundaries of this region of feasible commercial argiculture were known, the social saving could be broken into two parts: (1) The difference between the cost of shipping agricultural commodities from farms lying within the feasible region to primary markets with the railroad and the cost of

---

[9] Cf. with discussion in Chapter II.

shipping from the same region without the railroad; (2) the loss in national product due to the decrease in the supply of agricultural land. The social saving estimated in this manner (estimate β) would be less than the previous measure since it allows for a partial adjustment to a non-railroad situation.

There are two major theoretical problems in executing estimate β. One is the determination of the boundaries of feasible commercial agriculture. The solution to this problem can best be explained by resorting to a hypothetical example. Suppose that Congress passed a law requiring all farmers in an area of land 1 mile wide and 100 miles long, running westward from the Mississippi River through the state of Missouri along the 40th parallel, to send their products to market (St. Louis) by wagon and boat. Suppose that Congress also prohibited these farmers from responding to the law by changing the kinds or the proportions of the commodities that were produced for the market. Finally, assume that the rates from all rail shipping points in the strip to St. Louis were exactly the same as Mississippi River rates from the 40th parallel to St. Louis.

Under these circumstances, how much of the land in the designated area would remain in commercial agricultural production after the Congressional enactment? Obviously farms lying along the Mississippi would be unaffected by the law as would all farms that were just as far from the Mississippi River as from a rail shipping point. For all other farmers the law would result in a decline in the prices they received at the farm for their various commodities. The fall in price would, in turn, lead to a corresponding decline in farm land values. Since the output of the farms in question is very small relative to total agricultural production, no output decisions on the part of these farmers could affect prices in primary markets. The reduction in prices paid at the farm and the corresponding fall in land values would be explained by the increased cost of transportation, that is, by the fact that farmers were now being forced to ship over longer distances at high wagon rates. The farther a farm was from the Mississippi, the greater would be the fall in the value of that farm land. At some distance from the Mississippi the increase in the cost of wagon transportation would be such that land values would be zero. All land lying beyond this distance would have a negative price. Hence given the value of each plot of land prior to enactment, the quantities of agricultural commodities shipped to St. Louis from each of the farms, the wagon rates, and the distance from each farm to a rail shipping point, one could determine the boundary of feasible commercial agriculture after the enactment. The boundary would be located along a set of points at which the increase in the cost of transporting the market bound output from a farm to a shipping point was exactly equal to the pre-enactment rental value of that land.

The hypothetical example indicates the basic procedure for establishing the boundaries of feasible commercial agriculture. There are, of course, several differences between the hypothetical example and the actual problem. First, transportation rates from rail and water shipping points to primary markets will not be the same for most farms. If water rates are less than rail rates the boundary of feasible production will be pushed out; if rail rates are less than water rates the boundary will be pushed closer to the navigable water route. Second, when the whole country is considered, one cannot ignore the effect of the cessation of agricultural production on land beyond the feasible range on the level of prices in primary markets. Given the relative inelasticity of the demand for agricultural products, the reduction in production would have tended to raise prices in primary markets. The rise in prices would have led to a more intensive exploitation of agriculture within the feasible region, thus raising land values. The rise in land values would have increased the burden of additional transportation costs that could have been borne by various farms. Thus calculation of the feasible range on the basis of the actual 1890 land values and shipment statistics tends to understate the limits of feasible commercial agriculture and over-states the amount of land that would have remained unused in the absence of the railroad. The net effect of these conflicting considerations on the interpretation of the β estimate is uncertain. Third, the mix of agricultural commodities undoubtedly would have changed in response to the changed structure of the transportation rates associated with a non-rail situation. To the extent that this influence would have been operative, acceptance of actual 1890 production and shipment figures introduces an upward bias in the β estimate. Since the available evidence suggests that water transportation was a constant or decreasing cost industry, acceptance of 1890 water rates introduces either no bias or an upward bias.[10] The use of published wagon rates also imparts an upward bias. Most farmers used their own wagons and teams when hauling their crops to a shipping point. They also usually provided the labor. Use of commercial wagon rates involves the dubious assumption

[10] There is less possibility of a bottleneck in the intraregional than in the long-haul case because no one water route would have had to carry the burden assigned to the Erie Canal in long-haul transportation.

that the marginal cost of farmer's labor and equipment was equal to the price of the professional service.[11]

The second major theoretical problem involved in the execution of estimate β is the determination of the loss in national income brought about by a decrease in the supply of land. Land values also provide the key to the solution of this problem. The 1890 value of the lands lying beyond the region of feasible commercial agriculture represents a capitalization of the amount by which the annual product of labor and capital utilized on this territory exceeded the value of the product of the same amount of labor and capital when applied at the margin. If the land in the non-feasible region had not been available, the labor and capital employed on it would have been invested either at the intensive or extensive margin. Hence, if the quantity of displaced factors had been small, the fall in the value of the output of these factors would have been equal to the annual rental value of the land they had previously occupied. This loss in national income could be estimated by decapitalizing the land values, i.e., multiplying land values by appropriate mortgage rates of interest. However, the amount of labor and capital employed on non-feasible terrain was quite large, so that their displacement would have led to a fall in national income which exceeded the decapitalized value of the non-feasible lands. Consequently the estimate of the loss in national income due to the decrease in the supply of land will contain an indeterminate downward bias.

How shall estimate β be interpreted? It contains both upward and downward biases. These will, of course, tend to cancel. However, there is no way of telling whether the residual will be positive, negative, or zero. My personal speculation is that the upward biases are greater and hence that estimate β is another (lesser) upper bound on the true social saving. However, it is perhaps more reasonable to treat estimate β as a fairly close approximation of the true social saving. If this interpretation were adopted one could say: "The social saving attributable to the railroad in the intraregional distribution of agricultural products was probably about β. But in any case it was less than α."

In order to use the data for 1890 as a basis for inferences about the importance of the railroad in earlier years, one must know how the intraregional social saving changed over time. The change in the social saving (relative to G.N.P.) will depend on several factors: the change

[11] Cf. with the discussion of wagon transportation in the next section of this chapter.

in the comparative efficiency of water and rail transportation; the change in the quantity of agricultural goods shipped intraregionally by rail; the change in the average distance of wagon hauls; the change in the average cost of wagon transportation per ton-mile; and the growth in G.N.P. Available evidence suggests that the movement of these variables was such that both the absolute and relative social saving increased over time. Since the relationships that must be considered are complex, an algebraic statement will be useful. In any particular year the social saving (estimate α) will be given by:

(3.1) $$\alpha = xk$$

where x is the tonnage of goods entering into intraregional transportation that was carried by rail, and k is the social saving per ton of x. If the determinants of k are specified, equation 3.1 becomes

(3.2) $$\alpha = x \left[w(D_{fb} - D_{fr}) + (BD_{bp} - RD_{rp}) \right]$$

where

$w =$	the average wagon rate per ton-mile
$B =$	the average water rate per ton-mile
$R =$	the average rail rate per ton-mile
$D_{fb} =$	the average distance from a farm to a water shipping point
$D_{fr} =$	the average distance from a farm to a rail shipping point
$D_{bp} =$	the average distance from a water shipping point to a primary market
$D_{rp} =$	the average distance from a rail shipping point to a primary market.

The first term within the square bracket of equation 3.2 can be interpreted as the social saving per ton attributable to the reduction in wagon transportation; the second term, as the social saving per ton attributable to the superiority of railroads over boats.

How did k change over time? There is no evidence that wagon rates (w) fell over the 50 years leading up to 1890. There were no major innovations in wagon construction nor any marked improvement in roads.[12] Indeed, the money cost of commercial wagon transportation appears to have risen during the period in question. Taylor states that "by the fifties, 15 cents [per ton-mile] was considered the usual rate on 'ordinary highways.'" By contrast, a Department of Agriculture study indicated an average rate of 20.5 cents per ton-mile in 1906. However, if the change in the price level is taken into account, the

---

[12] Cf. with the discussion of wagon transportation in the last section of this chapter.

discrepancy disappears.[13] The average distance of a wagon haul from farms to a water shipping point (D_{fb}) increased as the interior of the North Central states became more heavily populated and the Trans-Missouri West was settled. At the same time the average wagon haul from a farm to a rail shipping point (D_{fr}) fell due to an increase in the density of the rail network. By 1906 the average distance from a farm to a rail stop was about 7 miles in corn territory and 12 miles in the cotton states.[14] Hence $w(D_{fb} - D_{fr})$ increased as the century progressed.

Table 3.2 suggests the perhaps surprising result that the social saving per ton attributable to the "superiority" of railroads over boats $(BD_{bp} - RD_{rp})$ was negative. However, it seems quite likely that this term became less negative over time. For the years 1871–75, the charge on wheat carried from Chicago to New York by rail exceeded the water rate by an average of 5.85 mills per ton-mile. By the quinquennium 1891–95, the differential had fallen to 3.66 mills.[15] On the other hand, there is no reason to suppose that the average distance from a rail shipping point to a primary market rose or, if it did, that it rose more than in proportion to the average distance from a water shipping point to a primary market. When agricultural production moved westward, new primary markets arose in Milwaukee, Minneapolis, Kansas City, and Omaha.

From the foregoing it seems quite likely that k rose, or at the least, remained constant as the country developed. If, in fact, k was constant or increased, the ratio $\dfrac{\alpha_n}{\alpha_{1890}}$ would be less than or equal to $\dfrac{x_n}{x_{1890}}$ where n is any year prior to 1890. It is possible to use this relationship to estimate the level of the intraregional social saving in the years preceding 1890—i.e., to determine the maximum value of the intraregional social saving.

In 1870, for example, agricultural commodities entering into intraregional trade amounted to approximately 26,746,000 tons. By 1890 the corresponding figure was 60,347,000 tons (see Table 3.1). Con-

[13] Taylor, *Transportation Revolution*, p. 134; *Industrial Commission*, X, 690; Frank Andrews, "Cost of Hauling Crops from Farms to Shipping Points," U.S.D.A., Bureau of Statistics, *Bulletin No. 49*. When the 1850 wagon rate is put in dollars of 1906 (using the Snyder-Tucker index) it becomes about 20.3 cents per ton-mile.

[14] Andrews, "Cost," pp. 20, 21.

[15] Frank Andrews, "Grain Movement in the Great Lakes Region," U.S.D.A., Bureau of Statistics, *Bulletin 81*, p. 71.

TABLE 3.1. TONNAGE ENTERING INTO INTRAREGIONAL TRANSPORTATION, 1870 AND 1890 (thousands of tons)

Commodity	Shipments from farms 1870	Shipments from farms 1890
1. Wheat	4,123	8,642
2. Corn	3,485	12,125
3. Oats	1,032	3,020
4. Barley	363	970
5. Rye	343	566
6. Buckwheat	83	119
7. Potatoes	2,675	4,071
8. Sweet potatoes	392	764
9. Flax seed	36	273
10. Hay	4,900	10,300
11. Cotton	1,005	1,785
12. Cottonseed	—	874
13. Tobacco	132	263
14. Rice	37	107
15. Dry edible beans	74	95
16. Beet sugar	—	4
17. Cane sugar	89	249
18. Fruits	741	2,117
19. Peanuts	8	47
20. Dairy products	2,674	6,346
21. Chickens	114	220
22. Eggs	54	172
23. Wool	81	138
24. Cattle	1,744	3,687
25. Calves	46	212
26. Hogs	2,397	2,913
27. Sheep and lambs	118	268
28. Totals	26,746	60,347

SOURCES AND NOTES: See Table 3.6.

sequently the absolute intraregional social saving of 1870 was, at most, 44 per cent of the absolute social saving of 1890. Since G.N.P. rose by approximately 52 per cent between the two dates, whatever the 1890 ratio of the intraregional social saving to G.N.P., the 1870 ratio was less than 67 per cent of that amount.[16]

THE DATA PROBLEM

To compute the intraregional social saving it is necessary to know: the quantity of agricultural commodities shipped by rail from the farms in each county to primary markets; the average wagon distances from

[16] U.S. Bureau of the Census, *Historical Statistics of the United States, 1789–1945* (Washington, 1949), p. 14; hereafter referred to as *Historical Statistics* (1949).

these farms to the rail and water shipping points; the distances from the rail and water shipping points to the primary markets; the wagon, rail and water rates on the commodities entering into intraregional trade; farm land values; and mortgage rates of interest. Unfortunately most of these figures are not directly available. This section deals with the problems involved in the derivation of desired information from available data. Once again it is important to emphasize that the results presented below are tentative; many obvious adjustments have not yet been made. Nevertheless, the results are sufficiently close to the truth to permit the computation of crude α and β estimates.

An α Estimate for the North Atlantic Region

Table 3.2 presents an α estimate of the intraregional social saving in the eight states that comprise the North Atlantic region. The estimate is based on a randomly drawn sample of 23 ($= n$) of the 215 ($= N$) counties in the region. The sample value $\dfrac{\hat{a}}{n}$ —i.e., the total sample social saving divided by the number of counties in the sample— is an unbiased and consistent estimate of the average social saving per county. Consequently $\dfrac{N}{n}\hat{a}$ is an unbiased and consistent estimate of the region's total social saving. However $\dfrac{N}{n}\hat{a}$ is not necessarily the most efficient estimator. It may be possible to reduce the variance of the estimator by using social saving per improved acre, social saving per farm or some similar variable. Of course, the data available for the 23 counties in the sample are also available for all the other counties so one need not resort to sampling techniques at all. The decision to rely on the sample was based on economic rather than technological considerations.

Shipments

The rail shipments of agricultural commodities from the counties are given in Column 1. Total shipments from the counties in the sample amounted to 761,314 tons. The last figure was obtained by subtracting from the production data contained in the 1890 census estimates of consumption within the counties. However, not all of this surplus was

TABLE 3.2. PRELIMINARY α ESTIMATE OF THE INTRAREGIONAL SOCIAL SAVING IN THE NORTH ATLANTIC DIVISION (in dollars)

	1	2	3	4	5	6	7	8	9
Commodity	Amount shipped out via rail in tons[b]	Wagon cost to water	Wagon cost to rail	Cost of water transportation	Cost of rail transportation	Cost of shipping without railroad Col.2 + Col.4	Cost of shipping with railroad Col.3 + Col.5	Social saving Col.6 − Col.7	Social saving per ton Col.8 ÷ Col.1
1. Corn	11,556	63,634	7,857	7,888	16,545	71,522	24,402	47,120	4.08
2. Wheat	51,731	222,771	44,217	45,327	74,128	268,098	118,345	149,753	2.89
3. Oats	30,759	296,399	31,388	38,008	62,752	334,407	94,140	240,267	7.81
4. Barley	18,453	37,161	12,470	21,076	27,846	58,237	40,316	17,921	0.97
5. Rye	15,701	44,216	12,349	17,263	24,736	61,479	37,085	24,394	1.55
6. Buckwheat	10,171	142,286	14,292	13,110	22,101	155,396	36,392	119,004	11.70
7. Potatoes	106,500	2,186,842	156,652	269,717	315,428	2,456,559	472,081	1,984,478	18.63
8. Beef	5,034	30,744	6,789	7,578	10,911	38,322	17,700	20,622	4.10
9. Pork	520	4,624	470	48	993	4,672	1,463	3,209	6.17
10. Chickens	70	467	56	78	210	545	266	279	3.99
11. Milk	112,316	393,185	103,736	583,129	762,331	976,314	866,067	110,247	0.98
12. Butter	4,700	59,704	5,817	5,038	17,168	64,742	22,985	41,757	8.88
13. Cheese	1,741	10,210	2,233	2,805	5,207	13,015	7,440	5,575	3.20
14. Eggs	2,894	13,484	2,799	6,814	8,894	20,298	11,693	8,605	2.97
15. Fruits	6,775	32,451	8,931	2,359	19,723	34,810	28,654	6,156	0.91
16. Hops	17	43	20	35	45	78	65	13	0.76
17. Dry Canada Pease	391	9,037	589	1,229	1,264	10,266	1,853	8,413	21.52
18. Cowpease	105	2,031	154	293	307	2,324	461	1,863	17.74
19. Beans	7,140	23,031	8,073	11,523	11,644	34,554	19,717	14,837	2.08
20. Peanuts[a]	0	0	0	0	0	0	0	0	0.00
21. Broom Corn	3	17	3	3	9	20	12	8	2.67
22. Flax[a]	0	0	0	0	0	0	0	0	0.00
23. Hemp[a]	0	0	0	0	0	0	0	0	0.00

24. Tobacco	946	2,631	511	1,148	1,876	3,779	2,387	1,392	1.47
25. Maple Sugar	1,388	25,726	2,074	475	2,457	26,201	4,531	21,670	15.61
26. Maple Molasses	527	4,860	689	382	968	5,242	1,657	3,585	6.80
27. Hay	222,450	1,883,970	282,298	261,720	376,240	2,145,690	658,538	1,487,152	6.69
28. Mutton	2,424	16,984	2,706	4,057	5,590	21,041	8,296	12,745	5.26
29. Wool	597	4,512	636	1,012	1,918	5,524	2,554	2,970	4.97
30. Column Totals	614,909	5,511,020	707,809	1,302,115	1,771,291	6,813,135	2,479,100	4,334,035	7.05
31. Estimated Regional Totals (line 30 × 9.347826)	5,748,062	51,516,056	6,616,475	12,171,944	16,557,720	63,688,000	23,174,195	40,513,805	

SOURCES AND NOTES: See text for sources and method of computation.

a No county produced as much as one half of 1 ton of peanuts, flax, or hemp.

a Only tonnage for which the social saving was positive, when computed on the assumption that all output was shipped at least part of the way by rail, is included here. The tonnage on which the social saving was negative (i.e., on which the cost of transportation without the railroad was less than with it) was assumed to have been shipped by wagon or by wagon and boat. The total of all the shipments from the counties in the region was 7,116,631 tons. The share shipped by rail (80.8 per cent) was well above the national ratio of 61.0 per cent (see below, pp. 74–75). The difference between the regional and national ratios of the share shipped by rail is probably due to the fact that the wagon rates used in computing the regional social saving exceeded the actual cost of wagon transportation to the farmer (cf. pp. 71–72, below). The overstatement of wagon rates and the consequent overstatement of outshipments via rail will impart an upward bias in the estimate of the regional social saving.

shipped from farms to primary markets via rail. The county by county computations summarized in Table 3.2 showed that for commodities weighing 146,405 tons, transportation costs from farms to primary markets were less when shipments were made exclusively by wagon or by wagon and water than when some railroad service was used. Consequently, it was assumed that only 80.8 per cent (614,909 tons) of the total shipments from the counties in the sample were carried at least part of the distance to primary markets by rail.

The major problem that had to be solved in preparing the entries in Column 1 was the estimation of local consumption. Since the nature and availability of the data needed to compute local consumption varied from commodity to commodity, three different methods of estimation were employed. In the case of commodities used primarily for food, the first step was the estimation of average per capita consumption in the region. Using butter as an example of the procedures followed for this class of commodities, an estimate of the national disappearance of butter per capita was obtained by following the method of the Department of Agriculture. The national disappearance figure was transformed into a regional consumption figure by multiplying the former by the estimated ratio of per capita consumption in the region to per capita consumption in the nation (see Table 3.3). This per capita consumption figure was multiplied by the population of the various counties in the sample to obtain consumption in the region (see Table 3.4).

TABLE 3.3. PER CAPITA CONSUMPTION OF BUTTER BY REGIONS

1. Production on farms (lbs.)	1,024,223,468
2. Production in factories (lbs.)	181,285,000
3. Total butter produced	1,205,518,468
4. + Imports (lbs.)	75,521
5. − Exports (lbs.)	29,748,042
6. Supply (lbs.)	1,175,845,947
7. Population	62,622,250
8. U.S. per capita consumption (lbs.)	18.7768

North Atlantic	1.0781	× 18.7768	=	20.2433
South Atlantic	0.9167	× 18.7768	=	17.2127
North Central	1.0809	× 18.7768	=	20.2958
South Central	0.7487	× 18.7768	=	14.0582
Western	1.1052	× 18.7768	=	20.7521

SOURCES: U.S. Bureau of the Census, *Eleventh Census, Agriculture; Eleventh Census, Manufacturing,* Part I.; U.S.D.A., Bureau of Statistics, *Bulletins 74, 75; Eighteenth Annual Report of the Commissioner of Labor.*

TABLE 3.4. BUTTER SHIPPED OUT OF COUNTY (pounds)

County and State	1 Butter made on farms	2 Off-farm butter factor	3 Butter made in factories Col. 1 × Col. 2	4 Total butter production Col. 1 + Col. 3	5 Human consumption of butter	6 Butter shipped Col. 4 − Col. 5
Aroostook, Me.	1,219,134	.0902	109,966	1,329,100	1,003,845 +	325,255
Cheshire, N. H.	918,636	.2417	222,034	1,140,670	598,777 +	541,893
Rockingham, N. H.	664,149	.2417	160,525	824,674	1,005,080 −	180,406
Washington, Vt.	3,071,176	.2181	669,823	3,740,999	599,323 +	3,141,676
Franklin, Mass.	1,348,523	.2455	331,062	1,679,585	781,594 +	897,991
Windham, Conn.	611,058	.4409	269,415	880,473	833,174 +	47,299
Allegheny, N. Y.	1,515,396	.1475	223,521	1,738,917	875,320 +	863,597
Dutchess, N. Y.	1,224,189	.1475	180,568	1,404,757	1,576,528 −	171,771
Herkimer, N. Y.	1,209,157	.1475	178,351	1,387,508	923,256 +	464,252
Oneida, N. Y.	2,507,681	.1475	369,883	2,877,564	2,488,347 +	389,217
Orleans, N. Y.	1,069,440	.1475	157,742	1,227,182	623,554 +	603,628
Sullivan, N. Y.	1,581,554	.1475	233,279	1,814,833	628,174 +	1,186,663
Tioga, N. Y.	1,700,181	.1475	250,777	1,950,958	650,983 +	1,344,975
Yates, N. Y.	773,705	.1475	114,121	887,826	425,130 +	462,696
Union, N. J.	49,839	.0598	2,980	52,819	1,466,971 −	1,414,152
Adams, Pa.	1,313,185	.2524	331,448	1,644,633	677,867 +	966,766
Allegheny, Pa.	2,102,964	.2524	530,788	2,633,752	11,173,472 −	8,539,720
Chester, Pa.	1,628,235	.2524	410,967	2,039,202	1,809,285 +	229,917
Forest, Pa.	140,373	.2524	35,430	175,803	171,704 +	4,099
Huntingdon, Pa.	678,864	.2524	171,345	850,209	723,718 +	126,491
Lehigh, Pa.	1,206,066	.2524	304,411	1,510,477	1,551,264 −	40,787
Perry, Pa.	617,056	.2524	155,745	772,801	531,913 +	240,888
Westmoreland, Pa.	1,845,031	.2524	465,686	2,310,717	2,283,829 +	26,888

SOURCES AND NOTES:

Column 1. *Census of Agriculture, 1890.*
Column 2. State ratios of production in factories to production on farms, *Census of Manufacturing, 1890.*
Column 5. Regional per capita consumption figure multiplied by population of county.
Column 6. A plus indicates the surplus shipped out; a minus indicates that the county was a deficit producer of butter by the amount shown.

The ratio of regional to national per capita consumption was based on the 1901 study of food consumption by urban workers,[17] but food consumption habits of the urban and rural populations differ. Given the available data, the alternative to using the urban consumption studies is the application of the national per capita figures to all regions. If urban consumption patterns in given regions are indicative of rural consumption patterns in the same region, then use of the regional urban consumption ratios will yield better results than use of unadjusted national averages. The essential assumption involved in the regional adjustment made in Table 3.3 is that regional rural consumption is systematically related to regional urban consumption for given foods. More specifically it is assumed that if the average southern urban person consumed y times as much corn as the average of all urban persons, then the average southern rural person consumed y times as much corn as the average of all rural persons. A comparison of the regional consumption patterns of farmers as revealed by Funk's study with the budget surveys of urban workers [18] indicates that this is a reasonable assumption. If the assumption is correct, the error involved in disregarding regional differences in the ratios of urban to rural population is quite small and can be neglected. Since the proof of this statement is complex, it is again helpful to resort to algebra.

The following notation will be used:

Let Z^i = the per capita consumption of the zth commodity in the ith region.

$\overline{Z}^i$ = per capita consumption of the zth commodity in the ith region on the assumption that it is not necessary to take account of the urban-rural population mix.

Z^i_u = urban per capita consumption of the zth commodity in the ith region.

Z^i_r = rural per capita consumption of the zth commodity in the ith region.

p^i_u = the proportion of all persons who are urban in the ith region.

p^i_r = the proportion of all persons who are rural in the ith region. When any of the above symbols are used without superscripts, they represent national averages.

[17] U.S. Bureau of Labor, *Eighteenth Annual Report of the Commissioner of Labor* (Washington, 1903).
[18] *Ibid.*; Funk, *Value to Farm Families.*

Then by assumption:

(3.3) $$\frac{Z^i{}_r}{Z_r} = \frac{Z^i{}_u}{Z_u}; \text{ therefore } \frac{Z^i{}_r}{Z^i{}_u} = \frac{Z_r}{Z_u} = K.$$

By definition

(3.4) $$\bar{Z}^i = \frac{Z^i{}_u}{Z_u} \cdot Z$$

and

(3.5) $$Z^i = p^i{}_u Z^i{}_u + p^i{}_r K Z^i{}_u = Z^i{}_u (p^i{}_u + p^i{}_r K).$$

The point at issue is the ratio of Z^i to $\bar{Z}^i$. Now

(3.6) $$\frac{Z^i}{\bar{Z}^i} = \frac{Z_u (p^i{}_u + p^i{}_r K)}{Z}.$$

But

(3.7) $$Z = p_u Z_u + p_r Z_r = Z_u (p_u + p_r K).$$

Therefore

(3.8) $$\frac{Z^i}{\bar{Z}^i} = \frac{p^i{}_u + p^i{}_r K}{p_u + p_r K}$$

In 1890 p_u was 0.29 and p_r was 0.71.[19] Substituting these values into the denominator and appropriate values of $p^i{}_u$ and $p^i{}_r$ into the numerator of equation 3.8 yields the results shown in Table 3.5.[20] Two features of the table stand out. $\bar{Z}^i$ underestimates Z^i and hence leads to an overstatement of tons shipped out of the counties. This overstatement is quite small even when the ratio of rural to urban per capita consumption (K) is quite large. These unexpected results are explained

TABLE 3.5. AMOUNT BY WHICH $\bar{Z}^i$ UNDERSTATES Z^i IN THE
NORTH ATLANTIC REGION

Value of K	Per cent understatement
1.00	0.0
1.25	0.8
1.50	2.2
1.75	2.9
2.00	3.4
3.00	4.7
4.00	5.4
5.00	5.9
10.00	6.8
100.00	7.5

[19] *Compendium of the Eleventh Census of the United States,* Part I, p. lxxv, Table 3.
[20] The value of $p^i{}_u$ is 0.23; $p^i{}_r$ is 0.77. These figures are averages of the county ratios weighted by tons shipped from the county.

by the fact that counties with predominantly urban populations shipped only a small amount of agricultural production beyond their borders. Counties with large surpluses had urban-rural population ratios which were, on the average, quite close to the national ratio.

In the case of feed grains and hay, it was not possible to take account of regional differences in the consumption of particular crops by particular animals. However allowance was, in most cases, made for differing mixes of livestock. The method and sources used were described in the discussion of corn consumption in Chapter II.

It was assumed that the entire production of the residual category of commodities was shipped from counties, i.e., that there was no local consumption. While this no doubt leads to an overstatement of out-shipments, the error is quite small relative to the total of outshipments in the North Atlantic region. The residual category represents less than 2 per cent of the total tonnage shown in Table 3.2.

Wagon, Rail, and Water Mileage

The measurement of the average wagon distance from all points within a county to a railroad would be a relatively simple task if only one line of track ran through the middle of each county or if all counties were square with rail tracks running only on county borders. In the former case the average "airline" distance would be one-half of the distance from the track to the county border. If, in the latter case, the side of a county were $2n$ miles long, the average "airline" distance (r) would be:

$$\frac{\int_0^n r\,(n-r)\,dr}{\int_0^n (n-r)\,dr} = \frac{n}{3}$$

where $(n-r)dr$ is the number of acres lying r miles from a railroad (see Figure 3.1).

Unfortunately counties are more often rectangular or irregular than square and railroads cut across them in a wide variety of complex patterns. Under these circumstances the measurement of average distances is a complex mathematical problem, the answer to which is not immediately obvious. One method of approximating the average is to break each county into very small squares, measure the distance of each small square from a railroad, and divide the sum of the distances by the number of squares. One can make the approximation as fine

FIGURE 3.1

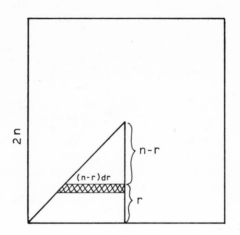

as desired by choosing squares of an appropriately small size. The difficulty with this method is its laboriousness.

A somewhat cruder but simpler approximation may be obtained by using one-third of the distance (n) from the farthest point in a county to a railroad. This method is demonstrated in Figures 3.2 and 3.3. Figure 3.3 shows that in the illustrative case 43 per cent of the county lies an average of $\frac{n}{3}$ miles from a railroad (area 2), 7 per cent averaged more than $\frac{n}{3}$ miles (area 3), and 50 per cent averaged less than $\frac{n}{3}$ miles (area 1). The average distance given by the simplified method differs from that of the method of small squares by only 11 per cent.

To transform the airline distance to a road distance it is necessary to multiply $\frac{n}{3}$ by 1.6, the average ratio of road to air distance.[21] Since 1.6 $\frac{n}{3}$ is approximately equal to $0.5n$, half the longest distance was used as the actual estimate of average miles of wagon haulage to a rail shipping point.

[21] The ratio was determined from a random sample in which modern highway distances were compared with straight line distances drawn on maps.

FIGURE 3.2

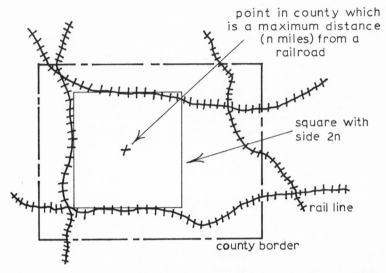

point in county which
is a maximum distance
(n miles) from a
railroad

square with
side 2n

rail line

county border

The estimates of average wagon haulage derived in the manner just described are close to the results of the 1906 survey of the Department of Agriculture. The U.S.D.A. study found that in the North Atlantic region the average wagon distance from farms to rail shipping points was 6.5 miles for hay, 7.0 miles for potatoes, and 6.2 miles for wheat.[22] The corresponding results for the method used in the present study are 6.5, 8.5, and 4.3. The divergences are not statistically significant.

The estimation of the average distances from farms to water shipping points was much simpler since there generally was only one water route near a county, and this usually fell beyond the county border. After ascertaining the "airline" distance from the center of a county to a water point, the "air" distance was multiplied by 1.4 to obtain a road distance.[23]

[22] Andrews, "Costs," pp. 24, 29, 33.

[23] The ratio was again determined from a random sample in which modern highway distances were compared with straight line distances drawn on maps. It will be noted that the ratio of "air" to road distance is lower in the water case than in the rail case. This is to be expected since the average distance of a wagon haul to water was 3.5 times as long as it was to a railroad, and the route from a farm to a shipping point generally involved a short first movement more or less parallel to a rail or water line, plus a second movement more or less perpendicular to the rail or water line.

FIGURE 3.3

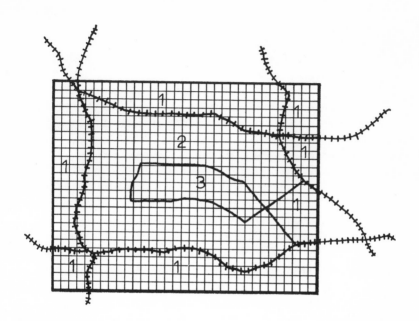

Distances from rail and water shipping points to primary markets were measured on the maps contained in the *Rand McNally Company's Business Atlas for 1891.*

Rail, Water, and Wagon Rates

Rail rates are less troublesome in the intraregional case than in long-haul movements. Shipments from farms to primary markets on most agricultural commodities in the North Atlantic region were sent in relatively small lots and usually traveled under class rates. The relative absence of references to rebating on intraregional shipments suggests that this practice does not represent a serious problem in the computation of local rates. The rail rates used in calculating Column 5 of Table 3.2 were estimated from regressions between rates and distances. The data were drawn from the local tariffs of five railroads that operated in the region: the New York, New Haven, and Hartford; the New York,

Lake Erie, and Western; the Lehigh Valley; the Pennsylvania Railroad; and the Buffalo, Rochester, and Pittsburgh. There were 117 observations available in each of six commodity classes for 1890, making a total of 702 observations.[24] The correlation coefficients were high, ranging between 0.76 and 0.90 and the regression coefficients were all significant. The classes under which various commodities were carried were determined from *Official Classification No. 7,* published by the Joint Traffic Committee in 1890.

The data on water rates thus far available are much more sparse. The largest single source of information was a 1912 study of inland water transportation which contained data on rates directly applicable to 12 of the 29 commodities listed in Table 3.2.[25] These 12 commodities represented 77 per cent of the tonnage shipped from counties. The rates in the study covered a fairly wide number of water routes in the North Atlantic region including the Hudson, Connecticut, and Delaware rivers; Lake Champlain and Lake George; and Long Island Sound. The number of observations available on each commodity ranged between 7 and 37. Most of the regressions were fairly well correlated with distance (the coefficients varied between 0.49 and 0.97) and the regression coefficients were generally significant. Since available data indicated that water rates in 1912 were virtually the same as those prevailing in 1890, no attempt was made to adjust for changes in the price level; the rise in the price level between 1890 and 1912 appears to have just offset the increase in the efficiency of water transportation.[26] Rates on pork and beef were based on data pertaining to coastwise shipping.[27] The regressions obtained yielded rates considerably higher than the only published meat rates available on inland water transportation in 1890. However, since these inland rates covered only southern routes, no adjustment was made.[28] The rates on the remaining items were made proportional to some commodity for which a regression

[24] U.S. House of Representatives, *Sixteenth Annual Report of the Interstate Commerce Commission,* Appendix G, Part II, Doc. No. 253, 58th Cong., 2d Sess. (4699), pp. 164–69.

[25] Frank Andrews, "Inland Boat Service," U.S.D.A., *Bulletin No. 74* (1914), pp. 17–31.

[26] Cf. U.S. Bureau of Statistics (Treasury Department), *Report on the Internal Commerce of the United States, 1891* (Washington, 1892), p. xxxiii; Chicago Board of Trade, *Annual Report, 1920,* p. 100; Buffalo Merchants' Exchange, *Annual Report, 1891,* p. 61.

[27] U.S.D.A., Division of Statistics, *Freight Charges for Ocean Transportation of Products of Agriculture, Bulletin No. 12* (1896), pp. 35–42.

[28] See, for example, Newcomb, *Changes in Rates,* p. 65.

equation existed. The proportions were calculated from a scattering of water tariffs that contained both a rate on the commodity in question and on the commodity for which the regression equation existed.[29]

The wagon rates for the computation in Table 3.2 were taken from a 1906 study of the cost of hauling crops from farms to shipping points.[30] This source contained the rates on 14 commodities representing 73 per cent of the tonnage shipped from counties in the North Atlantic division. The average wagon rate on these 14 commodities (weighted by the tons shipped) was 24.8 cents per ton-mile. Hence a wagon rate of 25 cents per ton-mile was assumed to have prevailed on those commodities for which individual rates were not available. Before turning to adjustments that must be made in these wagon rates, it is worth noting that the cost of wagon transportation in the North Alantic region was 4 cents per ton-mile (or 20 per cent) greater than the national average.[31]

The wagon rates contained in the 1906 study clearly overstate the 1890 cost of transportation. This overstatement flows partly from the manner in which the Department of Agriculture arrived at its figures. The Department computed its rates by determining the cost of hiring a team, wagon, and driver in the 1,894 counties covered by the survey.[32] However, very few farmers actually engaged in such hiring. They usually used their own labor, equipment, and animals. Since farmers preferred to perform these activities themselves rather than hire, the presumption is that the actual cost of wagon transportation to the farmer was below the hire rate. The Department's estimates are also biased by the presumption that wagons carried no back loads.[33] In actual fact, farmers carried loads on the return trip. Hence the Department's estimates of rates on shipments from the farms should be reduced to take account of the tonnage hauled on return trips. To put it another way, the figures in the 1906 study include not only the cost of hauling commodities from farms but also the cost of hauling goods to farms. Finally, the 1906 study overstates 1890 rates because of the general rise in prices between the two dates. Labor accounted for 43 per cent

[29] Providence and Stonington Lines, *Tariff of Rates* (1888); Norwich and New York Transportation Company, *Rates of Freight* (1887); Evansville, Paducah and Tennessee River Packet Company, *Tennessee River Freight Tariff* (1892); Kansas City and Missouri River Transportation Co., *Tariff No. 3* (1892); Union Steamboat Company, *Freight Tariff No. 1* (1891).

[30] Andrews, "Cost."

[31] *Ibid.*, and p. 56 above.

[32] *Ibid.*, pp. 11–12.

[33] *Ibid.*, pp. 12–13.

of the cost of wagon haulage in the U.S.D.A. study. However, wages in the North Atlantic region rose by 22 per cent.[34] Since there were virtually no improvements in either roads or wagons over the 16 years in question, it must be presumed that other costs also rose with the change in the price level. The 1906 rates were therefore deflated by a weighted average of a wage index and the Snyder-Tucker price index which reduced the rates by 17.6 per cent.[35] These deflated figures were then used to calculate the cost of wagon transportation in Table 3.2. Since no adjustment was made for back hauls, the computed social saving includes a non-agricultural as well as an agricultural component.

The Social Saving in the North Atlantic Region

Several features of the computation shown in Table 3.2 are surprising and conflict with commonly held notions. First, the cost of shipping goods from rail points to primary markets is 36 per cent higher than the cost of moving the same commodities from water points to primary markets. This is particularly odd in view of the fact that the average water rate per ton-mile was—in contradistinction to the long-haul case—slightly higher than the rail rate. The respective figures are 2.60 and 2.50 cents per ton-mile. This double mystery is explained by still a third oddity: the average distance which a ton moved by rail was 115 miles while the average distance a ton would have moved by water

[34] The last two figures were obtained in the following manner. The regional average daily wage for hauling in 1890 was computed by weighting the average daily wage for labor other than harvest work in each state as given in George K. Holmes, *Wages of Farm Labor,* U.S.D.A. Bureau of Statistics, *Bulletin 99* (Washington, 1912), pp. 40–41, by the total number of tons shipped from the farms in each state. The regional average daily wage for hauling in 1906 was obtained in the same way. The ratio of the average 1890 wage to that of 1906 was 0.7819. The average 1906 daily wage was then multiplied by the average number of days required to haul each commodity as given in Andrews, "Costs," for the North Atlantic region. The result was a series on the average wage cost per haul by commodity. This series was converted into the average wage cost per haul on all commodities, using the number of tons of each commodity shipped from the farms in the region as weights. The average total cost of wagon hauls in the region was also computed, with the total cost per round trip on each commodity as given by Andrews again weighted by the tons of each commodity shipped. The ratio of the average wage cost per haul to the average total cost per haul was 0.433.

[35] The price index of wagon hauling was computed as follows:

$$78.19 \times 0.433 + 85.71 \times 0.567 = 82.45$$

where 78.19 is the wage index described in the previous note, 85.71 is the Snyder-Tucker index (*Historical Statistics* [1949], p. 231), and 0.433 and 0.567 are the weights.

is only 81 miles. That water hauls are shorter than rail hauls is partly attributable to the fact that the canals, rivers, and lakes of the North Atlantic region provided relatively straight routes. However the major factor is a substitution of wagon for non-wagon transportation. Thus in the absence of railroads the average wagon haul would have been 44 miles; with the railroad wagon hauls averaged only 5.7 miles.

Because of these factors the entire social saving in the North Atlantic region is attributable to the reduction in wagon transportation made possible by the introduction of the railroad. This part of the social saving $w(D_{fb} - D_{fr})$ is \$7.81 per ton. By contrast, the social saving in movements between water or rail shipping points and primary markets $(BD_{bp} - RD_{rp})$ is negative by 76 cents per ton.

Another interesting fact which emerges from the computations connected with Table 3.2 is the relative bulkiness of farm shipments from the North Atlantic division. Whether calculated on the basis of tons shipped per acre of all farm land or tons shipped per acre of improved land, the rate in this division is higher than the national average.[36] For while it is true that farmers in the region specialized in production of dairy products with a high value relative to weight, they also specialized in two bulky, low-value products: hay and potatoes. Hay and potatoes represented 50 per cent (by weight) of all the commodities that farmers shipped across county lines.

PRELIMINARY α AND β ESTIMATES

The most desirable way of estimating the total intraregional social saving is to extend the calculation shown in Table 3.2 to all other regions. An aggregate estimate based on the social saving of individual counties would permit a clear delineation of those areas falling beyond the feasible region and would yield detailed information on regional differences in the social saving. The enormous amount of time required for such a computation puts the endeavor beyond the reach of an individual scholar. Still it is possible to arrive at national estimates by another route. The computation of the α and β values presented in this section will be less detailed than an aggregation over counties. It will also involve certain approximations that would have been more certain were the study built up from county data. Despite these limitations,

[36] *Census of Agriculture, 1890,* p. 74; Table 3.1 above.

the order of magnitude shown by the computation that follows seems fairly reliable. The most likely errors are in the direction of an over-estimation of the social saving.

Shipments Via Rail

The volume on transportation in the Eleventh Census gives three sets of figures on the agricultural commodities carried by railroads during the census year of 1890. These categories are "Freight originating on all roads," "Freight received from connecting roads and other carriers," and "Unsegregated tonnage." Agricultural commodities listed under the first heading amounted to 39,362,821 tons. Unsegregated agricultural freight was 20,879,197 tons. If it is assumed that un-segregated freight was divided between agricultural freight originating on roads and agricultural freight received from connecting lines in the same proportions as was true for the freight that was segregated, the total weight of all agricultural freight originating on roads in 1890 was 48,240,798 tons.[37]

Now all agricultural commodities shipped from farms via the railroad must be included in the figure on "Freight originating," but not all "Freight originating" was shipped from farms. Agricultural commodities sent to primary markets and put in storage will again be counted as "Freight originating" when they are taken out of storage and shipped to deficit centers in the East and South. In Chapter II it was shown that 10,070,000 tons of 12,750,000 tons or 79 per cent of the wheat and corn received from the West by secondary markets was stored in primary markets; that is, only 21 per cent of the grain shipped to deficit markets from the farms of the Midwest went under through bills of lading. If it is assumed that the same ratio applied to pork and beef, then 79 per cent of the 14,494,000 tons of corn, wheat, pork, and beef which entered into interregional trade via rail has been counted twice and should be deducted from the estimated total of 48,240,798 tons of agricultural freight originating on railroads.[38] The resulting figure, 36,794,000 tons, represents the total tonnage of agricultural commodities shipped from farms via railroad in the census year of 1890.

It is interesting to compare this figure with the estimated tonnage

[37] *Eleventh Census, Transportation,* Part I, Table 8.

[38] Tables 2.1, 2.2, 2.4, and 2.6 above. This is, of course, a conservative assumption since virtually all of the livestock shipped from the Midwest to the East and South was first sent to stockyards in the primary markets.

of agricultural commodities shipped out of counties by farmers (see Table 3.6). The latter amount is 60,347,000 tons. The data thus suggest that 39 per cent of all agricultural tonnage that entered into intraregional trade as defined in this chapter was carried by wagon and boat.

If true, these figures point to an underestimation in the literature of the continuing importance of non-rail forms of transportation in intraregional movements even at the height of railroad supremacy. Scattered information on the movement of individual commodities gives strong support to this conclusion. In the case of hay, for example, the Department of Agriculture reported that over the years 1911–15 only 63 per cent of the quantity entering intraregional trade was carried by railroads.[39] Scattered data on even as perishable an item as milk presents a similar picture. Another U.S.D.A. study revealed that 12 per cent of all milk reaching New York City in 1900 was carried by wagon and another 3 per cent was carried by boat. For most of the 15 largest cities the proportion of milk received by means other than railroad was higher. St. Louis received 57 per cent of its milk by wagon; San Francisco received 45 per cent by wagon and about 4 per cent by river boat; and in the hot city of New Orleans, 86 per cent of all milk arrived by wagon. If New York and Chicago are excluded from the list of the 15 largest cities, the remaining 13 received an average of 33 per cent of milk shipments by wagon and an undisclosed additional percentage by water. With respect to smaller cities, the Department of Agriculture reported that wagons were "the principal means by which the supply of small cities is procured, and is very often the only means." [40]

The Limits of the Feasible Region

Scattered bits of evidence suggest that in the absence of railroads, the boundaries of the region of feasible commercial agriculture would have fallen a considerable distance from navigable waterways. Describing the transportation of wheat to Minnesota markets during the

[39] U.S.D.A., *Agricultural Yearbook, 1924,* p. 356. Motor trucks were only a minor factor in transportation during the years cited. Total truck registrations were 20,000 in 1911 and rose to only 158,000 in 1915. The big increase in truck utilization took place in the next five years. By 1920 registrations had risen to 1,108,000. *Historical Statistics* (1960), p. 462.

[40] Edward G. Ward, Jr., *Milk Transportation,* U.S.D.A., Division of Statistics, *Bulletin No. 25* (1903), pp. 10–12, 21, 22, 52.

TABLE 3.6. AGRICULTURAL PRODUCTS SHIPPED FROM COUNTIES, 1890
(in thousands of tons)

		1 Gross pro- duction	2 Proportion shipped from county	3 Amount shipped from county Col. 1 × Col. 2
1.	Wheat	15,135	0.571	8,642
2.	Corn	14,225	0.8524	12,125
3.	Oats	3,989	0.7571	3,020
4.	Barley	970	1.0	970
5.	Rye	620	0.9123	566
6.	Buckwheat	205	0.5793	119
7.	Potatoes	5,428	0.75	4,071
8.	Sweet potatoes	1,019	0.75	764
9.	Flax seed	273	1.0	273
10.	Hay	10,300	1.0	10,300
11.	Cotton	1,785	1.0	1,785
12.	Cottonseed	874	1.0	874
13.	Tobacco	263	1.0	263
14.	Rice	107	1.0	107
15.	Dry edible beans	95	1.0	95
16.	Beet sugar	4	1.0	4
17.	Cane sugar	249	1.0	249
18.	Fruits	5,143	0.4116	2,117
19.	Peanuts	47	1.0	47
20.	Dairy products	21,600	0.2938	6,346
21.	Chickens	588	0.3741	220
22.	Eggs	849	0.2026	172
23.	Wool	138	1.0	138
24.	Cattle	5,015	0.7352	3,687
25.	Calves	288	0.7352	212
26.	Hogs	5,645	0.5160	2,913
27.	Sheep and lambs	288	0.93	268
28.	Totals	95,142		60,347

SOURCES AND NOTES:

Column 1. Gross production equals total production less quantities used for feed and seed. Strauss and Bean, *Gross Farm Income.*

Column 2. Line 1. U.S.D.A., *Annual Report of the Secretary of Agriculture, 1892,* p. 450.

Line 2. Holbrook Working's estimate of domestic corn meal consumption was converted into a grain equivalent using the 1890 Census ratio. The grain equivalent was divided between farmers and others in the ratio of population. Corn production shipped from the county was gross production less consumption by farmers. Holbrook Working, "The Decline in Per Capita Consumption of Flour in the United States," *Wheat Studies,* II (July, 1926), 279; *Census of Manufacturing, 1890,* pp. 702–5.

Line 3. Consumption by farmers was estimated by multiplying the ratio of oatmeal production to that of corn meal by the estimated farm consumption of corn. Funk, *Value to Farm Families.*

Line 5. The ratio of rye consumed as food to total production over the years 1910–14 was multiplied by the 1890 ratio of farm to total population. This resulting figure was taken to be the share of gross production consumed on farms as food. U.S.D.A. Stabilization and Conservation Service, *Rye: U. S. Supply and Disposi-*

tion, Annually 1909 to Date (May, 1959). Martin S. Cooper, Glen T. Barton and Albert P. Brodell, *Progress of Farm Mechanization*, U.S.D.A., *Misc. Publication No. 630* (1947) is the source of the estimate of farm population.

Line 6. The entry is the proportion of total output sold by farmers during 1949–52 divided by the 1890 ratio of gross production to total production. U.S.D.A., *Agricultural Statistics, 1959*, p. 28; Strauss and Bean, *Gross Farm Income*, p. 50.

Lines 7 and 8. Computed for the years 1909–13 from data in U.S.D.A., *Statistical Bulletin No. 251*.

Lines 10 and 27. Strauss and Bean, *Gross Farm Income*, pp. 59, 62, 121–22.

Lines 18, 21, 22, 24, 25, and 26. Per capita consumption of the farm population was computed from Funk's study and multiplied by the estimated farm population in 1890. The amount shipped out of the county was taken to be equal to gross production less farm consumption.

Line 20. Computed from *Census of Agriculture, 1900*, Part I, p. clxxvi.

Lines 4, 9, 11, 12, 13, 14, 15, 16, 17, 19, 23. The proportion of gross production shipped out of the county was arbitrarily assumed to be one. While this is no doubt an overstatement, the effect of even a very large error will be quite small since the entries in these lines represent only 4.9 per cent of gross production. Moreover in the case of cotton, which represents more than a third of the residual group, it was possible to establish that the error in the assumed ratio is probably quite small. Census data relating to the manufacture of cotton textiles in southern states indicated that in more than half the counties in which southern cotton textile plants were located consumption by these plants exceeded the counties' production of cotton. Consequently, if one abstracts from the possibility of home production, then the amount of cotton retained for consumption within counties must have been less than that used by southern textile manufacturers. A computation based on the assumption of zero home production implies that the least the ratio of out-shipments to gross production could have been is 0.958.

---

years immediately preceding the construction of that state's first railroad, Henrietta M. Larson wrote: "The river-town newspapers often recorded the arrival of wheat teams from points 150 miles to the west. A committee in the state legislature reported in 1861 that the mean distance for the farmers of the state to the nearest navigable river was 80 miles." [41]

Even as late as 1906 when most of the country was laced with a dense rail network, wagon hauls of considerable length were not unheard of. One of the questions asked in the U.S.D.A. study on wagon transportation in that year was: "Greatest distances of haul to railroad or steamboat shipping points by any considerable number of farmers?" The reply to this question revealed hauls up to 50 miles on apples, 60 miles on corn, and 110 miles on cotton. Indeed the average distance of these "common" long hauls for cotton was 40 miles. The average distance of "common" long hauls of corn in the North Central states was 25 miles.[42] It should be noted that these figures do not represent

[41] Henrietta M. Larson, *The Wheat Market and the Farmer in Minnesota, Studies in History, Economics and Public Law*, CXXII, No. 2 (New York, 1926), p. 24. A mean distance of 80 miles suggests a boundary of 160 miles.

[42] Andrews, "Costs," pp. 9, 35–37.

the maximum distances of commercially feasible wagon transportation; rather they are reports of distances over which it was relatively "common" to transport agricultural products. In states where the rail network was less dense than the South Atlantic or North Central regions, much longer wagon hauls were reported. Texas, for example, reported that the distance of wagon haulage from some counties to shipping points was 110 miles for cotton, 47 miles for corn, 47 miles for hay, 42 miles for oats, 46 miles for potatoes, and 60 miles for wheat. In such areas there arose companies specializing in the sale of wagon transportation services ("freighters") with rates as much as 50 per cent below the average rate indicated in the U.S.D.A. study.[43]

Without county by county information on land values, tonnages shipped by rail per acre, and the difference per ton in the cost of shipping from water and rail points to primary markets ($BD_{bp} - RD_{rp}$), it is not possible to determine definitively the boundaries of feasible commercial agriculture. While such an analysis is beyond the scope of this study, it is possible to use the data in Table 3.2 to say something about the limits of the boundary of feasible commercial agriculture in the North Atlantic region.

According to Table 3.2 a total of 5,748,062 tons of agricultural commodities were shipped by rail from counties in the region. Since the total number of acres in farms was 62,743,525,[44] an average of 0.0916 tons were shipped per acre. For simplicity of exposition this amount will be referred to as an "acre-weight." The average cost of hauling a ton 1 mile by wagon was 20.32 cents; the cost of hauling an acre-weight was 1.86 cents. Table 3.2 also indicates that transportation from water shipping points to primary markets was 76.30 cents cheaper per ton or 6.99 cents per acre-weight less than the cost of shipping the same amounts from rail points to primary markets. This saving would have permitted an increase in wagon haulage of 3.8 miles per acre-weight.[45] That is, given the negative value of 76.30 cents in ($BD_{bp} - RD_{rp}$), a typical acre just 3.8 miles farther from a water shipping point than it was from a rail shipping point would, *ceteris paribus,* have had the same value in the absence of the railroad as it did with the railroad.

Table 3.7 indicates that the value of all land in farms in the North Atlantic region was $1,092,281,000 or $17.41 per acre. Since the median

[43] *Ibid.,* pp. 35–44.
[44] *Census of Agriculture, 1890,* p. 74.
[45] The mileage is obtained by dividing 6.99 cents by 1.86 cents.

mortgage rate of interest was 5.72 per cent, the annual rental value of an average acre was 99.59 cents. Consequently an acre-weight would have had to have traveled 53.5 more miles (99.59 ÷ 1.86) by wagon than it actually did in 1890 to exhaust the average rental value of the land. If one adds to the last figure the additional mileage permitted because of the negative value of $(BD_{bp} - RD_{rp})$ and the average 1890 wagon haul (5.7 miles), the total is 63.1 miles. When this figure is divided by the ratio of road to air distance it becomes 45.1 miles. Thus the data on the North Atlantic region indicate that, on the average, the boundary of feasible agricultural production would have been located between 40 and 50 straight-line miles from a navigable waterway.

It is important to point out that the feasible boundary was probably closer to waterways in the North Atlantic region than in other sections of the country. This is suggested by the fact that farm land values relative to outshipments were probably lower in this area than in all other areas except the Mountain states. At the same time the cost of wagon transportation was higher on the average in the North Atlantic region than outside it. Nevertheless, for the purposes of this discussion it will be assumed that in all regions of the country the boundary of feasible commercial agriculture fell 40 "straight" or "airline" miles from a navigable waterway.[46]

The shaded area on the map (see Figure 3.4) represents all land within 40 miles of natural waterways and canals actually used for commercial navigation in 1890 as well as abandoned canals that would have been in use in the absence of railroads.[47] While the shaded area covers less than half of the land mass of the United States, it includes 76 per cent of all agricultural land by value. This is in part explained by the fact that the third of the land mass falling between the hundredth meridian and the Sierra Nevada Mountains was of extremely limited usefulness for agricultural purposes. By value this area represented only 2 per cent of all agricultural land.

[46] The preceding calculation understates the limits of feasible commercial agriculture for still another reason. It was assumed that 81 per cent of the commodities shipped from counties were transported to primary markets by rail. However, as was previously shown, it appears that 61 per cent is the appropriate figure for the nation as a whole.

[47] Permission has been granted by Rand McNally and Company for use of the map underlying Figure 3.4. Navigable waterways in use in 1890 are shown in the map in front of the 1890 Census volume on transportation, Part II; see also the tables in *Preliminary Report*, pp. 39–93; and the last map in the same volume. For canals see Carter Goodrich and others, *Canals and American Economic Development* (New York, 1961), pp. 184–85.

Table 3.7 shows that the loss in national income due to the diminished supply of land would have been $154,000,000. It is interesting to note that only 1.3 per cent of this amount is in the North Atlantic region while 1.5 per cent is in the Mountain states. About 75 per cent of the loss is concentrated in the North Central states. Indeed, more than half of the decline in national income associated with the diminished supply of land falls in just four states: Illinois, Iowa, Nebraska, and Kansas.

It might be thought that the large social saving in the North Central states supports the frequently met contention that railroads were essential to the development of agriculture in the prairies.[48] Such an inference would be erroneous. The prairies were settled at a time when the railroad had achieved clear technological superiority over canals. As a consequence, the movement for canal construction which played such an important role in the development of Ohio and the states to the east of it was aborted in the prairies. The fact that the major loss of agricultural land is concentrated in a compact space suggests an entirely different conclusion: a relatively small extension of the canal system would have brought most of the productive agricultural land shown in white in Figure 3.4 into the region of feasible commercial agriculture.

Another fact implicit in Table 3.7 is that land close to the main navigable waterways was more valuable than land farther away from it. Thus within the feasible region, the land value per improved acre was $25.16; the corresponding figure for improved land outside of the feasible region is only $17.34. The case of Iowa is particularly instructive. As is shown by Figure 3.4, land falling within the feasible range in this state is limited to strips along the Missouri River in the West and Mississippi River in the East. The entire central portion of the state, representing 70 per cent of the land mass, is outside of the feasible range. A glance at a railroad map will indicate that railroads were virtually equally dense in all portions of the state in 1890. Yet the value per acre of improved land was 37 per cent greater in the feasible region than outside of it ($32.11 per acre as opposed to $23.42 per acre). In other words, land was not homogeneously distributed over space in most states. It tended to be much more productive, perhaps for natural reasons, along navigable waterways than elsewhere. Consequently the assumption made in computing the loss in national income

---

[48] See, for example, Dillon's statement on pp. 5–6 above.

FIGURE 3.4

AREA OF FEASIBLE COMMERCIAL AGRICULTURE

TABLE 3.7. Loss in National Product due to the Decrease in the Supply of Land (thousands of dollars)

	1	2	3	4	5
	Value of farm land 1890	Value of farm land beyond feasible region 1890	Col. 2 as a per cent of Col. 1	State mortgage rate of interest 1889	Loss in national product Col. 2 × Col. 4
Maine	9,137	195	2.1	0.0624	12
New Hampshire	9,890	2,264	22.9	0.0598	135
Vermont	8,536	1,595	18.7	0.0592	94
Massachusetts	45,673	0	0.0	0.0560	0
Rhode Island	8,655	0	0.0	0.0577	0
Connecticut	31,803	0	0.0	0.0572	0
New York	443,461	45	0.0	0.0571	3
New Jersey	65,964	0	0.0	0.0566	0
Pennsylvania	469,162	1,538	0.3	0.0565	87
North Atlantic Div.	1,092,281	5,637	0.5	0.0587	331
Delaware	20,265	0	0.0	0.0577	0
Maryland	88,300	0	0.0	0.0590	0
District of Columbia	5,461	0	0.0	0.0577	0
Virginia	129,570	38,053	29.4	0.0593	2,257
West Virginia	85,743	8,590	10.0	0.0599	515
North Carolina	89,281	42,348	47.4	0.0775	3,282
South Carolina	44,401	12,266	27.6	0.0856	1,047
Georgia	50,621	15,933	31.5	0.0809	1,289
Florida	43,757	676	1.5	0.0912	62
South Atlantic Div.	557,399	117,866	21.1	0.0717	8,452
Ohio	666,118	20,205	3.0	0.0659	1,332
Indiana	481,684	38,783	8.1	0.0667	2,587
Illinois	964,612	174,567	18.1	0.0670	11,696
Michigan	301,739	106,110	35.2	0.0702	7,449
Wisconsin	264,049	53,483	20.3	0.0675	3,610
Minnesota	254,261	81,649	32.1	0.0796	6,499
Iowa	678,364	372,339	54.9	0.0741	27,590
Missouri	443,611	68,891	15.5	0.0804	5,539
North Dakota	51,257	19,483	38.0	0.0928	1,808
South Dakota	79,676	43,114	54.1	0.0904	3,898
Nebraska	310,302	187,149	60.3	0.0819	15,328
Kansas	435,934	276,179	63.3	0.0838	23,143
North Central Div.	4,931,607	1,441,952	29.2	0.0766	110,479
Kentucky	178,670	1,893	1.1	0.0631	119
Tennessee	123,633	7,936	6.4	0.0599	475
Alabama	32,795	1,223	3.7	0.0834	102
Mississippi	51,166	342	0.1	0.0954	33
Louisiana	42,901	0	0.0	0.0801	0
Texas	265,841	145,248	54.6	0.0913	13,261
Arkansas	43,327	2,224	5.1	0.0903	201
South Central Div.	738,333	158,866	21.5	0.0893	14,191
Montana	11,575	7,948	68.7	0.1079	858
Wyoming	11,027	11,027	100.0	0.0954	1,052
Colorado	63,259	63,259	100.0	0.0853	5,396
New Mexico	4,576	4,576	100.0	0.0790	362

TABLE 3.7. LOSS IN NATIONAL PRODUCT DUE TO THE DECREASE IN THE SUPPLY
OF LAND (thousands of dollars) (continued)

	1	2	3	4	5
		Value of farm land beyond feasible region 1890	Col. 2 as a per cent of Col. 1	State mortgage rate of interest 1889	Loss in national product Col. 2 × Col. 4
	Value of farm land 1890				
Arizona	5,099	4,853	95.2	0.1135	551
Utah	14,720	14,720	100.0	0.0959	1,412
Nevada	8,643	8,613	99.7	0.1084	934
Idaho	10,756	8,020	74.6	0.1028	824
Washington	63,625	8,703	13.7	0.0800	696
Oregon	64,902	9,310	14.3	0.0928	864
California	542,770	77,187	14.2	0.0903	6,970
Western Div.	800,952	218,216	27.2	0.0913	19,919
United States	8,120,572	1,942,537	23.9	0.0791	153,572

SOURCES AND NOTES:

Columns 1 and 2. The figures in these columns are estimates of the value of
"pure" farm land. They were constructed by subtracting from data published in
the Eleventh Census on the value of land, buildings and fences, estimates of the
value of buildings, of fences, and of land improvements.

The Census first collected separate data on the value of buildings in 1900. The
value of buildings in 1890 was estimated on the assumption that the county ratios
of the value of buildings to the value of land, buildings, and fences did not change
between the two dates.

The number of rods of fencing in a specified county was taken to be equal to
four times the square root of the average number of square rods of improved farm
land per farm in that county, multiplied by the number of farms in the county.
The estimates obtained in this manner are an average of 30 per cent below those
given by Martin Primack in his study of capital in American agriculture. The
value of fences per rod is a linear interpolation of prices given by Department of
Agriculture studies for 1871 and 1909.

Primack's data on the labor cost of land clearing were used to estimate the
value of land improvements. However, in the forested regions only the cost of
removing stumps was treated as an investment in the improvement of land. The
cost of cutting trees down (60 per cent of Primack's figure) was treated as a cost
associated with another enterprise—the production of forest products. Primack's
labor cost in man hours, thus adjusted, was multiplied by the daily wage rate paid
in 1890 for outdoor farm labor. Since Primack omitted non-labor costs of land
improvement (e.g., the cost of equipment, special teams, etc.), the value of land
improvements may be understated.

Census of Agriculture, 1890, Table 6; *Census of Agriculture, 1900,* Part I, Table
19; "Statistics of Fences in the United States," U.S.D.A., *Annual Report of the
Commissioner of Agriculture, 1871,* p. 510; H. N. Humphrey, "Cost of Fencing
Farms in the North Central States," U.S.D.A., *Bulletin No. 321* (1916), p. 2;
Martin L. Primack, *Farm-formed Capital in American Agriculture, 1850-1910*
(unpublished Ph.D. dissertation, University of North Carolina, 1962), Chapter IV;
Martin L. Primack, "Land Clearing Under Nineteenth-Century Techniques: Some
Preliminary Calculations," *Journal of Economic History,* XXII (December, 1962),
484–97; Holmes, *Wages,* p. 40.

Column 4. U. S. Bureau of the Census, *Eleventh Census of the United States,
1890, Report on Real Estate Mortgages,* XII, 248.

due to the diminished supply of land—that within counties land was
homogeneously distributed—probably biases the estimate upward.

The First Approximations

The first approximation of the β estimate is composed of two
elements. The loss in national income due to the decrease in the supply
of land (L) and an α estimate for the shipments from the feasible
region $(\bar{\alpha})$. The β estimate is shown in Table 3.8. The value of $\bar{x}$ was
determined by multiplying the total tonnage of agricultural commodities
shipped from farms via rail by the ratio of the value of agricultural
products produced in the feasible region to the value of all agricultural
production. The straight-line average distance from a farm in the
feasible region to a navigable waterway must be less than 20 miles
since some navigable waterways were within 40 miles of each other.
Nevertheless, $\overline{D}_{fb}$ was taken to equal 20 miles multiplied by the ratio
of the road to "air" distance. $\overline{D}_{fr}$ is a weighted average of the wagon
distances given for individual commodities in the U.S.D.A.'s 1906
study. The weights were the tonnages shipped from counties as shown
in Table 3.6. From Table 3.2 $(B\overline{D}_{bp} - R\overline{D}_{rp})$ was obtained by dividing
the difference between the sums of Columns 4 and 5 by the sum of
Column 1. The national average wagon rate per ton-mile (w) was
computed from the rates in the Andrews study. The method was the
same as that used in the computation of the average wagon rate in the
North Atlantic region except that figures on the value of farm products
rather than tonnages shipped were used as weights in constructing the
wage component of the price index.[49]

Table 3.8 shows that the β estimate of the intraregional social saving
is on first approximation $221,000,000 or 1.8 per cent of gross national
product in 1890.[50]

---

[49] Andrews, "Costs," p. 16; Table 3.6 above and notes 34 and 35 of this chapter.

[50] It will be noted that the values substituted in equation 3.10 are estimates of
national totals and averages except for $(B\overline{D}_{bp} - R\overline{D}_{rp})$ which is taken from the
North Atlantic sample. In order to test whether the use of the values which
obtained in this region introduces a bias into the first approximation of β, a
sample of 50 counties was drawn from the 1,059 counties in the North Central
division. The distances from rail and water shipping points to the primary markets
were determined for each county in the new sample. These distances were then
averaged using the value of the agricultural output of each county as weights. The
resulting figures for the North Central region were 155.3 miles by water and 145.0
miles by rail.

The α estimate can also be broken into two parts. It is the sum of an α estimate for the feasible region $(\bar{\alpha})$ and an α estimate for the non-feasible region $(\overset{*}{\alpha})$. This computation is shown in Table 3.9. The average distance from the non-feasible region in each state to a navigable waterway was estimated from maps. The average of these state figures weighted by the value of agricultural land in the non-feasible region of each state yielded $\overset{*}{D}_{fb}$. The figure for $\overset{*}{x}$ was obtained by subtracting $\bar{x}$ from the total tonnage shipped from farms via rail. All the other values of the variables in equation 3.15 were taken from Table 3.8.

The α estimate of the intraregional social saving is \$300,000,000 or 2.5 per cent of gross national product.[51]

The Indirect Costs

It is now necessary to add to the first approximations of α and β certain transportation costs that have been neglected thus far. In the interregional case it was shown that the first approximation of the social saving omitted six charges of considerable importance. These were: wagon haulage costs, transshipping costs, capital costs not in-

---

That the ratio $\overline{D}_{bp}/\overline{D}_{rp}$ is higher in the North Central region than in the North Atlantic region (the figures are 1.07 and 0.70 respectively) does not imply that the use of North Atlantic sample data introduces a downward bias into the first approximation of β. Such a conclusion would be warranted only if the change in the ratio of distances was not offset by a change in the ratio of rail and water rates. However, in contradistinction to the North Atlantic region where the average water rate exceeded the average rail rate, in the North Central region water rates were well below rail rates. Using rates by rail and water along the upper Mississippi as typical of those prevailing in the Midwest, we find that if a one ton market basket of goods (with items represented in the proportions indicated by column 3 of Table 3.6) were shipped 155 miles by water and 145 miles by rail, the value of $(BD_{bp} - R\overline{D}_{rp})$ would be $-\$0.89$. But this is 13 cents lower than the value actually used in Table 3.8. Consequently it appears likely that reliance on the data obtained from the North Atlantic sample introduces an upward rather than a downward bias into the first approximation of β. The same argument applies to the first approximation of α. (Rail and water rate regressions were computed from data contained in *Preliminary Report*.)

If $-\$0.89$ were used in equation 3.10, β would decline to \$218,000,000.

[51] If $-\$0.89$ were used in place of $-\$0.76$ as the value of $(B\overset{*}{R}_{bp} - R\overset{*}{D}_{rp})$ and a similar adjustment was made in the value of $\overline{\alpha}$, α would decline to \$295,000,000.

TABLE 3.8. FIRST APPROXIMATION OF THE β ESTIMATE

Let L = loss in national income due to withdrawal of land beyond the feasible region

$\bar{a}$ = an α estimate for the feasible region

$\bar{x}$ = the tonnage of agricultural produce shipped out of counties in the feasible region by rail

w = average wagon rate per ton-mile

B = average water rate per ton-mile

R = average rail rate per ton-mile

$\bar{D}_{fb}$ = average distance from a farm in the feasible region to a water shipping point

$\bar{D}_{fr}$ = average distance from a farm in the feasible region to a rail shipping point

$\bar{D}_{bp}$ = average distance from a water shipping point within the feasible region to a primary market

$\bar{D}_{rp}$ = average distance from a rail shipping point within the feasible region to a primary market

then

$(3.9) \quad \beta = L + \bar{a}$

$(3.10) \quad \beta = L + \bar{x} \ [w \ (\bar{D}_{fb} - \bar{D}_{fr}) + (B\bar{D}_{bp} - R\bar{D}_{rp})]$

$L = \$154,000,000$

$\bar{D}_{fb} = 28.0$ miles

$\bar{D}_{fr} = 8.6$ miles

$B\bar{D}_{bp} = \$2.12$

$R\bar{D}_{rp} = \$2.88$

$\bar{x} = 27,600,000$

$w = \$0.165$

Then substituting into equation 3.10

$(3.11) \quad \beta = \$154,000,000 + 27,600,000 \ [.165(28.0-8.6) + (\$2.12 - \$2.88)]$

or $\qquad \beta = \$221,000,000$

and

$(3.12) \quad \dfrac{\beta}{\text{G. N. P.}} \times 100 = 1.8$ per cent.

cluded in water rates, cargo losses in water transportation, the cost resulting from the use of a slow medium of transportation, and the cost of being unable to use water routes during certain months of the year.[52]

With respect to the first three items listed, no additions to α and β are required. Wagon haulage costs are included in the computations shown in Tables 3.8 and 3.9. Transshipment costs would have been no greater in the non-rail case than in the rail case. In both situations

[52] Above, pp. 41–47.

bulk would have been broken when the wagons reached the rail or water shipping points and no further transshipments would have been required between these points and the primary markets. Since all government expenditures on rivers and canals financed out of taxes rather than tolls were assigned to interregional agricultural shipments,

TABLE 3.9. FIRST APPROXIMATION OF THE α ESTIMATE

$\overset{*}{\alpha}$ = an α estimate for the non-feasible region

$\overset{*}{x}$ = the tonnage of agricultural commodities shipped out of counties in the non-feasible region by rail

w = average wagon rate per ton-mile

B = average water rate per ton-mile

R = average rail rate per ton-mile

$\overset{*}{D}_{fb}$ = average distance from a farm in the non-feasible region to a water shipping point

$\overset{*}{D}_{fr}$ = average distance from a farm in the non-feasible region to a rail shipping point

$\overset{*}{D}_{bp}$ = average distance from a water shipping point within the non-feasible region to a primary market

$\overset{*}{D}_{rp}$ = average distance from a rail shipping point within the non-feasible region to a primary market

then

(3.13) $\quad \alpha = \bar{\alpha} + \overset{*}{\alpha}$

(3.14) $\quad \alpha = \bar{\alpha} + \overset{*}{x} \, [w \, (\overset{*}{D}_{fb} - \overset{*}{D}_{fr}) + (B\overset{*}{D}_{bp} - R\overset{*}{D}_{rp})]$

$\qquad \bar{\alpha} = \$67,300,000$

$\qquad \overset{*}{D}_{fb} = 166.6$ miles

$\qquad \overset{*}{D}_{fr} = 8.6$ miles

$B\overset{*}{D}_{bp} - R\overset{*}{D}_{rp} = \$0.76$

$\qquad \overset{*}{x} = 9,200,000$ tons.

Then substituting into equation 3.14

(3.15) $\quad \alpha = \$67,300,000 + 9,200,000 \, [\, .165 \, (166.6 - 8.6) - .76]$

or $\qquad \alpha = \$300,000,000$

and

(3.16) $\dfrac{\alpha}{\text{G. N. P.}} \times 100 = 2.5$ per cent.

their inclusion in intraregional shipments would represent double counting. One could, of course, distribute the $18,000,000 allowed in Chapter II for uncompensated capital used in water transportation between inter- and intraregional movements. If the distribution were made proportional to the ton-miles of water transportation required in each instance, the α and β estimates would have to be increased by about $2,000,000 and the interregional social saving would have to be reduced by the same amount.[53]

The three remaining items do require additions to the first approximations of α and β. The cost of the cargo losses that would have occurred with the increase in intraregional water transportation is small. As previously noted, insurance rates are a measure of the expected social cost of such losses. If the average intraregional water haul would have been about 150 miles, the insurance charge would have been about 0.15 per cent of the value of the commodities shipped.[54] Under the assumptions of the α estimate, the total value of the additional agricultural commodities that would have been shipped by water is $897,000,000. Therefore, cargo losses not reflected in the first approximation of α amount to only $1,300,000. Under the assumptions of the β estimate the value of the additional cargo loss is $1,000,000.[55]

The cost of the slow medium of transportation is measured by the cost of the increased inventory required to compensate for longer

[53] Cf. with discussion on pp. 46–47 above. Since non-agricultural commodities would have made use of waterways subsidized by the government, a part of the uncompensated capital costs of water transportation assigned to the shipment of agricultural commodities should be assigned to the shipment of non-agricultural commodities. Consequently, as in the case of wagon haulage charges (see pp. 71–72 above), the allowance for the uncompensated cost of capital used in the computation of the agricultural social savings is too large. It includes part of social saving on the movement of non-agricultural commodities.

[54] See p. 41 above and notes to Table 2.6. In computing the indirect costs, I have used the water and rail distances of the sample drawn from the North Central region rather than the shorter distances of the North Atlantic region. See note 50 of this chapter.

[55] As shown above (p. 74), only 39 per cent of the gross product of agriculture was shipped by rail. But not all agricultural commodities hauled by rail would have been hauled by water in the non-rail situation. The North Atlantic sample indicated that about 11 per cent of the tonnage carried by railroads would have been shipped to market exclusively by wagon. Under the assumptions of the α estimate, this implies that products representing 34 per cent of gross farm income would have entered into intraregional water transportation. (Gross farm income is taken from Strauss and Bean, *Gross Farm Income*.) Under the assumptions of the β estimate, shipments, and therefore the value of cargo losses, fall by 25 per cent.

delivery times. The average intraregional haul would have required, under the assumptions of the α estimate, 54 additional miles of wagon transportation. At the rate of 20 miles per day, the added wagon transportation would have increased delivery time by somewhat over two days. Both the rail and water haulage distances are about 150 miles. If the average rail speed is taken at 12 miles per hour and the average water speed at 7 miles per hour, the substitution of water for rail transportation would have increased the delivery time by about 13 hours.[56] Hence, under the assumptions of the α estimate, the cost of the time lost in slower forms of transportation would have equalled the cost of carrying increased inventories in primary markets equal to a mere 2.8 times the average daily rail shipments of agricultural commodities to these markets. Under the assumptions of the β estimate, the cost of slow transportation is equal to the cost of increasing agricultural inventories in primary markets by 1.1 times their average actual daily rail receipts in 1890. Consequently, under either set of assumptions the cost of using a slow medium of transportation would have been less than $2,000,000.[57]

The cost of the limited season of navigation can also be measured by determining the expense of the additional inventory required to compensate for the disadvantage of an extended interruption in deliveries.[58] Three factors combine to make this cost relatively small. First, the relevant inventory charges on corn, wheat, pork, and beef were implicitly included in the computation of the interregional social saving when inventories were increased in the deficit markets of the North Atlantic and southern regions without a reduction on inventories held in the primary markets of the Midwest.[59] The average daily inventory of wheat held by the ten primary grain markets of the Midwest in 1890 was 522,000 tons.[60] However, most of this amount was used to cover shipments to deficit markets. A regression relating the average daily inventory to the average daily shipments and the population of each of

[56] Note 53, Chapter II, above.

[57] The method of computation is that indicated below in note 66 of this chapter except that the inventories of all commodities were assumed to have increased.

[58] pp. 44–46 above.

[59] *Ibid.*

[60] Minneapolis Chamber of Commerce, *Annual Report, 1889*, pp. 86–88; and *Annual Report, 1890*, pp. 89–91. The annual average daily inventory of each city is the average of twelve observations. Each observation is the inventory on a given day of the first week of each month. In the case of Kansas City, inventory figures for 1889 were used, since data on inventories in 1890 were not reported.

the ten primary markets revealed that 97 per cent of the daily stock (505,000 tons) was due to shipping requirements and only 3 per cent (17,000 tons) to the support of the local population.[61] In the absence of railroads, the additional average daily inventory required to cover local consumption during the stoppage of navigation would have been 85,000 tons.[62] The increment is only 13 per cent of the daily inventory that was actually held in connection with shipping transactions—transactions that would have halted during winter months in the absence of railroads.[63]

The amount of the additional inventory costs in the intraregional case is also affected by the fact that in the territory below the 37th parallel, navigable waterways were open virtually all year round. Hunter reported that below Cairo on the Mississippi "the operation of the largest steamboats was rarely suspended by low water." Similarly, "steamboats of medium tonnage" on the Red River could ascend to Natchitoches, "some two hundred miles from the mouth, during the entire year save for a period of extremely low water in the summer," and "on the Arkansas River vessels of medium tonnage could operate to Little Rock ... most of the year."[64] Consequently for commodities produced in the South virtually no increase in inventories is required for the limited season of navigation. In many instances, it would not even have been necessary to increase inventories because boats were a slower medium

[61] The equation is:

$$I = 0.4321S + 0.0635P$$
$$(0.0549)\quad(0.2357)$$

where I is average daily inventory in hundreds of tons, S is average daily shipments in tons, and P is population in thousands.

[62] The non-rail inventory requirement is estimated on the assumption that the annual consumption of each person in the local population was 5 bushels of wheat per year.

[63] This argument implicitly assumes that farmers would have kept the wheat stocks normally shipped to primary markets during the winter months until the spring. Shipping and inventory data on grains at Chicago in 1859, before the railroad became a significant factor in interregional grain movements, support the assumption (cf. Chicago Board of Trade, *Annual Report, 1859*, pp. 30–32, 35). One might, nevertheless, want to argue that farmers would have shipped greater amounts of grain before navigation was closed for the winter and that these increments would have been stored in the primary markets until the opening of navigation in the spring. Still, such behavior does not necessarily imply an increase in the social cost of storage. As noted in Chapter II, the increase in winter inventories in receiving centers would have been offset, at least in the case of crops, by declines in the inventories held on farms. The social cost would have risen only to the extent that storage costs in primary markets exceeded those on farms.

[64] Hunter, *Steamboats*, pp. 224–25.

of transportation than railroads. According to the Inland Waterways Commission, in parts of the South there was "greater certainty as to time of delivery by the river" than by rail. "When a planter ships by river he knows that his commodity will reach its destination on a certain day, and that he can take advantage of ruling market quotations, steamboat sugar and cotton being considered as 'spot' for the purpose of sale. On the other hand, rail shipments are frequently delayed for many days, and it is often a matter of weeks after application is made for cars before they are furnished for loading, to say nothing of the delay that is likely to occur in transit." [65]

Finally, the harvest and shipping season of certain crops, such as deciduous fruits, coincided with the season of navigation.

When the above factors are taken into account, the cost of holding the inventories required to compensate for the limited season of navigation is somewhat smaller in the intraregional case than it was in the long-haul case. Under the assumptions of the α estimate the cost is $34,000,000; under the β assumptions it is $25,000,000.[66]

Table 3.10 shows the adjustment of the first approximations of the social saving for indirect costs. The α estimate rises to $337,000,000 and the β estimate to $248,000,000. These figures are 2.8 per cent and 2.1 per cent respectively of gross national product.

THE POSSIBILITY OF TECHNOLOGICAL ADAPTATION TO A NON-RAIL SITUATION

The discussion thus far has been based on the assumption that in the absence of the railroad all other aspects of technology would have remained fixed in the 1890 pattern. This is a severe assumption. It

[65] *Preliminary Report*, pp. 328–29.

[66] Under the assumptions of the α estimate the interest cost of increasing inventories is $9,200,000 and the storage cost is $24,800,000. Under the β assumptions the corresponding figures are $6,900,000 and $18,600,000.

Additional inventories were assumed to be zero for wheat, corn, beef, pork, cotton, cottonseed, tobacco, rice, cane sugar, and deciduous fruits. On all other items inventories were increased by an amount equal to five-twelfths of the annual rail shipments. It was assumed that meats, dairy products, and certain vegetables and fruits would have been placed in cold storage. Storage rates were taken from Buffalo Merchants' Exchange, *Annual Report, 1890*, pp. 88–90; U.S.D.A., *Statistical Bulletin, No. 93*, p. 44; *Transportation by Water, III*, 315; U.S.D.A., *Farmers' Bulletin No. 847* (1917), p. 25; U.S.D.A., *Farmers' Bulletin No. 977*, (1921), p. 24.

TABLE 3.10. PRELIMINARY α AND β ESTIMATES (in millions of dollars)

	1 α	2 β
1. First approximation	300.2	220.9
2. Cargo losses	1.3	1.0
3. Cost of the slow medium of transportation	1.7	0.7
4. Cost of the limited season of navigation	34.0	25.5
5. Totals	337.2	248.1
6. Social saving as a per cent of G. N. P.	2.8	2.1

SOURCES: See text.

seems quite likely that in the absence of railroads much of the capital and ingenuity that went into the perfection and spread of the railroad would have been turned toward the development of other cheap forms of land transportation. Under these circumstances it is possible that the internal combustion engine would have been developed years sooner than it actually was, thus permitting a reduction in transportation costs through the use of motor trucks.

While most such possibilities of a speed-up in the introduction and spread of alternative forms of transportation may be too speculative to permit meaningful quantification, there are two changes about which one can make fairly definitive statements. They are the extension of the existing system of internal waterways and the improvement of common roads. Neither of these developments required new knowledge. They merely involved an extension of existing technology.

The Extension of Internal Navigation

Figure 3.5 and Table 3.11 present a system of canals that could have been constructed in the absence of railroads. Although the 37 canals and feeders proposed are only 5,022 miles in length, their construction would have brought almost all of the agricultural land in the Midwest within 40 straight-line miles of a navigable waterway. As a result, the value of agricultural land falling beyond the boundary of feasible commercial production in 1890 would have been reduced from 24 per cent to 7 per cent of the national total. Hence the loss in national income due to the diminished supply of land would have been not $154,000,000 but only $47,000,000 (see Table 3.12). Part of this reduction in the intraregional social saving would have been offset by the annual cost of the capital required to build the canals, and (in the

FIGURE 3.5

PROPOSED CANALS

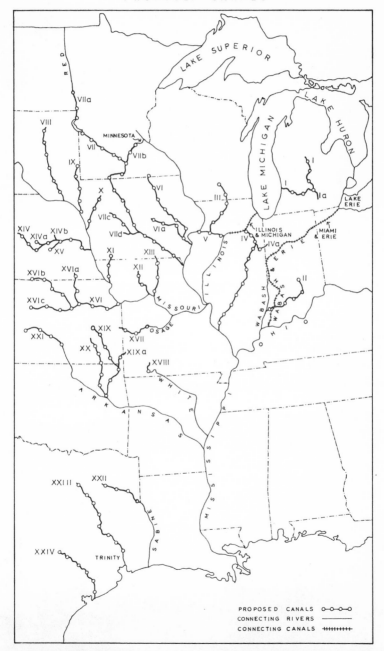

TABLE 3.11. PROPOSED CANALS

1	2	3	4	5	6	7
Canal number	Endpoints of canals	Names of adjacent rivers	Length of canals (miles)	Average rise and fall per mile (feet)	Estimated cost of construction (thousands of dollars)	Per cent of water supply available at summit required for full capacity operation
I	Mt. Pleasant (Mich.) and Lake Michigan	Chippewa, Maple Grand, Kalamazoo	232	3.0	6,244	9 18
Ia	Eaton Rapid (Mich.) and Jackson (Mich.)	Grand	29	0.9	847	35
II	Edinburg (Ind.) and Wabash River near Mt. Carmel (Ill.)	Driftwood, East Fork	163	1.8	4,601	3
III	McFarland (Wis.) and Illinois and Mississippi Canal Feeder	Yahara, Rock	153	1.6	4,370	25
IV	Illinois and Michigan Canal near Blodgett (Ill.) and the Mississippi River	Kankakee, Iroquois Sangamon, Kaskaskia	327	1.5	21,198	25
IVa	Foresman (Ind.) and Spring Creek (Ill.)	Iroquois	32	1.6	934	14
V	Bureau Junction (Ill.) and Green Rock (Ill.)	Rock	77	3.1	5,068	1
VI	Austin (Minn.) and Mississippi River near New Boston (Ill.)	Cedar, Iowa	261	2.3	6,701	21
VIa	Marshalltown (Iowa) and Columbus Junction (Iowa)	Iowa	128	2.3	3,945	6

VII	Ortonville (Minn.) and Mississippi River near Keokuk	Minnesota, Blue Earth, West Fork of Des Moines, Des Moines	549	3.3	13,143	31 / 9
VIIa	Ortonville (Minn.) and Breckenridge (Minn.)	Big Stone Lake, Traverse Lake, Bois De Sioux	83	0.2	2,856	65
VIIb	Mankato (Minn.) and Le Sueur (Minn.)	Minnesota	24	1.5	701	2
VIIc	Grant City (Iowa) and Des Moines (Iowa)	Racoon	104	3.4	3,538	5
VIId	Dale (Iowa) and Racoon River	South Racoon	28	3.6	818	9
VIII	Startford (S.D.) and Missouri River	James	211	0.5	5,327	37
IX	Flandreau (S.D.) and Missouri River near Sioux City (Iowa)	Big Sioux	136	2.9	4,182	20
X	Peterson (Iowa) and Missouri River	Little Sioux	101	2.2	3,373	10
XI	Clarinda (Iowa) and Missouri River near St. Joseph (Mo.)	Nodaway	62	2.4	2,576	13
XII	Mill Grove (Mo.) and Missouri River near Brunswick (Mo.)	Weldon, Thompson, Grand	86	2.3	3,070	17
XIII	Centerville (Iowa) and Missouri River near Glasgow (Mo.)	Chariton	106	1.6	3,423	11
XIV	Milburn (Nebr.) and Platte River near Columbus (Nebr.)	Middle Loup, Loup	154	6.4	5,021	5
XIVa	Scotia (Nebr.) and Loup River	North Loup	22	4.5	642	5

TABLE 3.11. PROPOSED CANALS (continued)

1	2	3	4	5	6	7
Canal number	Endpoints of canals	Names of adjacent rivers	Length of canals (miles)	Average rise and fall per mile (feet)	Estimated cost of construction (thousands of dollars)	Per cent of water supply available at summit required for full capacity operation
XIVb	St. Edward (Nebr.) and Loup River	Beaver Creek	15	8.3	438	44
XV	Central City (Nebr.) and Missouri River near Plattsmouth (Nebr.)	Platte	142	5.2	4,579	5
XVI	Salina (Kans.) and Missouri River near Kansas City	Smokey Hill, Kansas	186	2.7	5,207	9
XVIa	Beatrice (Nebr.) and Manhattan (Kans.)	Big Blue	84	2.7	3,054	15
XVIb	Franklin (Nebr.) and Junction City (Kans.)	Republican	166	4.5	5,050	6
XVIc	Wilson (Kans.) and Salina (Kans.)	Salina	50	4.0	2,394	26
XVII	Trading Post (Kans.) and Warsaw (Mo.)	Maris Des Cygnes, Osage	117	1.3	3,608	2
XVIII	Jamesville (Mo.) and Point Lookout (Mo.)	James, White	71	4.2	2,876	5
XIX	Emporia (Kans.) and Arkansas River near Ft. Gibson (Okla.)	Neosho	262	2.2	6,702	33
XIXa	Waco (Mo.) and Neosho River	Spring	36	2.8	1,051	4

XX	Altoona (Kans.) and Arkansas River near Ft. Gibson (Okla.)	Verdigris	153	2.1	4,435	7
XXI	Larned (Kans.) and Wichita (Kans.)	Arkansas	116	6.1	4,072	15
XXII	Sabine River near Roberts (Tex.) and Sabine River near Tenaha (Tex.)	Sabine	134	1.5	3,970	18
XXIII	Dallas (Tex.) and Romayor (Tex.)	Trinity	225	1.1	5,720	3
XXIV	Austin (Tex.) and mouth of Colorado River	Colorado	197	2.3	5,360	2
	Total or Grand Average		5,022	2.6	161,103	

SOURCES AND NOTES:

Columns 2, 3, 4, and 5. The routes of the canals and their profiles were constructed from the 1:250,000 series of topographic maps of the Geological Survey. These maps were supplemented by the 1:24,000 scale topographic maps; *The Rand McNally Commercial Atlas for 1957;* Henry Gannett, "Profiles of Rivers in the United States," U. S. Geological Survey, *Water Supply Paper, No. 44* (Washington, 1901); *Cram's Standard American Railway System Atlas, 1892;* and various reports of the U.S. Corps of Engineers.

Column 6. The cost of canals over 49 miles long was computed from a regression relating cost to the length of canals, the area of the cross section of the prism, and the total rise and fall. The regression was computed by H. Jerome Cranmer from data on 44 canals built prior to 1860. To adjust the estimated cost of construction for changes in the price level, an index of the average cost of construction prior to 1860 was computed by weighting the Snyder-Tucker price index by the amount of construction over the years from 1817 through 1860. The ratio of this weighted index to the Snyder-Tucker index for 1890 provided the price correction factor.

For all canals longer than 49 miles, except Canals IV and V, the area of the cross section of the prism was taken to be 300 square feet (60 feet at the surface, 40 feet at the bottom with a depth of 6 feet). In the case of Canal IV, the same dimensions were assumed for all of the canal except 35 miles which would have required a deep cut averaging about 61 feet. At the cost of excavation prevailing along the route of the Illinois and Mississippi Canal in 1890, the cut would have added $13,369,000 to the cost of the canal. It should be noted that the deep cut is not necessary to bring all of Illinois within 40 straight-line miles of a navigable waterway. The cut was made only to provide Canal IV with a direct link to the Illinois and Michigan Canal. Moreover, it is possible that such a connection could have been made without the cut. The assumption of excavation through several high ridges was necessary because of the absence of data on the discharge of small rivers and streams. Given such information it might have been possible to plan a route that avoided the ridges. Canal V covers the same route that was subsequently taken by the Illinois and Mississippi Canal. It was assumed that Canal V was built according to the dimensions and at the cost of the Illinois and Mississippi.

Cranmer's equation does not provide good estimates for canals under 50 miles. Seven of the proposed canals, representing 4 per cent of the total mileage, are under 50 miles. In these cases the average cost per mile was taken to be equal to the average cost per mile on all the other canals except IV and V.

H. Jerome Cranmer, "Canal Investment, 1815-1860," Conference on Income and Wealth, *Trends,* pp. 553–64; Carter Goodrich and others, *Canals and American Economic Development* (New York, 1961), pp. 208–9; U.S. Corps of Engineers, *Annual Report, 1890,* table following p. 2596.

Column 7. The water requirements of the summit levels of the canals were computed from the formulas of the U.S. Corps of Engineers. The computations were based on the assumption of canals with prisms having a cross section of 300 square feet and a width at the surface of 60 feet. Locks were assumed to be 15 feet wide and 100 feet long with an average lift of 10 feet. Such canals could have handled boats with a burden of 120 tons. At 170 lockages per day, the daily capacity of each canal (except V) would have been 20,400 tons; during a season of 200 days the capacity would have been 4,080,000 tons. The gross capacity of Canal V is 28,600,000 tons. The data on the supply of water were obtained from the *Water Supply Papers* of the Geological Survey. U.S. Corps of Engineers, *Annual Report, 1874,* I, 504–7; *Annual Report, 1876,* II, 60–78, 97–101; *Annual Report, 1908,* p. 2012; U.S. Geological Survey, *Water Supply Papers, Nos. 1385–93;* cf. Otto Franzius, *Waterway Engineering* (Cambridge, Mass., 1936).

TABLE 3.12. LOSS IN NATIONAL PRODUCT DUE TO DECREASE IN LAND SUPPLY AFTER CONSTRUCTION OF PROPOSED CANALS

	1	2	3	4	5	6
	Value of farmland in 1890	Value of land beyond feasible regions before new canals	Col. 2 as a per cent of Col. 1	Value of land beyond feasible region after new canals	Col. 4 as a per cent of Col. 1	Loss in national product after new canals
North Atlantic Div.	1,092,281	5,637	0.5	5,637	0.5	331
South Atlantic Div.	557,399	117,866	21.1	117,866	21.2	8,452
Ohio	666,118	20,205	3.0	20,205	3.0	1,332
Indiana	481,684	38,783	8.1	18,150	3.8	1,211
Illinois	964,612	174,567	18.1	0	0.0	0
Michigan	301,739	106,110	35.2	61	0.0	4
Wisconsin	264,049	53,483	20.3	16,636	6.3	1,123
Minnesota	254,261	81,649	32.1	12,023	4.7	957
Iowa	678,364	372,339	54.9	0	0.0	0
Missouri	443,611	68,891	15.5	1,260	0.3	101
North Dakota	51,257	19,483	38.0	19,483	38.0	1,808
South Dakota	79,676	43,114	54.1	3,267	4.1	295
Nebraska	310,302	187,149	60.3	21,373	6.9	1,750
Kansas	435,934	276,179	63.3	29,798	6.8	2,497
North Central Div.	4,931,607	1,441,952	29.2	142,256	2.9	11,078
Kentucky	178,670	1,893	1.1	1,893	1.1	119
Tennessee	123,633	7,936	6.4	7,936	6.4	475
Alabama	32,795	1,223	3.7	1,223	3.7	102
Mississippi	51,166	342	0.1	342	0.1	33
Louisiana	42,901	0	0.0	0	0.0	0
Texas	265,841	145,248	54.6	73,854	27.8	6,742
Arkansas	43,327	2,224	5.1	2,224	5.1	201
South Central Div.	738,333	158,866	21.5	87,472	11.8	7,672
Western Div.	800,952	218,216	27.2	218,216	27.2	19,919
United States	8,120,572	1,942,537	23.9	571,447	7.0	47,452

SOURCES AND NOTES:

Columns 1, 2, and 3. Table 3.7

Column 4. Computed in the same manner as Column 2 of Table 3.7 after determining counties brought into the region of feasible commercial agriculture as a result of the proposed canals.

Column 6. Entries in Column 4 above multiplied by corresponding entries in Column 5 of Table 3.7.

case of the β estimate) by the increased cost of wagon haulage on shipments originating within the enlarged feasible region. After taking such factors into account, the revised α estimate of the social saving is $214,000,000 and the revised β estimate is $175,000,000 (see Table 3.13).

This proposed extension of internal water transportation is more than a historian's hallucination. In the absence of railroads, the canals shown in Figure 3.5 would have been both technologically and economically feasible. This assertion can be verified by considering the two main issues on which the question of feasibility turns: the nature of the terrain over which the canals would have been built and the water supply available for the operation of the canals.

Far from presenting insuperable obstacles, the terrain of the proposed system is generally more favorable than that over which the actual canal system was constructed. Figures 3.6 through 3.9 show the profiles of the routes of each of the proposed canals. Figure 3.10 shows the profiles of canals actually constructed in New York. A comparison of the proposed system with the canals built by the State of New York reveals that proposed canals with about 30 per cent of the total mileage have an average rise and fall per mile below that which prevailed on the fabled Erie; 41 per cent of the proposed system would have been constructed through terrain more favorable than that of the Champlain Canal; and no canal in the proposed system has an average rise and fall per mile as great as that which prevailed on the Genesee Valley, the Chenango, the Black River, or the Chemung Canals.[67] The unusually

TABLE 3.13. α AND β ESTIMATES ADJUSTED TO TAKE ACCOUNT OF THE POSSIBILITY OF EXTENDING INTERNAL NAVIGATION (millions of dollars)

	1 α	2 β
1. Preliminary estimates	337.2	248.1
2. Change in L		−106.1
3. Change in $\bar{\alpha}$	16.1	16.1
4. Change in $\overset{*}{\alpha}$	−148.9	
5. Change in indirect costs	9.8	16.6
6. Totals	214.2	174.7
7. Social saving as a per cent of G. N. P.	1.8	1.5

SOURCES: See text.

[67] U. S. Census Office, *Tenth Census of the United States: 1880, Report on the Agencies of Transportation* (Washington, 1883), pp. 752–53 (hereafter referred to as *Census of Transportation, 1880;* Table 3.11 above).

FIGURE 3.6

PROFILES OF PROPOSED CANALS IN MICHIGAN, INDIANA, ILLINOIS, WISCONSIN, MINNESOTA AND IOWA

HORIZONTAL SCALE IN MILES
VERTICAL SCALE IN FEET

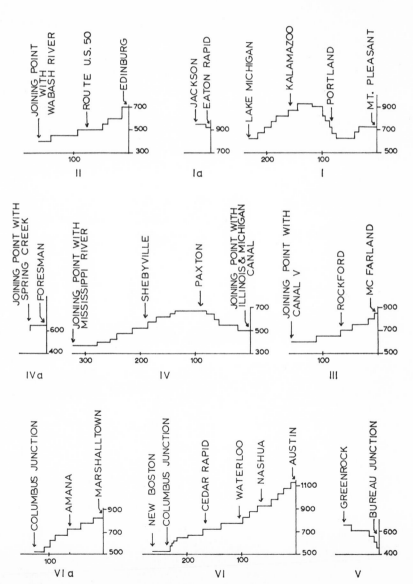

FIGURE 3.7

PROFILES OF PROPOSED CANALS IN MINNESOTA, IOWA,
NORTH DAKOTA AND SOUTH DAKOTA

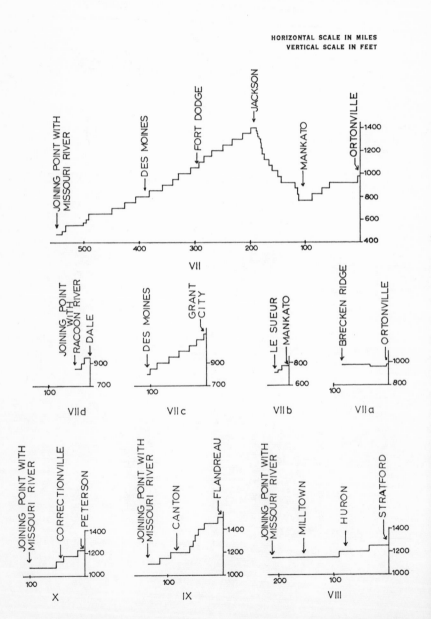

FIGURE 3.8

PROFILES OF PROPOSED CANALS IN IOWA, MISSOURI, NEBRASKA
AND KANSAS

HORIZONTAL SCALE IN MILES
VERTICAL SCALE IN FEET

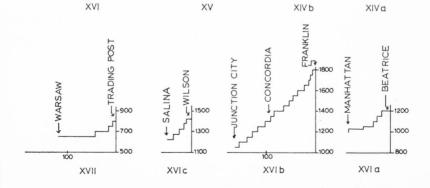

FIGURE 3.9

PROFILES OF PROPOSED CANALS IN MISSOURI, KANSAS AND TEXAS

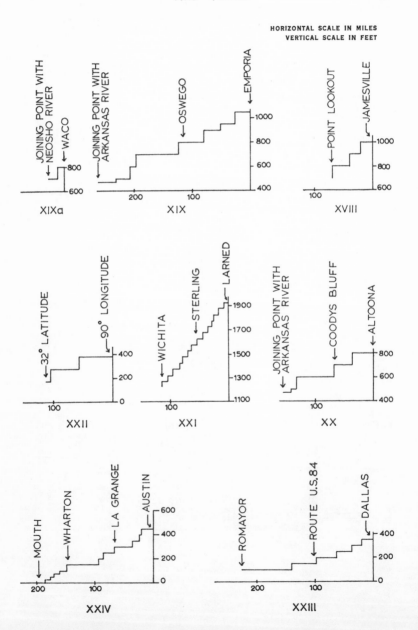

HORIZONTAL SCALE IN MILES
VERTICAL SCALE IN FEET

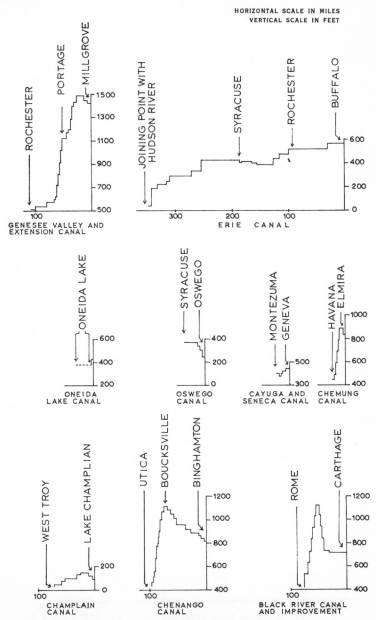

FIGURE 3.10

CANALS IN NEW YORK

SOURCE PROFILES OF THE NEW YORK STATE CANALS,
ANNUAL REPORT OF THE CANAL COMMISSIONERS, 1867, NEW
YORK STATE, ASSEMBLY DOCUMENTS, 19th SESSION, 1867, No.7

favorable character of the proposed routes is even more strongly emphasized by a general comparison. The average rise and fall per mile on the proposed system is 29 per cent less than the average on those canals that were successful enough to survive railroad competition through 1890. [68]

With respect to the water supply, the crucial issue is the adequacy of the supply at the summit level of each of the canals. Three factors must be considered in estimating water consumption at summit levels: evaporation, percolation, and lockage. The largest losses at a summit are due to lockage which is generally responsible for 80 per cent or more of water consumption. However, since the water released from the summit lock of a canal passes on to the next level with the boat, the summit level of a canal provides the water required for lockage at lower levels. The water requirement of each of the canals in the proposed system was determined from the consumption formulas used by the Corps of Engineers. [69] Column 7 of Table 3.11 shows that even if worked at full capacity, no canal in the proposed system would have required more than 65 per cent of the supply available at the summit. Indeed if two canals totaling 98 miles are excluded (VIIa and XIVb), no canal operating at full capacity would have required as much as 40 per cent of the available supply. The highly favorable situation of the canals in the proposed system with respect to the availability of water is further underscored by the information that in no case would the agricultural tonnage carried by a canal have exceeded one-third of its capacity. [70]

The new values of α and β given in Table 3.13 do not show the full extent of the reduction in the social saving that could have been brought about by an improvement in the system of internal water transportation. The preliminary value of β was not adjusted to reflect the fact that the average transportation rate on the proposed canals would have been below the average water rate used in the initial computation.

[68] *Census of Transportation, 1880*, pp. 752–55; *Census of Transportation, 1890*, II, 474–77.

[69] U.S. Army, Corps of Engineers, *Report of the Chief of Engineers, Annual Report, 1874*, pp. 504–7; *Annual Report, 1876*, Part II, pp. 61–78 and 97–101. Cf. Otto Franzius, *Waterway Engineering* (Cambridge, Mass., 1936), especially, pp. 461–64.

[70] Perhaps the most surprising finding is the relatively small per cent of the available supply of water that would have been required for the canals built through Nebraska and Kansas. Although the Platte may be "a mile wide and a foot deep at the mouth," the discharge from such a stream is more than adequate to keep a channel 50 feet wide and 6 feet deep supplied with water.

Moreover, the proposed canals do not exhaust the improvements in internal navigation that would have been socially profitable in the absence of railroads. Significant reductions in the social saving could have been achieved by the construction of additional canals in the South Atlantic states, Texas, and California. Finally, the estimated cost of the proposed system is probably higher than the actual cost would have been. In some cases it would have been cheaper to have extended internal navigation through the improvement of rivers rather than through the construction of canals. The cost of constructing the proposed system was also exaggerated by certain constraints imposed by the availability of data. For example, published information on water flows is limited to very large rivers. Hence it was necessary to propose more circuitous routes than would have been necessary with information on the water flows of smaller rivers.

The Improvement of Country Roads

Historians have focused considerable attention on the great highway movement following the Rural Post Roads Act of 1916. The widespread improvement of common roads that followed this act, together with the development of motor trucks, significantly reduced the cost of short-haul transportation. However, the movement for the improvement of common roads began more than two decades prior to this enactment. Agitation for improved highways became prominent in the 1880's. The first major state program of road improvement was launched by New Jersey in 1891. In 1893 the Department of Agriculture established the Office of Road Inquiry (later called the Office of Public Roads) to disseminate information on rural roads and to promote state and local improvement programs. Yet by 1904 just 7.14 per cent of all country roads were classified as "improved." In 1909 the figure stood at 8.66 per cent.[71]

The meager success achieved by the good-roads movement during a period of nearly 30 years is puzzling if one accepts the estimate of the Department of Agriculture on the reduction in wagon transport costs that could have been achieved by the proposed improvements. Of the

[71] Maurice O. Eldridge, "Public-Road Mileage, Revenues and Expenditures in the United States in 1904," U.S.D.A., Office of Public Roads, *Bulletin No. 32* (1907), p. 7; J. E. Pennybacker, Jr. and Maurice O. Eldridge, "Mileage and Cost of Public Roads in the United States in 1909," U.S.D.A., Office of Public Roads, *Bulletin No. 41* (1912), p. 8.

several estimates published by the Department betwen 1895 and 1912, the most conservative put the annual saving—after allowance for the capital cost of the improvements—at 76.28 cents per acre of farm land. This saving multiplied by the 623,200,000 acres in farms in 1890 would have produced a total saving of $475,400,000. Since the traffic on country roads was put at 3,791,000,000 ton-miles, the Department's estimates implied that improved roads would reduce the cost of wagon transportation by 50 per cent—from 25 to 12.5 cents per ton-mile. A less conservative computation put the fall in the wagon rate at 60 per cent—from 25 to 10 cents per ton-mile.[72]

Assuming an amortization period of ten years, the Department's estimates imply a rate of return of over 29 per cent on capital invested in road improvements. At the time, the yield on railroad bonds varied between 4 and 5 per cent. If the Department's estimates were correct, the political pressure for so highly profitable an enterprise was unusually modest—far more modest and less successful than the political movements for publicly aided railroad construction had been in earlier decades.

It should therefore not be surprising to find that the Department's estimates were severely criticized by leading civil engineers and journals of civil engineering. Interestingly, the critics argued not that the U.S.D.A. underestimated the cost of wagon transportation over improved roads, but rather that it grossly overestimated the cost on ordinary ones. The *Engineering News* said that the claim that haulage costs averaged 25 cents per ton-mile "must be set down, we believe, by any impartial critic as a wild exaggeration. Such ridiculous statements must injure rather than aid the cause they are put forth to serve." [73] The *Engineering News* based its argument on the doctrine of alternative cost: [74]

The real measure of the cost to the farmer is what he can afford to pay for having the work done for him. How much would his expense be reduced if the hauling to market were done for him gratis? We have already pointed out that the teams which do the plowing and harrowing and mowing and reaping also draw the

[72] U.S.D.A., Office of Road Inquiry, *Circular Nos. 19 and 23;* U.S.D.A., Office of Road Inquiry, "Proceedings of the National Road Conference," *Bulletin No. 10* (1894), pp. 8–9; cf. U.S.D.A., "Benefits of Improved Roads," *Farmers' Bulletin 505* (1912).

[73] *Engineering News,* XXXIV (Dec. 5, 1895), 378.

[74] *Ibid.,* (Dec. 19, 1895), p. 410.

product to the railway, and would manifestly be standing idle in the fall after the crops are harvested and when the grain is ready for market, were they not employed to draw it.

Ira O. Baker, Professor of Civil Engineering at the University of Illinois and author of one of the standard textbooks on road construction used at the turn of the century, held that if one took account of the fact that most of the hauling of farm crops took place when farmers, horses, and equipment were otherwise idle and that wagons usually carried goods back to farms on the return trip, the actual cost of hauling farm products was about 60 per cent below the figure put forth by the U.S.D.A. "In the crop season," said Baker, "with little choice as to the time of doing the work the cost on fairly level loam or clay roads is probably not more than 10 to 12 cents per ton-mile; and when farm work is not pressing, the cost is not more than 8 to 10 cents per ton-mile." In support of his contention Baker stated that "non-resident land owners in central Illinois frequently hire corn delivered for 9 to 11 cents per ton-mile. This price has obtained over large areas for 10 or 15 years. The contract is usually taken by the man who does the shelling, he hiring farmers to do the hauling." [75]

Whether the Department or its critics were correct is too complex an issue to be resolved in this study. It is part of the larger, neglected problem of the extent and developmental significance of the investment in non-railroad forms of overland transportation during the nineteenth century. However, regardless of which side was right, the debate points to the necessity of recomputing the previous estimates of the intraregional social saving on the basis of a reduced wagon rate. If the critics were right, a computation based on a wagon rate of 10 cents per ton-mile merely removes one of the upward biases in the earlier estimates. If the U.S.D.A. was right, the recomputation measures the amount by which the social saving could have been reduced by the improvement of roads.

The results of the new computation are summarized in Table 3.14. A wagon rate of 10 cents per ton-mile implies that the boundary of the region of feasible commercial agriculture fell 80 straight-line miles from navigable waterways. The doubling of the distance of this boundary together with the construction of the canals shown in Figure 3.5

[75] Ira Osborn Baker, *A Treatise on Roads and Pavements* (2d ed., enl.; New York, 1913), pp. 8, 16–17.

TABLE 3.14. α AND β ESTIMATES ADJUSTED TO REFLECT BOTH THE EXTENSION OF INTERNAL NAVIGATION AND A REDUCTION IN WAGON RATES (millions of dollars)

	1 α	2 β
1. Preliminary estimates	337.7	248.1
2. Change in L		−130.3
3. Change in $\bar{\alpha}$	− 18.6	− 18.6
4. Change in α^{*}	−188.0	
5. Change in indirect costs	9.8	17.9
6. Totals	140.9	117.1
7. Social saving as a per cent of G. N. P.	1.2	1.0

SOURCES: See text.

would have brought all but 4 per cent of agricultural land within the feasible region. As a consequence, the loss in national income due to the reduction in the supply of land would have been only $23,300,000. The social saving on direct shipping costs within the enlarged feasible region would have been $48,700,000. When the indirect costs are included, the β estimate is $117,000,000 or slightly less than 1 per cent of G.N.P. The new value of α is $141,000,000 or just 1.2 per cent of G.N.P.

It thus appears that while railroads were more important in short-haul movements of agricultural products than in long-haul movements, the differences are not as great as is usually supposed. It is very likely that even in the absence of railroads the prairies would have been settled and exploited. Cheap transportation rather than railroads was the necessary condition for the emergence of the North Central states as the granary of the nation. The railroad was undoubtedly the most efficient form of transportation available to the farmers of the nation. But the combination of wagon and water transportation could have provided a relatively good substitute for the fabled iron horse.

CHAPTER IV

Railroads and the "Take-Off" Thesis:
The American Case

Every economic historian should, however, have acquired what might be called the statistical sense, the habit of asking in relation to any institution, policy, group or movement the questions: how large? how long? how often? how representative? The requirement seems obvious; but a good deal of the older . . . economic history was less useful than it might have been through neglect of it.—SIR JOHN CLAPHAM

It is quite true that our knowledge of facts is very often too incomplete to admit of a clear answer to what constitutes the real economic meaning of what has happened. But even in that case it is necessary not to stop at a so-called fact which is meaningless in itself; what explanation it really points to must be investigated, and often it will be found out that the sources will yield all the knowledge wanted, if only properly questioned. It is the lack of that questioning which is most usually at the bottom of the difficulty.—ELI F. HECKSCHER

In his widely discussed book, *The Stages of Economic Growth,* and in other works, W. W. Rostow divides the process of economic development into a series of five temporal stages. These stages are: *traditional society,* an era in which limited knowledge and use of modern science places a ceiling "on the level of attainable output per head"; *the preconditions for the take-off,* a period when traditional society is transformed so as to provide a social, political, intellectual, scientific, and institutional framework favorable for economic growth; *the take-off,* a "brief time interval of two or three decades . . . during which the rate of investment increases in such a way that real output *per capita* rises and this initial increase carries with it radical changes in production techniques and the disposition of income flows which perpetuate the new scale of investment and perpetuate thereby the rising trend in *per capita* output"; *the drive to maturity,* a "long interval of sustained if fluctuating progress" marked by the application of the range of "modern technology to the bulk of its resources"; *the age of high mass consumption,* the stage beyond maturity during which an increasing proportion of resources is allocated to the production of "durable consumers' goods and services."[1]

Rostow suggests that all developed nations have passed through this sequence of stages and that it is possible to identify all societies as lying in one or another of them. But by far the most crucial category in his theory is the middle or "take-off" period which Rostow calls the "great watershed in the life of modern societies." The other four stages are so constructed that they lead up to the "take-off" or follow from it. Although it occupies a relatively brief interval of time, the "take-off" emerges as the strategic objective toward which all nations desiring growth must aspire. Without achieving it, sustained economic growth is impossible; once it is achieved, all further economic growth becomes "more or less automatic."[2]

Rostow presents a number of definitions and characterizations aimed at identifying the unique quality of this important juncture.[3] The "take-off," he writes, is that "decade or two" during which "both the basic structure of the economy and the social and political structure of the society are transformed in such a way that a steady rate of growth can be, thereafter, regularly sustained"; it is the time when the "forces of modernization make a decisive break-through," the "early stage when industrialization takes hold," the epoch when growth becomes a "normal condition"; it is the era during which "the scale of productive activity reaches a critical level and produces changes which lead to a massive and progressive structural transformation," a transformation "better viewed" as a change "in kind" rather than "in degree"; it is "an industrial revolution, tied directly to radical changes in methods of production, having their decisive consequence over a relatively short period of time." Thus, the "take-off" is above all the period of "decisive," "rapid," "radical" structural change, structural change that makes further growth more or less automatic is the essence of Rostow's "take-off."[4]

[1] Rostow, *Stages*, pp. 4, 6, 7, 9, 10, 59; W. W. Rostow, *The Process of Economic Growth* (2nd ed.; Oxford, 1960), p. 274.

[2] Rostow, *Stages*, p. 7; Rostow, *Process*, p. 274.

[3] The "take-off" is more than just the time interval during which nations first begin to grow or the period during which the rate of growth accelerates. Rostow suggests that substantial economic progress, including rises in per capita income, can take place in "pre-take-off" societies. Moreover, his dating of some "take-offs" suggests that a rising per capita income is not a necessary characteristic of this stage. Rostow, *Stages*, pp. 38–40.

[4] *Ibid.*, pp. 8, 9, 36, 39, 40, 57.

Yet, despite the colorful language used to describe it, the exact nature of this crucial structural transformation never becomes very clear in *The Stages of Economic Growth*. One perceives a series of adumbrations rather than a clearly specified theory. What precisely does "industrialization taking hold" mean? How far must industrialization proceed before it is adjudged to have "taken hold"? What is a "decisive" breakthrough for the "forces of modernization"? How does one recognize it? Exactly what does Rostow mean by the structure of the economy? And how far does structural change have to go before it is "better viewed" as a change "in kind" rather than "merely in degree"?

Rostow does not answer these questions. Instead he lists three conditions that are necessary for a "take-off"; "(1) a rise in the rate of productive investment from, say, 5 per cent or less to over 10 per cent of national income (or net national product [NNP]); (2) the development of one or more substantial manufacturing sectors, with a high rate of growth; (3) the existence or quick emergence of a political, social, and institutional framework which exploits the impulses to expansion in the modern sector and the potential external economy effects of the take-off and gives to growth an on-going character." Although he never specifies what he means by a "substantial manufacturing sector" or a "high rate of growth," Rostow places particularly heavy emphasis on the second of these three conditions. He holds that aggregative variables such as the aggregate marginal capital/output ratio tell "little of what actually happens and of the causal process at work in a take-off." Moreover, "the overall growth of an economy must be regarded in the first instance as the consequence of differing rates of growth in particular sectors of the economy." Hence, one must know "not merely how a rise in the investment-rate is brought about" but "how rapidly growing manufacturing sectors emerged and imparted their primary and secondary growth impulses to the economy." His argument, says Rostow, "is that one or more new manufacturing sectors is a powerful and essential engine of economic transformation." The "take-off," then, is a process dominated by a "limited number" of rapidly expanding "primary growth sectors" whose own "expansion and technical transformation induce a chain of requirements for increased capacity and the potentiality for new production functions in other sectors." [5]

Rostow introduces greater specificity into the discussion when he presents the bounds of the "take-off" period of 13 countries. Among

---

[5] *Ibid.*, pp. 39, 46, 52, 53, 57, 58.

these dates are: Great Britain, 1783-1802; France, 1830-60; the United States, 1843-60; Germany, 1850-73; and Russia, 1890-1914. The American "take-off" is described "as the upshot of two different periods of expansion: the first, that of the 1840's, marked by railway and manufacturing development" in the East; "the second, the great railway push into the Middle West during the 1850's. . . . By the opening of the Civil War the American economy of the North and West, with real momentum in its heavy-industry sector, is judged to have taken off." Rostow stresses that while the cotton textile industry triggered the British "take-off," the railroad "was decisive" in the American case and in a number of other countries where "the growth of modern basic industrial sectors can be traced in the most direct way to the requirements for building and, especially, for maintaining substantial railway systems."[6]

In stressing the nexus between the construction of railroads and the American "take-off," Rostow relied on the widely accepted view that railroad construction during the nineteenth century had a crucial impact on the growth of manufacturing. Thus a discussion of the applicability of the "take-off" thesis to the American case serves a dual purpose. It bears on both the historical relevance of Rostow's view of economic development and on the broader issue of the relationship between railroad construction and growth of the capital-good industries in the antebellum period. In the pages that follow I first present data pertaining to structural change in the American economy during the years 1843-60. I then attempt to evaluate the significance of the indicated transformation and the extent to which it can be attributed to the influence of a "limited number of primary growth sectors"—particularly the railroad sector.

STRUCTURAL CHANGE DURING THE "TAKE-OFF"

There are two problems involved in the attempt to measure structural change during the "take-off" period. The first stems from Rostow's failure to define precisely what he means by a change in the structure of the economy. In economic literature, as Fritz Machlup has recently pointed out, the term "structure" is used to connote a wide, and frequently confusing, if not contradictory, array of ideas.[7] What assump-

[6] *Ibid.*, pp. 38, 55.
[7] Fritz Machlup, "Structure and Structural Change: Weaselwords and Jargon," *Zeitschrift Für Nationalökonomie*, XVIII (1958), 280–98.

tion should one make about the particular way in which the term is used in *The Stages of Economic Growth*? Does Rostow have in mind (1) a change in the percentage distribution of output among the various industries that make up the economy? Or does he mean (2) a change in the percentage distribution of inputs? Perhaps he uses the term merely (3) to differentiate between temporary (e.g., cyclical) and secular or "permanent" changes? Or again he may intend the term (4) principally as a description of changes in the parameters of supply and/or demand functions, regardless of the effect of such changes on the percentage distribution of outputs and inputs. Clearly, the author's intent would determine the particular set or sets of data to be examined in searching for evidence of structural changes during the "take-off." The ensuing discussion concentrates on data bearing on the first alternative. This focus is more than expedient. The doctrine that the "take-off" is the product of an uneven development of industry in general, and of a few very rapidly expanding industries in particular, leads one to expect large changes in the percentage distribution of outputs.

The second problem pertains to the nature of the available data. The two main statistical series that can be used to measure the percentage change in the distribution of output among industries for the period in question are those provided by R. F. Martin and Robert E. Gallman.[8] The accuracy of Martin's estimates are open to question in a number of important respects.[9] Moreover, Martin's estimates are given only in current prices. Gallman, on the other hand, limits himself only to the commodity producing industries. The output of these is measured by value added rather than by the income originating within each sector. However, Gallman's estimates seem to rest on a sounder methodological footing than Martin's; his results are given both in current and constant prices; and while he excludes the large and important service sector of

[8] Robert F. Martin, *National Income in the United States 1799–1938*, National Industrial Conference Board Studies No. 241 (New York, 1939); Gallman, "Commodity Output," pp. 13–67. Martin's main series are reprinted in *Historical Statistics* (1949).

[9] Simon Kuznets, "Long-Term Changes in the National Income of the United States of America since 1870," International Association for Research in Income and Wealth, *Income and Wealth of the United States,* Income and Wealth Series II (Baltimore, 1952), pp. 221–41; William N. Parker and Franklee Whartenby, "The Growth of Output Before 1840," Conference on Research in Income and Wealth, *Trends,* pp. 191–212.

the economy, it is presumably in the commodity producing areas that Rostow finds most of his "modern" industries.

Martin's Data

Martin divides the economy into nine categories: agriculture; mining and quarrying; electric light, power, and gas; manufacturing; construction, transportation, and communication; trade; service; and miscellaneous. His figures are for census years. Table 4.1 gives the percentage distribution of income among Martin's categories for the years 1839, 1849, and 1859. The significant feature of this table is the steady decline—amounting to about 4 percentage points—in agriculture's share of total output. In contradistinction to the movement of agriculture, Table 4.1 indicates a rise in the share of manufacturing of about two points and a rise of about three and one-half points in the trade share. Table 4.2 compresses Martin's nine categories into three—the A, M, and S sectors. This table shows that most of the decline in agriculture was absorbed not by the M but by the S sector. Table 4.3 presents the distribution of income originating in the sphere of commodity production. The pattern it displays is similar to the previous tables. Of particular interest is the fact that all three tables place the increase in the manufacturing share entirely in the first decade of the period. In the fifties, the shift toward manufacturing is reversed or comes to a virtual halt. The general impression conveyed by Martin's data is one of relatively moderate change in the structure of the economy.

TABLE 4.1. THE PERCENTAGE DISTRIBUTION OF INCOME IN CURRENT PRICES BY NINE SECTORS—MARTIN'S DATA

| | 1 | 2 | 3 | 4 | 5 | 6 | 7 | 8 | 9 |
Year	Agriculture	Mining and quarrying	Electric light, power, and gas	Manufacturing	Construction	Transportation and communication	Trade	Service	Miscellaneous
1839	34.6	0.3	0.1	10.3	6.0	17.6	8.6	14.1	8.6
1849	31.7	0.7	0.1	12.5	5.7	17.1	8.4	15.3	8.5
1859	30.8	1.1	0.1	12.1	4.5	16.9	12.1	14.0	8.4

SOURCE: *Historical Statistics* (1949), p. 14.

TABLE 4.2. THE PERCENTAGE DISTRIBUTION OF INCOME IN CURRENT PRICES BY THREE SECTORS—MARTIN'S DATA

Year	1 A	2 M	3 S
1839	34.6	16.6	48.8
1849	31.7	18.9	49.4
1859	30.8	18.6	51.5

SOURCE: Same as Table 4.1.

Note: The M sector comprises columns 2, 4, and 5 of Table 4.1.
The S sector comprises all the other categories of Table 4.1 except agriculture.

Gallman's Data

Table 4.4 is a sectoral distribution of the shares of value added in commodity production. Based on Gallman's current price series, it shows a more precipitous fall in the share of agriculture and a more rapid rise in the share of manufacturing over the two-decade period than does Table 4.3. However, part of this phenomenon may be due to the nature of the indexes involved. It is quite possible to have the

ratio $\dfrac{\text{value added in manufacturing}}{\text{value added in all commodity production}}$ rise, while the ratio

$\dfrac{\text{net income in manufacturing}}{\text{net income in all commodity production}}$ remains constant. For value

added includes depreciation and purchase of services. Hence, if the ratio

$\dfrac{\text{depreciation} + \text{purchases of services}}{\text{net income}}$ increased more rapidly in manu-

facturing than in agriculture, the use of value added as an index of structural change would impart a bias toward manufacturing and against

TABLE 4.3. PERCENTAGE DISTRIBUTION OF INCOME ORIGINATING IN COMMODITY PRODUCTION—MARTIN'S CURRENT PRICE DATA

Year	1 Agriculture	2 Mining and quarrying	3 Manufacturing	4 Construction
1839	67.5	0.6	20.1	11.8
1849	62.7	1.4	24.7	11.3
1859	63.6	2.2	24.9	9.3

SOURCE: Same as Table 4.2.

TABLE 4.4. PERCENTAGE DISTRIBUTION OF VALUE ADDED IN COMMODITY PRODUCTION—GALLMAN'S CURRENT PRICE DATA

Year	1 Agriculture	2 Mining	3 Manufacturing	4 Construction (Variant A)
1839	68.8	0.9	23.1	7.2
1844	62.8	1.2	28.5	7.4
1849	59.1	1.2	31.9	7.8
1854	61.3	1.3	27.8	9.6
1859	58.1	1.3	31.7	8.9

SOURCE: Gallman, "Commodity Output," p. 43.

agriculture. Between 1805 and 1880, the percentage increase in the value of business structures and equipment was ten times as large as the percentage increase in the value of agricultural structures and equipment. Over a similar period (1809–79) the percentage increase in manufacturing income was only four times as large as the increase in agricultural income.[10] It seems likely, therefore, that the bias alluded to is present in the value-added series.

Fortunately, Gallman's data are given by quinquennia. Table 4.4 not only agrees with the previous tables in placing all of the shift toward manufacturing betwen 1839 and 1849 but also suggests that this shift was probably well under way before the onset of Rostow's "take-off" period. Manufacturing increased its share of commodity output by 5.4 points during the first quinquennium, most of which predates the "take-off." Furthermore, the shift towards manufacturing during the fifteen years from 1844 to 1859 (3.2 points) is smaller than the one which occurred during the five years ending in 1844.

Current price data are, of course, a rather poor index of changes in the distribution of physical output. Since Rostow's discussion of structural change is presumably cast in real rather than value terms, a constant price series would provide a more appropriate instrument for analyzing "the inner structure" of the "take-off." However, the material presented so far is germane to one of Rostow's points, the proposition that the rapid growth of modern industry during the "take-off" significantly shifted the flow of income away from the old and to the new, more productive sectors. This, he argues, was one of the main

[10] Raymond Goldsmith, "The Growth of Reproducible Wealth of the United States of America from 1805 to 1950," International Association for Research in Income and Wealth, *Income and Wealth of the United States,* Income and Wealth Series II (Baltimore, 1952), p. 306; *Historical Statistics* (1949), p. 14.

means of procuring the capital required to finance the "take-off." [11]
The previous tables clearly indicated that the "take-off" years were not
ones of radical alteration in the sectoral distribution of income. The
increased flow toward manufacturing was quite moderate, considerably
more moderate, as will be shown, than the change in the relative shares
in real output.

Table 4.5 presents a distribution of value added in commodity production in constant dollars. Use of constant dollars does not materially
alter the pattern of development in mining and construction. However,
it increases both the rate of decline in the share of agriculture and the
rate of increase in the share of manufacturing. The relative gain in
manufacturing between 1844 and 1859 is three times as great in real
terms as it was in value terms (10.1 points as opposed to 3.2 points).
The over-all impression is one of very rapid growth in manufacturing.
Still there remain two points of similarity between the constant and
current dollar series. First, almost all of the shift toward manufacturing
shown by Table 4.5 took place during the years 1839–49. Over 80 per
cent of the increase in the manufacturing share came during this decade.
Second, the 3.7 per cent increase in the manufacturing share during the
first quinquennium again suggests that the process of structural transformation was well under way prior to the start of the "take-off" period.

The Significance of the Data

Do Tables 4.1–4.5 support the view that the years 1843–60 should be
singled out as years of decisive change, as years during which the
economy underwent a unique structural transformation that built growth
into the economy? It might be argued that the rapid increase in the

TABLE 4.5. PERCENTAGE DISTRIBUTION OF VALUE ADDED IN COMMODITY
PRODUCTION—GALLMAN'S CONSTANT DOLLAR SERIES

Year	1 Agriculture	2 Mining	3 Manufacturing	4 Construction (Variant A)
1839	71.9	0.7	17.4	10.1
1844	68.7	1.0	21.1	9.2
1849	59.7	1.1	29.5	9.8
1854	56.8	1.1	29.2	12.9
1859	55.5	1.2	32.0	11.2

SOURCE: Same as Table 4.4

[11] Rostow, *Stages*, pp. 46–47, 49.

manufacturing share of commodity output shown by Gallman's constant price series provides such support. But while a high rate of structural transformation is a necessary condition for the verification of the Rostow thesis, it is not a sufficient condition. To attach special significance to the fact that the manufacturing share of commodity output increased by an average of 3.6 points per quinquennium during Rostow's "take-off" years, we need evidence that such a transformation was unique in some respect. It must be shown either that this rate of change was significantly higher than the rate of change in adjacent time periods, or that 1843-60 marked the onset of the rapid shift toward manufacturing, or that there were qualitative changes not disclosed merely by statistics on shifts in sectoral shares.

Available data appear to contradict the first two of these possibilities. The Gallman series extends from 1839 to 1899. Of the 12 quinquennia included in the study, the manufacturing share increased by 3.0 points or more in half. However, only one of these high-rate-of-change periods falls during Rostow's "take-off" years. Four belong to the epoch following the Civil War. Indeed, the increase in the manufacturing share during the fifteen years from 1879 to 1894 exceeded that of 1844–59 by over 50 per cent. Thus the rate of structural transformation during the "take-off" was not uniquely different from the rates that prevailed in the years that followed it (see Table 4.6).[12]

[12] The measure of structural change used in Table 4.6, the increase in the manufacturing share of value added in commodity production, depends on the rate of growth of manufacturing, the rate of growth of the other commodity producing sectors, and the relative size of the manufacturing sector. This relationship can be stated as follows:

Let D = the increase in the manufacturing share of commodity output

m = value added by manufacturing in the base year

a = value added by all other commodity sectors in the base year

μ = 1 + the rate of growth of m

α = 1 + the rate of growth of a

$x = \dfrac{a}{m}$.

Then

$$D = \frac{\mu m}{\alpha a + \mu m} - \frac{m}{a + m} = \frac{x\left(\dfrac{\mu}{\alpha} - 1\right)}{x^2 + \left(1 + \dfrac{\mu}{\alpha}\right)x + \dfrac{\mu}{\alpha}}.$$

The ratio of μ to α required for a particular D is given by:

$$\frac{\mu}{\alpha} = \frac{Dx^2 + Dx + x}{x - Dx - D}$$

(*continued*)

TABLE 4.6. ABSOLUTE INCREASES IN MANUFACTURING'S SHARE OF VALUE ADDED IN COMMODITY PRODUCTION—GALLMAN'S CONSTANT DOLLAR SERIES

Quinquennium		Absolute increase in manufacturing's share (percentage points)
1.	1839-44	3.7
2.	1844-49	8.4
3.	1849-54	—0.3
4.	1854-59	2.8
5.	1859-64	—
6.	1864-69	—
7.	1869-74	6.4
8.	1874-79	—2.4
9.	1879-84	7.0
10.	1884-89	4 0
11.	1889-94	5.4
12.	1894-99	—0.1
		Average increase per quinquennium.... 3.0

SOURCE: Same as Table 4.4.

Evidence on Structural Changes Prior to the "Take-off"

What of the years that preceded the "take-off"? Unfortunately, Gallman's data only go back to 1839. As previously noted, there was a shift toward manufacturing of 3.7 points during the 1839–44 quinquennium, most of which precedes the onset of the "take-off." There may have been additional quinquennia of rapid increase in the manufacturing share of commodity output prior to 1839. The decade of the 1820's is of particular interest. According to Martin's current price data, the shift toward manufacturing during this decade exceeded that of the forties.[13] While there is no global index of the change in physical terms, certain events suggest that the real shift was quite high.

For one thing, the decade of the 1820's was marked by a sharp decline in household manufactures. Household production appears to have reached a peak about 1815. Yet according to Tryon, "the transfer from home- to shop- and factory-made goods was rather generally com-

---

Consequently, for value of $x > 0$, $\dfrac{\mu}{\alpha}$ and x are related by a "U" shaped function which reaches a minimum when $x = \dfrac{1 + D}{1 - D}$; that is the ratio of μ to α required for a given D is at a minimum when the value added by all commodity producing sectors except manufacturing is just slightly larger than the value added by the manufacturing sector.

[13] *Historical Statistics* (1949), p. 14.

pleted before the close of the third decade of the nineteenth century." The last lingering item in home manufacturing was textiles. But home production of this item declined precipitously during the last half of the third decade. Census data for 1825 and 1835 indicate that in New York the annual home production of textiles during the period fell by 55 per cent, from 9 to 4 yards per capita.[14] The decade of the twenties was also a period of rapid urbanization. Between 1820 and 1830 city population increased at twice as great a rate as the population as a whole, adding almost half a million urban dwellers to the population.[15]

The impression of a rapid rise in the manufacturing share of commodity output during the twenties is buttressed by the extremely rapid rate at which a number of leading manufacturing industries expanded. One of the most important of these is cotton textiles. Up to 1807 the expansion of this industry was slow and uncertain. In that year there were only 15 or 20 mills in existence using approximately 8,000 spindles.[16] But after 1807 "the interruption of importations, the low price of raw cotton and the high selling price of yarn, the development of markets in the middle and western states tempted capital and managerial ability, particularly from foreign trade, into the industry." [17] In a report sent to Congress in 1810, Albert Gallatin estimated that 87 firms would have 80,000 spindles in operation during the following year.[18] By 1815 the number of spindles increased to at least 130,000.[19] This rapid rise appears to have been slowed by foreign competition in the years following the close of the War of 1812. According to the census of manufactures for 1820, the number of spindles in operation had still to reach the 200,000 mark (see Table 4.7).

A new period of expansion in cotton textiles began about 1822 when the first large mill was established in Lowell. A second Lowell firm opened in 1825, two more in 1828, and three more in 1830. By 1833 these seven firms alone contained 97,400 spindles, 50 per cent of the national total a scant dozen years earlier.[20] But if Lowell led the advance

[14] Rolla Milton Tryon, *Household Manufacturers in the United States, 1640–1860* (Chicago, 1917), pp. 268, 305; Taylor, *The Transportation Revolution*, p. 211.

[15] *Historical Statistics* (1949), p. 25.

[16] Caroline F. Ware, *The Early New England Cotton Manufacture* (Boston, 1931), pp. 37–38; U.S. Congress, *American State Papers, Finance*, II, 427.

[17] Edward C. Kirkland, *A History of American Economic Life* (3rd ed.; New York, 1951), p. 299.

[18] U.S. Congress, *American State Papers, Finance*, II, 427.

[19] U.S. Congress, *American State Papers, Finance*, III, 53.

[20] Timothy Pitkin, *A Statistical View of the Commerce of the United States of America* (New Haven, 1835), p. 529.

TABLE 4.7. COTTON SPINDLES IN OPERATION IN TWELVE STATES, 1820 AND 1831

State	1 Spindles in operation in 1820	2 Spindles in operation in 1831
Maine	1,064	6,500
Vermont	2,074	12,392
New Hampshire	9,872	113,776
Massachusetts	29,379	339,777
Connecticut	20,682	115,528
Rhode Island	49,489	235,753
New York	33,910	157,316
New Jersey	12,274	62,979
Pennsylvania	14,401	120,810
Delaware	7,902	24,806
Maryland	8,721	47,222
Virginia	1,284	9,844
Total	191,052	1,246,703
Column 2 as a percentage of Column 1		652.5

SOURCES AND NOTES:

Column 1. "Digest of Manufacturing Establishments in the United States," U.S. Congress, *American State Papers, Finance*, IV, 22–28.

The following adjustments were made in the census data. In some instances the number of spindles in operation was estimated by multiplying the cotton consumption of a given firm by the Massachusetts ratio of spindles in use to pounds of cotton consumed. Where both data on the number of spindles in use and cotton consumption were lacking, it was presumed that all the spindles in existence were in use. In the case of factories which produced both cotton and woolen goods, spindles used for cotton production were assumed to be equal to the total number of spindles in use multiplied by the ratio of the pounds of cotton consumed to the pounds of cotton plus wool consumed. In cases where firms produced satinets and similar products, 10 per cent of the spindles in use were assigned to cotton. For one Virginia firm, the number of spindles in use was taken to be equal to the capital of that firm multiplied by the Maryland ratio of spindles per dollar of capital.

Column 2. These are the estimates of the *General Convention of the Friends of Domestic Industry, Assembled at New York, October 26, 1831*, as cited in Timothy Pitkin, *A Statistical View of the Commerce of the United States of America* (New Haven, 1835), pp. 482, 526.

of the industry, other areas did not lag far behind. Table 4.7 contains estimates of the number of spindles in operation in 12 states for the years 1820 and 1831. Using spindles in operation as an index of the growth of the industry, this table shows a five and one-half fold increase in the scale of operations in 11 years.[21] By 1831 cotton textiles had become a very substantial industry. Indeed, judging by statistics of cotton consumption, production was 40 per cent greater in America in

[21] Victor S. Clark (*History of Manufacturers in the United States* [3 vols.; New York, 1929], I, 544) indicates a somewhat slower rate of growth than that shown in Table 4.7. Clark appears to have compared estimates of the total number of spindles *in existence* in 1820 with the total number *in use* in 1831.

1831 than it had been in Great Britain in 1801, *the year preceding the close of the British "take-off."* Even on a per capita basis production was 14 per cent greater in the United States in 1831 than in England in 1801.[22]

The decade of the twenties was also a period of rapid expansion in iron making. The development of the iron industry, one of the oldest manufacturing industries—and during the colonial period, one of the largest—was quite erratic in the first four and one-half decades following independence. During the Revolution pig iron production probably rose to about 35,000 tons. However, peace brought increased British competition and the industry went into half a decade of decline. Beginning about 1790, tariffs, a rise in the price of British iron, and later the Embargo Act carried the industry to a new high. According to Tench Coxe, production reached 54,000 tons in 1810, a level which apparently was maintained through most of the war years. This appears to have been followed by a half decade of stagnation and decline.[23] The output of pig iron in 1820 was estimated at 20,000 tons, less than two-thirds of the revolutionary peak.[24]

While the tariffs of 1824 and 1828 may have played some role in the forward surge of domestic iron production during the twenties, what transpired was more than a reallocation of a fixed total between foreign and domestic suppliers. Despite the tariffs, imports of British iron increased 400 per cent in the 11 years following 1820.[25] The rise in

[22] Pitkin, *A Statistical View,* p. 483; *Historical Statistics* (1960), p. 7; U.S. Congress, House, *Letter from the Secretary of the Treasury Transmitting Tables and Notes on the Cultivation, Manufacture and Foreign Trade of Cotton,* Doc. No. 146, 24th Cong., 1st Sess. (Ser. No. 289), p. 40; Michael G. Mulhall, *Dictionary of Statistics* (4th ed.; London, 1899), p. 444. Rostow based his demarcation of the British "take-off" largely on the rate of growth of cotton-textiles production and the size of that industry relative to the rest of the British economy. Cf. Rostow, *Stages,* pp. 53–56.

[23] Benjamin F. French, *History of the Rise and Progress of the Iron Trade of the United States from 1621 to 1857* (New York, 1858), pp. 11–20.

[24] *Historical Statistics* (1960), p. 366; the figure in the source is in net tons; that given in the text above is in gross tons. In his unpublished paper, "A Review of the Statistics of Pig Iron Production," Peter Temin points out that this widely cited figure is of unknown origin and therefore of unknown reliability. The sharp downward movement in iron prices and the 60 per cent fall in iron imported from Great Britain between 1816 and 1820 give some credence to the estimate. Stephen Colwell, "Special Report No. 12, Report on Iron," U.S. Revenue Commission, *Reports of a Commission Appointed for a Review of the Revenue System* (Washington, 1866), p. 330; hereafter referred to as Colwell, "Special Report."

[25] *Ibid.*

domestic production clearly reflected a sharp increase in domestic demand. The expansion of the internal market was described by Timothy Pitkin in this manner:

> Many new branches of the manufacture of iron have been established, and are now almost daily being established in different parts of the United States, and which it is impossible to particularize— among these, however, may be enumerated, in addition to steam engines and machinery for a great variety of purposes, the manufacture of stoves, chain cables, mill and cross cut saws, spades and shovels, wood screws, sickles, hammers, gimblets, brazier's roads, door locks of various kinds, latches, surgical instruments, knives, razors, and many other articles of cutlery, various kinds of carpenter's tools; and there is a vast increase in the manufacture of muskets and rifles, and of edge tools generally.[26]

The rise of the domestic industry also appears to have been stimulated by cost-reducing technological innovations. The puddling and rolling process was introduced in the United States in 1817, and the opening of the Schuylkill and Lehigh canals gave Pennsylvania easy access to the coal used in the rolling process. [27] As a result of these developments, pig iron production rose to 192,000 tons in 1830.[28] Over the decade of the twenties, the percentage increase in the output of this item was 25 times as large as the percentage increase in population. By 1830 iron, like textiles, was a substantial industry. In this branch of manufacture too, American production in 1830 was greater by 12 per cent than British production at the close of the British "take-off" period in 1802.[29]

The high rate of growth of cotton textiles and iron during the 1820's must have had a perceptible influence on the share of manufacturing in commodity output. This influence can be illustrated by referring back to Gallman's data. According to Gallman, value added in commodity

---

[26] Pitkin, *A Statistical View*, p. 496.

[27] French, *History*, pp. 21–22.

[28] *Historical Statistics* (1960), p. 366, gives a figure of 185,000 net tons (165,000 gross tons). However Temin, "A Review," points out that this figure was corrected by a later survey which raised output to 192,000 gross tons. Cf. French, *History*, pp. 32–33, 47–48.

[29] Arthur D. Gayer, W. W. Rostow, Anna Jacobson Schwartz, *The Growth and Fluctuation of the British Economy, 1790–1850* (2 vols.; Oxford, 1953), p. 72. Per capita production of pig iron was about the same in both countries at the respective dates.

production in 1839 was $1,094,000,000 in constant prices of 1879. Value added in manufacturing was $190,000,000. At the same time Gallman provides a series in current dollars which indicates that cotton textiles accounted for 9.87 per cent and metals for 10.5 per cent of value added in manufacturing for the same year.[30] Applying these percentages to the constant price figure for manufacturing, one obtains $18,800,000 as the amount of value added in constant prices for cotton textiles and $20,000,000 for metals. Since metals were almost completely dominated by iron, cotton textiles and iron together may be taken to have amounted to approximately $39,000,000 in 1839. If it is assumed that all commodity production between 1820 and 1839 grew at the rate of growth of population, except for cotton and iron which grew at the rates indicated by the physical indexes discussed above, the manufacturing share of commodity production would have been 14.7 per cent in 1820 and 16.2 per cent in 1830. In other words, even if one assumes that all manufacturing industries except cotton textiles and iron just kept pace with the rate of population growth, there would have been an increase of 1.5 per cent in the manufacturing share of commodity ouput.

However, available evidence seems to indicate that the production of most manufactured articles during the twenties grew at decade rates which exceeded by far the 35 per cent increase in population. Cole estimated that factory consumption of wool increased from 400,000 pounds in 1810 to 15,000,000 pounds in 1830 and allocated "fully half the increase in manufacturing capacity to the period after the peace" (i.e., 1816–30).[31] Even more spectacular was the rate of growth in carpet production which increased from an output of 9,984 yards in 1810 to 1,147,500 in 1834, with most of the increase taking place during a four or five year period beginning in 1827.[32] According to the *Eighth Census of Manufacturing* the value of paper production doubled between 1820 and 1830 and since the decade of the twenties was one of declining prices, it is very likely that the real output of paper more

---

[30] Gallman, "Commodity Output," p. 43; Robert E. Gallman, *Value Added by Agriculture, Mining and Maunfacturing in the United States, 1840–1880* (Unpublished doctoral dissertation, University of Pennsylvania, 1956), pp. 249–58, 357–58.

[31] Arthur Harrison Cole, *The American Wool Manufacture* (2 vols.; Cambridge, Mass., 1926), I, 249.

[32] U.S. Census Office, *Eighth Census of the United States, Manufactures* (Washington, 1865), pp. liv–lv; hereafter referred to as *Eighth Census of Manufacturing, 1860.* Cf. Arthur H. Cole and Harold F. Williamson, *The American Carpet Manufacture* (Cambridge, Mass., 1941), pp. 12–14.

than doubled.[33] There was also rapid growth in the production of primary refined lead, the most important metal after iron, with output eleven times greater in 1830 than in 1820.[34] In the food processing industries, the output of sugar and molasses in Louisiana, the main center of production, increased by 200 per cent over a ten year period ending in 1830–31; salt production tripled between 1810 and 1830; and fragmentary evidence, such as the fact that the number of hogs slaughtered in Cincinnati increased by 600 per cent in eight seasons ending in 1830–31, suggests rapid growth in the meat processing industry.[35] The production of steam engines also appears to have increased precipitously. The first engine was not produced commercially in the United States until 1805. In subsequent years, especially after 1815, output was spurred by the development of steamboats; 359 engines were required for this purpose alone during the twenties. By 1830 Pittsburgh was producing 100 engines per year and Cincinnati another 150.[36] Finally, Pitkin reported that while the first American flint-glass factory was not established until 1812, by 1831 domestic manufacture was "almost equal to domestic consumption." [37] The only major industry that seems to have languished was ship production; statistics on tonnage reveal a growth of only 7 per cent over the decade in question.[38] If in light of the foregoing one assumes that on the average manufacturing industries other than cotton textiles and iron grew at twice the rate of population during the twenties, the manufacturing share of commodity production would increase by 3.9 points for the decade. And if it is assumed that the other industries grew three times as fast as population, the decade increase in the manufacturing share would be 5.7 points.

The Continuity of Structural Change

This discussion is not aimed at producing a specific estimate of the increase in the manufacturing share of commodity output during the twenties. Obviously the data now available are too crude for this.

[33] *Eighth Census of Manufacturing, 1860,* pp. cxxvi–cxxvii; *Historical Statistics* (1960), p. 115.

[34] *Historical Statistics* (1960), p. 370.

[35] Pitkin, *A Statistical View,* p. 499; Thomas Senior Berry, *Western Prices Before 1861* (Cambridge, Mass., 1943), pp. 219–20, 289.

[36] U.S. Census Office, *Tenth Census of the United States,* IV, *Report on the Agencies of Transportation* (Washington, 1883), p. 662; Clark, *History,* I, 507.

[37] Pitkin, *A Statistical View,* p. 500.

[38] *Historical Statistics* (1960), p. 449. This result obtains when end years are compared. When quinquennial averages are compared, a rise of 47 per cent is indicated.

However, there does seem to be a prima facie case for the view that the third decade of the nineteenth century was one in which the shift toward manufacturing approached the rate that prevailed during Rostow's "take-off" years. The point at issue is not merely that the dates Rostow assigned to the American "take-off" may be wrong.[39] More tenuous than the dating is Rostow's dictum that the "decisive" consequences of changes in methods of production were confined to a very short period of time. In the American case the available evidence tends to contravert the view that the period from 1843 to 1860 or any other 18-year period was one of unique structural change.[40] Instead, the data suggest a process of more or less continuous increase in the absolute and relative size of manufacturing extending from 1820—a good argument can be made for viewing 1807 as the starting date—through the end of the century. The process appears to have been interrupted only during the last half of the 1830's, the first half of the 1850's, the Civil War decade, the last half of the 1870's, and the last half of the 1890's.

If the "take-off" years are not unique with respect to the rate of structural change, neither are they unique in the quality or degree of technological innovation. The most important changes in the technology of the cotton industry took place prior to 1830. In the woolen industry,

---

[39] Cf. with the discussion of Douglass C. North, *The Economic Growth of the United States, 1790–1860* (Englewood Cliffs, N. J., 1961), especially pp. 165–66 and 189–90.

[40] One might, of course, argue that the first phase in the process of the modern economic growth of a nation is more crucial than any other. But this point must be established. Of course it is true that a child cannot live to be an adult unless he survives his first year of life. From this point of view, one might call the first year of life crucial, but then so is the second and all other intervening years.

The special thing about Rostow's "take-off" is that it is an era in which growth becomes "self-sustained." It is the absence of any evidence to support this notion which makes Rostow's thesis so questionable. As Simon Kuznets has pointed out, the process of economic development always contains both self-sustaining and self-limiting factors. "If then Professor Rostow characterizes one stage of growth as 'self-sustaining' and others, by inference, as not, he must mean that in the latter stages the obstacles generated by past and current growth outweigh the self-sustaining impacts; whereas in the former stage the self-sustaining impacts outweigh the self-limiting ones. . . . Given the two sets of impacts of economic growth just suggested, the outcome is uncertain; and the process can never be *purely* self-sustained, since it always generates *some* self-limiting effects. In this sense economic growth is always a struggle; and it is misleading to convey an impression of easy automaticity, a kind of soaring euphoria of self-sustained flight to higher economic levels." Simon Kuznets, "Notes on the Take-Off," *The Economics of Take-Off into Sustained Growth: Proceedings of a Conference Held by the International Economics Association,* ed. W. W. Rostow (New York, 1963), p. 40. The volume will be referred to hereafter as Rostow, *Economics of Take-Off.*

as Cole points out, the factory form was established by the end of the third decade; the next crucial turning point was about 1870; and the intervening forty years were a period of gradual movement toward maturity. In the iron industry, two of the three major pre-Civil War innovations were introduced by 1820. Similarly, the mechanization of the paper industry was well under way before the end of the fourth decade.[41] Again, the argument is not that all important innovations preceded the "take-off" years, but rather that the process of innovation was, like the progressive shift toward manufacturing, continuous, so that practically every decade of the nineteenth century produced important and far-reaching technological advances.

The doubt attached to Rostow's dictum on the existence of short periods of decisive structural transformation does not imply that historians must abandon the concept of "industrial revolution." One should not, however, require a revolution to have the swiftness of a coup d'etat. That manufacturing accounted for about 10 per cent of commodity production in 1820 and 48 per cent in 1889 is certainly evidence of a dramatic change in what was, by historical standards, hardly more than a moment of time. One need not arbitrarily abstract 18 years out of a continuum to uphold the use of a venerable term.

RAILROADS AND THE LEADING SECTORS THESIS

One of the most interesting aspects of Rostow's stages-of-growth theory is the concept of leading sectors and particularly the proposition that the American "take-off" was triggered by the railroad, the rapid expansion of which generated a series of "secondary" growth sectors. "The development of railways," Rostow writes, "has led on to the development of modern coal, iron and engineering industries. In many countries the growth of modern basic industrial sectors can be traced in the most direct way to the requirements for building and, especially, for maintaining substantial railway systems." [42]

Is there, in the American case, an actual historical counterpart to Rostow's generalization? To what extent can the rapid growth of American manufacturing and the concomitant increase in the manufacturing share of commodity output during the "take-off" years be at-

---

[41] Cole, *American Wool Manufacture,* I, 265; French, *History,* pp. 20–21; *Census of Manufacturing, 1860,* pp. cxxvi–cxxvii.

[42] Rostow, *Stages,* p. 55.

tributed to the railroad's consumption of manufactured goods? In answering these questions data bearing on five industries will be examined. The industries are coal, iron, machinery (the three emphasized by Rostow), transportation equipment, and lumber.[43]

Some objection might be raised to so limited a focus. For while it is true that railroads did not directly consume large amounts of the output of other industries, Rostow has suggested that the repercussions of the consumption of the primary growth sector may "have to be tracked many stages back into the economy." [44] It might be argued that if such a line of analysis were followed, the number of industries in which a substantial proportion of output was indirectly used for railroad construction would exceed the five selected. However, an attempt to find the total demand for goods required by a given industry by summing the successive increments of demand generated at receding stages of the production results in series with terms which rapidly approach zero. Suppose, for example, that railroads did not directly consume chemicals but that the iron industry consumed 10 per cent of the output of the chemical industry. Suppose also that railroads purchased 10 per cent of the output of the iron industry. Then the error involved in neglecting the second stage demand for chemicals—the output of chemicals consumed in the production of railroad iron—would amount to 1 per cent of chemical production. Quite clearly, if none of the other industries from which the railroads made large direct purchases used significant amounts of chemicals, the error involved in neglecting the tertiary and subsequent stages of demand would be negligible. Thus, if it is found that the railroad's direct and second stage demand for the output of given industries was small, it is unlikely that the track-back suggested by Rostow would significantly alter the relevant conclusions.

The Iron Industry

No industry in nineteenth-century America is said to have leaned more heavily on railroads as a market than the iron industry. This dependency has been referred to by many historians. However, the fact that 1,000,000 tons of rails were produced in 1872 (about 35 per cent of the weight of pig iron production) and that 1,461,000 tons of steel rails (75 per cent of all rolled steel) were turned out in 1882 is irrele-

[43] The industrial classification followed here is that contained in Gallman, "Value Added," pp. 357–58.
[44] Rostow, *Stages*, p. 52.

vant here.[45] The issue posed by the designation of the railroad as a "primary growth sector" cannot be resolved by citing, as Rostow does, evidence which suggests that rails may have dominated iron production in the post-Civil War era.[46] The point at issue is the share of the output of the iron industry consumed by railroads between 1843 and 1860; it is the extent to which the growth of the iron industry *during the "take-off" years* can be attributed to railroads.

Column 1 of Table 4.8 reveals that amount of domestic crude iron consumed in the production of the final products of the domestic iron industry more than trebled between 1840 and 1860, although this growth was uneven. After an initial decline, consumption of domestic crude iron rose steadily from 1842 through 1847, reaching a peak of nearly 900,000 tons in the latter year. The increase in the five-year period was over 230 per cent. Following 1847, the industry's consumption of domestic crude iron declined steadily until 1851 when it stood at 58 per cent of the previous peak. The industry recovered during the next two years and consumption hovered at about 900,000 tons from 1853 through 1858. The final two years of the period show a new rise of about 30 per cent over the level prevailing in 1858.

If the 20 years from 1840 through 1859 are broken into four quinquennia, corresponding to Gallman's time periods, one finds that the second quinquennium was the most important with respect to the rise in crude iron consumption (see Table 4.8). The average annual consumption of that quinquennium was 775,000 tons, 99 per cent above the average of the previous five years. Average consumption in the third quinquennium fell slightly below, and in the fourth quinquennium it rose somewhat above, the level achieved in the second one. Thus during the years 1845–49 the iron industry appears to have ascended a plateau on which it remained for the most of the rest of the "take-off" years.

Table 4.8 also reveals that the amount of domestic crude iron consumed by domestic firms in manufacturing the iron products used in the construction and maintenance of railroads constituted only a minor part of total consumption. Far from dominating the iron industry, crude iron used in the domestic production of rails averaged less than 12

---

[45] A.I.S.A., *Annual Report, 1883,* pp. 23, 28, 41. The use of tons of rails produced divided by tons of pig iron production as an index of the position of rails in the market for iron leads to a large upward bias. See the discussion of this point in the next chapter.

[46] Rostow, "Leading Sectors and the Take-Off," *Economics of Take-Off,* p. 5.

Table 4.8. The Consumption of Domestic Iron by Railroads, 1840-60 (in thousands of net tons)

	1 Domestic crude iron consumed by the domestic iron industry	2 Domestic crude iron used for the domestic production of rails	3 Domestic crude iron used in rail fastening	4 Domestic crude iron used in locomotives	5 Domestic crude iron used in freight, passenger and baggage cars	6 Railroad consumption of domestic crude iron sum of Cols. 2, 3, 4, 5	7 Share of domestic crude iron consumed by iron industry going into rails Col. 2÷Col. 1	8 Share of domestic crude iron consumed by the iron industry going into all railroad construction and maintenance Col. 6÷Col. 1
1. 1840	394	5	6	1	5	17	1.3	4.3
2. 1841	317	20	7	0	4	31	6.3	9.8
3. 1842	267	29	7	1	8	45	10.9	16.9
4. 1843	412	13	5	1	7	26	3.2	6.3
5. 1844	558	9	4	2	13	28	1.6	5.0
6. 1845	661	31	6	2	16	55	4.7	8.3
7. 1846	790	48	7	4	25	84	6.1	10.6
8. 1847	881	58	8	4	23	93	6.6	10.6
9. 1848	809	54	10	2	10	76	6.7	9.4
10. 1849	733	42	13	3	15	73	5.7	10.0
11. 1850	574	44	15	3	18	80	7.7	13.9
12. 1851	502	47	16	5	24	92	9.4	18.3
13. 1852	651	58	20	5	24	107	8.9	16.4
14. 1853	864	84	23	6	31	144	9.7	16.7
15. 1854	802	102	23	7	31	163	12.7	20.3
16. 1855	869	143	22	5	24	194	16.5	22.3
17. 1856	989	196	28	7	33	264	19.8	26.7
18. 1857	932	172	27	9	38	246	18.5	26.4
19. 1858	868	168	27	4	18	217	19.4	25.0
20. 1859	1,036	198	24	10	38	270	19.1	26.1
21. 1860	1,146	206	25	12	46	289	18.0	25.2
Period Averages								
22. 1840-44	390	15	6	1	7	29	3.8	7.4
23. 1845-49	775	47	9	3	18	76	6.1	9.8
24. 1850-54	679	67	19	5	26	117	9.9	17.2
25. 1855-59	939	175	26	7	30	238	18.6	25.3
26. 1855-60	973	181	26	8	33	247	18.6	25.4
27. 1840-49	582	31	7	2	13	53	5.3	9.1
28. 1850-59	809	121	23	6	28	178	15.0	22.0
29. 1850-60	839	129	23	7	30	188	15.4	22.4
30. 1840-60	717	82	15	4	21	124	11.4	17.3

SOURCES AND NOTES:

Column 1. Table 5.14, Column 4.

Column 2. Table 5.16, Column 1 minus Table 5.15, Column 7.

Column 3. According to data in Henry S. Tanner, *A Description of the Canals and Railroads of the United States* (New York, 1840), fastenings on roads with heavy plate or edge rails averaged 18.36 net tons per track-mile in 1840. Those laid with light plate averaged 3.52 tons. In 1840 a little less than 54 per cent of roads were laid with light plate and the rest were laid with heavy rails (L. Klein, "Railroads in the United States," *Journal of the Franklin Institute*, Vol. 30 [1840], pp. 89–102, 227–30, 301–7). These proportions indicate that the average weight of fastenings on roads in 1840 was 10.8 tons per track-mile. Bell put the average weight of fastenings in the United States in the post-Civil War period at 6.4 tons per track-mile (Sir I. Lowthian Bell, *The Iron Trade of the United Kingdom Compared with That of the Other Chief Iron-Making Nations* [London, 1886], p. 143).

It was assumed that the average weight of fastenings declined linearly from 10.8 tons in 1840 to 6.5 tons per track-mile in 1860. The weight of fastenings was multiplied by 1.125 to obtain a crude iron equivalent on the assumption that half of the fastenings were made from wrought iron and half from cast iron.

The number of track-miles laid each year was taken from Table 5.8.

Track-miles multiplied by the average amount of crude iron required for a track-mile of fastenings yielded the total crude iron requirement in each year. The amount of domestically produced crude iron consumed in fastenings was found by multiplying the entries in the last series by the corresponding entries for the share of crude iron consumed by the domestic iron industry that was domestically produced.

Column 4. The number of locomotives produced in each year was taken to be equal to the number produced by the Baldwin Locomotive Works multiplied by the ratio of national production in the census year of 1859–60 to a weighted average of the Baldwin production in 1859 and 1860. *Eighth Census, Manufacturing*, p. clxxxix; *History of the Baldwin Locomotive Works, 1831–1923* (n.p., n.p., n.d.), p. 182.

The average weight of locomotives was assumed to have increased linearly from 12 to 27 tons over 1840–60 on the basis of the weights given in *ibid*, pp. 24, 35; cf. Ringwalt, *Development, passim; Tenth Census, Manufacturing*, pp. 661–62; and Stephen Roper, *Handbook of the Locomotive* (Philadelphia, 1874), p. 126.

In 1880, 90 per cent of a locomotive by weight was iron (*Tenth Census of Manufacturing*, p. 662). This factor was applied to all the years from 1840–60. The proportion of iron in locomotives was probably less during the ante-bellum era, especially during the earlier years when considerable amounts of lumber were still used in the construction of the locomotive frame.

The total weight of locomotives produced in a given year multiplied by 1.0125 (on the assumption that half of the iron in locomotives was wrought and half was cast) yielded the amount of crude iron required for locomotives. This was dividing between domestically produced crude and imported crude in proportion to the share of total crude iron consumed by the domestic iron industry that was domestically produced in the corresponding years.

Column 5. Data contained in Ringwalt, *Development,* p. 338, and *Eighth Census, Manufacturing*, p. clxxxv, indicate that the amount of iron in the "first class," eight-wheeled freight car of 1886 was approximately 8,000 pounds, of which 6,500 pounds was in the trucks (including the wheels). Cast iron represented about 74 per cent of the total; the remainder was primarily wrought iron. Hence the indicated amount of crude iron per car is 4.262 net tons.

A sample of 29 roads drawn from H. V. Poor, *History of Railroads and Canals of the United States of America* (New York, 1860), revealed that the average number of freight cars per locomotive in 1859 was 15.92. However, since the ratio increased over time, one would expect dF/dL to be larger than F/L (where $F = $ the number of freight cars and $L = $ the number of locomotives). A linear regression was fitted to the sample data. The first derivative of the equation was dF/dL =23.09. The number of freight cars constructed each year was estimated by multiplying the estimated number of locomotives produced each year by 23.09. (This value of dF/dL is very close to the first derivative of a second degree equation forced through the origin and fitted to data in *Poor's Manual of Railroads* on the aggregate number of freight cars and locomotives in the United States over the years 1871–95. In this case $dF/dL = 23.82 + 0.000562L$. Since L varied between 56 and 517 over the years 1840–60, dF/dL only varied between 23.85 and 24.11.)

The tons of crude iron required for freight cars in each year was thus the estimated number of cars produced each year multiplied by 4.262 net tons. The total requirement was again divided between domestically produced crude and imported crude in proportion to the share of total crude iron consumed by the domestic iron industry was domestically produced in each year.

The procedure followed in estimating the domestic crude iron consumed in passenger and baggage cars was similar to that employed for freight cars. According to data cited by Ringwalt, (*Development*, pp. 338–39), there were 9,449 pounds of iron in the standard passenger car built for the Pennsylvania Railroad in 1876. This figure was turned into a crude iron equivalent by multiplying it by 1.091. The conversion factor was obtained in the manner indicated for freight cars. The resulting figure, 5.155 net tons per passenger (or baggage) car, probably overstates the average amount of crude iron consumed for such cars during 1840–60. Passenger cars were generally larger and used more iron after the Civil War than before it. However the data needed for an adjustment have not been located.

The number of passenger and baggage cars was obtained in the manner indicated for freight cars, the relevant derivative being $dP/dL = 1.673$, where P stands for passenger and baggage cars. (The derivative obtained by fitting a second degree equation forced through the origin to data on national totals over the years 1871–95 as contained in *Poor's Manual* was $dP/dL = 0.9214 + 0.0000026L$. Consequently, the use of 1.673 as the marginal rate may lead to an overstatement of the production of passenger and baggage cars.)

Column 7. This is index I_3 which is discussed in Chapter V.

Lines may not add across because of rounding.

---

per cent of the total over the 21-year period. All the other forms of iron used by railroads raised the share to an average of only 17 per cent.[47] While it is true that in the final six years of the period the railroad's share rose to 25.4 per cent, more significant for this discussion is the fact that during the quinquennium ending in 1849, railroad consumption of domestic crude iron was just 10 per cent of the total. Even if there had been no production of rails or railroad equipment whatsoever, the domestic crude iron consumed by the iron industry would have reached an average of 700,000 tons in the second quinquennium. The rise over the previous quinquennium would still have been 338,000 tons—an increase of 94 per cent as opposed to the 99 per cent rise that took place with the railroads. Clearly railroad consumption of iron had little effect on the rate of growth of the industry during the crucial first decade of Rostow's "take-off" period; the new high level of produc-

---

[47] An index based on value added would make the railroad share substantially smaller. See Appendix B.

tion attained by the iron industry during 1845–49 did not depend on the railroad market.

The strongest statement that can be made in support of Rostow's thesis is that the demand for railroad iron played an increasingly important role during the fifties in maintaining the *previous* level of production when the demand for other items sagged. Otherwise one could just as well argue that nails rather than rails triggered the 1845–49 leap in iron production. Indeed, in 1849 the domestic production of nails probably exceeded that of rails by over 100 per cent.[48] Whatever role rail production might have played in growth of the iron and steel industry during the seventies and eighties, the construction and maintenance of railroads in the "take-off" did more to build up the British than the American industry. From 1840 through 1860 only 40 per cent of the rails required by the United States were supplied by domestic industry. The rest of the demand was satisfied in the English Market.[49]

Coal

The direct demand for coal by the railroad during the two decades ending in 1860 was negligible. Coal had been used to fire the vertical boilers of some of the early engines, but first attempts to use mineral fuel on locomotives with horizontal boilers failed due to the serious damage caused by "the destructive effects of a coal fire." While the pace of experimentation increased during the fifties, few coal burners were in regular service at the end of the decade.[50] In later decades the switch to coal became more rapid. By 1921 locomotives consumed about one-quarter of the annual output of coal.[51] But this was more

[48] Approximately 30,300 net tons of nails were produced in Pennsylvania in 1849 (Charles E. Smith, "The Manufacture of Iron in Pennsylvania," *Merchants' Magazine,* vol. 25 [Nov., 1851], p. 578). The national tonnage (88,800) was obtained by multiplying 30,300 by the 1856 ratio of U.S. to Pennsylvania production as given in J. P. Lesley, *The Iron Manufacturer's Guide to the Furnaces, Forges and Rolling Mills of the United States* (New York, 1859), p. 758; hereafter referred to as Lesley, *Guide.*

[49] Table 5.15 below.

[50] Ringwalt, *Development,* pp. 135, 161–62. Albert Fishlow states that the problem of the firebox was not solved until 1854. He points to estimates that put the total number of coal burning locomotives in early 1859 at between 250 and 400. Albert Fishlow, *The Economic Contribution of American Railroads Before the Civil War* (Unpublished doctoral dissertation, Harvard University, 1963), pp. 180, 183.

[51] *Historical Statistics* (1960), pp. 356, 359, 436.

than half a century after the close of the "take-off." Wood was the fuel that powered the land leviathan prior to 1860.

If the analysis is pushed back to the second stage of demand, the picture changes slightly. The iron industry was a major consumer of coal during the "take-off" years. Approximately 2.5 tons of coal were required to produce 1 ton of pig iron and another 2.5 tons were needed to turn the crude metal into a rail.[52] Over the 21 years from 1840 through 1860, some 1,372,000 tons of pig iron were transformed into rails.[53] At the specified rate, this transformation required 6,860,000 tons of coal. Another 579,000 tons of rails were rerolled and, at a rate of 2.5 tons of fuel per ton of reworked rail, rerolling required an additional 1,448,000 tons of coal.[54] The manufacture of the iron used in fastenings, locomotives, and cars involved still another 4,335,000 tons of coal.[55] All told, railroads consumed 12,643,000 tons of coal from 1840–60 through purchases of rail and other products made of iron. Over the same period total coal production was 211,680,000 tons.[56] Thus coal consumed by railroads through consumption of iron products represented only 5.97 per cent of the coal produced during the "take-off." Even this low figure is biased upwards, since the calculation is based on the assumption that all pig iron was produced with coal. Yet as late as 1860, 30 per cent of domestic pig iron still spilled from charcoal furnaces.[57]

Lumber

As a consumer of goods, railroads exercised even less influence on the development of the modern lumber industry than on the expansion of coal production—this despite the huge quantities of wood used by the railroads as fuel and in the construction of track. The paradox is

[52] French, *History*, pp. 69, 100–2, 152.

[53] Table 5.15 below.

[54] *Ibid.* The rate of fuel consumption used here is probably too high because old rails did not have to be puddled, and because some of the pig in new rails was imported.

[55] Table 4.8 above, Columns 3, 4, 5. This calculation is based on the assumptions that the items shown in Columns 3–5 were domestically produced, and that all of the crude iron was rolled from domestic pig. Undoubtedly some of the crude iron was scrap and some was imported pig. There was also a considerable amount of cast iron used in locomotives and cars. Consequently the figure given in the text overstates the amount of coal required for the specified items.

[56] *Historical Statistics* (1960), pp. 357, 360.

[57] A.I.S.A., *Annual Report, 1877*, p. 16.

partly explained by the fact that wood used as fuel in the fire boxes of railroad engines was not lumber. Chopping trees into fire wood was as distinct from the manufacture of boards and planks as the picking of cotton was from the manufacture of cloth. While the railroad's fuel requirements served to swell the output of forest products, it did not provide a market for the output of the nation's saw and planing mills.

A similar consideration is involved in connection with the railroad's consumption of cross ties. According to E. E. R. Tratman, the author of the leading manual on track construction at the turn of the twentieth century, the largest ties then in general use were 7x9 inches by 9 feet. Approximately 2,700 ties were laid per mile of track.[58] Hence, railroads required a maximum of 127,575 feet of wood, board measure, for each mile of track. Taking account of both the ties needed for new construction and for replacement, Column 2 of Table 4.9 indicates that railroads required a total of 5,844,000,000 feet B.M. in ties over the 21 years from 1840 through 1860. Only a small proportion, however, of this amount was supplied by lumber mills. Throughout the nineteenth century railroad men believed that ties hewed by axe would resist decay better than sawed ties.[59] Thus as late as 1889, only 7.68 per cent of all ties were produced by lumber mills.[60] Applying this ratio to the 1840–60 output of ties, one finds that, at most, lumber mills supplied 449,000,000 feet B.M. during the 21-year period. This was less than one-half of 1 per cent of all lumber production. When the lumber required for car construction is included, the figure rises by half a percentage point to 0.96 per cent. Indeed, even if all the ties that were required by the railroad were arbitrarily lumped into the category of mill products, railroad consumption of lumber over the 21-year period would still have constituted only 5.43 per cent of the estimated total production. The relatively modest position of railroads in the market for lumber products emphasizes the large volume of the consumption of lumber by other sectors of the economy.

Transportation Equipment

Perhaps the most surprising aspect of the impact of railroad construction and maintenance on the markets of manufacturing industries is the relatively small share of the output of the transportation equipment

---

[58] See note to Column 2 of Table 4.9.

[59] E. E. Russel Tratman, *Railway Track and Track Work* (3rd ed.; New York, 1909), pp. 32–40.

[60] See note to Column 3 of Table 4.9.

TABLE 4.9. THE CONSUMPTION OF LUMBER BY RAILROADS, 1840–60
(in thousands of feet B.M.)

	1 Total lumber production	2 Wood used for ties	3 Ties supplied by mills Col. 2 × .07683	4 Lumber consumed by cars	5 Total mill- produced lumber con- sumed by railroads Col. 3 + Col. 4
1. 1840	1,982,800	79,734	6,126	6,945	13,071
2. 1841	2,361,600	105,377	8,096	6,200	14,296
3. 1842	2,740,400	87,899	6,753	10,790	17,543
4. 1843	3,119,200	56,005	4,304	9,292	13,596
5. 1844	3,498,000	56,516	4,342	16,977	21,319
6. 1845	3,876,800	73,738	5,665	20,823	26,488
7. 1846	4,255,600	87,516	6,724	32,473	39,197
8. 1847	4,634,400	114,945	8,831	30,125	38,956
9. 1848	5,013,200	157,428	12,095	15,491	27,586
10. 1849	5,392,000	230,273	17,692	23,181	40,873
11. 1850	5,655,700	270,969	20,819	28,627	49,446
12. 1851	5,919,400	299,291	22,995	38,672	61,667
13. 1852	6,183,100	376,729	28,944	37,799	66,743
14. 1853	6,466,800	417,298	32,061	46,362	78,423
15. 1854	6,710,500	446,257	34,286	47,849	82,135
16. 1855	6,974,200	417,043	32,041	36,314	68,355
17. 1856	7,237,900	519,230	39,892	45,617	85,509
18. 1857	7,501,600	500,987	38,491	50,948	89,439
19. 1858	7,765,300	528,926	40,637	25,540	66,177
20. 1859	8,029,000	498,308	38,285	54,036	92,321
21. 1860	8,501,654	519,358	39,902	64,085	103,987
22. Totals	113,799,154	5,843,827	448,981	648,146	1,097,127

23. Total Col. 2 + total of Col. 4 as a per cent of
    (total of Col. 1 + total of Col. 2)............................ 5.426

24. Total of Col. 3 as a per cent of total of Col. 1.................... 0.395

25. Total of Col. 4 as a per cent of total of Col. 1.................... 0.570

26. Total of Col. 5 as a per cent of total of Col. 1.................... 0.964

SOURCES AND NOTES:

Column 1. The census year figures are taken from U.S.D.A., *Yearbook of Agriculture, 1933* (Washington, 1933), p. 748. The other entries are linear interpolations.

Column 2. According to Tratman, the largest ties required 127,575 board feet per mile of track (E. E. Russel Tratman, *Railway Track and Track Work* [3rd ed.; New York, 1909], pp. 32, 40). The yearly estimates of wood consumed in ties were obtained by multiplying the entries in Column 3 of Table 5.8 below, by 127,575.

Column 3. *Census of Manufactures, 1890,* Part III, p. 620; *Historical Statistics* (1960), p. 427; Tratman, *Railway Track,* p. 32. According to Tratman, about 2,700 ties were required for each new track mile constructed and replacements ran at the rate of about 250 ties for each mile of old track. At the end of 1888 there were 191,376 miles of track in existence. Hence at Tratman's rate, about 47,844,000 ties were required for replacements during the census year of 1889. Approximately 8,775 miles of new track were built in the census year (this figure is a weighted average of construction in 1889 and in 1890), requiring another 23,693,000 ties, for a total of 71,537,000 ties. However, mills produced only 5,496,174 ties or 0.07683 of the requirement. The column entries were obtained by multiplying the entries in Column 2 by the last figure. This procedure overstates the purchases from mills during the "take-off" years because the size of ties, the number used per mile of track, and probably also the proportion purchased from mills, increased over time.

Column 4. According to Ringwalt, *Development,* pp. 338–39, there were 4,474 feet of lumber in a "first class," 1886 freight car and 12,340 feet in the 1876 passenger cars built by the Pennsylvania Railroad. These figures, multiplied by the corresponding series on passenger and freight cars described in the notes to Table 4.8, yielded the desired estimates of lumber consumed in the construction of cars. Since cars were generally smaller during 1840–60 than in 1876 or 1886, the resulting series probably overstates lumber consumption.

---

industry accounted for by railroads. Historians have stressed the rapid progress of the railroad during the decade of the fifties. From 1850 through 1860 some 26,300 miles of new track were laid.[61] During the same time about 3,800 locomotives, 6,400 passenger and baggage cars, and 88,600 freight cars were constructed.[62] Yet value added in the construction of railroad equipment in 1859 was only $12,000,000 or 25.4 per cent of value added by all transportation equipment (see Table 4.10). During the years leading up to the Civil War, the rapid progress of the railroad captured the American mind. But popular reaction is not always a sound basis for evaluating the strategic significance of economic events. In 1859 the dollar value of the output of vehicles drawn by animals was still almost twice as great as the output of equipment for the celebrated iron horse.

Machinery (Other Than Transportation Equipment)

The relatively small share of the output of the iron, coal, lumber, and transportation equipment industries accounted for by the railroad purchases suggests that the railroad was also a relatively small consumer of machinery. This possibility is supported by Table 4.11 which indicates that the locomotive and car construction industries utilized machinery requiring only 11,500 horsepower. Assuming that the output of

[61] Table 5.8 below.
[62] The derivation of these estimates is discussed in the notes to Table 4.8 above.

TABLE 4.10. VALUE ADDED IN 1859 BY INDUSTRIES SUPPLYING TRANSPORTATION EQUIPMENT FOR STEAM RAILROADS

Industry	Value added
1. Locomotive engines and repairing	$ 2,454,946
2. Springs	1,024,142
3. Cars, construction and repairing by firms other than steam railroads	2,461,269
4. Cars, construction and repairing by steam railroads	5,371,087
5. Car wheels	753,150
6. Axles	86,372
7. Car brakes	7,800
8. Car linings	12,193
9. Total	12,170,959
10. Value added by all transportation equipment in 1859	47,827,000
11. Line 9 as a per cent of line 10	25.4

SOURCES AND NOTES:

All lines except lines 4 and 10 were taken directly from the *Census of Manufacturing, 1860*. Line 4 was estimated by multiplying the figure in line 3 by the 1889 ratio of value added in the construction of cars by steam railroads to the value added in the construction of cars by firms other than steam railroads as contained in the *Census of Manufacturing, 1890*.

Line 10 is from Gallman, "Value Added," p. 357.

machinery in 1859 was distributed among the various industries in proportion to the distribution of horsepower, the railroad directly consumed less than 1 per cent of machine production. Again, the situation does not change appreciably when indirect purchases from industries at more remote levels of production are considered. If the share of machinery consumed by the lumber, iron, and machine industries attributable to the railroad is added to that of transportation equipment, the railroad would have still accounted for only 6 per cent of machine production in 1859 (see Table 4.11).

Manufacturing as a Whole

Table 4.12 shows that the value added in the manufacturing of those goods which railroads purchased, directly and indirectly, from the transportation equipment, iron, lumber, and machinery industries amounted to only $22,500,000 or 2.76 per cent of all value added in manufacturing. Thus if, in the absence of railroads, there had been no increase in the demand for these goods by other forms of transportation, value added in manufacturing would have declined to $792,000,000. But then the market provided by the *non-railroad* demand for manufactured commodities would still have resulted in a 230 per cent rise in the output of manufacturing over the years from 1840 to 1859—as opposed to an increase of 240 per cent with the railroad market.[63]

Of course, this calculation is based on a consideration of direct and indirect purchases by railroads in only four of the 18 industries into which Gallman divides manufacturing. And even here the repercussions of railroad consumption are tracked back through just two or three stages of productive activity. While no attempt will be made to arrive at detailed estimates of the share of the products of other manufacturing industries consumed by railroads, it is possible to estimate the aggregate amount of the neglected items (in terms of value added). The estimate pivots around the fact that the value added in manufacturing all of the goods consumed in the construction of a railroad must be less than the cost of construction. The procedure will be to deduct from an estimate of the total cost of railroad construction in 1859 purchases of labor and other non-manufactured items as well as those manufactured items already taken into account. The residual will be an estimate of the total value of the neglected items which railroads purchased from manufacturing. The residual multiplied by a suitable ratio of value added to value of the final product will yield the desired estimate.

Over the decade from 1850 through 1860 the average cost of new railroads, including equipment, etc., was $38,416 per mile.[64] At this rate, the estimated total cost of the construction of the 2,118 miles of new road built during the census year of 1859–60 was $81,365,000.[65] Of

[63] Gallman, "Value Added," p. 357. In calculating the rate of growth of manufacturing output in the absence of railroads, the value added in the manufacture of commodities consumed by railroads has been deducted from the figure for all value added in manufacturing only for the year 1859. If a similar reduction were made for 1839, the resulting rate of growth would, of course, be higher than 230 per cent.

[64] U.S. Census Office, *Preliminary Report of the Eighth Census* (Washington, 1862), p. 231. According to data in Poor, *History*, the average cost of constructing roads in the New England and Middle Atlantic states in 1859 was $38,835 per mile. E. R. Wicker, "Railroad Investment Before the Civil War," Conference on Income and Wealth, *Trends*, p. 516.

[65] Table 5.8 below. The mileage is a weighted average of the entries for 1859 and 1860.

TABLE 4.11. AN ESTIMATE OF THE PROPORTION OF VALUE ADDED IN THE PRODUCTION OF MACHINERY ATTRIBUTABLE TO RAILROADS, 1859

Industry	1 Horsepower used in 1900	2 Number of workers in 1900	3 Horsepower per worker in 1900 Col.1 ÷ Col.2	4 Number of workers in 1860	5 Estimated horsepower in 1860 Col.3 × Col.4	6 Proportion of output attributable to railroads	7 Horsepower attributable to railroads in 1859 Col.5 × Col.6
1. Locomotives	29,806	24,806	1.20156	4,174	5,015	1.0	5,015
2. Lumber	1,889,050	378,840	4.98641	75,595	376,948	0.01180	4,448
3. Iron and steel rolling mills	1,164,035	183,023	6.36005	22,014	140,010	0.41638	58,297
4. Iron and steel blast furnaces	50,965	39,241	12.89378	15,927	205,350	0.08422	17,295
5. Railroad cars	134,117	210,105	0.63833	10,116	6,457	1.0	6,457
6. Machinery	818,441	528,390	1.54893	63,078	97,703	0.06092	5,952

7. Horsepower used in manufacturing attributable to railroads in 1859 (sum of Col. 7) 97,464

8. Total horsepower used in manufacturing in 1859 1,600,000

9. Proportion of total horsepower used in manufacturing in 1860 attributable to railroads (line 7 ÷ line 8) 0.06092

10. Value added in the production of machinery attributable to railroads in 1859 (line 9 × $54,117,000) $3,297,000

SOURCES AND NOTES:

Columns 1 and 2, Line 1. The figures are for 1904 and are taken from *Thirteenth Census, Manufacturing*, VIII, 612. Line 2. *Thirteenth Census, Manufacturing*, X, 488. Lines 3, 4, and 5. *Twelfth Census, Manufacturing*, X, 80, 84, 88, 272, 274. Line 6. The figures are for 1904. The industries included under the heading of machinery are those designated in Gallman, "Value Added," pp. 357–58. The source is *Thirteenth Census, Manufacturing*, VII, 552, 584, 590, 632.

Column 4, Line 5. The number of workers in "Cars, construction and repairing by steam railroads" was determined by multiplying the figure in Table 4.10, line 4, by the ratio of workers to value added for "Cars, construction and repairing by firms other than steam railroads" as taken from the *Eighth Census, Manufacturing*. Lines 1–4, 6. *Eighth Census, Manufacturing*. Cf. note to Columns 1 and 2, line 6, of this table.

Column 5. The figures in this column probably overstate estimated horsepower used in the specified firms in 1860. For manufacturing as a whole, the horsepower per worker was 1.64 in 1900 but only 1.23 in 1860. Carroll R. Daugherty, "An Index of the Installation of Machinery in the United States Since 1850." *Harvard Business Review*, VI (April, 1928), 283; Gallman, "Commodity Production," p. 30; *Historical Statistics* (1960), p. 74.

Column 6, Line 2. The entry is a weighted average of the share of lumber used in ties and in the construction of cars for the years 1859 and 1860. The weights are 0.5833 and 0.4167. Table 4.9, lines 20 and 21 of Columns 1 and 5. Line 3. The following equation was computed from state production data on rolled iron given in *Census of Manufacturing, 1860,* p. clxxxiii :

$$V = 17.61R + 29.19B$$
$$(5.57) \quad (5.52)$$

where V is the value added in rolling all iron, R is the gross tonnage of rails rolled, and B is the tonnage of all other rolled iron. The coefficient of R is the average amount of value added in dollars per gross ton of rail; the coefficient of B is the average amount of value added in dollars per ton of all other rolled iron. Total value added in the production of rails then is equal to \$17.61 multiplied by the census figure for the production of rails. The value added in the rolling of the wrought iron used for fastenings, locomotives, and cars is equal to \$29.19 multiplied by the tonnage of this iron (as computed in Table 4.8). The sum of the two products divided by value added in the production of all rolled iron (as computed from the equation) is the estimated proportion of the output of rolling mills consumed by railroads. Line 4. The coefficient is the sum of the additional domestic pig iron used for rails plus all domestic crude iron used in other iron products by railroads divided by the total production of pig iron. Both the numerator and denominator are a weighted average of the entries for the years 1859 and 1860. Table 5.15, Column 10, lines 20 and 21; Table 5.14, Column 1, lines 20 and 21; Table 4.8, lines 20 and 21 of Columns 3, 4, and 5. Line 6. This coefficient was obtained iteratively; i.e., by making the ratio of the sum of Column 7 divided by line 8 equal to the coefficient. In other words the coefficient includes machinery required to produce the machines used for the production of the railroad goods in the first five industries.

Line 8. Daugherty, "An Index," p. 283.

Line 10. Gallman, "Value Added," p. 357.

this amount at least 50 per cent appears to represent the cost of the labor required for grading, track laying, and the erection of structures; the purchase of other services (engineering, surveying, legal); interest charges; land; and the cost of non-manufactured commodities (e.g., forest products).[66] Consequently, the total cost of the manufactured materials purchased by railroads was probably less than $40,683,000.

To obtain the value of the neglected items one must subtract from this figure the items which have already been taken into account. One of the items previously considered is locomotives, the 1859 value of which was $4,867,000.[67] A second deduction must be made for the value of all cars manufactured by firms other than railroads, $4,303,000, and for 56.75 per cent of the value of the product of the car shops of steam railroads, $4,510.000—the remaining 43.25 per cent represent the repair and maintenance of existing rolling stock.[68] Previous account

---

[66] The ratio is based on an examination of the listed construction costs of various railroads built during the 1850's and 1860's. In the case of the Illinois Central, for example, only 33.3 per cent ($6,863,000) of the total expenditures on the road, as listed in an 1856 report, was for rails, fastenings, rolling stock, machinery, furniture, and other equipment. While this figure included the purchase of some services (insurance and transportation charges), most of the $6,863,000 represented payments to the manufacturing sector. On the other hand, 47.5 per cent ($9,978,000) of the total expenditure was for construction activities in which labor was virtually the only cost (grading, construction of the superstructure), the purchase of non-manufactured materials (ties), the purchase of services (engineering, advertising), promotional expenses (interest, charter expenses), and the purchase of land. The final 19.2 per cent ($3,954,000) was for the erection of buildings and structures (terminals, engine houses, bridges, fencing) in which labor and other service charges probably represented over half of the total cost. *American Railroad Journal*, Vol. 30 (April 19, 1856), p. 250; cf. *ibid.*, Vol. 30 (March 8, 1856), p. 148; *ibid.*, Vol. 27 (February 25, 1854), pp. 123–26, 215–16; *Annual Report of the State Engineer and Surveyor of the State of New York in Relation to Railroad Reports, 1850–1861* (Albany, 1851–62), *passim;* U.S. Congress, Senate, *Reports of the Government Directors of the Union Pacific Railroad Company,* Exec. Doc. No. 69, 49th Cong., 1st Sess. (Ser. No. 2336), p. 54; Wicker, "Railroad Investment," pp. 521–22.

[67] *Census of Manufacturing, 1860*, p. clxxxix.

[68] The value of the product of car shops not connected with railroads is taken from the *ibid.*, p. 734. The value of the product of railroad car shops was determined by multiplying the 1859 figure for non-railroad shops by the 1889 ratio of the value of the product of the rail to the value of the product of non-rail shops (car shops of steam railroads not only built and repaired cars but also repaired engines). It was assumed that the per cent of the value of the product of rail shops which represented new construction was the same in 1859 as in 1900 (*Census of Manufacturing, 1900*, Part IV, pp. 278, 279).

TABLE 4.12. VALUE ADDED IN MANUFACTURING ATTRIBUTABLE TO RAILROAD
CONSUMPTION OF MANUFACTURED GOODS, 1859

Industry	1 Value added in 1859 (dollars)	2 Proportion of output purchased by railroads	3 Value added in 1859 attributable to railroads (dollars) Col. 1 × Col. 2
1. Transportation equipment	42,827,000	0.2545	12,171,000
2. Machinery	54,117,000	0.06092	3,297,000
3. Rolled iron	12,646,000	0.41638	5,266,000
4. Pig iron	8,577,000	0.08422	722,000
5. Lumber	90,755,000	0.01180	1,071,000
6. Total of Column 3...			22,527,000
7. Value added by all manufacturing in 1859			814,888,000
8. Line 6 as a per cent of line 7			2.76

SOURCES AND NOTES:
   Column 1, Lines 1, 2, 5: Gallman, "Value Added," p. 357. Lines 3, 4: *Census of
Manufacturing, 1860,* p. clxxxiii
   Column 2. Tables 4.9–4.11.
   Line 7. Gallman, "Value Added," p. 357.

has also been taken of the rails used in new construction which amounted
to approximately $5,843,000.[69]

Deduction of the sum of these items from $40,683,000 leaves a
residual of $21,160,000. This residual probably overstates the value
of the neglected purchases from manufacturing since, in addition to the
other upward biases, it still includes the value of spikes, rail chairs,
and similar items of iron which were taken into account in the calculation shown in Table 4.12. Multiplying the residual by the ratio of value
added to the value of all manufactured goods in 1859, one obtains
$9,585,000 as the value added in the manufacturing of the neglected
items.[70] No addition need be made to this figure for manufactured
goods used in the maintenance of track and equipment since these items
are covered by Table 4.12.

Consequently, the total amount of the value added in manufacturing
the goods purchased from that sector in 1859 was probably less than

[69] A weighted average of the A.I.S.A. data for 1859 and 1860 indicates that
200,000 net tons of domestic rails were produced in 1859. The average price of
rails was $54.83 per net ton, indicating a total value of $10,966,000. This figure was
divided between new construction and replacement in proportion to the ratio of
the track-miles of new construction to the track-miles of replacements. Tables
5.8 and 5.15 below; A.I.S.A., *Annual Report, 1878,* p. 47.
[70] *Census of Manufacturing, 1860,* p. 742.

$32,112,000, or 3.94 per cent of the figure for all manufacturing. It would be wrong, however, to interpret $32,112,000 as a measure of the amount by which railroad purchases increased the market for manufactured goods. As the discussion in Chapters II and III indicated, in the absence of railroads there would have been a considerable increase in the consumption of wagon and water transportation services. To determine the incremental contribution of railroad purchases to the market of each particular industry as well as to manufacturing as a whole, it is necessary to subtract from railroad purchases the increase in the purchases of corresponding items that would have been made by other forms of transportation. The incremental contribution of railroad purchases to the market for various manufactured goods is still to be determined—but it is clearly smaller than the limited amount of railroad purchases already derived.

CHAPTER V

The Position of Rails in the Market for American Iron, 1840–60: A Reconstruction

A qualitative change in the structure or functioning of an economic institution . . . is of uncertain import until it is translated, with the help of quantitative data and statistical analysis, to show what these qualitatively identified events mean in terms of measurable modifications in the substantive performance of economic institutions.—SIMON KUZNETS

There is no way of avoiding the problem of quantification in the study of the influence of railroads on economic growth. Apparently qualitative analyses always contain implicit quantifications. To eschew the application of quantitative techniques because the data are too poor, while at the same time asserting that railroads had an enormous qualitative impact on the economy, involves a gross inconsistency. For if the proposition asserted is correct, it is because the railroads had a significant quantitative impact on such variables as the cost of transportation, speed of movement, the concentration of wealth and power, and the rate of growth in the output of various industries. If the quantitative impact of the railroad on these and other variables is unmeasurable (even roughly), then the qualitative significance of railroads is indeterminate.

The ostensibly qualitative statement that the growth of the American iron industry prior to the Civil War depended on railroad consumption of iron is, in fact, an assertion that the proportion of the output of iron purchased by railroads was of such a magnitude that the absence of these purchases would have significantly diminished the demand for iron and retarded the growth of the industry. Yet this statement has been made without a rigorous examination of the available data on either the volume of iron production or the consumption of railroad iron. Of course the data on these matters are extremely poor and fragmentary. But the data problem is not surmounted by relying on the opinions of eminent and knowledgeable persons who lived during the ante-bellum period. The belief that the views of historical contem-

147

poraries is a superior form of evidence is open to question because the data on which such views were based were often no better than those now available. To accept the conclusions of historical contemporaries does not avoid the problem of working with fragmentary data; it merely covers it up.

Determination of the position of rails in the market for iron must be based on a reconstruction of both the volume of total iron consumption and the volume of iron used for rails. Since only fragmentary data on these matters are available, the method of performing these reconstructions becomes of paramount importance. The procedure of just using one or a few items of arbitrarily selected information about rails and the iron industry is akin to a palaeontologist who attempts to reconstruct the shape of a whole animal from a tooth. Of course in palaeontology no fragment, however small, will be discarded. Indeed, with a tooth and a knowledge of statistical correlations between teeth and bone structures, it may be possible to make a sound inference about the jaw from which the tooth came. However, the particular jaw formation which is suggested may be consistent with a large variety of structures in other parts of the body so that no reliable inference can be made about the shape of the entire animal. On the other hand, if in addition to a tooth one has a part of the skull, some bones from the spine and legs, etc., the range of reconstructions consistent with biological knowledge may be reduced to the point where one can have considerable confidence in the shape of the animal that emerges.

The absence of a systematic reconstruction of the position of rails in the market for iron between 1840 and 1860 cannot be explained by an insufficiency in the number of available data fragments. In addition to several series revealing the number of new miles of railroad opened, scattered information is available on the weight of rails, the length of life of rails, the amount of rails rerolled, the amount of rails scrapped, etc. Paradoxically, the explanation for the lack of a systematic reconstruction appears to be the very volume of these fragments and the absence of well worked out procedures for their combination.

The problem of how to proceed will be more obvious if it is recognized that all reconstructions of the type being discussed here are theories. The prehistoric animal we see in a museum is not the animal as it actually was but a theory of the animal built up from fossil fragments on the basis of biological principles. Similarly, the reconstruction attempted in this chapter should be interpreted not as representing the actual position of rails in the market for iron but as a theory of that position built up from data fragments on the basis of economic principles. But since it is a theory, one can draw on well known standards for evaluating the quality and relevance of theories. These standards include the internal consistency of the theory and the "goodness of the fit" of the theory to the available data. The reconstruction presented in this chapter, then, is an attempt to evolve a model which incorporates the largest number of available data fragments in an internally consistent manner. If more than one internally consistent model is possible, the choice between alternatives must be based on the ability of the differing models to "explain" the available data; that is, the model which incorporates the maximum amount of data in a consistent manner, in economic history as in any other science, should be considered the superior one. Of course since the reconstruction presented below is only a model, it is subject to change either because new information becomes available which contradicts the model or because of advances in economic theory. But this is certainly no special limitation of economic history. In any field, the prevailing theories are merely the best ones currently available. That the models of economic history may change is an expression of the fact that economic history is not yet a closed field of research.[1]

THE INDEX OF THE POSITION OF RAILS IN THE MARKET FOR AMERICAN IRON

The problems involved in the reconstruction of the position of rails in the market for iron can be divided into four categories: the selection of an index of the share of the output of the iron industry represented by rails; the determination of pig iron production; the determination of the amount of iron consumed in the manufacture of rails; and the determination of total domestic crude iron production and consumption. This section deals with the first of these problems.

---

[1] A literature dealing with the specific problems and approaches to the utilization of fragmentary data in the systematic statistical reconstruction of American economic history is just beginning to emerge. Helpful discussions of these matters are contained in Conference on Income and Wealth, *Trends,* and in Albert Fishlow's review of this book, "Trends in the American Economy in the Nineteenth Century," *Journal of Economic History,* Vol. 22 (March, 1962), pp. 71–80. Cf. Robert William Fogel, ["A Provisional View of the 'New Economic History,'"] *American Economic Review,* LIV (May, 1964), 377–89.

Since the iron industry did not produce one homogeneous product, the usual problem of how to aggregate these products arises. One desirable procedure would be to aggregate by prices and to use

$$I_1 = \frac{\text{value of domestically produced rails}}{\text{value of all final products of the iron industry}}$$

as an index of the proportion of the output of the American iron industry represented by rails. The numerator of I_1 is defined to exclude rails purchased from abroad. The denominator is defined to exclude double counting. Unfortunately the available data are not complete enough to permit the construction of this index. Even for the years following the Civil War, the breakdown of production by type of product is not detailed enough and prices of many individual products are not available.

As a consequence, writers dealing with the impact of railroads on the iron industry have resorted to indexes based on the tonnage of iron production and consumption. One measure of this type is

$$I_2 = \frac{\text{tons of rails used in the construction and maintenance of railroads}}{\text{tons of pig iron produced}}.$$

The implicit assumption made in using I_2 is that $I_1 = I_2$. This assumption would be true if (1) all rails were purchased from domestic producers; (2) the amount of pig iron required to produce a ton of more highly manufactured iron was the same for all products, namely one ton; (3) only pig iron was used to produce more highly manufactured iron; and (4) the values of final products of the iron industry were directly proportional to the amount of pig iron used in their production.

In actual fact all of these conditions were violated in such a way that $I_2 > I_1$ by a substantial amount. A large part of the rails consumed during the years in question was purchased from abroad; in the decade of the 1850's, foreign rails represented nearly two-thirds of all rail purchases. The pig iron requirement of a ton of rolled iron differed from that of cast iron and hammered iron. Pig iron was not the only form of crude iron used in the production of final products; scrap iron became an increasingly important part of total crude iron consumption in the years leading up to 1860. Finally, the value of all final products was not directly proportional to the amount of pig required to produce them; the ratios of the price of a ton of steel and the price of a ton of hammered bar to the amount of pig used in their production exceeded the ratio of the price of a ton of rails to its pig iron content. Consequently the use of I_2 as a measure of the share of the output of the domestic iron industry consumed by railroads contains a considerable upward bias.

It is possible, even within the limitations imposed by aggregation based on tonnages rather than prices, to define two indexes that reduce the upward bias of I_2. These are

$$I_3 = \frac{\text{tons of domestic crude iron used in domestically produced rails}}{\text{tons of domestic crude iron consumed in the iron industry}}$$

and

$$I_4 = \frac{\text{tons of all crude iron used in domestically produced rails}}{\text{tons of all crude iron consumed in the iron industry}}.$$

If imported crude iron were distributed betwen the production of railroad iron and other items in proportion to the amount of domestic crude iron each consumed, I_3 would equal I_4. While I_4 is less than I_2, it is still greater than I_1 because the ratio of price per ton of finished product to crude iron per ton of finished product was greater in the production of hammered iron, cast iron, rolled bar other than rails, and in steel than in the production of railroad iron.[2] However, it is closer to I_1 than previously used indexes based on tonnage and, as will be demonstrated below, it represents a significant improvement over these measures.

THE DOMESTIC PRODUCTION OF PIG IRON

The largest component in the denominator of I_4 is domestically produced pig iron. From 1854, annual estimates of the output of this product were published by the American Iron and Steel Association. The A.I.S.A. estimates were based on industry-wide surveys and appear to be reliable. Domestic production of pig iron prior to that year, particularly during the decade of the 1840's, is wrapped in confusion. The most widely quoted series pertaining to the forties is the one published in *Historical Statistics* (1960). As Peter Temin has shown, this series is derived from the work of Henry Carey.[3] Carey's estimates were severely criticized by W. H. Grosvenor who held that

[2] See Appendix B.
[3] Temin, "A Review."

Carey distorted the course of pig iron production during the forties so that it would conform with Carey's views on tariffs. Grosvenor replaced Carey's series with one of his own (see Table 5.1). Grosvenor's criticism was taken up almost three decades later by F. W. Taussig. While Taussig used Carey's estimates, he wrote:

> One point seems clear: there could not have been an increase during the five years between 1842 and 1847 from 230,000 to 800,000 tons, such as is indicated by Carey's figures, which Mr. Raymond follows. The total production of anthracite iron in 1847 was not 120,000 tons. Deducting this from the supposed total of 800,000, we have 680,000 as the production of charcoal iron in 1847 as against 230,000 (chiefly charcoal) in 1842. Considering the small scale on which charcoal iron was made, and the difficulty of increasing rapidly the supply of fuel, it is not possible that the product should have been tripled in five years. Either the figure for 1842 is too low or that for 1847 is too high.[4]

A logical starting point in the determination of pig iron production prior to 1854 is a detailed examination of the series put forth by Carey and of the criticisms that have been made of Carey's estimates. The fragmentary data that form the basis for this examination include a survey of pig iron production in Pennsylvania, a compendium of blast furnaces published in 1859, the data in the Sixth, Seventh, and Eighth Censuses, indices of the price movements of pig iron, reports on business conditions in the iron industry published in commercial journals and statements made by ironmasters.

Taussig's criticism of Carey appears to be technological; it actually turns on the consistency between the production increase stipulated by Carey and the fragmentary data available on the growth of furnace capacity during the 1840's. Considerable light is shed on this point by a survey of production in Pennsylvania commissioned by a convention of ironmasters which met in Philadelphia in December, 1849.[5] The

---

[4] F. W. Taussig, "The Tariff, 1830–1860," *Quarterly Journal of Economics,* Vol. 2 (April, 1888), pp. 380–81.

[5] A summary of the findings of the survey and its basic tables appeared in an article written by the chairman of the survey committee, Charles G. Smith, "The Manufacture of Iron in Pennsylvania," *Merchants' Magazine and Commercial Review,* Vol. 25 (November, 1851), pp. 574–81 and tables following p. 656; a more complete report on the Philadelphia convention is contained in *Documents Relating to the Manufacture of Iron* (Philadelphia, 1850), and in *The American Railroad Journal,* Vol. 23 (July 27, August 3, 17, 24, and August 31, 1850).

survey tables of the Philadelphia convention list 298 blast furnaces and provide information on capacity, greatest output prior to 1850, actual output in 1849, and furnace construction by date. Some of the furnaces failed at various times during the decade; the year of such bankruptcies is also given. Table 5.2 was constructed from the Philadelphia survey, with greatest previous production used as a measure of capacity (rather than the higher but more questionable capacity ratings). Table 5.2 probably understates Pennsylvania capacity. The survey of the Philadelphia convention was not a complete census of all blast furnaces in the state. Only 148 furnaces are listed as having been in existence in 1840, although the Sixth Census reported the existence of 213. Like the survey made in 1842 by the Harrisburg convention of ironmasters, the 1849 convention apparently failed to obtain reports from a large number of "inferior" furnaces.[6] Even so, Table 5.2 indicates a capacity of 377,000 tons at the end of 1847.

Given the data on Pennsylvania, the issue posed by Taussig reduces to whether the capacity of other states could have been in the neighborhood of 425,000 gross tons in 1847. Unfortunately capacity data comparable to the Pennsylvania series are not available for other states. However, according to the Sixth Census, Pennsylvania produced 34 per cent of the national production of pig iron.[7] If the capacity throughout the country was utilized to the same degree as it was in Pennsylvania, and if errors in reporting were no worse outside of Pennsylvania than in it, the 1840 capacity of other states was 326,000 tons. This

---

[6] Cf. the letter to S. J. Reeves in U.S. Congress, Senate, *Annual Report of the Secretary of the Treasury*, 1849, Doc. No. 2, 31st Cong., 1st Sess. [Ser. No. 552], p. 809 (hereafter referred to as Reeves, "Letter") ; and C. G. Child, "The Iron Trade of Europe and the United States," *Merchants' Magazine and Commercial Review*, Vol. 16 (June, 1847), pp. 586–91.

A survey of iron production in 1844 was taken by the Home League, a New York organization formed in 1841 to promote protective tariffs. A complete set of their documents is still to be located. However, an article by E. A. J. Merchant, "The Iron Trade," *Merchants' Magazine*, Vol. 12 (March, 1845) reports on the result of a survey which appears to be the one attributed to the Home League in John B. Pearse, *A Concise History of the Iron Manufacture of the Colonies up to the Revolution and of Pennsylvania until the Present Time* (Philadelphia, 1876), p. 278. According to Merchant, there were 235 blast furnaces in Pennsylvania in 1844, 51 more than the number indicated by the Philadelphia convention.

Part of the omission was due to the fact that the 1849 convention did not report on furnaces which were abandoned at various dates between 1840 and 1850. The failures listed in the convention tables pertain only to furnaces that were still active in 1850. Cf. p. 157 below.

[7] James M. Swank, *History of the Manufacture of Iron in All Ages* (2nd ed.; Philadelphia, 1892), p. 510.

TABLE 5.1. PRODUCTION OF PIG IRON AS ESTIMATED BY GROSVENOR AND CAREY

| | Carey | | Grosvenor | |
| | 1 | 2 | 3 | 4 |
Year	Gross tons	Net tons	Gross tons	Net tons
1840	315,000	353,000	347,000	389,000
1841			360,000	403,000
1842	200,000 to 230,000	224,000 to 258,000	376,000	421,000
1843			386,000	432,000
1844			427,000	478,000
1845			486,000	544,000
1846	765,000	857,000	551,000	617,000
1847	800,000	896,000	597,674	669,395
1848	800,000	896,000	570,000	638,000
1849	650,000	728,000	542,903	608,051
1850	563,755	631,406	564,000	632,000

SOURCES: Temin, "A Review"; W. H. Grosvenor, *Does Protection Protect?* (New York, 1871), pp. 215–18; Henry Carey, "Harmony of Interests," *Miscellaneous Works* (Philadelphia, 1872), pp. 11–12.

TABLE 5.2. CAPACITY[1] OF BLAST FURNACES IN PENNSYLVANIA AT YEAR END
(in gross tons)

| | New Construction in Given Year[2] | | | Cumulated Totals | | |
| | 1 | 2 | 3 | 4 | 5 | 6 |
Year	Charcoal	Coal	Col. 1 + Col. 2	Charcoal	Coal	All Furnaces
1840				141,621	28,452	170,073
1841	3,414	2,000	5,414	145,035	30,452	175,487
1842	8,700	11,153	19,853	153,735	41,605	195,340
1843	4,585	3,500	8,085	158,320	45,105	203,425
1844	15,300	5,978	21,278	173,620	51,083	224,703
1845	13,041	43,627	56,668	186,661	94,710	281,371
1846	27,427	37,973	65,400	214,088	132,683	346,771
1847	7,129	22,768	29,897	221,217	155,451	376,668
1848	5,400	14,547	19,947	226,617	169,998	396,615
1849	807	4,363	5,170	227,424	174,361	401,785

SOURCE: Smith, "Manufacture of Iron," tables following p. 656.

[1] Capacity is defined as maximum previous production. However in the case of three furnaces for which no data was presented on maximum product, capacity ratings were used.

[2] Two furnaces were converted from charcoal to coal, one in 1845, the other in 1848. These were included in new charcoal construction in the years in which they were originally erected. In the years of conversion a deduction was made from new charcoal construction and an addition of a like amount was made to new anthracite construction.

implies that Carey's estimates are consistent with a 30 per cent increase in furnace capacity outside of Pennsylvania during the seven years ending in 1847. But such a rate of increase is far less than that which actually took place in Pennsylvania. Indeed, it represents less than two-thirds of the percentage increase in Pennsylvania's charcoal furnaces alone. Under these circumstances one cannot rule out the possibility that the nation's capacity reached 800,000 tons in 1847. Since production could have been 800,000 tons in 1847, it certainly could have been 230,000 tons in 1842. The latter figure merely implies that the iron industry went through a depression that left it operating at about 50 per cent of its potential.

Grosvenor's criticisms of Carey rested on the proposition that the domestic market was too small to absorb the amount of product indicated by Carey's estimates. Grosvenor argued that 192,000 tons of iron were used in building and repairing railroads in 1850. This he held was "more than half as large" as the total quantity of pig iron produced in that year. On the other hand, he estimated that railroads only used 58,000 tons in 1848 and implied that consumption was even less in earlier years. With such a small railroad demand for iron, said Grosvenor, "with scarcely any railroad building" until after 1846 when the high protective tariff on iron was repealed, the country could not have consumed "the quantity it is asserted was produced—[a quantity] vastly in excess of the known product of 1850." [8]

Grosvenor attributed Carey's high figures for 1846, 1847, and 1848 to a series of false premises. Carey had supported his estimates by arguing that all furnaces were being worked at full capacity during these years. This enabled him to estimate production by using data on the number of furnaces built between 1840 and 1848. He assumed that capacity was 430,000 tons in 1840, 85,000 tons above the production figure cited by the Home League survey for that year. He assumed further that the average capacity of an anthracite furnace was 5,000 tons and that the average capacity of charcoal furnaces was substantially increased after 1840.[9] Grosvenor attacked these assumptions vigorously. He held that furnaces were operating at full capacity in 1840 so that the Home League estimate of production also represented

---

[8] W. M. Grosvenor, *Does Protection Protect?* (New York, 1871), p. 207; hereafter referred to as Grosvenor, *Protection*.

[9] Henry Carey, "Review of the Report of Hon. D. A. Wells," 3rd letter, *Miscellaneous Work* (Philadelphia, 1872); cf. with his estimates in "The Harmony of Interests," *ibid.*, pp. 11–12.

capacity. He put the average capacity of anthracite furnaces at only 3,000 tons and argued that data in the Sixth and Seventh Censuses conflicted with Carey's assumptions concerning the increase in the size of charcoal furnaces. Grosvenor also attacked Carey's failure to take account of the Philadelphia convention data on furnace failures. These furnaces, he said, were abandoned and should have been deducted from Carey's estimates of capacity. Finally, he contended that Carey overstated the increase in the number of furnaces built after 1840.[10]

Rejecting Carey's estimates, Grosvenor adopted Carey's method to derive his own series. He assumed that the Home League figure of 347,000 tons represented capacity in 1840. Of this amount he assigned 130,000 tons to Pennsylvania and the balance to other states. He derived his estimates for the years 1841–46 by adding to 1840 capacity 3,000 tons for each new anthracite and 1,000 tons for each new charcoal furnace. The number of new furnaces built in each year was based on the listing of furnaces in the compendium prepared by J. P. Lesley.[11] The estimates thus derived, said Grosvenor, were the upper limits of production since he had made no deduction for furnaces which failed. His figure for 1847 was reached by adding to the Philadelphia figure on the output of charcoal furnaces, 57,000 tons for the production of anthracite furnaces. The national total was taken to be approximately twice this sum. The 1848 and 1849 figures were based on similar modifications of the data of the Philadelphia convention and on Lesley's *Guide*. The 1850 estimate was taken from the Seventh Census.[12]

How well do Grosvenor's criticisms and his substitute series stand up? Grosvenor's contention that Carey overestimated the average production of anthracite furnaces appears to be well founded. According to the documents of the Philadelphia convention, the average maximum product of these furnaces was about 2,900 tons.[13] Available data also seem to confirm his conclusion that rather than holding steady, production declined in 1848.[14] Beyond this, Grosvenor's analysis collapses. His basic presumption that the absence of heavy railroad construction precluded a market for iron as large as that suggested by Carey rests on a gross overestimation of the amount of domestic pig iron that went into rails in 1850 and subsequent years. As is shown below, the addi-

---

[10] Grosvenor, *Protection*, pp. 210–15.
[11] Lesley, *Guide*.
[12] Grosvenor, *Protection*, pp. 215–18.
[13] Smith, "Manufacture of Iron," Table 2.
[14] See p. 160 below.

tion to the domestic production of pig iron directly attributable to domestic pig iron used for rails probably averaged under 50,000 net tons per year over the 11 years from 1850 through 1860. Indeed the amount of domestic pig iron used for rails in 1850 was probably a third less than that used in 1848.[15] In placing such heavy stress on the fact that railroad consumption of iron in 1850 was "more than half as large" as total domestic pig iron production, Grosvenor fell victim to the index problem discussed in the previous section; he implicitly based his calculations on I_2 rather than I_4.

Grosvenor was also wrong in his contention that furnaces which the Philadelphia convention listed as having failed at various dates during the forties were abandoned and permanently out of production. Grosvenor was apparently unaware of the fact that these tables were put forth not as representing all furnaces which had existed during the forties but those which were "running, or in running order" in 1850.[16] But even if this information were not available to him, the tables of the convention on which he drew clearly contradict his position. Thus of nine anthracite furnaces that failed between 1843 and 1848, four were in blast in 1849 and one returned to blast in 1850, this despite the fact that 1849 and 1850 were depressed years for the industry. Of five anthracite furnaces that failed in 1849, two were in blast in 1850. Failure did not even mean that furnaces were out of blast for the entire year in which they failed. Of the 15 furnaces of all types that failed during the first four months of 1850, three were listed as being in blast at the end of the period.[17]

Grosvenor's most serious errors were made in the construction of his alternative series. The data of the Philadelphia convention and his own assumptions on the capacity of individual furnaces conflict with Grosvenor's contention that the Home League's estimate of production in 1840 also represented capacity. The tables of the Philadelphia convention indicate that there were at least 135 charcoal and 10 coal furnaces in existence in Pennsylvania in that year. Grosvenor assumed 3,000 tons as the average capacity of coal furnaces and 1,000 tons for charcoal furnaces. At these rates, Pennsylvania capacity in 1840 would have been 165,000 tons, or 35,000 tons more than the "productive

---

[15] See Table 5.15 below. Grosvenor also miscalculated total domestic consumption of iron. Cf. Grosvenor, *Protection*, p. 210 (footnote) and Table 5.14 below.

[16] *American Railroad Journal*, Vol. 23 (August 3, 1850), p. 482.

[17] Smith, "Manufacture of Iron," tables. Forty-eight per cent of all active furnaces in Pennsylvania were out of blast in the Spring of 1850. *Ibid.*, p. 576.

power" stipulated by Grosvenor. Applying Grosvenor's ratio of U.S. to Pennsylvania capacity for 1840 yields an indicated national capacity of 440,000 tons, 93,000 tons above the Home League figure and 10,000 tons above the capacity assumed by Carey in his calculation. Yet 440,000 tons is probably a conservative estimate of capacity for, as was previously noted, the tables of the Philadelphia convention failed to include over 60 furnaces reported by the Sixth Census.[18]

Grosvenor stumbled even more badly in his effort to use Lesley's *Guide* to reconstruct capacity in later years. In culling data from this compendium he incorrectly presumed that it contained a listing of all the furnaces of the 1840's. As a result he omitted five of the anthracite furnaces shown in the tables of the Philadelphia convention. He also omitted, or included in the category of charcoal, several large coke and bituminous furnaces. Grosvenor's estimate of capacity outside of Pennsylvania was also erroneous. Lesley's *Guide* lists 33 anthracite furnaces in these states. However, it gives the date on which production commenced for only 19. Of these, seven began between 1840 and 1849 and 12 at other times. Grosvenor incorrectly assumed that all of the 14 undated furnaces were built after 1849. He further assumed that 69 charcoal furnaces which were undated were all built either before 1840 or after 1849. These and other errors introduced a considerable downward bias into Grosvenor's series. His low estimate of pig iron production in 1847, for example, involved, in addition to the previous errors, the arbitrary substitution of a figure on anthracite production in Pennsylvania which was 64,000 tons (53 per cent) below the estimate of the Philadelphia convention, and the omission of 17,800 tons of pig iron produced in coke and bituminous furnaces.[19]

What has been said so far is largely negative. To demonstrate that there was no technological barrier to an increase in production of the magnitude set forth by Carey does not reveal what actually happened to production. Nor is this task accomplished by showing that Grosvenor's major assumptions and his substitute series were erroneous. But the preceding discussion does dispel some of the confusion that has enveloped Carey's estimates. It also sets the stage for a consideration of the most important of the propositions set forth by Carey in the defense of his estimates—the proposition that from 1845 to 1847

[18] Grosvenor, *Protection,* pp. 215, 216; Smith, "Manufacture of Iron," tables; Carey, "Review," 3rd letter.

[19] Grosvenor, *Protection,* pp. 215–18; Smith, "Manufacture of Iron," p. 576, tables; Lesley, *Guide,* tables A, B, E, H, and K.

furnaces were "being driven to their utmost capacity." [20] If true, this information enables one to use the only sound, continuous statistical series available for the 1840's—the Philadelphia convention data on capacity—to estimate production during the all important middle years of the decade. Table 5.1 and Chart 5.1 show that if, as Carey claimed, production during 1844–47 rose at the rate of about 100,000 gross tons per year, the basic course of production during the decade is clearly established. Alterations in Carey's estimates for 1840, 1842, 1848, and 1849, such as those made by Grosvenor, do not substantially modify the pattern.

Both the commentary in the commercial journals and the movement of prices lend strong support to Carey's contention that 1845–47 was a boom period for the iron industry—a span of years during which capacity was rapidly expanded and furnaces were being worked at peak capacity. In the *Merchants' Magazine,* March, 1845, E. A. J. Merchant wrote that the iron "trade, at present, is in a very flourishing condition; and this year, no doubt, there will be a considerable addition to yield, in the great seat of this manufacture." [21] By mid-1845, *Niles Register* reported that the prosperity in the iron trade was "among the wonders of commercial fluctuation. From a long depression, dragging on for years with the most discouraging results, it has suddenly burst forth into almost boundless prosperity so as to become one of the great leading branches of business, and immensely profitable. . . . Our numerous iron districts have assumed new life and energy . . . accomplishing in months what formerly would have been considered the labor of years;—yet notwithstanding all of this energy and enterprise, there still exists an inability to supply the demand, so far are the orders in advance of demand. . . . Almost every mail brings intelligence of the erection of some new furnace or rolling-mill, or the blowing in of some one that has long been out of blast. . . ." [22] A similar note was struck by a correspondent for the *London Mining Journal* in the spring of 1846. Lamenting the increased difficulty of selling British iron in American markets, the writer concluded that "some demand for Scotch pig must continue" because "that country [the United States] is not yet capable of supplying is own requirements." Unable to restrain itself, the *American Railroad Journal,* which reprinted the British article, noted: "There

---

[20] Carey, "Review," 3rd letter. Interestingly, neither Taussig nor Grosvenor questioned this point.
[21] Merchant, "Iron Trade," p. 231.
[22] *Niles Weekly Register,* Vol. 68 (June 7, 1845), p. 219.

is evidently apprehension in England, of greater competition in the trade in this country than has ever existed—and well there may be, as the time will come when we shall export more iron than we ever imported." [23]

The movement of relative prices during this period further buttresses Carey's most crucial proposition. The average price of charcoal pig rose by 46 per cent in 21 months—from a low of $25.00 per ton in August, 1843, to a high of $36.50 in May, 1845—while the Warren-Pearson index of wholesale prices increased by only 9 per cent.[24] Especially significant is the decline in the differential between the average price of British pig at American ports and the average price of domestic pig as shown in Table 5.3.

In view of this evidence, Carey's assumption that existing firms were operating at full capacity during 1845–47 appears to be sound. While there was a perceptible jump in the rate of furnace failures during 1847, this occurrence was not inconsistent with production at or near full capacity.[25] Some furnaces may have failed and changed management during the spring slump in prices. However, prices surged upward again in the summer and reached $35 per ton in November. That month may have marked the peak of the boom. According to Samuel Reeves, a president of the A.I.S.A. and one of the leading iron manufacturers of the period, "the last half of 1847 and the first part of 1848" was the period of "greatest production." After November, prices moved steadily downward. By September, 1848, prices had fallen 27 per cent to their lowest point since December, 1843, and the commercial journals began to publish reports of hard times in the iron industry.[26]

Given that 1845–47 was a boom period during which furnaces were worked to capacity, production in Pennsylvania can be determined

[23] *American Railroad Journal,* Vol. 19 (May 2, 1846), p. 277.

[24] A.I.S.A. *Annual Report, 1877,* pp. 48, 50; Cornell University Agricultural Experiment Station, *Wholesale Prices for 213 Years, 1720–1932,* Memoir 142, 1932, Part I, p. 8; hereafter referred to as Warren and Pearson.

[25] Smith, "Manufacture of Iron," p. 581. In his summary Smith attributed one anthracite and 15 charcoal failures to 1847. However, the tables only list a total of 15 failures in that year. The maximum previous production of these 15 was 12,515 tons—3.6 per cent of Pennsylvania capacity at the end of 1846. Nine of the 13 furnaces are listed as having been in blast in 1849.

Some additional support for the proposition that production was very near capacity is to be found in a survey which reported that 40 of 41 anthracite furnaces were in blast in early 1847. C. G. Child, "The Iron Trade of Europe and the United States," *Merchants' Magazine and Commercial Review,* Vol. 16 (June, 1847), p. 592.

[26] A.I.S.A., *Annual Report, 1877,* pp. 48, 50; Reeves, *Letter.*

TABLE 5.3. PRICES OF BRITISH AND AMERICAN PIG IRON

Period	(1) Average price of imported pig plus duty at port of entry	(2) Average price of charcoal pig at Philadelphia	(3) Average price of anthracite pig at Philadelphia	(4) Col. 2 — Col. 1	(5) Col. 3 — Col. 1
9 mos. ending 6/30/43	$21.46	$27.94	$ ..	$ 6.48	$ ..
year ending 6/30/44	22.42	26.46	..	4 04	..
year ending 6/30/45	27.40	31.40	28.65	4.00	1.25
year ending 6/30/46	29.24	32.04	28.19	2.80	−1.05
year ending 6/30/47	26.34	30.21	28.19	3.87	1.85
year ending 6/30/48	20.53	31.52	29.72	10.99	9.19
year ending 6/30/49	17.29	25.79	24.69	8.50	7.40

SOURCES AND NOTES:

Column 1. The figures in this column were obtained by dividing the value of imports by the quantity and then adding the duty. U.S. Congress, Senate, *Annual Report of the Secretary of the Treasury, 1851*, Doc. No. 11, 32d Cong., 1st Sess. (Ser. No. 614), pp. 83, 85; U.S. Congress, Senate, *Report on Foreign Commerce and Navigation, 1846, 1847.*

Column 2 and Column 3. A.I.S.A., *Annual Report, 1877*, pp. 48, 50. The prices listed are simple averages of monthly prices.

from the data of the Philadelphia convention. These estimates are shown in Table 5.4 and are based on the assumption that new construction was spread evenly through the year.[27] No deduction has been made for furnaces which failed. As shown previously, failure was not equivalent to a cessation of production. Moreover, of the furnace failures during the three years in question only two occurred in 1845 and three in 1846; 15 or 16 occurred in 1847.[28] The number of failures was probably less than the number of furnaces that were in existence during 1845–47 but which did not find their way into the Philadelphia survey. In any case, it seems likely that if some furnaces went out of blast in 1847, the interruption was brief; the sharp upward movement in prices during the year created favorable conditions for a rapid resumption of operations.[29]

[27] The estimates differ from the summary of the Philadelphia convention tables presented by Smith, "Manufacture of Iron," p. 376. Smith included the production of several furnaces not built until after 1847 and assumed that all furnaces built in 1847 operated throughout the year. Smith also failed to take account of five furnaces that did not report their maximum previous product. In these cases, the figures on rated capacity were used in the calculation shown in Table 5.4.

[28] Cf. note 25 above.

[29] Although the index of wholesale prices declined moderately between July and November, 1847, the price of pig iron rose by 20 per cent. Warren and Pearson, p. 8; A.I.S.A., *Annual Report, 1877*, pp. 48, 50.

TABLE 5.4. ESTIMATED PRODUCTION OF PIG IRON IN PENNSYLVANIA, 1845-47

	Gross tons	Net tons
Maximum product of 184 furnaces built through 1844	224,703	251,667
One-half of maximum product of 28 furnaces built in 1845	28,334	31,734
Estimated product in 1845	253,037	283,401
Maximum product of 212 furnaces built through 1845	281,371	315,136
One-half of maximum product of 41 furnaces built in 1846	32,700	36,624
Estimated product in 1846	314,071	351,760
Maximum product of 253 furnaces built through 1846	346,771	388,383
One-half of maximum product of 20 furnaces built in 1847	14,948	16,742
Estimated Product in 1847	361,719	405,125

SOURCE: Table 5.2 above.

Existing data do not permit a direct determination of production outside of Pennsylvania. An alternative approach involves the "inflation" of the Pennsylvania data by an appropriate ratio of U.S. to Pennsylvania production. Three such ratios are available for the decade of the forties: the census ratio for 1839–40 (2.916); the ratio of the 1844 Home League survey (2.298); and the Seventh Census ratio (1.973).[30] If the last of these figures were applied to Pennsylvania product for 1847, national output would be 715,000 gross tons. If the ratio of the Sixth Census were used, national output would be over 1,000,000 gross tons. The spread indicated by the alternative calculations is quite large. While the true figure probably falls between these extremes, no evidence presently available enables one to fix the point with certainty.[31] There seems to be little doubt, however, that Pennsylvania's share of total output increased over the decade, although at a decreasing rate. This impression is further buttressed by an A.I.S.A. survey which put the ratio of national to Pennsylvania production at 2.006 in 1854, 1.852 in 1855, and 1.812 in 1856.[32] Taken as a

[30] Swank, *History,* p. 510; Merchant, "Iron Trade," p. 231.
[31] It is worth noting that the lower of the two figures indicates a national production of pig iron which is almost 120,000 tons (20 per cent) above Grosvenor's calculation.
[32] Lesley, *Guide,* p. 750.

group, the six ratios suggest that the changing position of Pennsylvania in the national market would be well described by a second degree equation. Such an equation was fitted to all six observations and used to estimate the desired ratios for years in which direct observations were not available. The results are shown in Table 5.5.[33]

When the relevant ratios in Table 5.5 are applied to the data of the Philadelphia convention, the indicated national production of pig iron is 574,000, 687,000, and 765,000 gross tons in 1845, 1846, and 1847 respectively. While these estimates will be used in the rest of the study, there is some reason to believe they may be low. As noted above, the Pennsylvania data excludes an unknown number of small firms. The results are also sensitive to the type of curve from which the ratios were interpolated. If the interpolation had been based on a linear rather than a second degree equation, estimated production in 1847 would have exceeded Carey's estimate by about 4 per cent. Although the 1846 figure would still have been less than Carey's, the difference would have been cut in half.

The data in Table 5.5 can also be used to obtain estimates for pig iron production in 1841, 1849, and 1850. The basis for the 1841 estimate is a survey conducted by the *Philadelphia Commercial List* which put production in Pennsylvania at 103,450 gross tons.[34] The *List* apparently gave special attention to the iron industry and its reports were considered reliable by both the *American Railroad Journal* and the *Merchants' Magazine*. Confidence in their 1841 estimate is enhanced by a *List* survey in 1847 which gives approximately the same output for Pennsylvania's anthracite furnaces as the tables of the Philadelphia convention.[35] If the *List's* figure is inflated by the 1841 ratio in Table 5.5, the resulting estimate of national production is 278,000 gross tons. The figure usually given for iron production in 1850 is the one contained in the Seventh Census. However, this datum represents output not of a calendar year but of the census year—June 1, 1849, to May 31, 1850. Since production appears to have declined rather steadily through 1849 and 1850,[36] use of the census figure as a calendar year estimate understates output in the former and overstates it in the latter one. The 1849 and 1850 estimates of production used in this paper are

---

[33] The equation is
$$Y = 2.9550 - 0.14259t + 0.004696t^2.$$ Year zero is 1839.
[34] Merchant, "Iron Trade," p. 231.
[35] Child, "Iron Trade," p. 592.
[36] Smith, "Manufacture of Iron," pp. 576–77.

TABLE 5.5. THE RELATIVE POSITION OF PENNSYLVANIA IN THE NATIONAL
OUTPUT OF PIG IRON

	1 Ratio of national to Pennsylvania production	2 Pennsylvania production as a share of national production (per cent)
1840	2.817	35.5
1841	2.689	37.2
1842	2.570	38.9
1843	2.460	40.7
1844	2.360	42.4
1845	2.269	44.1
1846	2.187	45.7
1847	2.115	47.3
1848	2.052	48.7
1849	1.999	50.0
1850	1.955	51.2

SOURCES: See text.

derived from the output data of the Philadelphia convention.[37] After
an appropriate correction of the understatement referred to previously,[38]
these figures on production in Pennsylvania were multiplied by the relevant ratios in Table 5.5. The resulting estimates of national output
were 627,000 gross tons in 1849 and 481,000 tons in 1850.

Of the remaining years during the decade of the forties, surveys by
the Home League are the basis for estimates in 1840 (347,000 gross
tons) and 1844 (486,000 gross tons). While the 1840 survey was far
from complete,[39] it appears to be closer to the truth than the Sixth
Census. The latter was widely criticized for under-reporting.[40] According to the Home League's "Committee on Iron," the iron industry
entered a depression at the close of 1840. Following that year, it said
in an 1842 report, iron manufacturers "suffered calamity and disaster.
Many works have already been stopped, and the workmen discharged."[41]

[37] *Ibid.*

[38] Smith's figures were increased by about 24 per cent to take account of
underenumeration in the survey. The correction factor was obtained by taking the
ratio of production in Pennsylvania as given by the Census to a weighted average
of Smith's 1849 and 1850 figures. The weights were 0.5833 for 1849 and 0.4167
for 1850.

[39] The Home League received reports from only 70 furnaces. Its estimate for
production in 1840 was the average product of these 70 multiplied by its estimate
of the total number of furnaces. *Proceedings of the National Convention for the
Protection of American Interests, Convened in the City of New York, April 5,
1842* (?), p. 21; hereafter referred to as Home League, *Proceedings.*

[40] Cf. Reeves, *Letter,* p. 809.

[41] Home League, *Proceedings,* p. 19.

Given the previous estimate of 278,000 tons as the national production of pig iron in 1841, the census figure is inconsistent with this widely reported depression in the iron industry. The Home League documents, commentary in journals, and the movement of iron prices also support Carey's contention that production fell off even further in 1842. Consequently, Carey's estimate of production in 1842 (230,000 gross tons) appears to be the best one available.[42] The estimates of output in 1843 and 1848 presented below are linear interpolations on adjacent years. The evidence which suggests that production declined in 1848 has already been cited. The upward movement in 1843 is far less certain. Despite the tariff of 1842, the price of pig iron continued to decline through August, 1843. Since 1842 and 1843 seem to have witnessed a widespread conversion to a hot blast, the further fall in prices may have been due to declining costs and may be consistent with the increase in demand suggested by some commentators.[43]

Data on production in 1851, 1852, and 1853 are also scanty. The 1851 estimate presented below appeared first in the *Annual Report of the Secretary of the Treasury* for 1851 and may have been based on a survey.[44] The 1852 estimate is taken from French; the increased production it suggests is consistent with the sharp rise in prices in the fall of that year.[45] The figure used for production in 1853 (723,000 gross tons) is taken from Raymond. There seems to be little doubt that 1853 was a boom year for the iron industry. The average price of pig iron in 1853 was 60 per cent above the previous year and stood at its highest level in a decade and a half.[46] The revised estimates for 1840–53 are presented in Table 5.6.

[42] Cf. Child, "Iron Trade," pp. 591–92. The formation of the Home League in 1841 and the holding of the Harrisburg convention of iron masters in 1842 also suggest that production was depressed. As Peter Temin has pointed out, such protectionist conventions tended to take place during periods of recession.

[43] French, *History,* p. 73; Reeves, *Letter,* p. 809. On the other hand, Merchant wrote, "In 1843, however, there was not much activity in the iron trade." "Iron Trade," p. 231.

[44] U.S. Congress, Senate, Doc. No. 11, 32d Cong., 1st Sess. (Ser. No. 614), p. 9; Pearse, *A Concise History,* p. 278, incorrectly attributed it to French.

[45] *History,* p. 145; A.I.S.A., *Annual Report, 1877,* p. 48. The A.I.S.A. *Annual Report of 1876* contains an estimate which is 8 per cent below the one cited by French. However, their figure is given in round numbers and was probably only a rough guess.

[46] Taussig, "The Tariff," p. 379; A.I.S.A., *Annual Report, 1877,* p. 49. French puts production during 1853–54 at 805,000 tons (*History,* p. 150). French's and Raymond's estimates together suggest that production rose rather sharply during the year 1853, ran at a rate exceeding 805,000 tons in the winter of 1853–54, and then declined sharply in 1854.

TABLE 5.6. THE REVISED ESTIMATES OF PIG IRON PRODUCTION (000 omitted)

		1 Gross tons	2 Net tons
1.	1840	347	389
2.	1841	278	311
3.	1842	230	258
4.	1843	358	401
5.	1844	486	544
6.	1845	574	643
7.	1846	687	769
8.	1847	765	857
9.	1848	696	780
10.	1849	627	702
11.	1850	481	539
12.	1851	413	463
13.	1852	541	606
14.	1853	723	810
15.	1854	657	736
16.	1855	700	784
17.	1856	789	883
18.	1857	713	798
19.	1858	630	705
20.	1859	751	841
21.	1860	821	920

SOURCES:
Lines 1–14. See text.
Lines 15–21. A.I.S.A., *Annual Report, 1877,* p. 16.

THE PRODUCTION AND CONSUMPTION OF RAILS

Rails were by far the most important form of iron used in railroad construction and maintenance. The American Iron and Steel Association published a series of annual estimates (beginning with the year 1849) of the production and consumption of this item.[47] Consumption in a given year was defined as domestic production plus imports; no adjustment was made for changes in inventories. With one modification, the A.I.S.A. series can be used in the preparation of the indexes discussed previously. In estimating annual consumption, the A.I.S.A. combined calendar year production data with fiscal year import data. To transform this hybrid into a calendar year series, adjoining fiscal year figures on imports were averaged and the averages used as estimates of calendar year imports.

Nothing comparable to the A.I.S.A. estimates is available on either the production or consumption of rails during the 1840's. It was therefore necessary to build a model which could be used to derive the desired

[47] A.I.S.A., *Annual Report, 1872–73,* p. 30.

Chart 5.1

THE PRODUCTION OF PIG IRON, 1840-1860

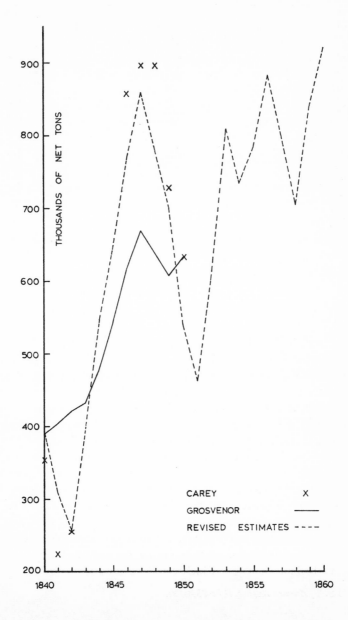

series from existing fragmentary data. There is an important conceptual difference between the derived estimates and the A.I.S.A. series: the A.I.S.A. figures are gross of inventory changes, while the estimates generated by the model are net of inventory changes. However, this element of incomparability does not significantly affect the analysis of trends in rail production and consumption, especially when the analysis is based on quinquennial averages. Moreover, the difference between the gross and net series reveals a hitherto neglected inventory cycle that will be discussed below.

The model of rail consumption involves the following variables:

R_t = tons of rails consumed in year t

R_{dt} = tons of rails produced domestically in year t

R_{ft} = tons of rails imported in year t

R_{jt} = tons of worn rails scrapped in year t

M_t = track-miles of rails laid in year t; a track-mile of rails is defined as one-half of the length of the rails in a mile of single track

w_t = the average weight of rails in year t per track-mile of rails laid in year t; i.e.,

$$w_t = \frac{R_t}{M_t}$$

M_{st} = track-miles of rails used in the construction of new single track in year t

M_{et} = track-miles of rails used in the construction of new extra track in year t; extra track refers to second and third tracks on a given line, sidings, etc.

M_{rt} = track-miles of rails used in the replacement of worn out rails in year t

t = time measured in years

The model can be set forth as follows:

(5.1) $$R_t = M_t w_t$$

(5.2) $$R_{dt} = R_t - R_{ft}$$

(5.3) $$M_t = M_{st} + M_{et} + \mathrm{M}_{rt}$$

(5.4) $$\frac{\overset{t}{\underset{0}{\Sigma}} M_{et}}{\overset{t}{\underset{0}{\Sigma}} M_{st}} = \alpha t$$

(5.5) $\qquad M_{rt} = \beta_1 M_{t-1} + \beta_2 M_{t-2} + \cdots + \beta_n M_{t-n}; \Sigma\beta_i = 1$

(5.6) $\qquad\qquad R_{jt} = \lambda_1 R_{t-1} + \lambda_2 R_{t-2} + \cdots + \lambda_n R_{t-n}$

Four of the variables in these equations, w_t, R_{ft}, M_{st}, and t, are determined exogenously.

Equations 5.3, 5.4, and 5.5 form a complete system and will be considered first. M_{st} (track-miles of rails used in the construction of new single track) was assumed to be equal to the annual increase (net miles added) in the miles of single road operated at the end of each calendar year. Several estimates of net miles added have been published. The most well known are the series taken from *Poor's Manual of Railroads* and the estimates of Armin Shuman published in the Tenth Census.[48] Unfortunately these sources give conflicting values for every year from 1830 through 1860, the differences between the two varying from 3 miles in 1839 to 2,200 miles in 1856. The discrepancies, as both E. R. Wicker and George Rogers Taylor recently pointed out, are due to the uncertainty of the dates of actual construction, differences in the definition of net miles added, and errors in reporting.[49]

Yet for the problem at hand, the discrepancies between Poor's and Shuman's series do not pose a severe problem. For one thing, the absolute annual differences during the decade 1840–49 are relatively small, averaging 58 miles per year in the first quinquennium and 292 miles in the second. Furthermore, annual discrepancies are offsetting so that the two series are quite close together in their estimates of construction per quinquennium. Poor's shows net mileage added as 2,075 miles for 1840–44 and 2,988 miles for 1845–49; Shuman's corresponding figures are 2,069 and 2,976. Consequently, despite differences in annual data, the two series give the same trend values. The variations introduced into M_t (total track-miles of rails laid) by use of one or the other of the two series is further damped by the fact that miles of single track added (M_{st}) is only one of the components of M_t. Track-miles of replacements (M_{rt}) were about half as large as M_{st} series. Thus, as Chart 5.2 demonstrates, use of either Poor's or Shuman's data results in negligible differences in the values of M_t for seven of the ten years

---

[48] Poor's series is published in *Historical Statistics* (1949), p. 200; Shuman's estimates are in *Census of Transportation, 1880,* Part I, pp. 288–89.

[49] E. R. Wicker, "Railroad Investment Before the Civil War," Conference on Income and Wealth, *Trends,* Table 1 and pp. 507–10; George Rogers Taylor, "Comment" (on Wicker's Paper), *ibid.,* pp. 525–37. See also the discussion in the next footnote.

between 1840 and 1849, and relatively small differences in the other three years. The series actually used to estimate M_t in the analysis presented below is the average of Poor's and Shuman's data on net miles added. Use of such an average series further reduces the effect of

Chart 5.2

THE VALUES OF M_t WHEN ESTIMATED FROM POOR'S DATA, SHUMAN'S DATA AND THE AVERAGE OF THE TWO SERIES

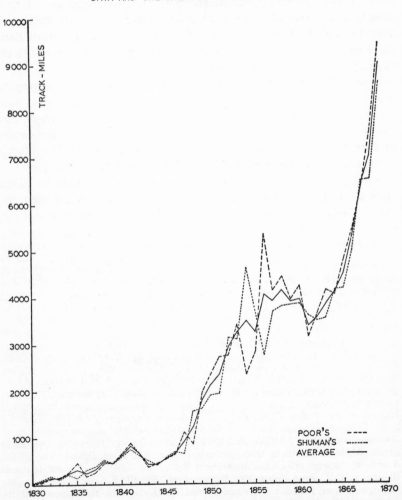

discrepancies in the underlying data on the value of M_t (see Chart 5.2).[50]

Equation 5.4 states that the ratio of total extra track to total single track increased linearly with time. The first date for which the aggregate mileage of extra track is available is 1876. In that year the ratio was 0.23.[51] Attempts to extrapolate the increase in extra track after 1876 to earlier years proved unsuccessful. Various fits either overstated or understated the value of M_{et} in earlier years by amounts too large to permit these equations to be used. Consequently, the value of α, the factor of proportionality in equation 5.4, was determined by fitting a straight line to the origin and 0.23. The decision to describe the movement from 1830 to 1876 by a straight line rather than a line linear in the logs was arbitrary. However, the difference in M_t produced by these alternatives is negligible for the years in question.

Equation 5.5 states that track-miles of rails required for replacement in any year was a weighted sum of the track-miles laid in previous years, the sum of the weights being equal to one. The various values of β_i (the weights) were determined from a model of rail wear. Fragmentary data indicate that the average length of life of an iron rail during the decades in question probably fell between 10 and 12 years. The data also suggest that few rails wore out in less than five years or lasted more than 20.[52] This pattern can be described by assuming that the wear of rails was log-normally distributed with a mean of 10.5 years

[50] If the true value of miles added fell between Poor's and Shuman's estimates, as seems likely for most years, the error in any given year, resulting from use of the average series would be less than or equal to one-half of the discrepancy in the values of M_t generated by Poor's and Shuman's estimates.

Albert Fishlow has put forth a substitute for both the Poor and census estimates of new construction during 1840–50. However, for reasons discussed in Appendix B, Fishlow's revision cannot be considered an improvement over those of Poor or Shuman.

[51] *Historical Statistics* (1949), p. 200.

[52] Sir I. Lowthian Bell, *The Iron Trade of the United Kingdom Compared with That of the Other Chief Iron-Making Nations* (London, 1886), p. 143; J. Elfreth Watkins, "The Development of American Rail and Track," U.S. Congress, House, *Annual Report of the Board of the Smithsonian Institution, 1889*; Misc. Doc. 224, Part 2, 51st Cong., 1st Sess. [Ser. No. 2780], *passim; Proceedings of the Annual Meeting of the American Iron and Steel Association,* February 11, 1875, paper by Z. E. Durfee; American Iron and Steel Association, *The Wearing Qualities of American Steel Rails* (Philadelphia, 1879); Charles Paine, "History of Iron Rails on the Michigan Southern and Northern Indiana Railway," *Transactions of the American Society of Civil Engineers* (1872); Philadelphia, Wilmington and Baltimore Rail Road Company, *Twenty-first Annual Report* (1859), p. 10; Michigan Central Rail Road Company, *Annual Reports,* 1847–1860, *passim*; Philadelphia and Reading Railroad, *Annual Reports, 1845–1860.*

Table 5.7. The Distribution of the Wear of Iron Rails

Age of rails in years	Proportion scrapped in given year
0–2	0.00
3	0.01
4	0.02
5	0.05
6	0.07
7	0.09
8	0.10
9	0.11
10	0.09
11	0.09
12	0.07
13	0.06
14	0.05
15	0.04
16	0.03
17	0.03
18	0.02
19	0.02
20–24	0.01
over 24	0.00

source: See text.

and a standard deviation of three years.[53] A discrete approximation of this distribution produced the weights shown in Table 5.7.

The rail consumption series (M_t) is fairly insensitive to changes in the assumed parameters of the distribution of rail wear and to a change in the form of that distribution from log-normal to normal. If the parameters are held constant and the form is changed (i.e., the assumed distribution is $N[10.5; 3]$), annual requirements change by an average

[53] The assumption of an average rail life of 10.5 years is supported by data in the 1880 *Census of Transportation*. The Census reports information on the road mileage, rail life, ton-miles, and passenger-miles of various companies. While many of these roads were laid with steel, 53 still had 90 per cent or more of their track laid with iron rails in 1880. The average length of life of rails in this sample of 53 companies was 10.48 years; the average amount of freight service per mile of track, 72,877 ton-miles, was quite close to the national average in 1860. The average life of rails was regressed on ton-miles per mile of road, passenger-miles per mile of road, weight of rails, and percentage of track in steel. Only ton-miles per mile of road was statistically significant. The linear equation between average rail life and this variable was:

$$L = 11.306 - 0.113 \, T$$
$$(0.062)$$

where T is measured in units of 10,000 ton-miles per mile of road. When Fishlow's estimate of ton-miles of freight transportation per mile of road in 1859 is substituted into the equation, the estimated average rail life in 1859 is 10.4 years. *Census of Transportation, 1880*, Tables III, VIII, and XI; Fishlow, *Economic Contribution*, Table A-5.

of less than 1 per cent. If the form and the mean of the distribution are held constant, but the standard deviation is reduced from three to two years (the assumed distribution is $LN[10.5; 2]$), annual replacements also change by less than 1 per cent. If the form of the distribution is changed and both the mean and standard deviation are reduced by one year (the assumed distribution is $N[9.5; 2]$), the average change in requirements is about 6 per cent (see Chart 5.3).

Chart 5.3

THE EFFECT OF CHANGES IN THE FORM AND PARAMETERS OF THE MODEL OF RAIL WEAR ON M_t

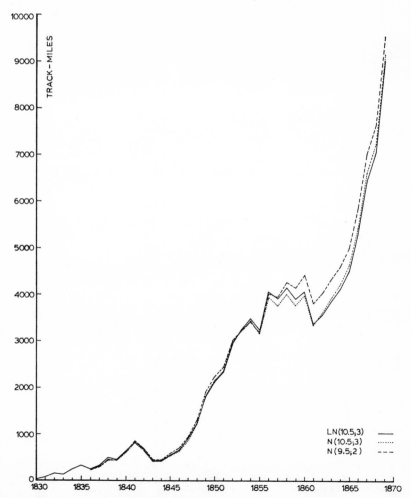

The estimates generated by equations 5.3, 5.4, and 5.5—total consumption of rails (M_t), track-miles of rails required for new construction ($M_{st} + M_{et}$), and track-miles required for replacement (M_{rt})—are shown in Table 5.8 and Chart 5.4. If correct, Chart 5.4 indicates that replacement became an important part of total rail consumption early in the 1840's. In 15 of the 30 years following 1839, replacements represented more than 40 per cent of total rail requirements; in five

TABLE 5.8. THE ESTIMATED CONSUMPTION OF RAILS, 1830–69 (in track-miles)

		1 New Construction ($M_{st} + M_{et}$)	2 Replacements (M_{rt})	3 Total consumption (M_t)
1.	1830	32	0	32
2.	1831	87	0	87
3.	1832	166	0	166
4.	1833	138	0	138
5.	1834	241	2	243
6.	1835	314	5	319
7.	1836	240	11	251
8.	1837	303	22	325
9.	1838	462	38	500
10.	1839	416	58	474
11.	1840	542	83	625
12.	1841	715	111	826
13.	1842	547	142	689
14.	1843	259	180	439
15.	1844	221	222	443
16.	1845	309	269	578
17.	1846	365	321	686
18.	1847	531	370	901
19.	1848	823	411	1,234
20.	1849	1,358	447	1,805
21.	1850	1,647	477	2,124
22.	1851	1,837	509	2,346
23.	1852	2,399	554	2,953
24.	1853	2,647	624	3,271
25.	1854	2,772	726	3,498
26.	1855	2,403	866	3,269
27.	1856	3,028	1,042	4,070
28.	1857	2,672	1,255	3,927
29.	1858	2,653	1,493	4,146
30.	1859	2,156	1,750	3,906
31.	1860	2,064	2,007	4,071
32.	1861	1,118	2,275	3,393
33.	1862	1,056	2,525	3,581
34.	1863	1,103	2,769	3,872
35.	1864	1,148	2,975	4,123
36.	1865	1,339	3,164	4,503
37.	1866	2,014	3,295	5,309
38.	1867	3,022	3,414	6,436
39.	1868	3,556	3,503	7,059
40.	1869	5,424	3,605	9,029

SOURCES: See text.

of these years, replacements accounted for more than two-thirds of requirements. Another important feature of Chart 5.4 is the contrast between the continuous upward movement of replacements and the wide fluctuations in rails used for new construction. The magnitude of, and the continuous upward movement in, replacements produce a

Chart 5.4

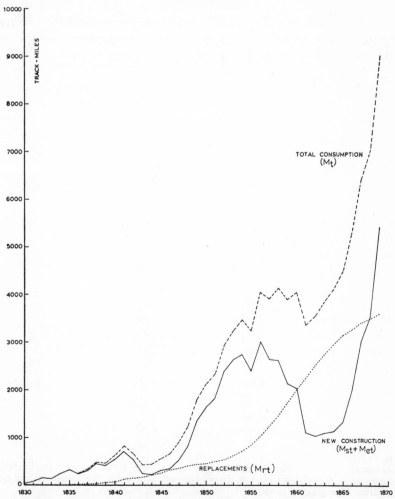

ESTIMATED QUANTITIES OF RAILS USED FOR NEW CONSTRUCTION AND REPLACEMENTS

pattern in total consumption which is markedly different from the pattern of new construction.

Before making use of the data presented in Table 5.8 and Chart 5.4, it is necessary to evaluate the realism of these estimates—that is, to test the empirical validity of the series generated by the model. The basis for this test is the consistency of various estimates produced by the model with data not used in the estimation of its parameters. One of the magnitudes implicit in the model is the ratio of rails used for new construction to total rail consumption. The only independent evidence available on this relationship comes from the report of a survey published in the *Bulletin of the American Iron Association*. According to this report, aggregate new construction requirements planned for 1856 represented 66 per cent of planned aggregate rail consumption.[54] For the same year the model "predicts" 74 per cent. A second ratio implicit in the model is that of annual rail replacements to the total mileage of main track. From the mid-fifties to the early seventies the iron industry used 8 per cent of the total mileage as the "rule-of-thumb" estimate of the amount of rails required annually for replacement.[55] Over the period from 1855 to 1869 the model indicates an average ratio of annual replacements to total track mileage of 7.64 per cent.

The A.I.S.A. estimates of rail consumption during 1849–69, the first two decades for which these estimates are available, provide a more substantial test of the model. If the model is empirically valid, the pattern of consumption represented by the M_t series on total track-miles of rails laid should conform closely to the pattern shown by the A.I.S.A. series on tons of rails consumed. The relationship between the two series is shown in Chart 5.5. The general trend depicted by both series is similar. The coefficient of correlation between the M_t and A.I.S.A. estimates is 0.93 and both it and the linear coefficient are significant at the 1 per cent level. Still, there are large deviations between the two series for a number of years (especially 1852, 1853, and 1857–63), and it seems evident that the value of the correlation coefficient is heavily influenced by the observations in the latter portions of the two series. The fact that the two series do not coincide in year to year estimates

---

[54] A.I.S.A., *Bulletin of the American Iron Association* (1856–57), p. 35.

[55] See, for example, A.I.S.A., *Bulletin* (1856), p. 28; and report by Z. E. Durfee in *Proceedings of the Annual Meeting of the American Iron and Steel Association, February 11, 1875*. The A.I.S.A. survey cited in the following note put replacements in 1856 at 5.1 per cent of the mileage of main track in existence at the end of 1855. The model "predicts" 5.4 per cent for the same year.

Chart 5.5

A COMPARISON BETWEEN M_t AND THE A.I.S.A. DATA

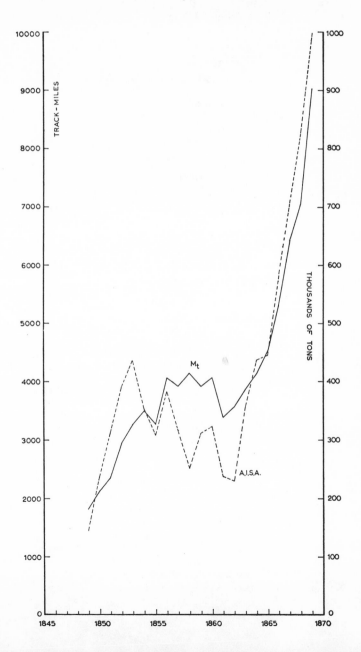

does not necessarily imply errors in the model, even if it is assumed the A.I.S.A. figures are perfectly accurate. It must be remembered that the A.I.S.A. series is gross of inventory changes while the M_t estimates are net. The two series would coincide exactly only if: (1) the average weight of rails remained constant and (2) inventory levels did not change over the two decades covered by Chart 5.5. However, it is clear that neither of these conditions obtained.

Data on rail weights are scanty, but the following information is available:

1. The average weight of rails on the main track of railroads in existence in 1840 showed marked regional differences (see Column 2 of Table 5.9). This factor combined with shifts in the regional focus of new construction led to a considerable fluctuation in the over-all average weight of the rails laid each year (w_t) from 1830 through 1839 (see Table 5.10).

2. There was a considerable rise in the over-all average weight of rails on main tracks between 1840 and 1869.[56] Regional differences in rail weights narrowed greatly over the same period (see Column 3 of Table 5.9).

3. The average weight of rails on siding, branch lines, and second track was generally below that of main track. Thus 37 per cent of the

---

[56] In 1856 the A.I.S.A. published the findings of a survey of 61 roads with main track totaling 5,840 miles at the end of 1855. The average weight of the rails on the roads of the sample was 58.11 pounds per yard, a figure somewhat higher than the average for 1869 given in Table 5.9. This high average weight appears to be due to the fact that the sample was biased toward large roads which tended to use heavier than average rails. The average length of the roads in the sample is 96 miles—a figure 94 per cent greater than the average length of all roads in 1850 and 44 per cent greater than the national average in 1860. A.I.S.A., *Bulletin of the American Iron Association* (1856), p. 35; U.S. Census Office, *Preliminary Report of the Eighth Census* (Washington, 1862), Table 38.

An alternative estimate of the average weight of rails in the late fifties can be obtained from the sample of 53 roads drawn from the 1880 *Census of Transportation*. As already noted, the average intensity of road utilizations in the sample was quite close to the national average in 1859 (see footnote 53 in this chapter); and the average length of the roads in the sample was within 14 per cent of the national average in 1860. A regression between the weight of rails and ton-miles per mile of road computed from the sample data produced the equation:

$$W = 53.91 + 0.085\,T$$
$$(0.046)$$

where T is measured in units of 10,000 ton-miles of freight transportation per mile of road and W in pounds per yard. Using the 1859 value of T computed from Fishlow's data, the estimated average rail weight in 1859 is 54.6 pounds. *Ibid.*, Table 38; Fishlow, *Economic Contribution*, Table A–5; footnote 53 of this chapter.

siding on the Baltimore and Ohio in 1853 was laid with plate rails and another 10 per cent with a mixture of plate and "T" or "U" rails. Similarly, the rails on the second track of the Syracuse and Utica in the early fifties were 9 pounds per yard (13 per cent) lighter than the rails on the main track. Again, while rails on the main track of railroads in Massachusetts in 1860 varied between 48 and 66 pounds, those on

TABLE 5.9. AVERAGE WEIGHT OF RAILS ON MAIN TRACK IN 1840 AND 1869
(pounds per yard of rail)

1 Region	2 1840	3 1869
I	51.9	57.8
II	28.1	58.2
III	19.3	54.5
IV	15.0	56.5
V	36.0	55.6
VI	—	55.7
National average	27.6	56.8

SOURCES AND NOTES:

Column 1. The regions are those given by the Census of 1880. The states included in each region are as follows: *Region I*. Maine, Vermont, New Hampshire, Massachusetts, Rhode Island, Connecticut. *Region II*. New York, Pennsylvania, Ohio, Michigan, Indiana, Maryland, Delaware, New Jersey. *Region III*. Virginia, West Virginia, Kentucky, Tennessee, Mississippi, Alabama, Georgia, Florida, North Carolina, South Carolina. *Region IV*. Illinois, Iowa, Wisconsin, Missouri, Minnesota. *Region V*. Louisiana, Arkansas, Indian Territory. *Region VI*. All other states and territories.

Column 2. Computed from the tables compiled by Francis Anthony Chevalier de Gerstner and published in the *Journal of the Franklin Institute* during 1840 by Gerstner's collaborator, L. Klein. This important source of information on railroads up to 1840 was rediscovered by Albert Fishlow who brought it to my attention. The tables provide information on the rails of 95 per cent of the rail network in early 1840. Plate rails which are given by dimension were converted to a weight equivalent on the basis of the conversion ratios of Frederic Overman. L. Klein, "Railroads in the United States," *Journal of the Franklin Institute,* Vol. 30 (1840), pp. 89–102, 227–30, 301–7; Frederic Overman, *The Manufacture of Iron* (Philadelphia, 1850), p. 492.

Column 3. Computed from a sample drawn from Henry V. Poor, *Manual of the Railroads of the United States for 1869–70* (New York, 1869). The sample contained railroads representing 83 per cent of the main track reported by the Census at the end of 1869. The data in this volume were supplemented by information taken from *Poor's Manual of Railroads, 1870–71* and from the *Census of Transportation, 1880*.

branch roads were as low as 37.5 pounds and no branch road had rails heavier than 60 pounds.[57]

4. There is a considerable discussion in the technical literature of a movement away from the use of heavy rails during the fifties. Colburn and Holly, writing in 1858, said that "the preference is now almost invariably in favor of lighter iron, as the heavy rails wear out soonest." The switch, they held, was due to the poor wear of heavy rails—a phenomenon they attributed to the inability of the existing equipment in rolling mills to process adequately the large iron piles from which heavy rails were rolled. This turn to light rails is illustrated by the Philadelphia, Wilmington, and Baltimore Railroad which in 1855 began substituting 50 and 51 pound rails for the 65 pound rails it had used previously. Further support for the tendency is to be found in a sample of New York railroads. According to this sample, which covers lines with 52 per cent of the state's track, the average weight of rails laid rose from 56 pounds in 1849 to 68 pounds in 1851 and then declined to 59 pounds in 1855.[58]

It appears likely that the downward trend in rail weights during the fifties was largely confined to the New England and Middle Atlantic states where most of the heavy rails were laid. In such states as Michigan, Illinois, and Indiana as well as in the South, the trend of rail weights appears to have been mainly an upward one. The early roads in the states west of Ohio—the Michigan Central during the midforties, the Galena and Chicago Union at the end of the forties and the beginning of the fifties, the New Albany and Salem prior to 1854—were laid largely with plate.[59] While the experience of the eastern roads may have prevented widespread use of rails over 60 pounds, the roads in the Midwest increasingly turned to the use of rails weighing in the

---

[57] Baltimore and Ohio R.R. Company, *Twenty-Seventh Annual Report* (1853), Appendix I; New York State, Assembly, *Annual Report of the State Engineer and Surveyor in Relationship to Railroads,* Assembly Docs. 1852, Vol. 1, No. 27, p. 138; Massachusetts, *Returns of Railroad Corporations together with Abstracts of Same Prepared by the Secretary of the Commonwealth,* Public Docs., 1860, No. 46.

[58] Zerah Colburn and Alexander L. Holly, *The Permanent Way* (New York, 1858), p. 80. Philadelphia, Wilmington, and Baltimore Rail Road Company, *Twenty-first Annual Report,* p. 10; New York State, Assembly, *Annual Report of the Railroad Commissioners, 1855,* Ass. Docs. 1856, Vol. 2, No. 12, Part 1, pp. 32–33; cf. John B. Jervis, *Railway Property* (New York, 1861), pp. 135–36.

[59] Michigan Central Railroad, *First Annual Report, 1847,* pp. 8–9; *Third Annual Report 1849,* pp. 18–19; *Fifth Annual Report, 1851,* pp. 15–16; *Census of Transportation, 1880,* pp. 330–31; Frank F. Hargrave, *A Pioneer Indiana Railroad* (Indianapolis, 1932), pp. 55, 62.

TABLE 5.10. AVERAGE WEIGHT OF RAILS LAID ON MAIN TRACK BY YEARS, 1830–40

Year	1 Average weight per yard of rail (lbs.)	2 Average weight per mile of single track (net tons)
1830	13.5	23.7
1831	14.7	25.9
1832	17.3	30.4
1833	28.7	50.5
1834	37.9	66.7
1835	30.1	52.9
1836	24.3	42.8
1837	25.7	45.2
1838	34.1	60.0
1839	30.8	54.3

SOURCES AND NOTES:

Computed from Gerstner's data on the assumption that rails were laid on roads over a two-year period ending in the year the roads were opened. Klein, "Railroads," pp. 89–102, 227–30, 301–7.

neighborhood of 56 pounds. The only general decline in rail weights between 1840 and 1869 appears to have been the one induced by the shortages of the Civil War years.[60]

The foregoing information together with data culled from the documents of some state railroad commissions and scattered reports of individual roads provided the basis for estimates of the trend in average rail weights in each of the six geographic regions into which the 1880 Census of Transportation divided the nation. The regional averages, weighted by each region's share of the total miles of new rails laid in each year, produced the series of Table 5.11.

With the data shown in Table 5.11, one can adjust the A.I.S.A. estimates of the consumption of rails for changes in the average weight of rails. This is done in Table 5.12 by dividing the weight of rails into the A.I.S.A. estimates. The procedure transforms the A.I.S.A. series from units of tons to units of track-miles. In addition to eliminating the weight factor, it has the virtue of making the A.I.S.A. and M_t series directly comparable. The adjusted estimates and the M_t series are juxtaposed in Chart 5.6. A comparison of Chart 5.6 with Chart 5.5 shows that fluctuations in rail weights do not explain the absence of coincidence. Elimination of the weight factor does not improve the relationship between the estimates generated by the model and the

[60] Watkins, "Development," p. 679.

TABLE 5.11. ESTIMATED AVERAGE WEIGHT OF RAILS LAID ON TRACK, 1830–69
(in pounds per yard of rail)

		1 Average weight of rails on main track	2 Average weight of rails on all track
1.	1830	13.5	13.5
2.	1831	14.7	14.7
3.	1832	17.3	17.3
4.	1833	28.7	28.4
5.	1834	37.9	37.5
6.	1835	30.1	29.8
7.	1836	24.3	24.1
8.	1837	25.7	25.4
9.	1838	34.1	33.8
10.	1839	30.8	30.5
11.	1840	30.7	30.3
12.	1841	30.8	30.4
13.	1842	37.3	36.7
14.	1843	32.8	32.1
15.	1844	39.4	38.6
16.	1845	42.6	41.8
17.	1846	43.6	42.8
18.	1847	48.2	47.3
19.	1848	49.8	48.8
20.	1849	51.5	50.5
21.	1850	51.9	50.8
22.	1851	53.8	52.6
23.	1852	54.6	53.4
24.	1853	55.4	54.1
25.	1854	54.2	52.9
26.	1855	55.0	53.5
27.	1856	54.5	53.1
28.	1857	54.8	53.3
29.	1858	54.8	53.3
30.	1859	53.8	52.2
31.	1860	54.3	52.6
32.	1861	54.4	52.7
33.	1862	51.0	49.4
34.	1863	51.1	49.4
35.	1864	51.9	50.2
36.	1865	53.8	52.0
37.	1866	55.1	53.2
38.	1867	56.3	54.4
39.	1868	57.6	55.6
40.	1869	59.5	57.4

SOURCES AND NOTES:

Column 1. Lines 1–10. Table 5.10. Lines 11–40. See the text for both sources and method. I am indebted to Albert Fishlow for criticism that led me to correct my original estimates of the course of average rail weight.

Column 2. Siding and other extra track were assumed to have been laid with rails that were an average of 20 per cent lighter than those on main track. The average weight of rails on all track follows from this assumption, the entries in Column 1 and the shares of main and extra track in the total track laid down each year as derived from equations 5.3, 5.4, and 5.5.

A.I.S.A. figures. The divergences between the two series are smaller in Chart 5.6 than in Chart 5.5 for some years, but larger in others.

The issue as to whether the residual discrepancy can be explained by inventory fluctuations still remains. That inventory levels must have changed between 1849 and 1869 seems apparent. Since consumption of rails increased sixfold over the 21 years, constant inventories imply an 85 per cent drop in the inventory-consumption ratio. Even if the stocks on hand at the end of 1848 equalled the whole consumption requirement of that year, the stocks in 1869 would have been reduced to a seven-week supply by the rapid rise in consumption. Beyond this deductive argument there are a few scattered items of direct testimony

TABLE 5.12. THE INVENTORY CYCLE IN RAILS (in track-miles)

		1	2	3	4	5	6
		Net consumption of rails in track-miles (M_t)	Gross consumption of rails in net tons (A.I.S.A. data)	Weight of rails in net tons per track-mile	Gross consumption of rails in track-miles Col. 2 ÷ Col. 3	Change in inventories Col. 4 − Col. 1	Cumulative change in inventories Sum of Col. 5
1.	1849	1,805	142,590	88.84	1,605	− 200	− 200
2.	1850	2,124	236,798	89.41	2,648	524	324
3.	1851	2,346	311,153	92.55	3,362	1,016	1,340
4.	1852	2,953	389,250	93.92	4,144	1,191	2,531
5.	1853	3,271	436,981	95.21	4,590	1,319	3,850
6.	1854	3,498	354,245	93.04	3,807	309	4,159
7.	1855	3,269	308,481	94.22	3,274	5	4,164
8.	1856	4,070	380,898	93.40	4,078	8	4,172
9.	1857	3,927	314,998	93.76	3,360	− 567	3,605
10.	1858	4,146	251,138	93.72	2,680	−1,466	2,139
11.	1859	3,906	310,738	91.92	3,381	− 525	1,614
12.	1860	4,071	323,037	92.56	3,490	− 581	1,033
13.	1861	3,393	237,605	92.75	2,562	− 831	202
14.	1862	3,581	229,258	86.88	2,639	− 942	− 740
15.	1863	3,872	357,250	86.97	4,108	236	− 504
16.	1864	4,123	438,261	88.35	4,961	838	334
17.	1865	4,503	446,895	91.53	4,882	379	713
18.	1866	5,309	582,137	93.65	6,216	907	1,620
19.	1867	6,436	704,608	95.71	7,362	926	2,546
20.	1868	7,059	825,044	97.77	8,439	1,380	3,926
21.	1869	9,029	998,034	100.98	9,883	854	4,780

SOURCES AND NOTES:

Column 1. See Table 5.8

Column 2. A.I.S.A., *Annual Report, 1873,* p. 30. The fiscal year import figures were averaged and the averages were used as estimates of calendar year imports.

Column 3. The entries in Column 2 of Table 5.14 were converted into net tons per track-mile by multiplying them by 1.76.

which suggest that inventories not only varied but varied substantially in relatively short periods of time. Thus a statement prepared by Senator William Bigler of Pennsylvania indicated that inventory accumulations during 1853 and 1854 amounted to approximately one year's consumption.[61]

The hypothesis that the discrepancy depicted by Chart 5.6 is due to inventory fluctuations can be tested by examining the inventory cycle implied by the differences between the M_t and the adjusted A.I.S.A. series. The necessary calculation is performed in Table 5.12 and the result is shown in Chart 5.7.[62] The most significant feature of this derived cycle in rail inventories is the close conformity with the cycle in new railroad construction, also shown in Chart 5.7. The diagram indicates that inventories rose during the building booms of the early fifties and the post-Civil War years. It also indicates that inventories declined after 1856 when the pace of new construction slackened. The striking conformity between the cycle in inventories and new construction is fully in keeping with the known conditions of railroad building and provides additional evidence of the consistency between the estimates generated by the model and the available data.

The circumstances under which rails were produced and distributed strongly suggest conformity between the movement of inventories and new construction. Rails were unstandardized in the fifties and sixties. They varied widely in weight (from as little as 18 to over 150 tons per track-mile), shape ("H", "T", "U", "I", inverted "T", fish-belly, box, etc.), basic structure (single, compound, continuous, etc.), and type of material used (anthracite iron, charcoal iron, cast iron, hammered iron, steel, etc.). Since the properties of the various types of rails were not well known, opinions about them differed markedly and changed rapidly.[63] As a result, rails were usually produced to fill specific orders and were not generally kept in stock by producers.[64] This made it necessary for railroads to order rails well in advance of anticipated use. To the extent that rail inventories accumulated they were held

[61] *Merchants' Magazine,* Vol. 37 (October, 1857), p. 497.

[62] Unfortunately the size of the rail inventory at the end of 1848 is unknown. The absence of this information does not affect the pattern of the inventory cycle but only its position. The addition of the 1848 inventory would merely shift the curve shown in Chart 5.7 upward.

[63] Cf. Watkins, "Development"; Swank, *History,* Chap. 48; *American Railroad Journal,* Vol. 24 (March 8, 15, and Aug. 30, 1851), pp. 145, 163, 547.

[64] See the ads in various issues of the *American Railroad Journal* by railroads desiring to place orders for rails; cf. A.I.S.A., *Annual Report, 1883,* p. 30.

Chart 5.6

A COMPARISON BETWEEN M_t AND THE A.I.S.A.
DATA ADJUSTED FOR CHANGES IN THE
AVERAGE WEIGHT OF RAILS

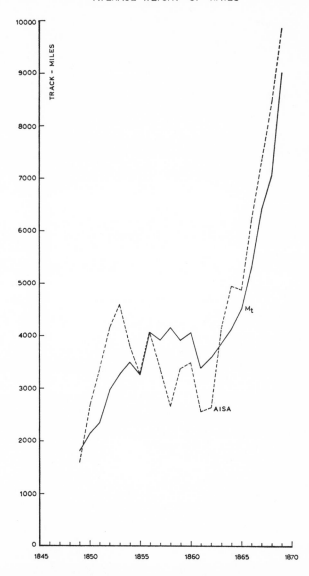

Chart 5.7

THE INVENTORY CYCLE IN RAILS

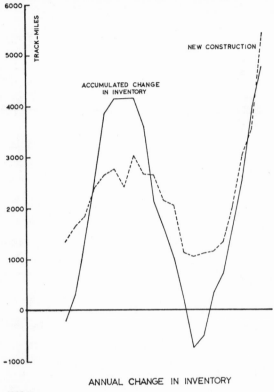

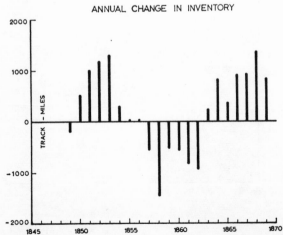

not primarily by producers but by consumers. The absence of producers' stocks that could serve as central depositories for railroads made aggregate inventories larger than they would otherwise have been.

The length of the time interval between order and delivery and the uncertainty of delivery schedules also suggest that inventories rose and fell with new construction. Consumers and producers of rail were separated by great distances and had to operate under conditions of poor communication and indefinite transportation schedules. This was particularly true in the case of rails imported from England (the bulk of consumption during the fifties). Deliveries of imports were subject to all the vagaries that then beset ocean transportation. Under these circumstances railroads in the process of expanding their lines ran a considerable risk of interruption if they failed to increase rail inventories beyond the levels needed for replacements. Such interruptions in construction activity were quite costly. In the case of the Illinois Central, for example, the labor cost involved in the loss of two days of activity per month (or 24 days per year) brought about by an absence of rails would have exceeded the interest cost of carrying a seven-month inventory of rails.[65] Additional costs of interruptions were the increase in interest payments necessitated by stretchouts of loans and other implied costs of delayed income.[66]

Chart 5.7 not only indicates that inventory cycles were correlated with new construction but that inventories were quite volatile, rising more rapidly than new construction in upswings and falling more rapidly in downswings. This relationship is also consistent with avail-

[65] The work force of the Illinois Central varied between 6,000 and 10,000 men, of which about 10 per cent were in the track-laying crew. The wages of unskilled labor ranged between $1.25 and $1.50 per day. Using the median values, the annual labor cost of two days' idleness each month would have been $26,400. Construction proceeded at an average of 169 miles per year. Since 56-pound iron was used, an average of 14,900 gross tons of rails were required each year. The average price of rails in 1851 was $45.63 per gross ton, making the total value of a seven-month inventory of rails $396,000. At an interest rate of 6 per cent (the company's 6 per cent bonds sold at a premium in 1851 and 1852), the interest charge on such an inventory would have been $23,700 per year. Howard Gray Brownson, *History of the Illinois Central Railroad to 1870* (Urbana, Ill., 1915), pp. 47, 59, 61, 62, 121, 122; Gates, *The Illinois Central Railroad*, pp. 94–98; A.I.S.A., *Annual Report, 1877,* p. 49.

It is interesting to note that the "first thing done [by the Illinois Central] was to buy the iron for the whole road at $45 per ton." Brownson, *History,* p. 59.

[66] Rails may also have been more expensive when ordered in small rather than in large quantities. Consequently the savings involved in ordering a year's supply of rails may have compensated for the cost of holding such a supply in inventory.

able information. As a boom in new construction developed and rail output pressed against capacity, the time interval between orders and deliveries increased. Given the high cost of interruptions, such stretch-outs appear to have led to a rise in the inventory-consumption ratio. This process continued well into the period when rails became more standardized and imports declined in importance. According to the American Iron and Steel Association, "so urgent in 1881 [the year before the peak of the third great railroad construction boom] were the wants of owners of established roads and projectors of new roads that they bought many tons of rails which were not laid until 1882." [67] The general impulse to increase the inventory-consumption ratio during the upswing in new constructions was reinforced during 1850–54 by a sharp rise in rail prices. In January, 1850, rails sold for $47 per ton; in October, 1854, the price was $81 per ton.[68] While prices of rails fell during the construction boom of the sixties, the rise in the inventory-consumption ratio during the early years of the boom is attributable to the low level to which stocks had been pushed during the war stringency. By 1862, rail stocks were below the level of 1851, although total consumption (replacements plus new construction) in 1862 was twice as great as in the former year.[69]

The fourth test of the model involves equation 5.6 which states that the tons of rails scrapped in a given year was a linear function of the tons of rails laid in previous years. The parameters of the equation (λ_i) are implied by the distribution of rail wear (see Table 5.7). The series generated by the sixth equation is shown in Table 5.13 and Chart 5.8. Alternative estimates based on independent sources are shown in Chart 5.8 for two years. They are 96,600 tons in 1856 and 325,000 tons in 1866.[70] The model deviates from the first estimate by 12 per cent and from the second by only 6 per cent.

---

[67] A.I.S.A., *Annual Report, 1882*, p. 27.

[68] *Ibid.*, p. 54.

[69] Chart 5.7 indicates that the ratio of inventory to consumption fell in 1869.

[70] The 1866 estimate was prepared by the A.I.S.A. and appears in their *Annual Report, 1868*, p. 16.

The 1856 estimate was computed from A.I.S.A. and census data. In 1856 rolling mills which produced 70.90 per cent of all rolled iron consumed 65,921 net tons of scrap, indicating that total scrap consumption of rolling mills was 92,971 tons. In 1869, however, the ratio of the total scrap consumed by the iron industry to scrap consumed by rolling mills was 1.423. Applying this ratio to 1856, and deducting imported scrap, total domestic production of scrap is 120,700 tons. According to the A.I.S.A., rails represented 80 per cent of all domestically generated scrap. Hence, the figure of 96,600 tons of rails scrapped in 1856.

TABLE 5.13. RAILS SCRAPPED, 1840–69 (thousands of net tons)

Year	Rails scrapped	Year	Rails scrapped
1840	4	1855	68
1841	5	1856	85
1842	7	1857	107
1843	9	1858	130
1844	11	1859	156
1845	14	1860	181
1846	17	1861	208
1847	19	1862	232
1848	23	1863	256
1849	25	1864	276
1850	28	1865	293
1851	31	1866	305
1852	36	1867	315
1853	43	1868	322
1854	54	1869	330

SOURCE: See text.

Another figure implicit in the model is the average weight of all the rails in use on main tracks in 1869. It forms the basis for the final test. As previously noted, a sample drawn from *Poor's Manual* covering 83 per cent of the mileage in use at the end of 1869 (see Table 5.9) revealed that the average weight of the rails on main tracks was 56.8 pounds. For the same year the model "predicts" an average weight of 55.3 pounds. The model differs from the sample average by only 2.6 per cent.

A.I.S.A., *Bulletin* (1858), p. 173, and Tables D, G, and J; *Census of Manufacturing, 1870,* pp. 601, 605, 607, 608, 625.

The A.I.S.A. put forward another and somewhat higher estimate of the amount of rails scrapped in 1856; 100,000 gross tons. This estimate appears to have been based on the survey of 61 railroads conducted by the Association in early 1856. The roads covered indicated that they planned to scrap 300 miles of track during the year. The Association inflated the last figure by an estimated ratio of the total miles of track in the nation to the miles of track in the sample. The computation indicated that 1,155 track-miles of rails were scrapped in 1856. This estimate differs from the figure produced by the model (1,042 track-miles) by only 9 per cent. The Association then proceeded to convert the mileage estimate into a tonnage estimate on the assumption that the average weight of rails scrapped in 1856 was equal to the average weight of rails then on the track. This biased their estimate upward. For the average age of rails scrapped was greater than the average age of rails still on the track. Given the upward trend in rail weights between 1840 and 1855, the average weight of rails scrapped must have been below the average weight of rails still in use in 1856. A.I.S.A., *Bulletin* (1856–58), pp. 35, 173; cf. note 56 of this chapter.

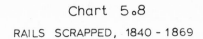

Chart 5.8

RAILS SCRAPPED, 1840 - 1869

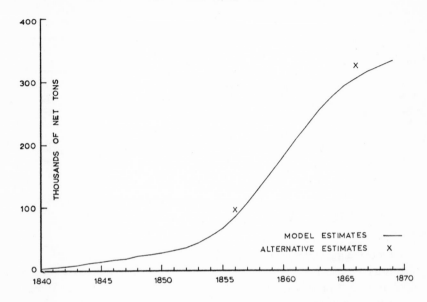

RAILS AND THE DOMESTIC CONSUMPTION OF IRON

The total domestic consumption of crude iron (C_t) can be divided into two parts: crude iron consumed by domestic manufacturers of iron products (C_{mt}), and crude iron used in the production of imported iron products (C_{it}). A major factor in overstatements of the influence of the demand for rails on the pre-Civil War development of the American iron industry has been the tendency to confuse domestic pig iron production (P_t) with C_{mt} and C_t. As Table 5.14 and Chart 5.9 show, there was a significant difference between domestic pig iron production and both the amount of crude iron consumed by the iron industry and the total consumption of crude iron.[71] Over the 21-year period from 1840 through 1860, C_{mt} exceeded P_t by over 20 per cent and C_t exceeded P_t by 59 per cent. Moreover, the gap between P_t and both C_{mt} and C_t increased as the period wore on. While C_{mt} was only 7 per cent greater

[71] This table understates C_t because of the ommission of imported finished iron products such as pots, anchors, etc. The omitted items probably represent less than 5 per cent of the total consumption of crude iron.

Chart 5.9

THE   PRODUCTION   OF   PIG   IRON   AND
THE   CONSUMPTION   OF   CRUDE IRON

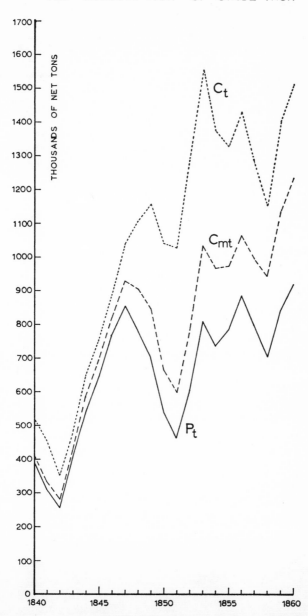

TABLE 5.14. THE PRODUCTION AND CONSUMPTION OF CRUDE IRON, 1840–60 (in thousands of net tons)

	1	2	3	4	5	6	7	8	9
	Production of domestic pig iron (P_i)	Old rails scrapped	Other domestic scrap Col. 2 × 0.25	Domestic production of crude iron Col. 1 + Col. 3	Imports of pig iron	Imports of scrap	Crude iron consumed by domestic iron industry (C_{mi}) Col. 4 + Col. 5 + Col. 6	Pig equivalent of imported rolled and hammered bar iron (C_{ii})	Domestic consumption of crude iron (C_i) Col. 7 + Col. 8
1. 1840	389	4	1	394	10	1	405	109	514
2. 1841	311	5	1	317	17	1	335	122	457
3. 1842	258	7	2	267	13	1	281	72	353
4. 1843	401	9	2	412	11	1	424	50	474
5. 1844	544	11	3	558	24	4	586	64	650
6. 1845	643	14	4	661	29	5	695	61	756
7. 1846	769	17	4	790	29	2	821	70	891
8. 1847	857	19	5	881	44	5	930	110	1,040
9. 1848	780	23	6	809	88	9	906	200	1,106
10. 1849	702	25	6	733	101	11	845	313	1,158
11. 1850	539	28	7	574	80	10	664	376	1,040
12. 1851	463	31	8	502	89	9	600	426	1,026
13. 1852	606	36	9	651	115	10	776	518	1,294
14. 1853	810	43	11	864	154	16	1,034	524	1,558
15. 1854	736	53	13	802	145	19	966	411	1,377
16. 1855	784	68	17	869	88	16	973	355	1,328
17. 1856	883	85	21	989	62	12	1,063	370	1,433
18. 1857	798	107	27	932	53	9	994	286	1,280
19. 1858	705	130	33	868	64	10	942	215	1,157
20. 1859	841	156	39	1,036	81	11	1,128	275	1,403
21. 1860	920	181	45	1,146	81	9	1,236	278	1,514
				Period Averages					
22. 1840–44	381	7	2	390	15	2	406	83	490
23. 1845–49	750	20	5	775	58	6	839	151	990
24. 1850–54	631	38	10	679	117	13	808	451	1,259
25. 1855–59	802	109	27	939	70	12	1,020	300	1,320
26. 1855–60	822	121	30	973	72	11	1,056	297	1,353
27. 1840–49	565	13	3	582	37	4	623	117	740
28. 1850–59	717	74	19	809	93	12	914	376	1,290
29. 1850–60	735	83	21	839	92	12	943	367	1,310
30. 1840–60	654	50	13	717	66	8	791	248	1,039

SOURCES AND NOTES:

Column 1. Table 5.6.

Column 2. Table 5.13.

Column 3. The ratio 0.25 is based on A.I.S.A. data in Lesley, *Guide,* p. 760, and *Annual Report, 1868,* p. 16.

Column 5. Colwell, "Special Reports," pp. 330–31. Fiscal year imports were averaged to obtain estimates of calendar year imports.

Column 6. *Annual Reports of Foreign Commerce and Navigation.* Fiscal year imports were averaged to obtain estimates of calendar year imports.

Column 8. *Ibid.;* note to Column 6 of Table 5.15. Fiscal year imports were averaged to obtain estimates of calendar year imports.

Lines may not add across because of rounding.

than P_t during 1840–44, the gap rose to a little over 28 per cent in 1855–60. This increasing disparity is attributable to the rapid rise in the use of scrap metal and to imports of pig. The pattern in the case of total consumption is similar. The ratio $\dfrac{C_t}{P_t}$ rose from 1.29 in 1840–44 to 1.65 in 1855–60. Thus the confusion between pig iron production and the consumption of crude iron has distorted the relationship between the demand for rails and the development of the iron industry.

Even more serious mistakes have been made in discussions of the amount of domestic pig iron used in rail production. The crudest error is the confusion between the production and consumption of rails. Table 5.15 shows that most of the rails consumed in the United States between 1840 and 1860 were imported. Domestic output during this period accounted for only 40 per cent of all rail consumption. A second and more common error is the assumption that all domestic rails were rolled from domestic pig iron. However, of those rails that were produced domestically between 1840 and 1860, 35 per cent were rolled from worn rails and another 14 per cent were rolled from imported pig. Moreover the importance of rerolling increased strikingly over the two-decade period, rising from 19 per cent of domestic rail production in 1845–49 to 42 per cent in 1855–60. As a consequence, rails rolled from domestic pig iron dropped to less than half of domestic production.

The effect of the errors discussed in the last two paragraphs on the analysis of the importance of the demand for rails in the development of the iron industry is shown in Table 5.17 and Chart 5.11. Index I_2, which incorporates all of these errors, gives the impression that rails represented a large and rapidly rising share of the output of the iron industry. I_2 increases from an average of 13 per cent in 1840–49 to

TABLE 5.15. PIG IRON AND THE PRODUCTION OF RAILS, 1840–60 (in thousands of net tons)

	1	2	3	4	5	6	7	8	9	10
	Rail consumption	Imports of rails	Domestic production of rails Col. 1 − Col. 2	Rails rerolled (domestic)	Domestic rails rolled from pig Col. 3 − Col. 4	Pig iron used in domestic production of rails Col. 5 × 1.25	Imported pig used in the domestic production of rails	Domestic pig used in the domestic production of rails Col. 6 − Col. 7	Railroad scrap substituted for pig iron in non-rail uses	Addition to domestic pig prod. directly attributable to rails Col. 8 − Col. 9
1. 1840	33	29	4	1	3	4	0	4	3	1
2. 1841	44	27	17	1	16	20	1	19	4	15
3. 1842	44	19	25	2	23	29	2	27	5	22
4. 1843	25	14	11	3	8	10	0	10	6	4
5. 1844	30	21	9	4	5	6	1	5	7	—2
6. 1845	43	16	27	5	22	28	2	26	9	17
7. 1846	52	11	41	6	35	44	2	42	11	31
8. 1847	75	24	51	7	44	55	4	51	12	39
9. 1848	106	55	51	9	42	53	8	45	14	31
10. 1849	160	118	42	11	31	39	8	31	14	17
11. 1850	237	193	44	13	31	39	8	31	15	16
12. 1851	311	261	50	14	36	45	12	33	17	16
13. 1852	389	327	62	17	45	56	15	41	19	22
14. 1853	437	349	88	22	66	83	21	62	21	41
15. 1854	354	246	108	28	80	100	26	74	26	48
16. 1855	308	170	138	37	101	126	20	106	31	75
17. 1856	381	201	180	48	132	165	17	148	37	111
18. 1857	314	153	161	62	99	124	14	110	45	65
19. 1858	251	87	164	78	86	108	18	90	52	38
20. 1859	311	115	196	96	100	125	23	102	60	42
21. 1860	323	118	205	115	90	113	22	91	66	25
					Period Averages					
22. 1840–44	35	22	13	2	11	14	1	13	5	8
23. 1845–49	87	45	42	8	35	44	5	39	12	27
24. 1850–54	346	275	70	19	52	65	16	49	20	29
25. 1855–59	313	145	168	64	104	130	18	112	45	67
26. 1855–60	315	141	174	73	101	127	19	108	49	59
27. 1840–49	61	33	28	5	23	29	3	26	9	17
28. 1850–59	329	210	119	42	78	97	17	80	32	48
29. 1850–60	329	202	127	48	79	99	18	81	35	46
30. 1840–60	201	122	80	28	52	65	11	54	23	31

SOURCES AND NOTES:

Column 1. Lines 1–10 are estimated from the model. Lines 11–21 are from A.I.S.A., *Annual Report, 1872–1873,* p. 30, with fiscal year imports averaged to obtain estimates of calendar year imports.

Column 2. Lines 1–11, Colwell, "Special Report," pp. 330–31; cf. A.I.S.A., *Bulletin* (1856), p. 35. Lines 10–21, A.I.S.A., *Annual Report, 1872–1873,* p. 30. For the years 1851–54 the A.I.S.A. added 7 per cent to the figures of the Treasury Department, apparently to take account of imports included in the category of bar iron. For the years 1855–60 the allowance was 7.5 per cent. Fiscal year imports were averaged to obtain estimates of calendar year imports.

Column 4. According to the A.I.S.A., *Annual Report, 1868,* the share of old rails rerolled in 1866 was 0.776. Data on the amount of rails rerolled for 1857, 1863, and 1864 together with data of Chart 5.13 indicate that this ratio rose over time. A linear regression fitted to the four observations yielded the equation $S = 0.255 + 0.019t$, where S is the share of worn rails rerolled and 1840 the year zero. Estimates of the share of worn rails rerolled computed from this equation were multiplied by corresponding entries in Chart 5.13 to obtain the estimated tonnage of rerolled rails in each year. Daddow and Bannon, *Coal, Iron and Oil,* pp. 683, 695.

Column 6. This estimate of the amount of pig iron (1.25 tons) used to produce a ton of rails is widely cited. See, for example, Lesley, *Guide,* p. 761; and *American Railroad Journal,* XX, 202. However, there is some reason for believing the consumption factor is too high. Swank, reporting the experience of eastern rail mills over the 16-year period from 1860 through 1875, put the ratio at 1.05 (Taussig, "The Tariff," p. 382). The last ratio was also put forth by French (*History,* pp. 63, 69) in 1858.

Albert Fishlow (*Economic Contribution,* pp. 202–3) has argued that one-third of each rerolled rail consisted of new pig iron. The basis for his statement is a description, published in the *American Railroad Journal* (1858), of a Cleveland mill that rerolled rails from three piles of iron, one of which was made from new pig. However, not all rerolled rails were rolled from three piles (the plate, flange, bridge, and compound were not) and not all rails rolled from three piles used new pig iron. Many, if not most, railroad men insisted on having their rails rerolled exclusively from old iron which they believed had wearing qualities superior to that of new iron. Colburn and Holly, also writing in 1858, stated that "the officers of many good roads go so far as to accuse iron masters of retaining old stock, sent them for re-rolling, and putting off their customers with new iron" (*The Permanent Way,* p. 88). The atypical nature of Fishlow's example is underscored by two additional facts: The firm he cites was the only one of the large western mills that produced new as well as rerolled rails (Daddow and Bannon, *Coal, Iron and Oil,* p. 695). More crucial is the information that none of the other large western mills built in the late fifties had any puddling furnaces that could serve to refine pig iron for use in rolling (A.I.S.A., *Bulletin* [1858], p. 155).

Even if it were true that one-third of each rerolled rail was manufactured from new pig, it would not follow that pig used in rerolling rails represented an increase in the net consumption of pig iron. For if as Colburn and Holly suggest, some of the metal from worn rails was used to produce new rails, a deduction must be made on this account. Moreover, since worn rails not used in rail production were substituted for pig iron in the production of non-rail products, the greater the amount of pig used in rerolling, the more the amount of worn rails substituted for pig in other processes. Hence, the net consumption of pig iron directly attributable to the domestic production of rails is unchanged, even if one grants Fishlow's contention.

Column 7. The ratio of imported pig iron consumed by rail mills in 1856 to total pig imports in the same year was extrapolated to other years between 1840 and 1860 by the ratio: domestic rail production divided by crude iron consumed in the domestic iron industry. The entries of the resulting series were then multiplied by pig iron imports. Table 5.14, Columns 5 and 7; Table 5.15, Column 1; A.I.S.A. *Bulletin* (1858), Tables D, G, and J.

Lines may not add across because of rounding.

TABLE 5.16. CRUDE IRON USED IN THE PRODUCTION AND CONSUMPTION OF RAILS, 1840–60 (in thousands of net tons)

	1 Crude iron used for domestic production of rails	2 Crude iron used in the production of imported rails	3 Crude iron represented by rail consumption Col. 1 + Col. 2
1. 1840	5	36	41
2. 1841	21	34	55
3. 1842	31	24	55
4. 1843	13	18	31
5. 1844	10	26	36
6. 1845	33	20	53
7. 1846	50	14	64
8. 1847	62	30	92
9. 1848	62	69	131
10. 1849	50	148	198
11. 1850	52	241	293
12. 1851	59	326	385
13. 1852	73	409	482
14. 1853	105	436	541
15. 1854	128	308	436
16. 1855	163	213	376
17. 1856	213	251	464
18. 1857	186	191	377
19. 1858	186	109	295
20. 1859	221	144	365
21. 1860	228	148	376
		Period Averages	
22. 1840–44	16	28	44
23. 1845–49	52	56	108
24. 1850–54	84	344	428
25. 1855–59	194	181	375
26. 1855–60	200	176	376
27. 1840–49	34	41	75
28. 1850–59	139	263	402
29. 1850–60	147	253	400
30. 1840–60	93	153	246

SOURCES AND NOTES:
   Column 1. Table 5.15, sum of Columns 4 and 6.
   Column 2. Table 5.15, Column 2 multiplied by 1.25.

46 per cent in the following decade. On the other hand, I_4 (crude iron used in the production of domestic rails as a per cent of all crude iron consumed by the American iron industry) behaves quite differently. Its average level for the 21-year period is only 12 per cent and the rise between the first and second decades is fairly moderate (from 6 to 15 per cent).

Chart 5.10

RAIL CONSUMPTION, CRUDE IRON USED
FOR THE DOMESTIC PRODUCTION OF RAILS,
AND NET CONSUMPTION OF DOMESTIC PIG
IRON DIRECTLY ATTRIBUTABLE TO RAILS

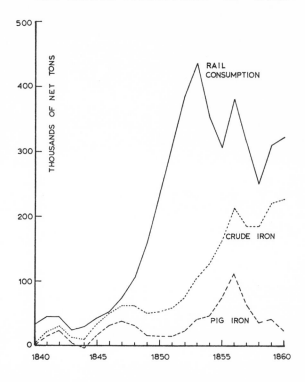

If one is interested in the importance of rails in the total output of
the iron industry, I_4 is an appropriate index. For an evaluation of the
narrower problem of the effect of the production of rails on the market
for pig iron, a preferable index is I_5 (the share of domestic pig iron
consumed in the production of rails). While I_5 indicates that the average
proportion of the output of blast furnaces that went into rails during
1840–60 was quite small (7 per cent), even it exaggerates the direct
influence of rails on pig iron production. I_5 fails to take account of the
fact that a by-product of the use of rails was the production of scrap
iron—a highly effective, and in some ways superior, substitute for pig.
Hence part of the pig iron absorbed by rail production was offset by

Chart 5.11

A COMPARISON OF INDEXES I_2, I_4, I_5 AND I_6

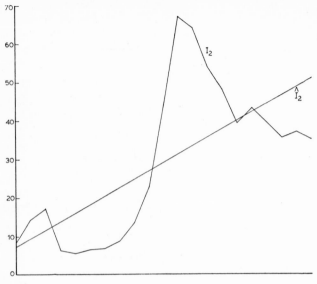

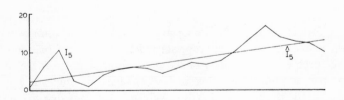

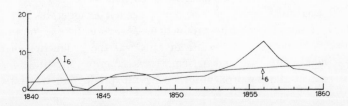

the substitution of worn rails for pig iron in the production of products other than rails. Index I_6 reflects this process of substitution. It not only shows that the net consumption of pig iron by rails was small (averaging less than 5 per cent) but also that this net consumption did not grow much faster than the production of pig iron for non-rail purposes. The coefficient of a linear term in a trend equation fitted to I_6 is only a little over two-tenths of 1 per cent.[72]

The preceding discussion and the data in Tables 5.14 through 5.17 indicate that the demand for rails did not dominate the development of the American iron industry during the two decades leading up to the Civil War. Rails represented only a small part of the total output of the iron industry. The direct effect of the demand for this item on growth in the industry was confined largely to one sector (rail mills) and within that sector to an even more specialized activity (rerolling). While it is possible that technological innovations in the rolling of rails may have affected the technology of other rolling activities, the significance of such possible technological leadership is still to be established. There was virtually no direct spillover effect on the growth of blast furnaces. The large rise in the average annual consumption of domestic pig iron between 1840–44 and 1855–60 did not go primarily into the production of rails but into other uses. Of the 440,000 ton increase, rails absorbed only 95,000 tons; and more than half of the last figure was offset by the substitution of worn rails for pig metal in the production of non-rail products.

Although the findings of this chapter contradict the "gross theory" that rails dominated the ante-bellum iron industry, they do not rule out a more subtle form of dependence. It may be possible to re-establish the crucial position of rails in the growth of the iron industry prior to 1860 by demonstrating that the *small* addition to iron consumption

[72] The trend functions fitted to the four indexes are:

$$\hat{I}_2 = 7.48 + 2.19t$$
$$\hat{I}_4 = 1.39 + 0.90t$$
$$\hat{I}_5 = 2.43 + 0.53t$$
$$\hat{I}_6 = 2.33 + 0.23t$$

The coefficients of the linear terms are significant in all cases. A regression coefficient of zero would indicate that pig iron consumed in rail production rose at the same rate as pig consumed in all other uses. Year zero is 1840.

The words "net" or "additional" applied to the numerator of I_6 should not be confused with the concept of "incremental" put forward in Chapter I. To determine the incremental consumption of pig iron attributable to rails one would have to subtract from the net figure the pig iron that would have been consumed by substitutes for the railroad.

TABLE 5.17. A COMPARISON OF INDEXES I_2, I_4, I_5 AND I_6

		1 I_2	2 I_4	3 I_5	4 I_6
1.	1840	8.5	1.2	1.0	0.0
2.	1841	14.2	6.3	6.1	4.8
3.	1842	17.1	11.0	10.5	8.5
4.	1843	6.2	3.1	2.5	1.0
5.	1844	5.5	1.7	1.0	0.0
6.	1845	6.7	4.8	4.0	2.6
7.	1846	6.8	6.1	5.5	4.0
8.	1847	8.8	6.7	6.0	4.6
9.	1848	13.6	6.8	5.8	4.0
10.	1849	22.8	5.9	4.4	2.4
11.	1850	44.0	7.8	5.8	3.0
12.	1851	67.2	9.8	7.1	3.5
13.	1852	64.2	9.4	6.8	3.6
14.	1853	54.0	10.2	7.7	5.1
15.	1854	48.1	13.3	10.1	6.5
16.	1855	39.3	16.8	13.5	9.6
17.	1856	43.2	20.0	16.8	12.6
18.	1857	39.4	18.7	13.8	8.2
19.	1858	35.6	19.8	12.8	5.4
20.	1859	37.0	19.6	12.1	5.0
21.	1860	35.1	18.5	9.9	2.7
			Period Averages		
22.	1840–44	9.2	3.9	3.4	2.1
23.	1845–49	11.6	6.2	5.2	3.6
24.	1850–54	54.8	10.4	7.8	4.6
25.	1855–59	39.0	19.0	14.0	8.4
26.	1855–60	38.3	18.9	13.1	7.2
27.	1840–49	10.8	5.5	4.6	3.0
28.	1850–59	45.9	15.2	11.2	6.7
29.	1850–60	44.8	15.6	11.0	6.3
30.	1840–60	30.7	11.8	8.3	4.7

SOURCES AND NOTES:

Column 1. $I_2 = \dfrac{\text{rail consumption of iron (Col. 1, Table 5.15)} \times 100}{\text{production of domestic pig iron (Col. 1, Table 5.14)}}$

Column 2. $I_4 = \dfrac{\text{crude iron used for the domestic production of rails}}{\text{crude iron consumed by the domestic iron industry}}$

$\dfrac{\text{(Col. 1, Table 5.16)} \times 100}{\text{(Col. 7, Table 5.14)}}$

Column 3. $I_5 = \dfrac{\text{domestic pig iron used in domestic production of rails}}{\text{production of domestic pig iron}}$

$\dfrac{\text{(Col. 8, Table 5.15)} \times 100}{\text{(Col. 1, Table 5.14)}}$

(*continued*)

$$\text{Column 4. } I_6 = \frac{\text{addition to domestic pig iron production directly attributable to rails}}{\text{production of domestic pig iron}}$$

$$\frac{(\text{Col. 10, Table 5.15}) \times 100}{(\text{Col. 1, Table 5.14})}$$

directly attributable to rails had far-reaching consequences. Indeed, one of the unfortunate effects of the reign of the gross theory is that it has choked off precisely such investigations. As long as one could explain the growth of the iron industry by the sheer size of rail consumption relative to pig iron production, there was little incentive to consider other alternatives.

A situation in which a small increase in the demand for pig iron consumed in rails can lead to a large increase in the total production of pig iron is presented in Figure 5.1. Part a of the diagram contains a completely inelastic demand curve for pig iron used in rails (R) and a highly elastic demand curve (O) for pig iron used in all other products. The total demand curve (R + O) is shown in part b of Figure 5.1 as is the industry supply curve (SS). Given the total demand and supply curves, output will be a_1. Now let the rail demand for pig iron increase by a small amount from R to R', the demand for pig iron in other uses remaining constant. The increase in the rail demand shifts the total demand curve to the position of R' + O as shown in part b. The new output of pig iron is now a_2. In this example an increase in the rail demand for pig iron equal to only 15 per cent of original production

FIGURE 5.1

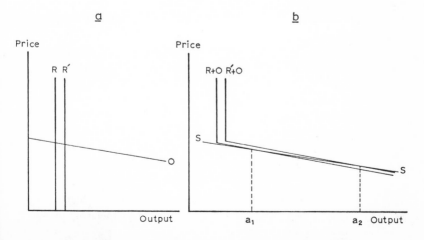

brought about an increase of 175 per cent in total pig output. It is not only a case in which a very large increase in production is attributable to a small rise in railroad consumption but also one in which the crucial role of rails is disguised by the fact that the observed rail share of pig iron production falls over time.

An alternative case in which an increase in the demand for rails leads to a fall in production is shown in Figure 5.2. Here LRS_u and LRS_e are the long run supply curves of rails in the United States and Great Britain respectively. S_u and S_e are corresponding short run supply curves. D_e represents the initial total demand for rails in Great Britain, including the excess demand for rails in the American market. The intersection of the demand curve (D_e) with the British short run supply curve (S_e) establishes a world price of P_1. At this price O_1 tons of rails are produced in the United States. Now let there be an increase in the demand for rails in the American market. The change results in an increase in the excess demand for British rails and shifts the total demand in Britain to the position shown by D'_e. As a consequence the world price rises to P_2, at which price American firms increase output to O_2. With the new world price, American firms are making large average profits of, say, about $P_2 - P_1$. While this will create an incentive to expand capacity in the United States, average British profits have also risen by an amount approximately equal to $P_2 - P_1$. Moreover, the increase in profit is, in the British case, an addition to a previously existing large average profit. All that is now necessary to obtain a result unfavorable to the American industry is to assume that the rate of expansion of capacity in both America and Britain is a function of average profit and that the second derivative of this function is positive and large. Then the increase in profits will lead to a much more rapid expansion of capacity in Britain than in the United States. After some time the American short run supply curve has shifted to S'_u. However, the British short run supply curve is at S'_e and the world price has fallen to P_3. At this price American production is only O_3. American firms are not covering costs and there is pressure to reduce American capacity. Here then is a case in which an increase in the American demand for rails stimulates a foreign competitor in a way that is detrimental to the development of the American iron industry.

Still other models could be developed. The point is that in theory small changes in the demand for iron due to rail consumption may

FIGURE 5.2

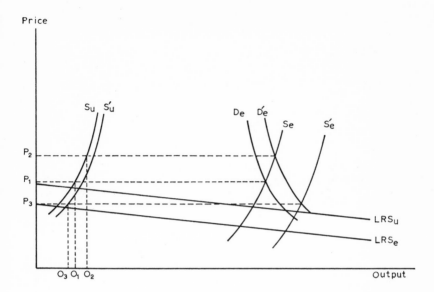

either stimulate the growth of the iron industry, leave it unaffected, or retard it. Which of these alternatives applies to the American iron industry of the mid-nineteenth century is an empirical question. The answer requires data not now available. Future attempts at statistical reconstruction may eventually provide the evidence needed to discriminate between the theories such as those presented in Figures 5.1 and 5.2. Until that time arrives, all that can be said with confidence about such alternatives is that the gross theory of the influence of rails on the growth of the American iron industry prior to the Civil War is unfounded.

While the model of rail consumption set forth in equations 5.1–5.6 was developed to provide information needed to construct indexes of the position of rails in the market for iron, it also has other uses. It can be disaggregated and examined in various ways to shed light on previously obscured aspects of the interaction between railroads and the growth of the ante-bellum iron industry.

In this connection, one further implication of the model is worth noting; that is the impulse given to the geographic decentralization of rolling mills by the rail replacement process. The effect is clearly evident in New England which witnessed a sharp decline in railroad construction after 1855. Over the next decade additions to the region's network averaged only 29 miles a year. Yet despite the decline in construction, the output of New England's rail mills expanded from 16,000 net tons in 1855 to 38,000 tons in 1863. Replacements stimulated this growth by sustaining the region's demand for rails at a high level (the model indicates that replacement requirements were over ten times as large as new construction requirements during 1856–65), and by providing New England with a substantial part of the raw materials she needed to supply the products wanted. According to the model, rails scrapped in 1859 exceeded 31,000 tons. This is more crude iron than spilled from New England's blast furnaces in the same year.[73]

A similar effect is evident in the states of the Old Northwest. The first rail mill in that region was completed in 1856. The production of rails increased from about 2,000 net tons in that year to 45,000 in 1860 and 73,000 in 1864. The rapid rise is not explained by the extension of the region's railroad network. New construction reached its antebellum peak two years before the first mill went into operation and then moved steadily downward. By 1864, when the mills of the Northwest produced a fifth of all domestic rails, the construction of new roads had fallen to a bare 40 miles. However, the growth of rail mills is positively and strongly correlated with the increase in the region's replacement requirements as indicated by the model.[74]

In the Northwest, as in New England, replacements stimulated the growth of rail rolling mills both from the demand and the supply side. According to the model over the years from 1858 through 1864, rail replacement requirements were more than twice as large as requirements for new construction. But in the case of the Northwest, the effect of the replacement process on supply was more important than its effect on demand. Illinois and Indiana, which produced 13 per cent of the nation's rail output in 1864, could not have competed with Pennsylvania in the production of rails if it had not been for the

[73] *Census of Transportation, 1880*, p. 290; A.I.S.A., *Bulletin* (1858), p. 79; Samuel Harris Daddow and Benjamin Bannon, *Coal, Iron and Oil* (Pottsville, Pa., 1866), p. 694; *Census of Manufacturing, 1860*, p. clxxx.

[74] Frederic L. Paxson, "The Railroads of the 'Old Northwest' before the Civil War," *Transactions of the Wisconsin Academy of Science, Arts and Letters*, XVII, Part 1, No. 4, pp. 268–74; *Poor's Manual, 1870–1871*, p. xlv; A.I.S.A., *Bulletin* (1858), pp. 155, 156; *Census of Manufacturing, 1860*, p. clxxxiii; Daddow and Bannon, *Coal, Iron and Oil*, p. 695. Five observations on rail production taken from the above sources showed a correlation with the replacement figures derived from the model of 0.94. The coefficient is significant at the 2 per cent level.

enormous quantity of scrap removed from the railroad tracks of the region. Lacking Pennsylvania's coal and iron resources, with only two small charcoal blast furnaces in operation in 1860 (neither of which survived the next decade), the rolling mills of the two states were almost completely dependent on scrap as the local source of crude iron. This situation explains why the mills of Illinois and Indiana were engaged exclusively in rerolling and why 95 per cent of the rails produced in Detroit and Cleveland in 1863 and 1864 were also rerolled.[75]

Changes in the supply of raw material rather than in the demand for rails appear to have determined the time that rail mills appeared in the Northwest as well as the time profile of production. The consumption of rails in the Northwest during 1850–54, which averaged 1,100 miles a year, certainly provided a substantial market. Rail consumption in this quinquennium was in fact 10 per cent higher than consumption during the quinquennium that witnessed the emergence of the region's rail mills. What was wanting during 1850–54 was not a market but a local supply of crude iron. According to the model, the average amount of rails scrapped during 1850–54 was about 3,500 net tons—hardly enough to sustain the operation of a single average sized rail mill, even if it were the only customer for scrap. By 1856 when the first rail mills of the Northwest began operations, the amount of old rails scrapped had jumped to 14,000 net tons. In 1857 some 20,000 tons of scrap were available to firms that produced nearly 17,000 tons of rails. And by 1864, when scrap amounting to 88,000 tons was removed from the tracks of the region, the production at local rail mills had risen to 73,000 tons, almost 97 per cent of which was rerolled from worn rails.[76]

* * *

Reconstruction of the past based on models that systematically incorporated widely dispersed data fragments thus does more than avoid the inconsistencies that are liable to develop when inferences are based on bits of information considered in isolation of each other. Such reconstruction also reveals significant processes that might otherwise be overlooked.

To relate railroad construction to the production of rails it was necessary to develop a model of rail consumption. One of the crucial

---

[75] *Census of Manufacturing, 1860*, p. clxxx; A.I.S.A., *Bulletin* (1858), pp. 159, 163; A.I.S.A., *Annual Report, 1872–1873*, rear section containing list of blast furnaces, p. 37; Daddow and Bannon, *Coal, Iron and Oil*, p. 695.

[76] A.I.S.A., *Bulletin* (1858), p. 155; Daddow and Bannon, *Coal, Iron and Oil*, p. 695.

links in the model is the distribution of rail wear. Investigation of this matter disclosed that, whether symmetric or skewed, a unimodal distribution of rail wear consistent with available evidence [77] implied the rapid emergence of replacements as an important factor in the demand for rails. It further revealed that the variability of rail life acted like a moving average, smoothing the peaks and troughs of new construction to produce a fairly continuous, predictable increase in replacements. While this situation has been overlooked by historians of the iron industry, it was perceived by the producers of iron. Such comprehension is implicit in their practice of estimating replacement sales in any given year as a fixed percentage of the existing track mileage. It is also explicit in their speeches and reports.[78] Hence, the model discloses that the use of rails gave rise to a mechanism that made the demand for the product considerably more stable than it would have been if demand depended only on new construction.

The model of rail wear also showed that replacements had different consequences for different sectors of the iron industry. The nature of the replacement process was such that it left the level of production in the smelting sector largely unaffected. For replacements generated their own supply of crude iron.[79] The same factor acted to liberate rolling mills from dependence on blast furnaces, thereby promoting the regional dispersion of the fabricating sector of the industry. The extent to which a non-railroad transportation system would have provided a similar stimulus to the growth and relocation of rolling mills is a question beyond the scope of this study.

[77] The hypothesis that the distribution of rail wear was log-normal with a mean of 10.5 years and a standard deviation of three years was tested against the sample of 53 roads drawn from the 1880 *Census of Transportation* (see footnote 53 of this chapter). A chi-square test for goodness of fit indicated that if, in fact, the true distribution of rail wear was $LN(10.5; 3)$, one would draw a sample yielding a chi-square value as high as that obtained from the census data more than one-third of the time.

[78] See, for example, A.I.S.A., *Proceedings of the Annual Meeting of the American Iron and Steel Association, February 11, 1875.*

[79] In this connection it should be noted that Table 5.15 understates the extent to which worn rails displaced pig iron. Since this scrap was highly refined, the amount of pig it displaced was greater than its own weight.

CHAPTER VI

Summary and Interpretation

Different approaches to history thus seem to represent, at least sometimes, substantive disagreements about the actual ways in which events are connected with one another, disagreements that are of the highest significance and cannot be dissolved simply by regarding them as expressions of different, and equally legitimate perspectives.—CHARLES FRANKEL

This chapter attempts to integrate and interpret the investigations reported in the preceding pages. The sequence of discussion is as follows: summary of findings on the primary effect of railroads; issues in extending the analysis of the primary effect to all commodities; the relationship between the primary and derived effects of railroads; summary of findings on the measurement of selected derived effects; implications for the theory of economic growth; implications regarding the role of measurement and theory in the study of economic history.

* * *

To establish the proposition that railroads substantially altered the course of economic growth one must do more than provide information on the services of railroads. It must also be shown that substitutes for railroads could not (or would not) have performed essentially the same role. Writers who have held either that railroads were crucial to American economic growth or enormously accelerated this growth implicitly asserted that the economy of the nineteenth century lacked an effective alternative to the railroad and was incapable of producing one. This assertion is without empirical foundation; the range and potentiality of the supply of alternative opportunities is largely unexplored.

In the investigation of the incremental contribution of the railroad to economic growth it is useful to distinguish between the primary and the derived consequences of this innovation. The primary consequence of the railroad was its impact on the cost of transportation. If the cost of rail service had exceeded the cost of equivalent service by alternative forms of transportation over all routes and for all items, railroads would not have been built and all of the derived consequences would have been

207

absent. The derived consequences or aspects of the innovation included changes in the spatial distribution of economic activity and in the mix of final products. They also included the demand for inputs, especially manufactured goods and human skills, required for railroad construction and operation as well as the effects of that construction and operation on human psychology, political power, and social organization. Those who have held that railroads were indispensable to American economic growth could have based their position either on the ground that the reduction in transportation costs attributable to railroads was large or on the ground that the derived consequences of railroads were crucial (even if the reduction in transportation costs were small) or on some combination of the two types of effects.

THE PRIMARY EFFECT OF RAILROADS

Summary of the Findings

In this study the investigation of the primary effect of railroads is limited to transportation costs connected with the distribution of agricultural products. Chapters II and III discuss the increase in the production potential of the economy made possible by the availability of railroads for the transportation of such goods. The main conceptual device used in the analysis of this problem is the "social saving." The social saving in any given year is defined as the difference between the actual cost of shipping agricultural goods in that year and the alternative cost of shipping exactly the same collection of goods between exactly the same set of points without railroads.

This cost differential is in fact larger than the "true" social saving. Forcing the pattern of shipments in a non-rail situation to conform to the pattern that actually existed is equivalent to the imposition of a restraint on society's freedom to adjust to an alternative technological situation. If society had had to ship by water and wagon without the railroad it could have altered the geographical locus of agricultural production or shifted some productive factor out of agriculture altogether. Further, the sets of primary and secondary markets through which agricultural surpluses were distributed were surely influenced by conditions peculiar to rail transportation; in the absence of railroads some different cities would have entered these sets, and the relative importance of those remaining would have changed. Adjustments of this sort would have reduced the loss of national income occasioned by the absence of the railroad.

For analytical convenience the computation of the social saving is divided into two parts. Chapter II deals with the social saving in interregional distribution. In 1890, interregional distribution began with the farm surpluses concentrated in the eleven great primary markets of the Midwest. Over 80 per cent of the agricultural products that entered into interregional trade were shipped from the farms to these markets. The surpluses were then transshipped to some ninety secondary markets located in the East and South. After arriving in the secondary markets the commodities were distributed to retailers in the immediately surrounding territory or were exported.

The interregional social saving is computed for only one year—1890. The social saving per ton-mile was greater, however, in 1890 than in previous years; the tonnage of agricultural goods carried by railroads increased more rapidly than gross national product; and the average distance of an interregional haul increased over time. Hence both the absolute interregional social saving and that social saving relative to total national product was greater in 1890 than in previous years.

Only four commodities are included in the interregional computation, but these—wheat, corn, pork, and beef—accounted for over 90 per cent of the tonnage of interregional agricultural shipments. While it is possible to include all commodities in the computation, the increase in the accuracy of the estimate would not justify the effort required to do so.

Of the various forms of transportation in use in 1890, the most relevant alternative to railroads were waterways. All of the eleven primary markets were on navigable waterways. Lakes, canals, rivers, and coastal waters directly linked the primary markets with secondary markets receiving 90 per cent of the interregional shipments. Consequently it is possible to compute a first approximation to the interregional social saving by finding the difference between payments actually made by shippers of agricultural products and the payments they would have made to water carriers if shippers had sent the same commodities between the same points without railroads.

The total quantity of corn, wheat, pork and beef shipped interregionally in 1890 was approximately equal to the local deficits of the trading regions of the East and South, plus net exports. The local net deficits of a trading area are computed by subtracting from the consumption requirements of the area its production and its changes in inventories. The average rail and water distances of an interregional shipment are estimated from a random sample of the routes (pairs of cities) that represent the population of connections between primary and secondary markets. The water and rail rates per ton-mile for the various commodities are based on representative rates that prevailed in 1890 over distances and routes approximating the average condition. The application of observed water rates to a tonnage greatly in excess of that actually carried by waterways is justified by evidence which indicates that water transportation was a constant or declining cost industry.

These estimates of tonnages shipped, rates, and distances reveal that the actual cost of the interregional transportation of corn, wheat, pork, and beef in 1890 was $87,500,000 while the cost of transporting the same goods by water would have been only $49,200,000. In other words the first approximation of the interregional social saving is negative by about $38,000,000. This odd result is the consequence of the fact that direct payments to railroads included virtually all of the cost of inter-regional transportation, while direct payments to water carriers did not. In calculating the cost of shipping without the railroad one must account for six additional items of cost not included in payments to water carriers. These items are cargo losses in transit, transshipment costs, wagon haulage costs from water points to secondary markets not on waterways, capital costs not reflected in water rates, the cost resulting from the time lost when using a slow medium of transportation, and the cost of being unable to use water routes for five months out of the year.

The first four of the neglected costs can be estimated directly from available commercial data.

It is more difficult to determine the cost of the time lost in shipping by a slow medium of transportation and the cost of being unable to use water routes for about five months during each year. Such costs were not recorded in profit and loss statements, or publications of trade associations, or the decennial censuses, or any of the other normal sources of business information. Consequently they must be measured indirectly through a method that links the desired information to data which are available. The solution to the problem lies in the nexus between time and inventories. If entrepreneurs could replace goods the instant they were sold, they would, *ceteris paribus,* carry zero inventories. Inventories are necessary to bridge the gap of time required to deliver a commodity from its supply source to a given point. If, on the average, interregional shipments of agricultural commodities required a month more by water than by rail and if water routes were closed for five months out of each year, it would have been possible to compensate for the slowness of water transportation and the limited season of navigation by increasing inventories in secondary markets by an amount equal to one half of the annual receipts of these markets. Hence the cost of the interruptions and time lost in water transportation is the 1890 cost of carrying such an inventory. The inventory cost comprises two elements: the foregone opportunity of investing the capital represented in the additional inventory (which is measured by the interest rate) and storage charges (which were published).

When account is taken of the neglected costs, the negative first approximation is transformed into a positive social saving of $73,000,000 (see Table 6.1). Since the actual 1890 cost of shipping the specified commodities was approximately $88,000,000, the absence of the railroad would have almost doubled the cost of shipping agricultural commodities interregionally. It is therefore quite easy to see why the great bulk of agricultural commodities was actually sent to the East by rail, with water transportation used only over a few favorable routes.

While the interregional social saving is large compared to the actual transportation cost, it is quite small compared to the annual output of the economy—just six-tenths of one per cent of gross national product. Hence the computed social saving indicates that the availability of railroads for the interregional distribution of agricultural products represented only a relatively small addition to the production potential of the economy.

The estimation of the social saving is more complex in intraregional trade (movements from farms to primary markets) than in long-haul trade. Interregional transportation represented a movement between

TABLE 6.1. THE SOCIAL SAVING IN THE INTERREGIONAL DISTRIBUTION
OF AGRICULTURAL COMMODITIES

First approximation	$-38,000,000
Neglected cargo losses	6,000,000
Transshipping costs	16,000,000
Supplementary wagon haulage	23,000,000
Neglected capital costs	18,000,000
Additional inventory costs	48,000,000
Total	$ 73,000,000

a relatively small number of points—eleven great collection centers in the Midwest and ninety secondary markets in the East and South. But intraregional transportation required the connection of an enormous number of locations. Considering each farm as a shipping point, there were not 11 but 4,565,000 interior shipping locations in 1890; the number of primary markets receiving farm commodities was well over a hundred.[1] These points were not all connected by the railroad network, let alone by navigable waterways. The movement of commodities from farms to primary markets was never accomplished exclusively by water or by rail. Rather it involved a mixture of wagon and water or wagon and train services.

This is the crux of the intraregional problem. If the evaluation of the impact of interior railroads merely involved an analysis of the substitution of water for rail transportation, there would be no reason to expect a large social saving. Considered in isolation, boats were a relatively efficient substitute for the iron horse. However the absence of the railroad would have required greater utilization not only of water service but also of wagon service. It is the additional amount of very costly wagon transportation that would have been needed for the shipment of each ton of agricultural produce leaving the farm which suggests that the social saving attributable to interior railroads probably exceeded the social saving of the more celebrated trunk lines.

The intraregional social saving—which covers twenty-seven commodities—is estimated in two ways. The first computation (estimate α) is a direct extension of the method used for long-distance shipments. It is the difference between the actual cost of shipping goods from farms to primary markets in 1890 and the cost of shipping in exactly the same pattern without the railroad. However, in the intraregional case the assumption that pattern of shipments would have remained unchanged despite the absence of railroads implies that wagons would have carried certain agricultural commodities over distances in which wagon haulage costs greatly exceeded the market value of the produce. As a result estimate α introduces an upward bias that is too large to ignore.

It is possible to estimate the intraregional social saving by a method that reduces this upward bias. Without railroads the high cost of wagon

[1] In the intraregional case the term "primary markets" refers not merely to the eleven great midwestern collection centers but also to cities that served as collection centers for intraregionally traded commodities. Thus while New York City was a secondary market for the corn, wheat, beef, and pork of the North Central states, it was a primary market for the dairy products, fruits, and other commodities produced by local farmers.

transportation would have limited commercial agricultural production to areas of land lying within some unknown distance of navigable waterways. If the boundaries of this region of feasible commercial agriculture were known, the social saving could be broken into two parts: (1) the difference between the cost of shipping agricultural commodities from farms lying within the feasible region to primary markets with the railroad and the cost of shipping from the same region without the railroad (i.e., an α estimate for the feasible region), and (2) the loss in national product due to the decrease in the supply of agricultural land. The social saving estimated in this manner (estimate β) would be less than the previous measure since it allows for a partial adjustment to a non-rail situation. Moreover, by disaggregating the social saving, estimate β provides additional information on the gestalt of the railroad's influence on the development of agriculture.

A first approximation of the α estimate can be computed on the basis of the relationship shown in equation 3.2.

$$(3.2) \qquad \alpha = x \left[w(D_{fb} - D_{fr}) + (BD_{bp} - RD_{rp}) \right]$$

where

$x =$ the tonnage of agricultural produce shipped out of counties by rail

$w =$ the average wagon rate per ton-mile

$B =$ the average water rate per ton-mile

$R =$ the average rail rate per ton-mile

$D_{fb} =$ the average distance from a farm to a water shipping point

$D_{fr} =$ the average distance from a farm to a rail shipping point

$D_{bp} =$ the average distance from a water shipping point to a primary market

$D_{rp} =$ the average distance from a rail shipping point to a primary market.

The first term within the square bracket $w(D_{fb} - D_{fr})$ is the social saving per ton attributable to the reduction in wagon transportation; the second term $(BD_{bp} - RD_{rp})$ is the social saving per ton on payments to water and rail carriers. One of the surprising results is that only the first term is positive. In the absence of railroads, wagon transportation costs would have increased by $8.92 for each ton of agriculture produce that was shipped interregionally by rail. Payments to water carriers, however, would have been $0.76 per ton less than the payments to railroads. In other words the entire first approximation of the α estimate of the social saving—which amounts to $300,000,000—is attributable not to the fact that railroad charges were less than boat charges but to the fact that railroads reduced the amount of expensive wagon haulage that had to be combined with one of the low-cost forms of transportation.

To the $300,000,000 obtained as the first approximation of α it is necessary to add certain indirect costs. In the long-haul case it was shown that the first approximation of the social saving omitted six charges of considerable importance. In the intraregional case, however, three of these items are covered by the first approximation. Wagon haulage costs are included in equation 3.2. Transshipment costs would have been no greater in the non-rail case than in the rail case. In both situations bulk would have been broken when the wagons reached the rail or water shipping points and no further transshipments would have been required between these points and the primary markets. Since all government expenditures on rivers and canals financed out of taxes rather than tolls were assigned to interregional agricultural shipments, their inclusion in the intraregional case would represent double counting.

Three indirect costs do have to be added to the first approximation of α. These are cargo losses, the cost of using a slow medium of transportation, and the cost of the limited season of navigation. As is shown by Table 6.2 these neglected items amount to only $37,000,000 which, when added to the first approximation, yields a preliminary α estimate of $337,000,000 or 2.8 per cent of gross national product.

Execution of the β estimate requires a theoretical structure that will make it possible to infer the location of the boundary of feasible commercial agriculture from observed data. The theory of rent provides such a structure. The applicability of the theory of rent can be demonstrated by considering a hypothetical example. Suppose that Congress passed a law requiring all farmers in an area of land one mile wide and a hundred miles long, running westward from the Mississippi River through the state of Missouri along the 40th parallel, to send their products to market (St. Louis) by wagon and boat. Suppose that Congress also prohibited these farmers from responding to the law by changing the kinds or the

TABLE 6.2. PRELIMINARY α ESTIMATE (in millions of dollars)

First approximation	300.2
Cargo losses	1.3
Cost of slow transportation	1.7
Cost of limited season of navigation	34.0
Total	337.2

proportions of the commodities that were produced for the market. Finally, assume that the rate from all rail shipping points in the strip to St. Louis were exactly the same as Mississippi River rates from the 40th parallel to St. Louis.

Under these circumstances farms lying along the Mississippi would be unaffected by the law as would all farms that were just as far from the Mississippi River as from a rail shipping point. For all other farmers the law would result in a decline in the prices they received at the farm for their various commodities. Since the output of the farms in question is very small relative to total agricultural production, no output decisions on the part of these farmers could affect prices in primary markets. The reduction in prices paid at the farm and the corresponding fall in land values would be completely explained by the increased cost of transportation. The farther a farm was from the Mississippi, the greater would be the fall in the value of that farm land. At some distance from the Mississippi the increase in the cost of wagon transportation would be such that land values would be zero. All land lying beyond this distance would have a negative price. Hence, given the value of each plot of land prior to enactment, the quantities of agricultural commodities shipped to St. Louis from each of the farms, the wagon rates, and the distance from each farm to a rail shipping point, one could determine the boundary of feasible commercial agriculture after the enactment. The boundary would be located along a set of points at which the increase in the cost of transporting the market bound output from a farm to a shipping point was exactly equal to the pre-enactment rental value of that land.

The hypothetical example indicates the basic procedure for establishing the boundaries of feasible commercial agriculture. There are, of course, differences between the hypothetical example and the actual problem. Thus, transportation costs from rail and water shipping points to primary markets will not be the same for most farms. Since water costs were in fact generally less than rail costs, the boundary of feasible production is pushed out. Moreover, when the whole country is considered, one cannot ignore the effect of the cessation of agricultural production in land beyond the feasible range on the level of prices in primary markets. Given the relative inelasticity of the demand for agricultural products, the reduction in production would have tended to raise prices in primary markets. The rise in prices would have led to a more intensive exploitation of agriculture within the feasible region, thus raising land values and increasing the burden of additional transportation costs that could have been borne by various farms. Hence, calculation of the feasible range on the basis of the actual 1890 land values and shipment statistics tends to understate the limits of feasible commercial agriculture, and overstates the amount of land that would have remained unused in the absence of the railroad.

The theory of rent can also be used to estimate the loss in national income brought about by the decrease in the supply of land. The 1890 rental value of the lands lying beyond the region of feasible commercial agriculture represents the amount by which the annual product of labor and capital utilized on this territory exceeded the value of the product of the same amount of labor and capital when applied at the margin. If the land in the non-feasible region had not been available, the labor and capital employed on it would have been utilized either at the intensive or extensive margin. Hence, if the quantity of displaced factors had been small, the fall in the value of the output of these factors would have been equal to the annual rental value of the land they had previously occupied. This loss in national income could be estimated by decapitalizing the land values, i.e., multiplying land values by appropriate mortgage rates of interest. The amount of labor and capital employed on non-feasible terrain, however, was quite large so that their displacement would have led to a fall in national income which exceeded the decapitalized value of the non-feasible lands.

Unlike the α estimate, the β estimate of the social saving has downward as well as upward biases. While the upward biases may be stronger than the downward ones, these conflicting errors tend to cancel, and make β a more acceptable approximation of the true social saving than α.

Data pertaining to the North Atlantic states indicate that in this region the boundary of feasible commercial agriculture would have been located between 40 and 50 airline miles from navigable waterways. The feasible boundary would probably have been closer to waterways in the North Atlantic region than in other sections of the nation. This is indicated by the fact that farm land values relative to outshipments were probably lower in this area than in all other areas except the Mountain states. At the same time the cost of wagon transportation was higher on the average in the North Atlantic region than outside it. Nevertheless, in computing the β estimate it is assumed that in all regions of the country the boundary of feasible commercial agriculture fell 40 airline miles from a navigable waterway.

Table 6.3 shows that 76 per cent of all agricultural land by value was within 40 miles of natural waterways and canals actually in use in 1890

TABLE 6.3. LOSS IN NATIONAL PRODUCT DUE TO THE DECREASE IN THE SUPPLY OF LAND (BY REGIONS) (thousands of dollars)

	Value of farm land	Value of farm land beyond feasible region	Col. 2 as a per cent of Col. 1	Loss in national product
North Atlantic	1,092,281	5,637	0.5	331
South Atlantic	557,399	117,866	21.1	8,452
North Central	4,931,607	1,441,952	29.2	110,476
South Central	738,333	158,866	21.5	14,191
Western	800,952	218,216	27.2	19,919
United States	8,120,572	1,942,537	23.9	153,572

as well as abandoned canals that would have been in use in the absence of railroads. Table 6.3 also shows that the loss in national income due to the diminished supply of land would have been $154,000,000. The loss is not equally distributed. Close to three quarters of it is concentrated in the North Central states. Indeed, more than half of the decline falls in just four states: Illinois, Iowa, Nebraska, and Kansas. This finding does not support the frequently met contention that railroads were essential to the development of commercial agriculture in the prairies. Rather, the concentration of the loss in a compact space suggests that most of the productive agricultural land that fell outside of the feasible region could have been brought into it by a relatively small extension of the canal system.

Adding an α estimate for the feasible region to the loss in national income attributable to the diminished supply of land yields a first approximation of β amounting to $221,000,000 (see Table 6.4). The further addition of indirect charges of $27,000,000 results in a preliminary β estimate of $248,000,000 or 2.1 per cent of gross national product.

TABLE 6.4. PRELIMINARY β ESTIMATE (in millions of dollars)

First approximation		220.9
Loss due to diminished supply of land	153.6	
α estimate for feasible region	67.3	
Cargo losses		1.0
Cost of slow transportation		0.7
Cost of the limited season of navigation		25.5
Total		248.1

The preliminary estimates of the intraregional social saving are based on the severe assumption that in the absence of railroads all other aspects of technology would have been unaltered. It seems quite likely, however, that in the absence of railroads much of the capital and ingenuity that went into the perfection and spread of the railroad would have been turned toward the development of other cheap forms of land transportation. Under these circumstances it is possible that the internal combustion engine would have been developed years sooner than it actually was, thus permitting a reduction in transportation costs through the use of motor trucks.

While most such possibilities of a speed-up in the introduction and spread of alternative forms of transportation have not been sufficiently explored to permit meaningful quantification at the present time, there are two changes about which one can make fairly definitive statements. These are the extension of the existing systems of internal waterways and the improvement of common roads. Neither of these developments required new knowledge. They merely involved an extension of existing technology.

Figure 3.5 presents a system of canals[2] that could have been built in the absence of railroads. Although the thirty-seven canals and feeders proposed are only 5,000 miles in length, their construction would have brought all but 7 per cent of agricultural land within 40 airline miles of a navigable waterway. Allowing for the projected waterways, the α estimate is reduced to $214,000,000 (1.8 per cent of gross national product) and the β estimate falls to $175,000,000 (1.5 per cent of gross national product).

Such an extension of internal water transportation is more than an historian's hallucination. The proposed canals would have been technologically and, in the absence of railroads, economically feasible.[3] Built across the highly favorable terrain of the North Central states and Texas, the average rise and fall per mile on the proposed system would have been 29 per cent less than the average rise and fall on those canals that were successful enough to survive railroad competition through 1890. The water supply along the routes would have been abundant. Even if worked at full capacity, no canal in the system

---

[2] See above, pp. 93–97.

[3] Even if the amortization period of canals is put as low as twenty-five years, the reduction in β implies a social rate of return of 45 per cent on the investment in the proposed canals. If the reduction in the α estimate is used, the implied return is 76 per cent.

would have required more than 65 per cent of the supply of water available to it. And in no case would the agricultural tonnage carried by a canal have exceeded one-third of its capacity.

According to data published by the Bureau of Public Roads, the intraregional social saving could have been further reduced by the improvement of common roads. The Bureau estimated that improvements would have reduced the cost of wagon haulage to ten cents per ton-mile. This rate implies a boundary of feasible commerical agriculture located at an average of 80 airline miles from navigable waterways. The doubling of the distance of this boundary together with the construction of the proposed canals would have brought all but 4 per cent of agricultural land within the feasible region. Under these circumstances the value of α is \$141,000,000 or just 1.2 per cent of gross national product. While the value of β is \$117,000,000 or slightly less than one per cent of gross national product.

It thus appears that while railroads were more important in short-haul movements of agricultural products than in long-haul movements, the differences are not as great as is usually supposed. It is very likely that even in the absence of railroads the prairies would have been settled and exploited. Cheap transportation rather than railroads was the necessary condition for the emergence of the North Central states as the granary of the nation. The railroad was undoubtedly the most efficient form of transportation available to the farmers of the nation. But the combination of wagon and water transportation could have provided a relatively good substitute for the fabled iron horse.

Extension to All Commodities

Of course the social saving has been computed only for agricultural commodities. Ultimate conclusions regarding the significance of the primary effect of railroads must await the computation of the social saving on non-agricultural items. It has been suggested that one can obtain a reasonable estimate of the social saving in the transportation of all freight by multiplying the combined inter- and intra-regional figures by four. The suggestion is rationalized on the ground that agricultural products probably accounted for about one-fourth of the ton-miles of transportation services provided by railroads in 1890. The procedure implies a total social saving of 7.1 per cent of gross national product if the α estimate of the intraregional saving is used

$$\left[\frac{\$214{,}000{,}000 \times 4}{\$12{,}000{,}000{,}000}\right]$$ or 6.3 per cent if the β estimate is used

$$\left[\frac{\$190{,}000{,}000 \times 4}{\$12{,}000{,}000{,}000}\right].$$ Unfortunately this simple way of moving from the agricultural to the total social saving probably leads to so large an overestimate of the true total that the figure derived from the computation is useless for most purposes.

Data on the ton-miles of railroad service utilized in shipping non-agricultural commodities can hardly be classified as decisive information. As has been shown, comparisons of transportation costs based only on direct payments to railroad and water carriers for the ton-miles of service provided by each introduced negative components into the social saving in both the inter- and intraregional cases. The important elements in the agricultural social saving were the cost of supplementary wagon transportation, the cost of increasing inventories to compensate for interruptions in navigation, and other indirect charges. The cost of increasing inventories alone equaled 65 per cent of the interregional social saving, and supplementary wagon transportation similarly dominated the intraregional computation.

However, there is no simple relationship between these all–important charges and the ton-miles of service actually provided by railroads. That is why it was not possible to estimate the intraregional social saving from the interregional one by extrapolating on the ton-miles of railroad service. Since intraregional shipments of agricultural products required only one-half of the ton-miles of railroad service consumed by shipments between regions, such an extrapolation would have led to the erroneous conclusion that interior railroads were considerably less important than the trunk lines. As pointed out in the introduction to Chapter III, the intraregional problem turned on the extent of the increase in supplementary wagon transportation that would have been required for each ton of freight shifted from railroads to boats. This increase could not have been derived from data on the amount of railroad service actually consumed.

Consequently no firm estimate of the social saving on non-agricultural items can be obtained without the detailed, protracted research required to determine such matters as: the geographic patterns of the production and consumption of non-agricultural goods, the extent to which the observed geographic patterns permitted the substitution of water for rail transportation, the amount of supplementary wagon transportation that would have been required in the non-rail case, the extent to which additions to the canal system would have permitted further reductions in the social saving through the substitution of water for wagon transportation, and the cost of the additional inventories of non-agricultural commodities required to compensate for the slowness and unavailability of water transportation during certain months of the year.

Such a study would probably reveal that the social saving per ton-mile of railroad service was lower for non-agricultural commodities than for agricultural commodities. This conclusion is suggested by the fact that products of mines dominated non-agricultural freight shipments in 1890. Coal alone accounted for 35 per cent of the non-agricultural tonnage. Iron and other ores brought the share to over 50 per cent.[4]

Unlike agricultural commodities which were produced on farms occupying nearly a million square miles of land in over 2,000 counties in every state of the nation, the production of coal was highly concentrated.[5] Nine states accounted for about 90 per cent of all coal shipped from mines in 1890. And within these states production was further concentrated in a relative handful of counties. Forty-six counties shipped 76,000,000 tons—75 per cent of all the coal sent from the mines in the nine states. Moreover, all of these counties were traversed by navigable rivers, canals actually constructed, or the proposed canals of Figure 3.5. Consumption of coal was also geographically concentrated. Just fifteen cities—all on navigable waterways—received 43 per cent of all coal shipped from mines.[6]

The production and consumption of iron ore were even more localized than coal. The *Report on Mineral Industries* prepared for the Eleventh Census reported that the

ranges embraced in the Lake Superior region are none of them of great extent geographically, and if a circle was struck from a center in Lake Superior with a radius of 135 miles, all of the present iron-ore producing territory of that region would be embraced within one-half of the circle, and most of the deposits would be near the periphery. The output of this section in 1889 was 7,519,614 long tons. A parallelogram 60 miles in length and 20 miles in width would embrace all of the mines now producing in the Lake Cham-

[4] *Eleventh Census, Transportation,* Part I, pp. 19, 384.

[5] *Eleventh Census, Agriculture,* p. 74.

[6] U.S. Census Bureau, *Eleventh Census of the United States: 1890, Report on Mineral Industries,* pp. 348, 355–417.

plain district of northern New York, whose output in 1889 aggregated 779,850 long tons. A circle of 50 miles radius, embracing portions of eastern Alabama and western Georgia, included mines which in 1889 produced 1,545,066 long tons. A single locality, Cornwall, in Lebanon county, Pennsylvania, contributed 769,020 long tons in 1889. . . . In the areas named, which are only occupied to a limited extent by iron-ore mines, there were produced in 1889 a total of 10,613,550 long tons, or 73.11 per cent of the entire output of iron ore for the United States.[7]

With respect to consumption, about 80 per cent of all iron ore was received by blast furnaces located in thirty-one counties.[8]

Consequently, the transportation pattern of minerals more nearly approximated the conditions of the *inter*regional than the *intra*regional distribution of agricultural commodities. Products of mines were carried from a relatively small number of shipping locations to a similarly small number of receiving locations. Many of these shipping and receiving centers were directly linked to each other by waterways, and a limited extension of the canal system could have provided water connections for many of those points that did not already have them. It thus appears likely that only a small amount of additional wagon transportation would have been required for each ton of coal or ore shifted from railroads to waterways. Moreover, the cost of increasing inventories to compensate for the slowness of and interruptions in water transportation would have been quite low. The total value of all products of mines in 1890 was well below the value of the agricultural commodities that entered intraregional trade.[9] Hence the opportunity cost of the increased inventories of minerals would have been well below that found for agriculture. Additional storage costs, if any, would have been trivial. Minerals required neither very expensive cold storage facilities nor shelters. They were stored on open docks or fields.

Still another consideration militates against an extrapolation from the agricultural to the total social saving by use of data on the tons of goods carried by railroads or the ton-miles of service railroads provided. That is the fact that the $214,000,000 presented as the agricultural social saving already includes substantial elements of the social saving on non-agricultural items. Although all of the capital costs of the improvement of waterways were charged to agricultural commodities,

[7] *Ibid.,* p. 9.

[8] *Eleventh Census of Manufacturing,* Part III, pp. 392–3.

[9] *Eleventh Census, Report on Mineral Industries,* p. xv.

most of this cost should be distributed among non-agricultural items. Similarly the wagon rates used in the computations assumed zero return hauls so that these rates cover most of the additional wagon cost that would have been incurred in shipping non-agricultural commodities to farms. It is possible that as much as 35 per cent of the $214,000,000 should be assigned to the social saving induced by railroads in transporting products of mines, forests, and factories. If the "pure" agricultural social saving is about $140,000,000, then extrapolation to the total saving on the basis of ton-miles yields an α estimate of $560,000,000 or 4.7 per cent of gross national product. This result, taken together with the earlier comments on the upward bias of such an extrapolation suggests that careful study will yield an α estimate for all commodities that is well below 5 per cent of gross national product.[10]

Ultimate judgment of the primary effect of railroads on American

[10] For theoretical reasons previously discussed, the α concept of the social saving developed in chapter II can only provide an upper bound to the true social saving. Of course many upper bounds are possible; the task is to find the least upper bound compatible with theoretical and data limitations.

In applying the α concept of the social saving to all items carried by railroads in the year 1860, Albert Fishlow *(Economic Contribution,* chap. II) produced an estimate equal to about 5 percent of gross national product. His estimate of the agricultural saving alone is about two and one-half per cent of gross national product. This result may seem to be in contradiction with the lower figures put forth here, especially since it is clear that the social saving increased over time.

The seeming contradiction is explained by the fact that in order to avoid the introduction of downward biases, Fishlow chose figures which, to quote him, made his estimate of the benefit of railroads "quite generous." Moreover, Fishlow did not take account of the reduction in water and wagon costs that could have been achieved by an extension of the canal system and improvements in common roads. Hence his computation of an α type estimate contains upward biases that put it well above a least upper bound.

Fishlow did attempt to compute an unbiased estimate of the social saving for agricultural commodities. This estimate is based on the assumption that the change in the value of agricultural land between 1850 and 1860 reflects the increase in national income attributable to railroads. If the circumstances of the situation examined by Fishlow approximated a partial equilibrium model, the assumption would be appropriate. (Cf. Fogel, *The Union Pacific Railroad,* chap. IV.) However when 10,000 miles of railroads are introduced and make supramarginal a land area equal to one-third of that previously in use, conclusions derived from a partial equilibrium rent model do not apply. Under such conditions a general equilibrium model must be used. It can be shown that in a general equilibrium model the change in agricultural rent arising from a reduction in transport costs may be less than, greater than, or equal to the change in income originating in agriculture. Indeed it is entirely possible that the effect of railroads per se was to reduce land rents and that the observed rise is attributable entirely to the increase in capital and labor that took place between 1850 and 1860. Without information on elasticities of substitution one cannot disentangle the effect of the introduction of railroads from the effect of changes in other endowments.

economic growth must not only await the computation of the social saving on non-agricultural items; it must also await research on the likelihood that the existing scientific and technological knowledge would have allowed society to find more effective substitutes for the railroad than were examined in this volume. The most interesting possibility is that in the absence of railroads, motor vehicles would have been introduced at an earlier date than they actually were. Another alternative is that inland navigation could have been kept open throughout the year. No less an engineer than R. H. Thurston pronounced as feasible a plan to keep the Erie Canal in operation during the winter by the application of artificially generated heat. He put the cost of such a scheme at $4,800 per mile.[11] At this rate, a canal system of 10,000 miles could have been kept in operation throughout the year for less than two-thirds of the inventory charges indicated for the compensation of interruptions in shipping agricultural products. The capacity of the economy to have adjusted to the absence of railroads cannot be fully ascertained without further research in the engineering and scientific literature of the nineteenth century.

THE DERIVED EFFECTS

To facilitate discussion, the derived effects of railroads will be divided into two groups. The term "disembodied" will be applied to those consequences that followed from the saving in transportation costs per se and which would have been induced by any innovation that lowered transportation costs by approximately the amount attributed to railroads. The term "embodied" will be applied to those consequences that are attributable to the specific form in which railroads provided cheap transportation services.

The Relationship between the Primary and Derived Effects

If it is assumed that the existence of railroads did not alter the stock of resources (e.g., the territory of the United States), then the combined inter- and intraregional (α) social saving of $214,000,000 may be interpreted as an upper limit estimate of the amount by which railroads changed the production potential of the economy through a reduction in the cost of transporting agricultural products per se. As such, the social saving subsumes all of the disembodied effects of railroads. In

[11] Robert A. Chesebrough, *Inland Transportation: Keeping the Canals Open for Navigation During the Winter Season* (New York, 1873).

particular, the social saving includes all of the increase in national income attributable to regional specialization in agriculture induced by the decline in shipping costs.[12] Based as it is on actual outputs and shipments, the social saving represents the increased cost of transportation that the nation would have incurred if, in the absence of railroads, it attempted to maintain the pattern of production and distribution that actually existed in 1890. In other words, by increasing its transportation bill on agricultural commodities by the amount of the social saving, the nation could have reaped all of the benefits of regional agricultural specialization and trade in the absence of railroads that it obtained with them. Hence the nation need not have been saddled with a geographic locus of production that reduced national income by more than the social saving.[13]

Of course, the social saving may exclude some disembodied effects because the stock of resources was altered by the existence of railroads. It has been suggested that without railroads the nation's income potential would have fallen not merely because the rise in transportation costs would have diverted resources from other productive activities but also because the rise in costs would have reduced the rate of growth of population. A decline of potential income by $214,000,000, with the 1890 population of 63,000,000 held constant, implies a fall in per capita income of about $3.40, i.e., a decline from about $190 per capita to somewhat under $187 per capita.[14] The contention that the absence of railroads would have reduced population, then, is based on the hypothesis that the rate of growth of the American population was a positive function of the level of per capita income.

But the empirical support for this hypothesis is slender. The population of the United States grew at a higher rate between 1800 and 1850

[12] Fishlow *(Economic Contribution,* especially chaps. V and VIII) incorrectly assumes that one can add the social saving and the gain from regional specialization without double counting.

[13] The normal operation of the market would have generated forces that led the economy to a geographic distribution of agriculture consistent with the production frontier implied by the social saving. Whenever the exploitation of land became so intensive that the marginal product of labor and capital in the East fell below that in the West by more than the extra cost of transporting western goods, the opportunity to increase profits would have directed resources to the more productive territories. As Healy ("American Transportation," p. 187) has pointed out, the shift of population into the West did not wait for the coming of the iron horse. By 1840, "before a single railroad had penetrated that area from the coast, some 40 per cent of the nation's people lived west of New York, Pennsylvania and the coastal states of the South."

[14] *Historical Statistics* (1960), p. 7.

than between 1850 and 1900, although both the level and rates of growth of per capita income were substantially higher in the latter period than in the former one. While the crude death rate fell during the nineteenth century, the crude birth rate fell even more rapidly. The consequence was a substantial decline in the American reproduction rate.[15] Since the same pattern was evident in the industrialized countries of Europe, one might well argue that—at least with respect to natural reproduction —a decrease in per capita income induced by the absence of railroads would have increased rather than retarded the rate of population growth.

The exact relationship between the rate of immigration and the level of per capita income in both the United States and the countries of emigration has not yet been clearly established.[16] Nevertheless, even if it is granted that immigration into the United States was strongly and positively correlated with the differential in per capita income, it by no means follows that the absence of railroads would have reduced immigration. The social saving implies a fall in the average income level of the United States relative to the rest of the world because the social saving was computed on the assumption that only the United States would have been deprived of railroads. This assumption obviously biases the estimated social saving upward. Given the highly favorable situation of the United States with respect to navigable waterways, it is possible that in a situation in which all nations were deprived of railroads, income would have fallen less in the United States than in the rest of the world. Under these conditions the suggested relationship between migration and income levels implies that the absence of railroads would have increased American immigration. Indeed, at this point one cannot rule out the possibility that in a world forced to rely on water and wagon transportation, the American advantage would have been so great that the turn in its terms of trade with the rest of the world would have more than offset the increased cost of transportation.[17]

It may be that the decisive feature of the railroad's contribution to economic growth was not that it allowed society to produce transporta-

[15] Simon Kuznets, "Toward a Theory of Economic Growth," *National Policy for Economic Welfare at Home and Abroad,* ed. Robert Lekachman (Garden City, 1955), pp. 19–24.

[16] *Ibid.*, pp. 45–46; Richard A. Easterlin, "Influences in European Overseas Emigration Before World War I," *Economic Development and Cultural Change,* IX (April, 1961), 331–51.

[17] That is, although the absence of railroads would have reduced the income of the world as a whole, the income of the United States would have been higher than it actually was.

tion service at a much lower cost than would otherwise have been possible but that it embodied low cost service in a distinctive and uniquely important form. Although other mediums may also have been able to provide cheap transportation, the optimum geographic locus of activity in railroad and non-railroad economies might have differed. In the absence of railroads the spatial distribution of population could have been altered in a manner unfavorable to economic growth. Under a changed dwelling pattern people given to extravagance might have received a larger share of the nation's income and thus retarded the accumulation of capital. Moreover, changes in the climatic or physiographic environment of sections of the population could have altered the way in which they allocated their time between leisure and income-producing activities. Such embodied consequences would not be subsumed by the estimates of the social saving given above.

Leaving aside disputes regarding the role of climatic conditions in economic growth, the force of this line of argument is undermined by the findings of Chapter III. Chapter III reveals that in the absence of railroads, extensions of canals and improvements in wagon roads would have kept in use all but 4 per cent of the land actually worked in 1890. Such a limited reduction in the supply of land leaves scant scope for alterations in the geographic locus of economic activity—hardly enough scope to warrant the assumption that aggregate propensities for saving and leisure would have been significantly altered by railroad–induced changes in the physiographic or climatic environment of the population.

One could also argue that shifts in political circumstances and social institutions would have reduced the production potential of the economy beyond the level indicated by the social saving. Thus one might conjecture that railroads gave the North a crucial edge in the Civil War—that in the absence of railroads Northern generals would not have developed a strategy capable of defeating the insurrection. It might be further argued that a Southern victory would have saddled the nation with institutional arrangements—such as slavery—that inhibited the growth of productivity in agriculture and in other sectors of the economy. While the possibility of such a course of development may be worth investigating, the currently available evidence is too tenuous to make this conjecture an acceptable basis for believing that national income would have fallen by more than the social saving. In the light of current knowledge one could just as well argue that in the absence of railroads the West would have been more closely allied with the South and hence a military conflict would have been avoided. It could be further asserted that whatever the moral repugnance and inefficiencies of slavery, the consequences of its continuation would not have reduced economic growth as much as did the destruction of resources and the disruption of Southern agriculture caused by the Civil War. The axiom of indispensability cannot be resurrected on socio-political grounds without stronger evidence than is now available.

The "Take-Off" Thesis

Perhaps the most persuasive theory of embodied consequences is the one which holds that the inputs required for railroad construction induced the rise of industries, techniques and skills essential to economic growth. Chapters IV and V examine the widely discussed version of this theory authored by W. W. Rostow. According to Rostow the growth of America's modern basic industrial sectors can be traced directly to the requirements for building and, especially, maintaining the railway system. Through their demand for coal, iron, machinery, and other manufactured goods railroads are supposed to have ushered the United States into a unique period of structural transformation that built modern growth into the economy. Rostow calls this period of radical transformation, the "take-off into self-sustained growth." He holds that it occurred between 1843 and 1860.

At first sight it might appear that available data support Rostow's contention that the eighteen years from 1843 through 1860 witnessed a unique structural transformation in the economy. According to data compiled by Robert Gallman the manufacturing share of commodity output increased from 21.1 per cent to 32.0 per cent over a period closely approximating the one singled out by Rostow—1844 through 1859. While this shift towards manufacturing is impressive, averaging 3.6 percentage points per quinquennium, it is by no means unique. Gallman's series extends from 1839 to 1899. Of the 12 quinquennia included in the study, the manufacturing share increased by 3.0 points or more in half. However, only one of these high-rate-of-change periods falls during Rostow's "take-off" years. Four belong to the epoch following the Civil War. Indeed, the increase in the manufacturing share during the fifteen years from 1879 to 1894 exceeded that of 1844–59 by 50 per cent.

Unfortunately there is no aggregate measure equivalent to Gallman's for the period prior to 1839. Available information indicates, however, that the decade of the 1820's may have witnessed a shift toward manufacturing comparable to that observed for the "take-off" years. This possibility is supported by the sharp decline in the home manufacture of consumer's goods and by the fact that urban population increased at twice the rate of the population as a whole. It is also buttressed by the rapid rise of the cotton textile and iron industries. The production of cotton cloth increased by over 500 per cent between 1820 and 1831. In the latter year the output of textiles was 40 per cent greater in America than it had been in Great Britain at the close of its "take-off." The growth of iron production outstripped that of cotton. The output of pig iron increased from 20,000 tons in 1820 to 192,000 tons in 1830, a rise of nearly 900 per cent. By 1830 iron, like textiles, was a substantial industry. In this branch of manufacture too, American production in 1830 exceeded British production at the close of the era that Rostow designated as the British "take-off."

The development of cotton textiles and iron during the 1820's was so rapid that even if all other commodity producing sectors grew no faster than the population, the manufacturing share of commodity output would have increased by 1.5 percentage points. And if manufacturing industries other than iron and cotton grew at three times the rate of population, the manufacturing share in commodity output would have risen by nearly 6 percentage points. Since the production of woolen textiles, carpets, paper, primary refined lead, sugar, and meat packing expanded from three to twenty-five times as rapidly as the population, the last alternative seems quite reasonable.

Available evidence thus tends to controvert the view that the period from 1843 to 1860 or any other eighteen-year period was one of unique structural change. Instead, the data suggest a process of more or less continuous increase in the absolute and relative size of manufacturing extending from 1820—a good argument can be made for viewing 1807 as the starting date—through the end of the century.

The doubt attached to Rostow's dictum on the existence of very short periods of decisive structural transformation does not imply that historians must abandon the concept of "industrial revolution." One should not, however, require a revolution to have the swiftness of a coup d'etat. That manufacturing accounted for about 10 per cent of commodity production in 1820 and 48 per cent in 1889 is certainly evidence of a dramatic change in what was, by historical standards, hardly more than a moment of time. One need not arbitrarily abstract eighteen years out of a continuum to uphold the use of a venerable term.

If the growth of manufacturing during the two decades prior to the Civil War was not the crossing of the Rubicon pictured by Rostow, it was nonetheless large and impressive. The question of the relationship between this growth and the materials required for the construction and maintenance of railroads still remains.

The Iron Industry

Iron is the most frequently cited example of an industry whose rise was dominated by railroads. Hofstadter, Miller, and Aaron, for example, report that the railroad was "by far the biggest user of iron in the 1850's" and that by 1860 "more than half the iron produced annually in the United States went into rails" and associated items.[18] Such reports, however, are not based on systematic measurements but on questionable inferences derived from isolated scraps of data. Casual procedures have led to the use of an index that grossly exaggerates the rail share, to the neglect of the rerolling process, and to a failure to consider the significance of the scrapping process.

The systematic reconstruction of the position of rails in the market for iron requires the development of a model of rail consumption that incorporates the largest number of available data fragments in an internally consistent manner. A model which meets this specification involves the following variables:

R_t = tons of rails consumed in year t

R_{dt} = tons of rails produced domestically in year t

R_{ft} = tons of rails imported in year t

R_{jt} = tons of worn rails scrapped in year t

M_t = track-miles of rails laid in year t; a track-mile of rails is defined as one-half of the miles of rails in a mile of single track

w_t = the average weight of rails in year t per track-mile of rails laid in year t; i.e., $w_t = \dfrac{R_t}{M_t}$

M_{st} = track-miles of rails used in the construction of new single track in year t

M_{et} = track-miles of rails used in the construction of new extra track in year t; extra track refers to second and third tracks on a given line, sidings, etc.

[18] Richard Hofstadter, William Miller, and Daniel Aaron, *The American Republic* (2 vols.; Englewood Cliffs, 1959), I, 557.

M_{rt} = track-miles of rails used in the replacement of worn out rails in year t

t = time measured in years.

The model can be set forth as follows:

(5.1) $R_t = M_t w_t$

(5.2) $R_{dt} = R_t - R_{ft}$

(5.3) $M_t = M_{st} + M_{et} + M_{rt}$

(5.4) $\dfrac{\overset{t}{\underset{0}{\Sigma}} M_{et}}{\overset{t}{\underset{0}{\Sigma}} M_{st}} = \alpha t$

(5.5) $M_{rt} = \beta_1 M_{t-1} + \beta_2 M_{t-2} + \cdots + \beta_n M_{t-n}; \Sigma \beta_i = 1$

(5.6) $R_{ft} = \lambda_1 R_{t-1} + \lambda_2 R_{t-2} + \cdots + \lambda_n R_{t-n}$

Four of the variables in these equations, w_t, R_{ft}, M_{st} and t, are determined exogenously.

The first three equations are definitional identities. The fourth equation states that the ratio of total extra track to total single track increased linearly with time. The fifth and sixth equations state that the amount of rails replaced in any given year and the amount of scrap generated by the replacement process were functions of the rails laid in all previous years. The parameters of the fifth and sixth equations were in turn determined by the assumption that rail life was a stochastic process that could be described by a log-normal distribution with a mean of 10.5 years and a standard deviation of 3 years. This hypothesis is strongly supported by data on rail life published in the Tenth Census. Moreover, the estimates produced by the model proved to be relatively insensitive to various other assumptions, consistent with the census data, regarding the parameters and form of the distribution of rail life.

Various tests indicate a high degree of conformity between estimates produced by the model and available data fragments. Thus the model is within one percentage point in predicting the iron industry's "rule-of-thumb" for the share of the track replaced during a year, within 8 per cent of the reported ratio of rails required for new consumption to total rail consumption for 1856, and within 3 per cent in predicting the average weight of rails on main track at the end of 1869. The estimates of rail consumption generated by the model for the years 1849 through 1869 are also consistent with the consumption series published by the American Iron and Steel Association.

The model does more than conform to alternative estimates. It reveals the substantial magnitude of two previously neglected processes. The first of these is replacements. The model shows that replacements became an important part of total rail consumption early in the 1840's. In fifteen of the thirty years following 1839, replacements represented more than 40 per cent of total rail requirements; in five of these years, replacements accounted for more than two-thirds of requirements. Moreover, the variability of rail life acted like a moving average, smoothing the peaks and troughs of new construction to produce a fairly continuous and predictable increase in the amount of rails required for replacements. Hence the use of rails gave rise to a mechanism that made the demand for the product considerably more stable than it would have been if demand depended only on new construction.

The model also reveals that the scrap metal generated in the replacement process rapidly became a significant part of the supply of crude iron. The availability of scrap in turn spurred the development of the rerolling of old rails. As early as 1849 one-fourth of all domestically produced rails were rerolled from discarded ones. By 1860, rerolling accounted for nearly 60 per cent of domestic production. Thus although replacements rapidly became a substantial part of total rail consumption, replacement demand had little effect on the growth of blast furnaces. Replacements generated their own supply of crude iron. And scrapped rails that were not rerolled supplanted pig iron as an input in the production of other products. Consequently the net addition to pig iron production required for rails between 1840 and 1860 amounted to less than 5 per cent of the output of blast furnaces.

The significance of railroads appears somewhat greater if account is taken of all forms of railroad consumption of iron from all sectors of the iron industry. On this basis railroads accounted for an average of 17 per cent of total iron production during the two decades in question. While it is true that the railroad share rose to 25 per cent in the final six years of the period, what is more germane to the evaluation of the Rostow thesis is the fact that during the quinquennium ending in 1849, railroad consumption of domestic crude iron was just 10 per cent of the total. Even if there had been no production of rails or railroad equipment whatsoever, the domestic crude iron consumed by the iron industry would have reached an average of 700,000 tons in the second quinquennium. The rise over the previous quinquennium would still have been 338,000 tons—an increase of 94 per cent as opposed to the 99 per cent rise that took place with the railroads. Clearly railroad consumption of iron had little effect on the rate of growth of the industry during the crucial first decade of Rostow's "take-off" period; the new high level of production attained by the iron industry during 1845–49 did not depend on the railroad market.

The strongest statement that can be made in support of Rostow's thesis is that the demand for railroad iron played an increasingly important role during the fifties in maintaining the *previous* level of production when the demand for other items sagged. Otherwise one could just as well argue that nails rather than rails triggered the 1845–49 leap in iron production. Indeed in 1849 the domestic production of nails probably exceeded that of rails by over 100 per cent.

Other Industries

The position of railroads in the market for the products of other industries designated by Rostow appears equally limited. In the case of coal, direct consumption during the two decades ending in 1860 was negligible. While the pace of experimentation increased in the fifties, few coal burning locomotives were in regular service until the last two years of the decade. Wood was the fuel that powered the land leviathan. On the second stage of demand the picture changes slightly. The iron industry was a major consumer of coal. It required 8,300,000 tons of this fuel to manufacture all of the domestic rails produced during 1840–60 and 4,300,000 tons to manufacture the iron required for rail fastenings, locomotives, and cars. All told, railroads consumed 12,600,-000 tons of coal through their purchases of rails and other products made of iron. Over the same two decade period total coal production was 211,700,000 tons. Thus coal consumed by railroads through consumption of iron products represented less than 6 per cent of the coal produced during the "take-off."

Railroads exercised a still more modest influence on the development of the modern lumber industry—this despite the huge quantities of wood consumed as fuel and in the construction of track. The paradox is partly explained by the fact that wood burned in the fire boxes of railroad engines was not lumber. A similar consideration is involved in connection with the railroads' consumption of cross ties. Throughout the nineteenth century railroad men believed that ties hewed by axe would resist decay better than sawed ties. Consequently lumber mills supplied ties amounting to only 450,000,000 feet B. M. during the "take-off" years. This was less than one-half of one per cent of all lumber production. When the lumber required for car construction is included, the figure rises by half a point to 0.96 per cent. The modest position of railroads in the market for lumber products emphasizes the scale of lumber consumption by other sectors of the economy.

The share of the output of the transportation equipment industry purchased by railroads is also surprising. From 1850 through 1860 some 26,300 miles of new track were laid. During the same time, about 3,800 locomotives, 6,400 passenger and baggage cars, and 88,600 freight cars were constructed. Yet value added in the construction of railroad equipment in 1859 was only $12,000,000 or 25.4 per cent of value added by all transportation equipment. The output of vehicles drawn by animals was still almost twice as great as the output of equipment for the celebrated iron horse.

As for other types of machinery, railroads directly consumed less than 1 per cent. Again, the situation does not change appreciably if indirect purchases at more remote levels of production are considered. When the share of machinery consumed by the lumber, iron, and machine industries attributable to the railroad is added to that of transportation equipment, the railroad still only accounts for about 6 per cent of machine production in 1859.

The transportation equipment, rolling mill, blast furnace, lumber, and machinery industries were the main suppliers of the manufactured goods purchased by railroads. Using value added as a measure, railroads purchased slightly less than 11 per cent of the combined output of the group in 1859. Since these industries accounted for 26 per cent of all manufacturing in that year, railroad purchases from them amounted to a mere 2.8 per cent of the total output of the manufacturing sector. Railroad purchases from all the other manufacturing industries raise the last figure to just 3.9 per cent. This amount hardly seems large enough to attribute the rapid growth of manufacturing during the last two ante-bellum decades to the "requirements for building and, especially, for maintaining substantial railway systems."

IMPLICATIONS FOR THE THEORY OF ECONOMIC GROWTH

The most important implication of this study is that no single innovation was vital for economic growth during the nineteenth century. Certainly if any innovation had title to such distinction it was the railroad.

Yet, despite its dramatically rapid and massive growth over a period of a half century, despite its eventual ubiquity in inland transportation, despite its devouring appetite for capital, despite its power to determine the outcome of commercial (and sometimes political) competition, the railroad did not make an overwhelming contribution to the production potential of the economy.

Economic growth was a consequence of the knowledge acquired in the course of the scientific revolution of the seventeenth, eighteenth and nineteenth centuries. This knowledge provided the basis for a multiplicity of innovations that were applied to a broad spectrum of economic processes. The effectiveness of the new innovations was facilitated by political, geographic and social rearrangements. All of these developments began before the birth of the railroad and the railroad was not needed for the transformation in economic life that followed from them.

The English industrial revolution did not wait for the coming of the iron horse. It was virtually completed before the first railroad was built. The millions that migrated to the American West before 1840 did not do so because they anticipated the windfall gains that the incipient competitor to waterways would bring. They moved to the West because even without railroads the growth of population and capital in Europe and the eastern portions of the United States made investment in the new lands more profitable than a comparable investment in the old ones. It was the heavy demand for nails, stoves and various forms of cast iron rather than rails that elicited the leap in the American production of pig iron during the 1840's. The acceleration in urbanization that paralleled the rapid expansion of industry and commerce also preceded the railroads. And the large market for their products that eastern textile firms found in upstate New York before 1835, and in territories further to the West before 1840, were reached by waterways and wagons.

The railroad—like the improvement of the steam engine, the mechanization of textile production, the development of refrigeration, or the introduction of the puddling and rolling process—was a part rather than a condition for the industrial revolution. Along with a series of other inventions, it emerged out of a widespread effort to apply scientific and technological knowledge to the improvement of products and the reduction of costs. This search for new methods was distinguished not only by the vigor with which it was pursued but also by the fact that it frequently yielded more than one solution. Arkwright and Hargreaves separately invented different spinning machines. Bessemer and the

Siemens brothers found alternative ways of producing cheap steel. Watt relied on the sun and planet while Pickard used the crank and connecting rod to transform reciprocating into rotary motion. In transportation too the search for cheap sources of service yielded more than one solution.

If correct, this stress on the multiplicity of solutions along a wide front of production problems clashes with the notion that economic growth can be explained by leading sector concepts. Such concepts suggest that the search for, or discovery of, new solutions was limited to narrowly selected industries and that growth in other sectors had to wait for breakthroughs in the anointed ones. It is the hero theory of history applied to things rather than persons. In the American case virtually every two–digit manufacturing industry was experiencing rapid growth during the last two decades of the ante–bellum era. The observed growth was not induced by a single technological change that linked all manufacturing enterprises to the railroad, like a string of freight cars attached to a locomotive. Rather it was induced by a multiplicity of innovations in these industries coupled with a series of cost saving developments in transportation as well as developments on the demand side that served to expand markets (accelerated population growth in Europe, rapid urbanization, etc.).

This view makes growth the consequence not of one or a few lucky discoveries but of a broad supply of opportunity created by the body of knowledge accumulated over all preceding centuries. Luck may have determined which breakthroughs came first or which of the many possible solutions was seized by society. It may have affected the timing of particular innovations and the relative rates of growth of particular industries. Chance factors no doubt affected the precise path that growth followed. But chance operated within the set of opportunities created by the scientific revolution.

The theory of overwhelming, singular innovations has probably been fostered by the modus operandi of competitive economies. Under competition firms tend to choose the most efficient of the available methods of production. Alternatives that could perform the same functions at somewhat greater cost are discarded and escape public attention. The absence from view of slightly less efficient processes creates the illusion that no alternatives exist. This illusion is heightened by the fact that the chosen process has an optimal set of institutional arrangements, appurtenances, and personnel. Given the fact that the operation of the economy has adjusted to the selected process, business success will frequently depend on the speed and effectiveness with which firms adopt these supplementary arrangements. Thus accessories of the innovation become *conditionally* indispensable and add to the impression of the massive and overwhelming character of the basic selection. Yet these accessories—in the case of railroads they were such things as automatic coupling devices, block signals, fast freight services, time tables, types of rails, varieties of freight cars, geographic locations—usually make no independent contribution. They are merely the conditions under which the primary innovation operates and through which it imparts its contribution to economic growth.

Emphasis on the multiplicity of opportunities does not mean that the particular nature of the solutions society selects are without significance. Cheap inland transportation was a necessary condition for economic growth. Satisfaction of this condition did not entail a specific form of transportation. The form by which the condition was in fact satisfied did effect, however, particular features of the observed growth process. It determined the names of some of the chief decision makers, it added new products to the bill of output and it modified the location of economic activity. Changes of this sort defined a particular path of economic growth, a path distinct from that which would have been followed if society had embraced some other solution. In other words the fact that the condition of cheap transportation was satisfied by one innovation rather than another determined, not whether growth would take place, but which of many possible growth paths would be followed.

MEASUREMENT AND THEORY IN THE STUDY OF ECONOMIC HISTORY

Analysis of the developmental role of railroads leads one unavoidably into the much disputed problem of the proper place of statistical methods in economic history. While considerable advances have been made in the application of these procedures to the data of American history, the advances have been confined largely to the measurement of national income and related aggregate variables. Professional discussions of most events in the domain of economic history are still carried on in qualitative terms with statistical data used largely as illustration.

If statistical methods could be applied only in the study of trivial issues or if, when applied, they yielded substantially the same conclusions as were obtained by qualitative analysis, a reluctance to exploit these techniques would be understandable. But in the case of the issues examined in this book, statistical methods yield results different from those that were obtained by more traditional approaches. Nor is railroad history the only area in which studies based on the analytical and quantitative techniques of contemporary economics have led to major departures in substantive findings. Estimates of returns on nineteenth-century land purchases computed by Allan and Margaret Bogue suggest the need for a re-interpretation of the position of the frontier land speculator in American economic development.[19] The application of capital theory to the study of slavery by Alfred H. Conrad and John R. Meyer produced evidence which strongly contradicts the long-standing view that the unprofitability of slavery had undermined that system.[20] And more recently, Thomas C. Cochran found that the failure of historians to take account of available quantitative data has resulted in "an exaggerated conception," if not misconception, of the role of the Civil War in the process of American industrialization.[21]

The inadequate exploration of the realm of issues to which modern statistical methods apply reflects, at least in part, the strong influence of that set of doctrines which philosophers of history refer to as "historicism." The premise that scientific methods are inappropriate for the study of history—the chief hallmark of "historicism"—has engendered in many historians a profound skepticism regarding the usefulness of statistics.[22] Charles H. Hull gave voice to this skepticism in his 1914 address to the 75th Anniversary Celebration of the American Statistical Association. "The majority of intelligent historians. . . ," said Hall, "would agree . . . that the statistical method, being a specific type of the method of natural science, is not their proper method and cannot become their principal tool. For the ultimate units with which the historian deals are not atoms, or any sort of instrumental abstractions, whose individual differences may be ignored, but they are men and

---

[19] " 'Profits' and the Frontier Land Speculator," *Journal of Economic History*, XVII (1957), 1–24.

[20] "The Economics of Slavery in the Ante Bellum South," *Journal of Political Economy*, LXVI (April, 1958), 95–130.

[21] "Did the Civil War Retard Industrialization?," *Mississippi Valley Historical Review*, XLVIII (1961), 197–210.

[22] A summary of the main tenets and present status of historicism is contained in the introductory essay to Hans Meyerhoff, *The Philosophy of History in Our Time* (Garden City, N. Y., 1959). The classic defense of the applicability of the scientific method in history is Carl G. Hempel, "The Function of General Laws in History," *The Journal of Philosophy*, XXXIX (1942), reprinted in Patrick Gardiner, *Theories of History* (Glencoe, Ill., 1959), pp. 344–56.

deeds of men." Men and their deeds, he asserted, are "too complex and too variously conditioned to be subject to the concept of general law."[23] The past half century has not significantly altered this predilection. In a recent article entitled "Scientific History in America: Eclipse of an Idea," Edward M. Saveth argued that the subject matter of history involved "a great number of variables distributed widely in space and time, whose interaction can rarely be precisely determined and, as a rule, cannot be measured quantitatively." As a result, said Saveth, the historian doubted

> the superiority of the quantitative measurements of the social scientist to his own informed guesses. The reaction of Dr. Henry David is typical of that of many historians when he asserts that the pollsters, had they been around in 1800, could not have done a better job of estimating popular attitude in the United States than did Henry Adams by using the historians' traditional sources.[24]

When applied to economic phenomena, the methodological precepts of "historicism" find expression in the view that qualitative analysis is the primary and distinctive feature of economic history. This view involves the premise that many, if not most, important issues in the economic history of societies are qualitative in nature and, therefore, not susceptible of quantitative analysis. It is further argued that the available data for periods as recent as the early nineteenth century are so fragmentary and of such poor quality that reliance on qualitative methods leads to false or misleading conclusions. Under such circumstances, it is held, qualitative analysis is to be preferred even for problems to which the application of statistical techniques are valid in principle.

However, these arguments are based on a fundamental misconception of the relationship between the qualitative and quantitative aspects of economic history. One cannot escape the ponderous problems of measurement in economic history by embracing qualitative analysis. The alternative is precluded by the subject matter of the discipline. "The special task of the economic historian," said Guy S. Callender, one of the first American claimants of the title,

> ought to be to analyze this all-embracing process [by which wealth is produced and distributed] as it has existed in each country at

[23] Charles H. Hull, "The Service of Statistics to History," *Journal of the American Statistical Association,* 75 (March, 1914), 35.

[24] Edward M. Saveth, "Scientific History in America: Eclipse of an Idea," Donald Sheehan and Harold C. Syrett, eds., *Essays in American Historiography* (New York, 1960), p. 15.

different times, and to explain it. His subject ought to be the *wealth of nations* in the literal sense of that phrase. He ought to make clear what factors have determined the ability of each nation to produce wealth in any particular time and what have influenced its distribution; and he should also reveal the forces which have acted to change economic conditions from time to time, producing economic progress or economic decline.[25]

Clearly the pursuit of the objectives outlined by Callender, and generally accepted by most economic historians, involves measurement in an essential and unavoidable manner. The description of the "wealth of nations" cannot be carried out purely or even primarily in qualitative terms; and to explain historical changes in the wealth (or national income or standard of living) of nations is to explain why wealth (etc.) rose or fell from one magnitude to another. In other words the central concern of economic historians is with phenomena which cannot be described without measurement and with the analysis of the effects of changes in institutions and processes on the measurable magnitudes of these phenomena.

Moreover, many qualitative differences in economic life are of such a nature that their explanation can only be cast in quantitative terms. The counterparts of American entrepreneurship, modern steel plants, railroads, airlines, IBM computers, coal and other mineral resources, skilled technicians, and virtually all the other endowments characteristic of a highly industrialized society are also to be found in India. At the same time, individuals who lack pecuniary incentive, who cannot cope with the technical problems of modern industry, who prefer to consume rather than save, who scorn the achievements of modern science, etc., are to be found in both nations. The *qualitative* difference between the developed and the underdeveloped nation is not explained by the presence or absence of qualitative endowments. Rather it is explained by the differences in the proportions and amounts in which the various qualitative endowments are found in the respective nations.[26]

Quantification insinuates itself in an essential way in virtually all the qualitative discussions of economic history. What is important here

[25] Guy S. Callender, "The Position of American Economic History," *American Historical Review*, XIX (October, 1913), 88.

[26] This relationship between the quantitative and qualitative aspects of phenomena is, of course, not limited to economics. After all, the difference between that gas which is inimicable to human life and a gas which makes soda pleasantly effervescent is one atom of oxygen.

is not that even the most literary essays tend to contain numerical illustrations. The important quantifications in such discussions enter more subtly, through statements which, while purely qualitative in *form*, are quantitative in *content*. These are statements in which quantification is assumed without explicit articulation, statements that have no warrant without prior measurement. Consider, for example, the following qualitative description of the effect of railroads on the American economy:

> Regional concentration of industries and specialized crops, though dependent on many factors, could not have developed so fully without railroad transportation. New England could find national markets for its textiles and shoes. Pennsylvania, with its coal and easy access to iron, could concentrate on basic iron and steel, shipping products wherever they might be wanted. Iowa could, with its specially adapted soils and climate, become a corn and hog country.[27]

This apparently qualitative description is permeated with implicit measurements. The "regional concentration" of industry referred to in the first sentence can only be defined in quantitative terms; the phrase implies the existence of a measure of the spatial distribution of productive activity. The sentence as a whole implies that the difference between the cost of transportation by railroad and the next most favorable medium was of such a magnitude that the absence of the railroad would have reduced regional concentration by a detectable, and, therefore, measurable amount.[28] The term "national market" (second sentence), if it is to have anything but a trivial meaning, implies that the amount of shoes and cotton goods sold by various firms beyond some region specified as local was large relative to their total output. The only significant economic interpretation of the phrase "easy access" (third sentence) is that the cost of obtaining iron in Pennsylvania was lower than in other designated areas. The statement that Pennsylvania "concentrated" on the production of basic iron and steel implies a system by which the amounts of the qualitatively different products of the state can be aggregated and against which the state's production of iron and steel products can be measured. Finally, the statement that Iowa's soil and climate were "specially adapted" to corn production (fourth

[27] George Soule, *Economic Forces in American History* (New York, 1952), p. 103.

[28] To be more precise, the sentence implies that such a measurement has in fact been performed.

sentence) presumes the existence of a measurable relationship between corn yields on the one hand and rainfall, temperature, and various soil properties on the other.

Even if it were possible to purge all qualitative discussions of implicit measurement, qualitative discussions would still be dominated by quantitative considerations. For which of the infinite number of the qualitative aspects of economic activity scholars choose to study is determined on quantitative grounds. If economic historians have written thousands of pages on the qualitative change from water to railroad transportation while slighting the qualitative changes in the treatment of the lumber used in the construction of wagons, it is because they believe that the first resulted in a major reduction in transportation costs and the second did not. Similarly, if economic historians were convinced that banking practices had absolutely no effect on the *supply* of money, the *rate* of interest, the *distribution* of income, the *amount* of saving and investment, the *rate* and *periodicity* of economic growth, the *extent* of the division of labor, the *size* of the market, and the *concentration* of wealth, they would devote no more attention to changes in the institutional arrangements and practices of the banking system than they do to the change from metallic to paper currency.

Authoritative Opinions as an Alternative to Statistical Measurement

The economic historian is thus more restricted in his capacity to disentangle the qualitative and quantitative aspects of his subject matter than is sometimes recognized. He is also much more restricted than is sometimes recognized in the choice of methods by which he can ascertain required magnitudes. Because of these restrictions the doctrine that opinions of authoritative historical persons regarding the magnitudes of economic phenomena are a satisfactory alternative to measurement based on modern statistical methods is frequently misleading.

Suppose, for example, that the evaluation of some historical problem required knowledge of the movement of the real wages of industrial workers during the panic of 1873. To determine this movement statistically one would have to have data on the wages of workers in various occupations at both the start and close of the designated period. These, together with information on the number of workers in the pertinent occupations, would make it possible to construct an index of money wages. To determine real wages, however, money wages need to be adjusted for changes in the prices of the things that workers purchased. The adjustment requires data on the prices of consumer goods as well as on the distribution of consumer expenditures among various alternatives.

Do the written opinions of authoritative individuals represent an alternative method of determining the course of real wages? Acceptance of the statement of some (or many) outstanding personalities merely indicates that the historian believes that these authorities had at their disposal the same data that the statistician would require. For without such information these authorities could not have known the course of real wages. It might be argued that a sample of opinions could be chosen in such a way as to be representative of the experiences of various categories of workers—for example, a suitable sample of the letters of workers. But the selection of a "suitable" sample requires the utilization of modern statistical techniques.[29] Moreover, unless these letters contained numerical information on prices, wage rates, etc., the most that could be inferred is the direction in which real wages moved —and then only on condition that all, or virtually all, the letters indicated changes in the same direction. Of course, the desired information could be obtained from such letters if they contained the relevant numerical data. However, in this case the method would be identical with that of the statistician; only the source of the data would differ.

The thrust of the preceding paragraph is that magnitudes can only be determined by measurement. The choice that confronts the economic historian is, therefore, not between measurement and something

---

[29] In this context, it is useful to examine the previously quoted statement that "pollsters, had they been around in 1800, could not have done a better job of estimating popular attitude in the United States than did Henry Adams by using the historians' traditional sources." Is this position tenable? Adams did not take a complete census of all the extant documents bearing on the questions in which he was interested. Consequently, the formal nature of his problem was the same as that which confronts pollsters—inferring the characteristic of a population from a sample. Thus if pollsters could not have improved on Adams' method, it can only be because he derived a sample in such a manner that his estimates had optimal properties (efficiency, unbiasedness, consistency, and sufficiency). But if his estimates lacked these properties, as they apparently do, pollsters could have improved on the work of Adams. Of course, if pollsters could not have improved on Adams, the historian's feat was even more remarkable than I have suggested. For all Adams had at his disposal were the documents left behind by the people of 1800 and not the people themselves. Thus Adams needed to know something which pollsters would not: how the distribution of opinions in surviving documents related to the distribution of opinions actually held in 1800.

else called "opinion" but between his own measurements and those on which the opinions of the past were based.

The issue under discussion is not fully joined unless the underlying data to which modern statistical methods may be applied are quite fragmentary and of poor quality. Then the claim that investigations based on the opinions of authoritative individuals are superior to statistical analyses is most appealing. However, the conditions under which this claim is valid are much more restricted than is often suggested. The requirements are that: (1) the extant data are so poor that little or no use can be made of them, (2) the authorities relied upon had superior data at their disposal, and (3) the authorities are known to have used appropriate quantitative techniques in the evaluation of the data.

These conditions are not usually fulfilled in nineteenth–century history. If we lack a series describing the year to year changes in American pig iron production between 1820 and 1854, it is not because annual surveys which contemporaries had at their disposal have subsequently disappeared. Rather it is because the desired surveys were not conducted in most of these years. One can conjure up endless arguments for the authoritativeness of the opinion of so notable a figure as David A. Wells—Special U.S. Commissioner of Revenue and eminent economist. But his belief that pig iron production increased steadily from 1840 through 1860 was based on data more fragmentary and less reliable than can be obtained in libraries today.[30]

The third condition is often more grossly violated than the second. When economic historians seek in the writings of historical personages the answer to such questions as "What share of the output of the iron industry was consumed by railroads in the decade preceding the Civil War?" or "Did interregional agricultural trade depend on the existence of long-haul railroads?", they put the writings to tests they cannot be expected to pass, except by chance. The answers to these questions require instruments of measurement which the men of the nineteenth century did not know or barely perceived. One cannot accurately determine the share of iron production purchased by railroads from the data available in the 1850's without a knowledge of the nature of index numbers—a problem not well explored until after the beginning of the twentieth century. The determination of the saving in cost attributable to railroads involves the use of linear programming and other techniques

[30] U.S. Congress, House, *Report of the Special Commissioner of Revenue for the Year 1868,* Exec. Doc. 16, 40th Cong., 3d Sess. (Ser. No. 1372), pp. 8–9.

of even more recent origin. On questions of this nature, a search for the estimates of authorities of the nineteenth century has little more value than a similar search for estimates of the atomic weight of elements in the eighteenth–century literature of chemistry.

Authoritative opinions of the past, on most quantitative matters which concern economic historians, are crude approximations derived from poor data on the basis of inadequate analytical tools. They should not be accepted without statistical verification unless the absence of data makes verification impossible. Such opinions then represent a superior choice because no alternative exists. But this statement still exaggerates the usefulness of contemporary opinions on quantitative matters. It presumes a unanimity of opinion among authorities. The usual state of affairs is one of conflict. If statistical verification is impossible, how is one to choose between contradictory statements? Whose testimony on the course of ante-bellum iron production is more reliable: that of the free trader W. M. Grosvenor or that of the protectionist Henry Carey? Are we to presume with the eminent ironmaster and innovator Abraham Hewitt that production stagnated between 1847 and 1860 or are we to accept the opinion of the equally eminent Special U. S. Commissioner of Revenue that production during the period increased fairly steadily at a rate of about 8 per cent a year? [31] If the data on iron production and consumption prior to the Civil War are too fragmentary to permit verification, conflicting views cannot be resolved; the position of railroads in the market for iron is then indeterminate and confident statements on this matter in history books are unwarranted.

That the data of economic history are often fragmentary, does not preclude the formulation of effective empirical tests of quantitative hypotheses. Other disciplines—archaeology and paleontology are examples—have achieved a high degree of success in establishing procedures for the utilization of fragmentary evidence. It is unduly pessimistic to assume that similar successes cannot be achieved in economic history.[32] There are no absolute standards regarding precision of measurement. The amount of error tolerable in a given set of estimates depends on the use to which they are put. Data wholly inadequate for the prediction of cyclical turning points may be quite suitable for the analysis of long-term rates of growth. More often than not, historical hypotheses turn on orders of magnitudes rather than particular values. In such

[31] *Ibid.,* and chapter V above.
[32] Cf. with discussion in chapter V above.

cases definite knowledge of the range within which crucial values lie, or merely knowledge of one of the limits of that range, may be all that is required to test a particular hypothesis. Then it is possible to utilize data with indeterminate errors as long as the direction of the errors is unambiguous. Instances in which the data thrown up by the nineteenth century are too poor or too fragmentary to work with are thus less common than is suggested by historicist doctrine.

The Role of Theory

All warranted statements regarding the contribution of railroads to economic growth must be based on hypothetico-deductive systems. These statements invariably imply or explicitly contain a comparison between actual events and relations, at least some of which can be (and were) observed, and those events and relationships that would have obtained in the absence of railroads. However, the latter category of phenomena were not (and cannot be) observed. Consequently statements about them can only be justified by hypothetico-deductive systems. Estimation of the social saving attributable to the railroads in the distribution of agricultural products, for example, requires a theory of how the absence of railroads would have affected the spatial distribution and rank of shipping and receiving centers, a theory of the way in which water haulage costs would have responded to an increase in the volume of freight shipments by water, a theory that enables one to quantify the cost of time lost in slow transportation and the cost of being able to use water routes during certain periods of a year, and a theory that enables one to state the areas in which the absence of the railroads would have led to an abandonment of commercial agricultural production.

The models of theoretical economics represent a library—very much like the library of computing routines at an IBM installation—which can be drawn on in the analysis of a wide range of historical problems. It is beside the point to argue that the many conflicting theories put forth by economists make it difficult for the economic historian to know which are right and which are wrong. To the extent that they are internally consistent, all the models (even though they yield conflicting conclusions) are "right," just as models of probability theory based on differently defined sampling spaces are all "right." [33] It is, of course,

---

[33] See William Feller's discussion of Maxwell-Boltzmann, Bose-Einstein, and Fermi-Dirac statistics in *An Introduction to Probability Theory and Its Applications,* Vol. I (2d. ed.; New York, 1957), pp. 38–40.

a difficult task to determine which of various alternative models, if any, conform to the reality with which the historian must deal. But the natural scientist faces essentially the same problem. The investigator attempting to explain a physical process does not find his material labeled with tags that direct him to the appropriate mathematical constructs. He is the one who must decide whether the process under examination corresponds to a random walk, a problem in the calculus of variations, or some other model.

The neglect of the theoretical constructs of economics in the study of history is only partly explained by the inadequacy of the existing models. The contention that models constructed to explain economic phenomena or analyze policies peculiar to the twentieth century are, for that reason, useless in investigations of earlier periods is not always right. It may be based on a failure to see that problems which vary widely in time and space, which outwardly are completely different, may nevertheless be all members of a set of problems with identical formal properties and therefore amenable to analysis by the same logical constructs. Students of economic history require the same knack that the biologist displays when he recognizes that a certain genetic process is "just like"a coin tossing game and therefore can be appropriately explained by a binomial distribution; or the quality that the physicist displays when he discovers that the process of heat exchange between two isolated bodies is "just like" the drawing of colored balls from a pair of urns. Although linear programming was developed during World War II to solve the logistic problems of military planners, it can nevertheless be used to estimate the social saving attributable to railroads in the interregional distribution of agricultural products during the nineteenth century. And the theory of rent can be used to estimate the social loss that would have been incurred in a given region by cessation of all railroad service, even though this theory was originally formulated to explain why early nineteenth–century landlords were getting richer.

That the library of models constructed by theorists may fail to contain constructs suitable to the specific phenomenon an historian wants to explain does not relieve him of the burden of having to employ hypothetico-deductive methods. It merely means that the historian must assume a task that would otherwise have been fulfilled by the economic theorist. While important amendments have been made to Carl Hempel's demonstration that historical explanations, no less than those of the natural sciences, require the formulation of hypothetico-deductive systems, these amendments do not appear to affect the main impact of his analysis.[34] For the practicing historian it is important to be aware that the models of history may be based on generalizations which are "law-like" rather than "laws," on generalizations that are not universal but, because they are based on "transitional regularities," may be temporally or otherwise limited.[35] Such considerations bear on the nature of the evidence that should be used to test the empirical validity of historical models. The suggestion that a more penetrating analysis may emerge if historical explanations are treated as complexes of related events rather than a single event defined by a large number of initial conditions has a similar usefulness.[36]

It is particularly important to stress that these amendments do not mitigate the force of Hempel's conclusion that most historical explanations are really "explanation sketches."

> Such a sketch consists of a more or less vague indication of the laws and initial conditions considered as relevant, and it needs "filling out" in order to turn it into a full-fledged explanation. This filling-out requires further empirical research, for which the sketch suggests the direction. . . .
>
> In trying to appraise the soundness of a given explanation, one will first have to attempt to reconstruct as completely as possible the argument constituting the explanation or the explanation sketch. In particular, it is important to realize what the underlying explaining hypotheses are, and to judge of their scope and empirical foundation. A resuscitation of the assumptions buried under the gravestones "hence," "therefore," "because," and the like will often reveal that the explanation is poorly founded or downright unacceptable. In many cases, this procedure will bring to light the fallacy of claiming that a large number of details of an event have been explained when, even on a very liberal interpretation, only some broad characteristics of it have been accounted for. . . .[37]

The disinclination of many writers dealing with the developmental impact of railroads to conduct their analyses along Hempelian lines, that is, to make explicit the assumptions that underlie their implicit

[34] Hempel, "The Function of General Laws," p. 351.

[35] Alan Donagan, "Explanation in History," *Mind* (1957), reprinted in Gardiner, *Theories of History,* pp. 428–43; Carey B. Joynt and Nicholas Rescher, "The Problem of Uniqueness in History," *History and Theory,* I (1961), 150–62.

[36] Maurice Mandelbaum, "Historical Explanations: The Problem of 'Covering-Laws'," *History and Theory,* I (1961), 229–42.

[37] Hempel, "The Function of General Laws," pp. 351–2.

hypothetico-deductive models, has led to numerous logical and empirical slips.

* * *

This discussion has stressed the usefulness of the analytical and quantitative techniques of contemporary economics. One could, of course, cite instances of disastrous misapplications of the same techniques. However, such misapplications do not invalidate the preceding arguments. They are caveats not against the use of statistics and theory in the study of economic history but merely against their misuse. The misuse of quantitative methods and hypothetico-deductive constructs will be minimized when they are applied by scholars deeply immersed in the materials of history. Only the scholar who knows what is *unique, special,* and *particular* about a given historical problem can successfully adapt powerful general methods to the study of that problem. The casual interloper cannot possess this knowledge.

APPENDIX A

An Extended System of
Internal Navigation in 1890

Figure A–1 combines the proposed canals discussed in Chapter III with navigable rivers actually in use about the year 1890 and the canals actually built prior to 1891. Figure A–1 is based largely on the data and maps contained in the *Census of Transportation, 1890,* Part II; *Preliminary Report*; and Goodrich, *Canals.* In a goodly number of cases the navigable routes shown in these sources were extended, shortened, or deleted on the basis of information contained or references cited in U.S. Congress, House, *Index to the Reports of the Chief of Engineers, U.S. Army, 1866–1912,* Doc. No. 740, 63d Cong., 2d Sess.

The waterways shown on the map do not represent all of the waterways that might have been brought into service in the absence of railroads. Among other feasible extensions of the canal system are the projects considered in U.S. Congress, Senate, *Transportation Routes to the Seaboard,* Report No. 307, 43d Cong., 1st Sess.; and U.S. Congress, Senate, *Final Report of the National Waterways Commission,* Doc. No. 469, 62d Cong., 2d Sess. In addition, many rivers not shown in Figure A–1 could have been made navigable with relatively modest expenditures.

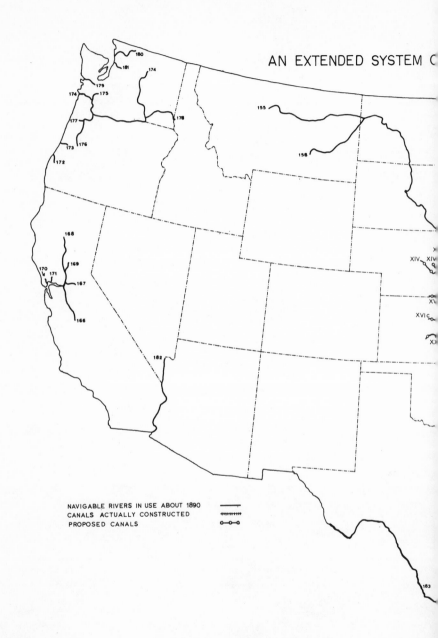

NAVIGABLE RIVERS IN USE ABOUT 1890
CANALS ACTUALLY CONSTRUCTED
PROPOSED CANALS

IRE A-I

ITERNAL NAVIGATION IN 1890

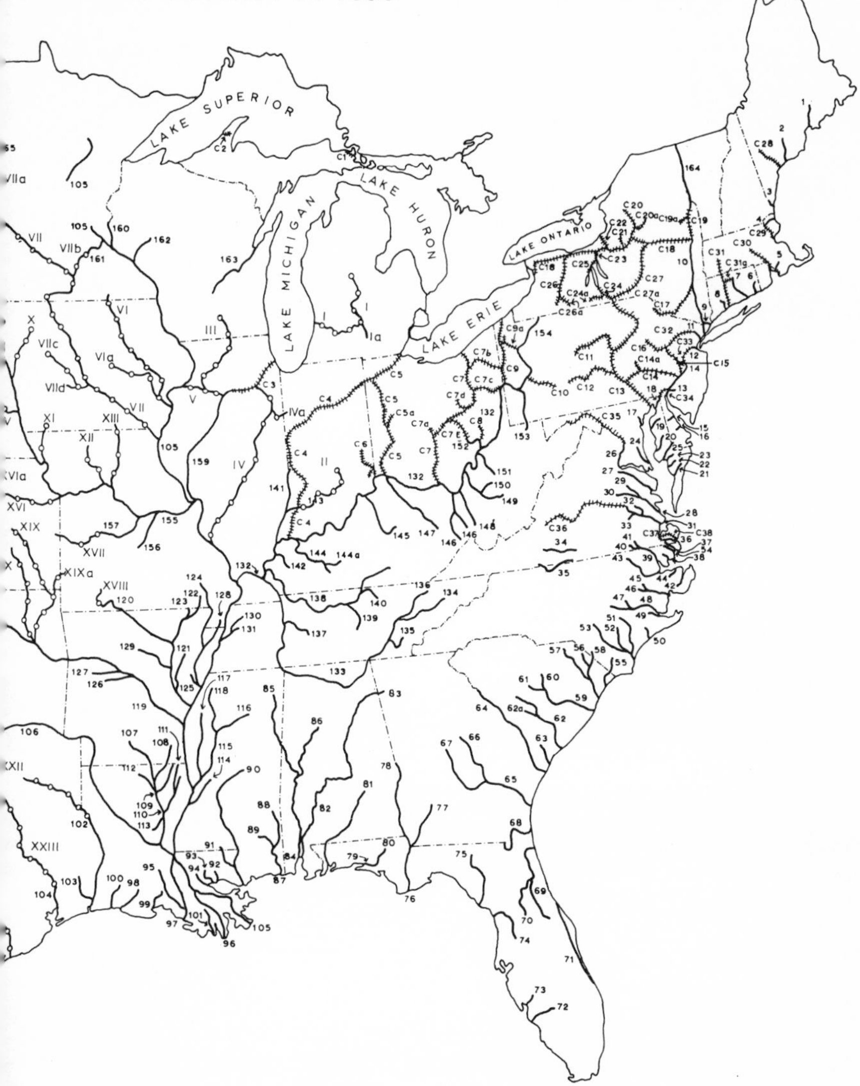

Navigable Streams and Rivers

1. Penobscot
2. Kennebec
3. Cochoeco
4. Merrimac
5. Taunton
6. Thames
7. Connecticut
8. Housatonic
9. East River
10. Hudson
11. Passaic
12. Raritan
13. Mantua Creek
14. Delaware
15. St. Jones
16. Mispillion
17. Patapsco
18. Elk
19. Chester
20. Choptank
21. Pocomoke
22. Manokin
23. Wicomico
24. Patuxent
25. Nanticoke
26. Potomac
27. Rappahannock
28. York
29. Mattaponi
30. Pamunkey
31. James
32. Chickahominy
33. Appomattox
34. Staunton
35. Dan
36. Nansemond
37. North
38. Perquimans
39. Chowan
40. Blackwater
41. Nottoway
42. Alligator
43. Roanoke
44. Scuppernong
45. Fishing Creek
46. Pamlico and Tar

47. Contentnia Creek
48. Neuse
49. Trent
50. New
51. Northeast
52. Black
53. Cape Fear
54. Pasquotank
55. Waccamaw
56. Little Pedee
57. Pedee
58. Lumber
59. Santee
60. Wateree
61. Congaree
62. Edisto
62a. South Edisto
63. Beaufort
64. Savannah
65. Altamaha
66. Oconee
67. Ocmulgee
68. St. Marys
69. St. Johns
70. Oklawaha
71. Indian
72. Caloosahatchee
73. Peace
74. Withlacoochee
75. Suwanee
76. Apalachicola
77. Flint
78. Chattahoochee
79. Choctawhatchee
80. Holmes
81. Escambia and
    Conecuh
82. Alabama
83. Coosa
84. Mobile
85. Tombigbee
86. Warrior and
    Black Warrior
87. Pascagoula
88. Chickasahay
89. Leaf

90. Pearl
91. Bogue Chitto
92. Chefuncte and
    Bogue Falia
93. Ticfaw
94. Amite and
    Bayou Manchac
95. Bayou Teche
96. Bayou Lafourche
97. Atchafalaya
98. Mermentau
99. Vermillion
100. Calcasieu
101. Bayou Terrebonne
102. Sabine
103. Neches
104. Trinity
105. Mississippi
106. Red
107. Black and Ouachita
108. Bayou Bartholomew
109. Boeuf
110. Tensas
111. Bayou Macon
112. Bayous D'Aarbonne
113. Little
114. Big Black
115. Yazoo
116. Tallahatchie
117. Big Sunflower
118. Coldwater
119. Arkansas
120. White
121. Cache
122. Black
123. Current
124. St. Francis
125. L'Anguille
126. Fourche le Fevre
127. Petit Jean
128. Little
129. Little Red
130. Obion
131. Forked Deer
132. Ohio
133. Tennessee

Navigable Streams and Rivers (continued)

134. French Broad
135. Clinch
136. Hiawassee
137. Duck
138. Cumberland
139. Caney Fork
140. Obey
141. Wabash
142. Tradewater
143. White
144. Green and Barren
144a. Green and Barren
145. Kentucky
146. Big Sandy
147. Licking
148. Guyandot
149. Kanawha
150. Elk

151. Little Kanawha
152. Muskingum
153. Monongahela
154. Allegheny
155. Missouri
156. Gasconade
157. Osage
158. Yellowstone
159. Illinois
160. St. Croix
161. Minnesota
162. Chipewa
163. Fox and Wisconsin, including Wolf
164. Lake Champlain
165. Red River of the North

166. San Joaquin
167. Mokelumne
168. Sacramento
169. Feather
170. Petaluma Creek
171. Napa
172. Coquille
173. Siuslaw
174. Columbia
175. Cowlitz
176. Willamette
177. Yamhill
178. Snake
179. Chehalis
180. Skagit
181. Skykomish
182. Colorado
183. Rio Grande

Canals Actually Built

C1. St. Marys Fall
C2. Portage Lake
C3. Illinois and Michigan
C4. Wabash and Erie
C5. Miami and Erie
C5-a. Feeder to Miami and Erie
C6. Whitewater
C7. Ohio and Erie
C7-a. Columbus Feeder
C7-b. Ohio and Pennsylvania
C7-c. Sandy and Beaver
C7-d. Walhonding
C7-e. Hocking
C8. Muskingum
C9. Erie Extension
C9-a. French Creek Erie Division
C10. Western Division
C11. West Branch
C12. Juniata Division
C13. Pennsylvania Canal Company
C13-a. Wiconisco Branch
C14. Union and Schuylkill Navigation
C14-a. Union Extension
C15. Delaware Division

C16. Lehigh Coal and Navigation Co.
C17. Delaware and Hudson
C18. Erie
C19. Champlain
C19-a. Glens Falls Feeder
C20. Black River and Feeder
　　　Black River Improvement
C20-a. Reservoirs Black River
C21. Oneida Lake
C22. Oswego
C23. Cayuga and Seneca
C24. Chemung
C24-a. Feeder
C25. Crooked Lake
C26. Genesee Valley
C26-a. Genesee Valley Branch
C27. Chenango
C27-a. Chenango Extension
C28. Cumberland and Oxford
C29. Middlesex
C30. Blackstone
C31. New Haven and Northampton
C31-a. Enfield Falls
C32. Morris Canal

CANALS ACTUALLY BUILT (continued)

C33. Delaware and Raritan   C36. James River and Kanawha
C34. Chesapeake and Delaware   C37. Dismal Swamp
C35. Chesapeake and Ohio   C38. Albermarle and Chesapeake

PROPOSED CANALS
(See Table 3.11)

APPENDIX B

Some Material Supplementary to the Chapter on Rails

1. On page 151 it was stated that I_4 exceeded I_1 because the ratio of the price per ton of finished product to crude iron per ton of finished product was greater in the case of other final products of the iron industry than it was for rails. The formal proof of this statement is as follows. Let

P_r = the average price of domestic rails
R = the total weight of domestic rails
P_a = the average price of all other final products of the iron industry
A = the total weight of all other final products of the iron industry
C_r = the weight of the crude iron required to produce R
C_a = the weight of crude iron required to produce A

(B1.1)

$$I_1 = \frac{\text{Value of all domestically produced rails}}{\text{Value of all final products of the domestic iron industry}}$$

or

(B1.2)
$$I_1 = \frac{P_r R}{P_r R + P_a A}.$$

Let

(B1.3)
$$\frac{P_r R}{C_r} = \alpha \text{ and (B1.4) } \frac{P_a A}{C_a} = n\alpha;$$

then

(B1.5)
$$I_1 = \frac{\alpha C_r}{\alpha C_r + n\alpha C_a} = \frac{C_r}{C_r + n C_a}.$$

However, since

(B1.6)
$$I_4 = \frac{C_r}{C_r + C_a}$$

$$I_4 > I_1 \text{ when } n > 1.$$

Now the statement that the ratio of the price per ton of finished product to crude iron per ton of finished product is greater for other final products of the iron industry than for rails means that

(B1.7) $$\frac{P_a}{\dfrac{C_a}{A}} > \frac{P_r}{\dfrac{C_r}{R}} \text{ or that (B1.8)} \frac{\dfrac{P_a A}{C_a}}{\dfrac{P_r R}{C_r}} > 1.$$

However the expression on the left side of the inequality sign in B1.8 is n. Therefore, $I_4 > I_1$.

2. It is possible to compute a value index (I_1) for two years near the end of the 1850's. Table B2.1 shows that in 1856 rails represented only 12.5 per cent of the final product of the iron industry by value. Hence for this year I_4 overstates I_1 by 60 per cent (cf. Table 5.17).

All of the data needed to compute I_1 for the 1859–60 except for the value of rails is reported in *Census of Manufacturing, 1860*. While the Census separates various products of rolling mills by weight, it does not break down the aggregate value of these products. It was therefore necessary to infer the rail share of the value of rolled iron. In the equation

(B2.1) $$\pi = P_r R + P_b B,$$

π stands for the value of all rolled iron, P_r is the average price of rails, R is the weight of rails, P_b is the average price of all other rolled iron and B is the weight of other rolled iron. When fitted to state data, the resulting regression is

(B2.2) $$\pi = 45.34R + 69.66B,$$
$$(8.27) \quad (8.17)$$

with the coefficients in units of dollars per gross ton.[1] Substituting for R and B, it appears that rails represented 35.84 per cent of the total value of rolled products produced in the census year or $11,428,000. Since the value of other final products of the iron industry was $68,691,000, I_1 is equal to 14.3 per cent.[2] The value of I_4 for the

---

[1] The coefficients are estimates of average producers' prices at the plant. *Census of Manufacturing, 1860*, p. clxxxiii.

[2] The denominator of the index of I_1 for this year differs from that used in Table B2.1. It includes the value of steel and wire which were omitted from the computation of I_1 for 1856. The weight of nail plate produced by rolling mills multiplied by $69.66 was subtracted from the value of nails to eliminate double counting. *Ibid.* pp. clxxxiii–clxxxv, clxxxvii, cxciv, cxcv.

TABLE B2.1. A VALUE INDEX (I_1) OF THE POSITION OF RAILS IN THE
MARKET FOR IRON, 1856

Product	1 Weight (thousands of gross tons)	2 Price (dollars per gross ton)	3 Value (Col. 1 × Col. 2)
1. Rails	161	63	10,143
2. Boiler and sheet	39	120	4,680
3. Nails	81	84	6,804
4. Bar, rod, band, hoop	235	65	15,275
5. Hammered	21	125	2,625
6. Castings	337	123	41,451
7. Totals	874		80,978
8. Value index (Col. 3, line 1 ÷ Col. 3, line 7).................12.5 per cent			

SOURCES AND NOTES:

Column 1. Lines 1–5. All entries are weights of finished products. Line 1 is
taken from Table 5.15, Col. 3, line 17. All other lines are from Lesley's, *Guide*,
p. 764. Line 6. This entry is the weight of the crude iron consumed in castings.
Ibid.

Column 2. Lines 1–5. Each entry is the average price per ton of finished
product. *Ibid.* Line 6. This entry is total value of the finished product divided by
the tons of crude iron consumed in castings. It was computed in the following
manner: Total crude iron consumed by the domestic iron industry in the census
year of 1859–60 was computed as a weighted average of the entries 1859 and 1860
in Col. 7, Table 5.14. This figure converted into gross tons was 1,047,000. The
crude iron consumed in rolling as reported by the census was 657,000 gross tons.
The difference, 390,000 tons, was assumed to have been consumed by foundries.
The value of all final products of foundries divided by the last figure ($92.65) was
extrapolated to 1856 by the average price of pig iron. Since some of the 390,000
tons of crude iron assigned to foundries was consumed by forges and steel producers, this procedure tends to understate the value of the final product per ton
of crude iron consumption. *Ibid.; Census of Manufacturing, 1860*, pp. clxxx,
clxxxiii, clxxxvii.

corresponding census year is 19.1.[3] In this case I_4 overstates I_1 by 34
per cent.

For many purposes the most relevant measure of the position of
rails in total iron production is an index based on value added such as

$$I_7 = \frac{\text{value added in the domestic production of rails}}{\text{value added by the domestic iron industry}}$$

This index can also be computed for the census year 1859–60. Regression analysis indicates that rails accounted for 34.11 per cent of value
added by rolling mills or $4,314,000. To this must be added 11.15

[3] The numerator is a weighted average of the 1859 and 1860 entries of Table 5.16,
Column 1. The denominator is a weighted average of the 1859 and 1860 entries of
Table 5.14, Column 7.

per cent of the value added in pig iron production or $956,000. The total value added by the iron industry was $49,593,000.[4] Hence I_7 is only 10.6 per cent; and I_4 overstates I_7 by about 80 per cent.

Available data thus suggest that rails represented an average of about 8 per cent of the value of the final product of the iron industry during 1840–60, and that the average share of rails in value added over the same period was probably less than 7 per cent.

3. In *The Economic Contribution of American Railroads Before the Civil War,* Albert Fishlow attempts to correct the estimate of new railroad construction compiled for the 1880 *Census of Transportation* by Armin Shuman. However Fishlow's adjustments, which lead to a considerable reduction in the estimate of construction during the 11 years from 1840 through 1850, cannot be considered an improvement over the series prepared by either Shuman or Poor. The attempted correction is invalidated by internal inconsistencies and empirically unwarranted assumptions.

Fishlow's study actually contains not one but two new figures for the construction of main road during 1840–50. Only one of these is made explicit. In Appendix B, Fishlow asserts that the true amount of new road built during the 11-year period in question was 5,627 miles. This figure, which is 680 miles below Shuman's and 1,092 below Poor's, is described as "the difference between the Gerstner total up to the end of 1839 minus 156 miles of failed road and the 1860 Census total of 8,590 up to the end of 1850 plus 53 miles of additional inclusions." To his figure on the construction of main line, Fishlow adds 563 miles for sidings and 600 miles for double tracks.[5]

Fishlow's second estimate of new main road is implied by the data shown in Tables III–4 and III–5 of his third chapter. Analysis of these data reveals that Fishlow based his estimate of the domestic consumption of rails on the assumption that only 5,336 miles of main road were built during 1840–50.[6] More surprising than the discovery that Fishlow

[4] Note to Table 4.11, Column 6, line 3. *Census of Manufacturing, 1860,* pp. clxxviii, clxxx, clxxxiii–clxxxv, clxxxvii, cxciv, and cxcv. Activities included in the computation of total value added were the production of pig iron, blooms, rolled iron, forged iron, castings, wire, steel, and nails.

The share of value added in pig iron production attributable to rails was computed from the 1859 and 1860 entries of Column 8, Table 5.15 and Column 1, Table 5.14.

[5] Fishlow, *Economic Contribution,* p. 536.

[6] *Ibid.,* pp. 198, 205, 536. Fishlow puts the total consumption of rails during 1840–50 at 672,000 gross tons. He allots 100,000 tons to the replacement of worn rails and 54,000 tons (90 gross tons per track-mile multiplied by 600 track-miles)

increased his deviation from the census estimate by an additional 291 miles is the manner that he distributes his new total between the six years from 1840 through 1845 and the five years from 1846 through 1850. Fishlow's implicit figure for construction during 1840–45 falls 1,207 miles short of the census estimate while his figure for 1845–50 exceeds the census estimate by 236 miles.[7] It is the drastic departure from both Shuman's and Poor's estimates of the construction of main road during 1840–45 (Fishlow's reduction is over 50 per cent) that is the most questionable feature of the revision.

The only evidence that Fishlow puts forth in support of his revision is Gerstner's survey of the construction of new roads during years ending 1839. Gerstner indicated that the main line in existence at the end of 1839 was 3,072 miles, a figure 807 miles greater than that reported by Shuman.[8] Fishlow proceeded on the assumption that most of the mileage reported by Gerstner through 1839 but not reported by Shuman was erroneously attributed to 1840–45 in the *Census of Transportation*. However, a road-by-road reconciliation of the Gerstner and Shuman surveys reveals that Gerstner's findings do not support Fishlow's drastic downward revision of construction during the first six years of the forties.

The discrepancies between Gerstner's and Shuman's findings can be divided into five categories:[9] Category A contains 27 roads. Gerstner's survey shows that the length of these roads at the end of 1839 was 191 miles more than is indicated by Shuman. Even if the Gerstner survey is flawless, the only correction required of the census is an addition to

---

to second track. The residual, 518,000 gross tons, represents the construction of main line and sidings. Since Fishlow placed the average weight of rails on such track at 88.25 gross tons per track-mile (0.9091 x 90.00 + 0.0909 x 70.71 = 88.25), the total mileage of both forms of track is 5,870. Hence 90.91 per cent of the last figure, or 5,336 miles, is Fishlow's implicit estimate of the construction of main road.

[7] *Ibid.* The distribution between the two time periods was computed in the manner indicated in the previous footnote on the assumption that all second track was built during 1846–50. It is not clear that this assumption was actually adopted by Fishlow. However any other assumption regarding the construction of second track would increase the disparity between Fishlow and Shuman on the amount of main line constructed in both 1840–45 and 1846–50.

[8] See the references in the next footnote.

[9] The reconciliation that follows is based on Klein, "Railroads in the United States," pp. 89–102, 227–30, 301–7; *Census of Transportation, 1880,* Table VIII; *Poor's Manual of Railroads, 1883,* pp. 1031–55; Poor's, *History;* various of the annual reports of the New York railroad commissioners; *Preliminary Report of the Eighth Census,* Table 38; and other scattered sources.

reported construction for 1830–39. No reduction of the census figures on construction during 1840–45 is possible since the census reports zero construction during the first six years of the forties for all of the roads in Category A.

Category B contains 25 roads. According to Gerstner's survey the total mileage of these companies at the end of 1839—none of which was reported by Shuman—was 310 miles. Although the census failed to attribute this construction to the thirties, it did not assign the neglected mileage to 1840–45 or any subsequent period. Indeed all of the mileage included in Category B was abandoned prior to or during 1880 and was not reported in the census for that reason. One of the overlooked features of Shuman's survey is that it only reported the progress of the construction of railroads still in use in 1880. Hence none of the mileage of Category B can be subtracted from the census estimates of 1840–45.

Category C includes 21 roads for which Gerstner's data indicate 298 miles of construction through 1839 that was not attributed to the period by Shuman. In each case the census reported substantial construction during 1840–45. Hence it is possible to subtract the omissions of 1830–39 from the reported construction of the subsequent six years. It by no means follows that such subtractions are automatically warranted. For example, according to Gerstner, at the end of 1839 the combined mileage of the roads that later merged to form the New York Central exceeded Shuman's report by 73.90 miles. At the same time the census puts construction of lines comprising the New York Central during 1840–45 at 176.36 miles. Independent sources verify that at least 142.49 miles of the construction reported during these years actually took place. Only 33.87 miles are unsubstantiated. But this is less than half of the 1839 discrepancy between Shuman and Gerstner. And even the unverified mileage may actually have been built at the time indicated by Shuman.

Category D contains 30 roads for which the census figures on construction through 1839 *exceed* those of Gerstner's by 238 miles. Since errors in the survey of the 1880 Census could have gone either way (i.e., listings too early as well as too late), if Gerstner is assumed to have been correct, the excess construction shown by the census for the years through 1839 should be applied to the subsequent period.

Category E contains four roads with 115 miles that could not be assigned to any of the previous categories because of insufficient information.

The foregoing reconciliation indicates that at most 373 miles of the discrepancy between the Gerstner and Shuman survey can be subtracted from the construction listed by the census for 1840–45. If any part of the mileage included in Category E was abandoned prior to 1880, the last figure is too high even as an upper limit. Moreover, the subtractable discrepancy is offset by the 238 miles of Category D. It is also offset by any mileage built between 1840 and 1845 that was subsequently abandoned. Hence Gerstner's data cannot be used to support a substantial reduction in the construction estimates of the 1880 Census, certainly not one of the magnitude assumed by Fishlow.

Restoration of the census mileage on railroad construction requires a revision of Fishlow's figure for the domestic production of rails during 1840–50. For if the census estimate is correct, then Fishlow's other assumptions [10] imply that the domestic production of rails during 1840–50 was 294,000 gross tons—an amount nearly 50 per cent greater than the 200,000 gross tons he designates. For the period 1840–46, restoration implies that domestic rail production was 147,000 gross tons, or nearly 400 per cent more than the 30,000 tons for which Fishlow argues.[11]

Fishlow justifies his low estimate of domestic rail production during 1840–45 on two grounds: (1) U.S. rolling mills did not have the equipment to produce edge rails until 1844, although edge rails were "in-

[10] On the mileage of sidings and second track, the average weight of rails per track-mile, and the amount of replacement.

[11] Fishlow's approach to the determination of the domestic production of rails during 1840–50 is circular. In the notes to Table III–5 he states that domestic rail production was obtained as the "residual of requirements after subtracting of imports." In Appendix B he divides requirements into two components: rails used in new construction and rails used as replacements. The new construction component is obtained by multiplying estimates of the new mileage of main track, siding, and second track by an estimate of the average weight of rails per track-mile. However, Fishlow's figure for the replacement component is obtained by first adding to imports *an assumed estimate of the domestic production of rails* and then subtracting his previous estimate of rails used in new construction! Hence Fishlow's "estimate" of domestic production is not an estimate at all, but an assumption. It is equal to 200,000 tons because in deriving his figure for replacements he assumed it was 200,000 tons.

It may also be noted that Fishlow's figure for the total consumption of rails for 1840–50 as derived from Tables III–4 and III–5 differs from that given in Appendix B by from 28,000 to 61,000 gross tons, depending on which of his alternatives is used. Since domestic production is supposed to be equal to the residual of total consumption less imports, the discrepancy implies a contradiction between the figure for domestic rail production given in Table III–5 and those implied in Appendix B of between 14 and 31 per cent. Fishlow, *Economic Contribution*, pp. 198, 205, 536, 551.

creasingly being used in place of strap iron in the early forties." (2) The difference between the price of domestically produced rails and imported rails during 1840–43 was so large as to preclude the possibility that domestic firms were the main suppliers of the American market.[12]

The first of these two assertions is irrelevant. Even if edge rails were being used in increasing amounts, it is still possible that the consumption of strap rails was large and that the supply of this type of rail came from domestic mills in sufficient quantities to boost domestic rail production to a point well above Fishlow's figure of 30,000 gross tons. No evidence presented by him excludes this possibility. While he quotes two iron masters who said, in early 1828, that domestic mills were incapable of supplying the strap rails needed to build the Baltimore and Ohio Railroad, such evidence has no bearing on the situation during 1840–44.[13] In 1840 there were nearly three times as many rolling mills in the United States as there were at the beginning of 1828, and the average capacity of these mills was substantially greater than the average capacity in 1828.[14]

Nor does Fishlow provide the evidence needed to support his contention regarding the relative prices of domestic and imported rails. For he compares not the prices of rails but the prices of common or assorted British bar iron and highly refined American country or merchant bar iron. The description of the American series from which he quotes clearly indicates that at least in 1842, and probably in 1840 and 1841, Fishlow's American prices pertain to hammered rather than rolled iron. But even if rolled iron prices were used, highly refined rolled iron of the type suitable for sale as merchant or country bar was much more expensive than the less refined iron rolled into rails. Over the first five years for which prices of both types of iron are available (1847–52), the price of rolled merchant iron exceeded that of rails by 22 per cent. On this basis, even after allowance for the present value of the tariff rebate for foreign rails, the American price would have been about the same as the British price during 1840–43.[15]

[12] *Ibid.*, p. 231.
[13] *Ibid.*, p. 190.
[14] The last two statements are based on evidence compiled by Stanley L. Engerman and Robert W. Fogel for a study tentatively entitled, *The Growth of the American Iron Industry, 1800–1860: A Statistical Reconstruction.*
[15] Fishlow, *Economic Contribution*, p. 231; Anne Bezanson, Robert D. Gray, and Miriam Hussey, *Wholesale Prices in Philadelphia, 1784–1861* (2 Vols.; Philadelphia, 1937), II, 103, 112; A.I.S.A., *Annual Report*, 1880, pp. 55, 56.

Selected Bibliography

GOVERNMENT DOCUMENTS

Indexes

Government documents are by far the most important source of information bearing on the subject matter of this volume. It is not feasible to list more than a small proportion of the reports, hearings, investigations, surveys, and articles that contain relevant material. The following indexes were particularly useful in locating desired information.

HASSE, ADELAIDE R. *Index of Economic Materials in Documents of the States of the United States: California, 1849–1904; Delaware, 1789–1904; Illinois, 1809–1904; Kentucky, 1792–1904; Maine, 1820–1904; Massachusetts, 1789–1904; New Hampshire, 1789–1904; New Jersey, 1789–1904; New York, 1789–1904; Ohio, 1787–1904; Pennsylvania, 1790–1904; Rhode Island, 1789–1904; Vermont, 1789–1904. Washington: Carnegie Institution of Washington, 1907–1919.*

U.S. DEPARTMENT OF AGRICULTURE. Office of Information, *Index to the Publications of the United States Department of Agriculture, 1901–1940.* 4 Vols. 1932, 1935, 1937, 1943.

U.S. DEPARTMENT OF INTERIOR. *Publications of the Geological Survey.* 1958.

U.S. HOUSE OF REPRESENTATIVES. *Index to the Reports of The Chief of Engineers, U.S. Army, 1866–1912.* Document No. 740, 63d Cong., 2d Sess. 2 Vols.

U.S. LIBRARY OF CONGRESS. Census Library Project. *Catalogue of U.S. Census Publications, 1790–1945.* 1950.

U.S. SUPERINTENDENT OF DOCUMENTS. *Checklist of United States Public Documents, 1789–1909.* 1911.

———. *List of Publications of the Agriculture Department, 1862–1902.* 1904.

Federal

ANDREWS, FRANK. *Cost of Hauling Crops from Farms to Shipping Points.* Bureau of Statistics (Department of Agriculture). Bulletin No. 49, 1907.

————. *Grain Movements in the Great Lakes Region.* Bureau of Statistics (Department of Agriculture). Bulletin No. 81, 1910.

————. *Inland Boat Service.* U.S. Department of Agriculture. Bulletin No. 74, 1914.

COLWELL, STEPHEN. "Special Report No. 12. Report on Iron." U.S. Revenue Commission. *Reports of a Commission Appointed for a Review of the Revenue System.* 1866.

COOPER, MARTIN S., BARTON, GLEN T., and BRODELL, ALBERT P. *Progress of Farm Mechanization.* U.S. Department of Agriculture. Miscellaneous Publication No. 630, 1947.

FUNK, W. C. *Value to Farm Families of Food, Fuel, and Use of House.* U.S. Department of Agriculture. Bulletin No. 410, 1916.

GANNETT, HENRY. *Profiles of Rivers in the United States.* U.S. Geological Survey. Water Supply Paper No. 44, 1901.

GREAT BRITAIN. Board of Trade. *Cost of Living in American Towns.* London: H. M. Stationery Office, 1911. Reprinted by U.S. Senate, Document No. 22, 62d Cong., 1st Sess.

HOLMES, GEORGE K. *Cold-Storage Business Features.* U.S. Bureau of Statistics (Department of Agriculture). Bulletin No. 93, 1913.

————. *Systems of Marketing Farm Products and Demand for Such Products at Trade Centers.* U.S. Department of Agriculture. Report No. 98, 1913.

————. *Wages of Farm Labor.* Bureau of Statistics (Department of Agriculture). Bulletin No. 99, 1912.

———— and OTHERS. *Meat Situation in the United States.* U.S. Department of Agriculture. Report No. 109, 5 Parts, 1916.

HUMPHREY, H. N. *Cost of Fencing Farms in the North Central States.* U.S. Department of Agriculture. Bulletin No. 321, 1916.

NEWCOMB, H. T. *Changes in the Rates of Charge for Railway and Other Transportation Services.* Bureau of Statistics (Department of Agriculture). Bulletin No. 15. Revised, 1901.

REEVES, S. J. "Letter." U.S. Senate. *Annual Report of the Secretary of the Treasury, 1849.* Document No. 2, 31st Cong., 1st Sess.

STRAUSS, FREDERICK and BEAN, LOUIS H. *Gross Farm Income and Indices of Farm Production and Prices in the United States, 1869–1937.* U.S. Department of Agriculture. Technical Bulletin No. 703, 1940.

U.S. BUREAU OF AGRICULTURAL ECONOMICS. *Consumption of Food in the United States, 1909–1952.* Agricultural Handbook No. 62, 1953.

U.S. BUREAU OF CORPORATIONS. *Report of the Commissioner of Corporations on Transportation by Water in the United States.* 3 Vols., 1909–13.

U.S. BUREAU OF FOREIGN AND DOMESTIC COMMERCE. *Atlas of Wholesale Grocery Territories.* Domestic Commerce Series No. 7, 1927.

―――. *Atlas of Wholesale Grocery Trading Areas.* Market Research Series No. 19, 1938.

―――. *The External Trade of New England.* Domestic Commerce Series No. 22, 1928.

―――. *Inland Water Transportation in the United States.* Miscellaneous Series No. 119, 1923.

U.S. BUREAU OF LABOR. *Annual Report of the Commissioner of Labor.* 1886–1910.

U.S. BUREAU OF PUBLIC ROADS. *Bulletin.* Nos. 1–48, 1894–1913.

―――. *Circular.* Nos. 1–100, 1893–1913.

U.S. BUREAU OF STATISTICS (Department of Agriculture). *Bulletin.* Nos. 1–103, 1890–1913.

―――. *Circular.* Nos. 1–47, 1896–1915.

―――. *Exports of Farm Products from the United States, 1851–1908.* Bulletin No. 75, 1910.

―――. *Freight Charges for Ocean Transportation of Products of Agriculture.* Bulletin No. 12, 1896.

―――. *Imports of Farm Products into the United States, 1851–1908.* Bulletin No. 74, 1910.

U.S. BUREAU OF STATISTICS (Department of Commerce and Labor). *Monthly Summary of Commerce and Finance of the United States.* New series, July, 1893–June, 1912.

―――. *Transportation Routes and Systems of the World.* 1907.

U.S. BUREAU OF STATISTICS (Treasury Department). *Annual Report on Commerce and Navigation.* 1840–71.

―――. *Report on the Internal Commerce of the United States, 1876–1891.* 1877–92.

U.S. BUREAU OF THE CENSUS. *Abstract of the Seventh Census. Report of the Superintendent of the Census for December 1, 1852.* 1853.

―――. *Eighth Census of the United States: 1860. Agriculture in the United States in 1860.* 1864.

―――. *Eighth Census of the United States: 1860. Manufactures of the United States in 1860.* 1865.

―――. *Preliminary Report on the Eighth Census, 1860.* 1862.

―――. *Ninth Census of the United States: 1870. The Statistics of the Wealth and Industry of the United States.* Vol. III, 1872.

―――. *Tenth Census of the United States: 1880. Report on the Manufactures of the United States.* Vol. II, 1883.

―――. *Tenth Census of the United States: 1880. Report on the Production of Agriculture.* Vol. III, 1883.

————. *Tenth Census of the United States: 1880. Report on the Agencies of Transportation in the United States,* Vol. IV, 1883.

————. *Eleventh Census of the United States: 1890. Report on Population of the United States.* Vol. I, 2 Parts, 1895–97.

————. *Eleventh Census of the United States: 1890. Reports on the Statistics of Agriculture in the United States.* Vol. V, 1895.

————. *Eleventh Census of the United States: 1890. Report on the Manufacturing Industries in the United States.* Vol. VI, 3 Parts, 1895.

————. *Eleventh Census of the United States: 1890. Report on Real Estate Mortgages in the United States.* Vol. XII, 1895.

————. *Eleventh Census of the United States: 1890. Report on Transportation Business in the United States.* Vol. XIV, 2 Parts, 1894–95.

————. *Compendium of the Eleventh Census: 1890.* 3 Parts, 1892–97.

————. *Twelfth Census of the United States: 1900. Agriculture.* Vols. V and VI, 2 Parts, 1902.

————. *Twelfth Census of the United States: 1900. Manufactures.* Vols. VII–X, 4 Parts, 1902.

————. *Thirteenth Census of the United States: 1910. Agriculture, 1909 and 1910. General Report and Analysis.* Vol. V, 1913.

————. *Thirteenth Census of the United States: 1910. Manufactures, 1909.* Vols. VIII–X, 1912–13.

————. *Transportation by Water, 1906.* 1908.

————. *Transportation by Water, 1916.* 1920.

————. *Historical Statistics of the United States, 1789–1945.* 1949.

————. *Historical Statistics of the United States, Colonial Times to 1957.* 1960.

U.S. Coast and Geodetic Survey. *Distances Between United States Ports.* Series No. 444. Rev. ed., 1938.

U.S. Congress. *American State Papers. Class III. Finance.* 5 Vols., 1832–59.

U.S. Department of Agriculture. *Agricultural Statistics.* 1936–.

————. *Atlas of American Agriculture.* 1936.

————. *Consumption of Feed by Livestock, 1909–1956.* Production Research Report No. 21, 1958.

————. *Consumption of Food in the United States, 1909–1952,* Agricultural Handbook No. 52, 1953.

————. *Report of the Secretary of Agriculture.* 1862–1902.

————. *Yearbook of Agriculture.* 1894–.

U.S. Engineer Department. *Report of the Chief of Engineers.* 1866–1912.

————. Board of Engineers for Rivers and Harbors. *Transportation in the Mississippi and Ohio Valleys.* 1929.

————. Board of Engineers for Rivers and Harbors. *Transportation on the Great Lakes.* 1936.

U.S. GEOLOGICAL SURVEY. *Water-Supply Papers.* 1896–.

U.S. HOUSE OF REPRESENTATIVES. *Documents Relative to Manufactures in the United States.* Executive Document 308, 22d Cong., 1st Sess. 2 Vols.

————. *Letter from the Secretary of the Treasury Transmitting Tables and Notes on the Cultivation, Manufacture and Foreign Trade of Cotton.* Document No. 146, 24th Cong., 1st Sess.

————. *Report on Steam Carriages.* Executive Document 101, 22d Cong., 1st Sess.

————. *Report on Steam Engines in the United States.* Executive Document No. 21, 25th Cong., 3d Sess.

U.S. INDUSTRIAL COMMISSION. *Reports of the Industrial Commission.* 19 Vols., 1900–2.

U.S. INLAND WATERWAYS COMMISSION. *Preliminary Report of the Inland Waterways Commission.* U.S. Senate, Document No. 325, 60th Cong., 1st Sess., 1908.

U.S. INTERSTATE COMMERCE COMMISSION. *Abstract of Statistics of Steam Railways in the United States.* 1916–.

————. *Annual Report.* 1887–1915.

U.S. NATIONAL WATERWAYS COMMISSION. *Final Report of the National Waterways Commission.* U.S. Senate, Document 469, 62d Cong., 2d Sess.

U.S. OFFICE OF EXPERIMENT STATIONS. *Bulletin.* Nos. 1–256, 1889–1913.

U.S. PAY DEPARTMENT (War Department). *Official Table of Distances.* 1888.

U.S. SENATE. *Andrews' Report.* Executive Document No. 136, 32nd Cong., 1st Sess.

————. Committee on Interstate Commerce. *Regulation of Railway Rates. Digest of Hearings.* Document No. 244, 59th Cong., 1st Sess.

————. Committee on Interstate Commerce. *Regulation of Railway Rates, Hearings.* Document No. 243, 59th Cong., 1st Sess. 5 Vols.

————. *Message of the President of the United States, Communicating a Digest of the Statistics of Manufactures According to the Returns of Seventh Census.* Executive Document No. 39, 35th Cong., 2d Sess.

————. *Reports of the Government Directors of the Union Pacific Railroad Company.* Executive Document No. 69, 49th Cong., 1st Sess.

————. *Select Committee on the Transportation and Sale of Meat Products.* Report No. 829, 51st Cong., 1st Sess.

————. *Select Committee on Transportation—Routes to the Seaboard.* Report No. 307, 43d Cong., 1st Sess. 2 Vols.

————. *Wholesale Prices, Wages and Transportation. Report of the Committee on Finance.* Report No. 1394, 52nd Cong., 2d Sess., 4 Parts.

U.S. SPECIAL COMMISSIONER OF THE REVENUE, 1866–70. *Annual Report, 1866–1869.* 1866–69.

WATKINS, J. ELFRETH. "The Development of American Rail and Track." U.S. House of Representatives. *Annual Report of the Board of The Smithsonian Institution, 1889.* Miscellaneous Document No. 224, Part 2, 51st Cong., 1st Sess.

WARD, EDWARD G., JR. *Milk Transportation.* Bureau of Statistics (Department of Agriculture). Bulletin No. 25, 1903.

WILLIAMS, FAITH M. and ZIMMERMAN, CARLE C. *Studies of Family Living in the United States and Other Countries.* U.S. Department of Agriculture. Miscellaneous Publication No. 223, 1935.

WRIGHT, CARROLL D. *The History and Growth of the United States Census.* U.S. Senate. Document No. 194, 56th Cong., 1st Sess.

State

ILLINOIS. Canal Commissioners. *Report, 1871/72–1916.* 1872–1916.

————. Railroad and Warehouse Commission. *Annual Report, 1870/ 71–1912/13.* 1872–1913.

MASSACHUSETTS. General Court. Committee on Railways and Canals. *Annual Reports of the Railroad Corporations in the State of Massachusetts, 1836–1856.* 1837–56.

————. Secretary of the Commonwealth. *Returns of Railroad Corporations in Massachusetts, 1857–1869.* 1858–70.

NEW YORK AGRICULTURAL EXPERIMENT STATION, ITHACA. *Wholesale Prices for 213 Years, 1720–1932.* Memoir 142, 1932.

NEW YORK (State). Engineer and Surveyor. *Annual Report 1850– 1920/21.* 1851–1922.

————. Engineer and Surveyor. *Annual Report of the State Engineer and Surveyor in Relation to Railroad Reports, 1848–1870.* 1849–71.

————. Legislature. Assembly. Special Committee on Railroads. *Proceedings and Report of the Special Committee on Railroads, 1879–80.* 8 Vols., 1879–80.

OHIO. Board of Public Works. *Annual Report, 1836–1904.* 1837–1905.

PENNSYLVANIA. Auditor-General's Office. *Annual Report of the Auditor-General.* 1860–75.

———. Department of Internal Affairs. *Annual Report.* Part IV. *Railroad, Canal, Telegraph and Telephone Companies.* 1875–1899/1900.

VIRGINIA. Board of Public Works. *Annual Report of the Board of Public Works.* 1830–60.

———. *Annual Reports of the Railroads of the State of Virginia.* 1853/54–1860/61.

WHITFORD, NOBLE E. *History of the Barge Canal of New York State.* New York (State). Engineer and Surveyor. *Annual Report, 1920/21.* Supplement, 1922.

———. *History of the Canal System of the State of New York.* New York (State). Engineer and Surveyor. *Annual Report, 1904/5.* Supplement, 1906.

BUSINESS RECORDS AND REPORTS, PUBLICATIONS OF TRADE ASSOCIATIONS, TRADE JOURNALS, AND TRADE MANUALS

All freight and passenger tariffs and other documents pertaining to railroad and boat rates filed with the Interstate Commerce Commission under the provisions of the Interstate Commerce Commission Act of 1887 are stored in the Federal Record Center at Alexandria, Virginia, under identification number 55A353.

AMERICAN IRON AND STEEL ASSOCIATION. *Bulletin of the American Iron Association.* Philadelphia, 1856–58.

———. *Bulletin of the American Iron and Steel Association.* Vol I–XLVI. Philadelphia, 1866–1912.

———. *Proceedings of the Annual Meeting of the American Iron and Steel Association, Feb. 11, 1875.*

———. *Statistics of the American and Foreign Iron Trades.* Annual Report. Philadelphia, 1868, 1871–1911.

———. *The Wearing Qualities of American Steel Rails.* Philadelphia, 1879.

The American Railroad Journal, Vols. I–XLIII. New York, 1832–70.

BALTIMORE CORN AND FLOUR EXCHANGE. *Annual Report.* 1880–1900.

BALTIMORE AND OHIO RAILROAD COMPANY. *Annual Report of the President and Directors.* 1846/47–1902/3.

BELL, SIR I. LOWTHIAN. *The Iron Trade of the United Kingdom Compared with that of the Other Chief Iron-Making Nations.* London, 1886.

BOSTON BOARD OF TRADE. *Annual Report.* 1854–1900.

BUFFALO MERCHANTS' EXCHANGE. *Annual Report.* 1886–1902.

BUREAU OF RAILWAY ECONOMICS. *An Economic Survey of Inland Waterways Transportation in the United States.* Washington, 1930.

CHICAGO AND NORTHWESTERN RAILWAY COMPANY. *Annual Report,* 1859/60–1907.

CHICAGO BOARD OF TRADE. *Annual Report of the Trade and Commerce of Chicago.* 1858–1900.

CHICAGO, BURLINGTON AND QUINCY RAILROAD. *Annual Report of the Board of Directors.* 1872–1901/2.

CINCINNATI CHAMBER OF COMMERCE AND MERCHANTS' EXCHANGE. *Annual Report.* 1849/50–1916.

CINCINNATI PRICE CURRENT. *Annual Report of Pork Packing in the West.* Cincinnati, 1880–90.

DeBow's Review. Vols. 1–34. New Orleans, 1846–64.

DULUTH BOARD OF TRADE. *Annual Report.* 1883–1900.

DUNLAP, THOMAS (ed.). *Wiley's American Iron Trade Manual.* New York, 1874.

Engineering News. Vols. 1–77. Chicago and New York, 1874–1917.

FRIENDS OF DOMESTIC INDUSTRY. *General Convention of the Friends of Domestic Industry, Assembled at New York, October 26, 1831.* Baltimore, 1832.

Hazard's United States Commercial and Statistical Register. Vols. 1–6. Philadelphia, 1839–42.

HOME LEAGUE. *Proceedings of the National Convention for the Protection of American Interests, Convened in the City of New York, April 5, 1842* (?)

IRON MASTERS' CONVENTION (Philadelphia, 1849). *Documents Relating to the Manufacture of Iron. Published on Behalf of the Convention of Iron Masters, which Met in Philadelphia, on the Twentieth of December, 1849.* Philadelphia, 1850.

JOINT TRAFFIC ASSOCIATION. *Proceedings of the Board of Managers.* 1896.

LESLEY, J. P. *The Iron Manufacturers' Guide to the Furnaces, Forges and Rolling Mills of the United States.* New York, 1859.

LOUISVILLE AND FRANKFORD RAILROAD COMPANY. *Annual Report of the President and Directors.* 1850–66.

LOUISVILLE AND NASHVILLE RAILROAD COMPANY. *Annual Report of the Board of Directors.* 1851/52–1902/3.

MARTIN, ROBERT F. *National Income in the United States, 1799–1938.* (National Industrial Conference Board Studies No. 241.) New York, 1939.

The Merchants' Magazine and Commercial Review. Vols. I–LXIII. New York, 1839–70.

MICHIGAN CENTRAL RAILROAD COMPANY. *Annual Report of the Board of Directors.* 1846/47–1907.

MICHIGAN SOUTHERN AND NORTHERN INDIANA RAILROAD COMPANY. *Report of the Directors,* 1852/53–1868/69.

MILWAUKEE CHAMBER OF COMMERCE. *Annual Report of the Trade and Commerce of Milwaukee.* 1880–95.

MINNEAPOLIS CHAMBER OF COMMERCE. *Annual Report.* 1884–1900.

MISSOURI RIVER NAVIGATION ASSOCIATION. *Railways and Waterways.* Kansas City, Mo., 1930.

NATIONAL ASSOCIATION OF IRON MANUFACTURERS. *Statistical Report of the National Association of Iron Manufacturers for 1872.* Philadelphia, 1873.

NEW YORK CHAMBER OF COMMERCE. *Annual Report.* 1858–1871/72.

NEW YORK PRODUCE EXCHANGE. *Annual Report.* 1872/73–1898/99.

PHILADELPHIA AND READING RAILROAD COMPANY. *Report.* 1845–70.

PENNSYLVANIA RAILROAD COMPANY. *Annual Report.* 1846/47–1908.

PITTSBURGH, FORT WAYNE AND CHICAGO RAILWAY COMPANY. *Annual Report.* 1862–79.

Poor's Manual of Railroads. 1868/69–1924. New York, 1869–1924.

ROPER, STEPHEN. *Handbook of the Locomotive.* Philadelphia, 1874.

ST. LOUIS MERCHANTS' EXCHANGE. *Annual Statement of the Trade and Commerce of St. Louis.* 1865–1900.

TRUNK LINE EXECUTIVE COMMITTEE. *Report upon the Relative Cost of Transporting Live Stock and Dressed Beef.* New York, 1883.

VOULLAIRE, FRANCOIS A. *How To Ship.* 2 Parts. New York, 1915.

BOOKS

ADAMS, CHARLES F., JR. *Railroads: Their Origin and Problems.* New York: G. P. Putnam's Sons, 1878.

ALBION, ROBERT G. and POPE, JENNIE B. *The Rise of the New York Port.* New York: Scribner's Sons, 1939.

ALLEN, HARRY C. and HILL, C. P. (eds.). *British Essays in American History.* London: Edward Arnold, 1957.

AMBLER, CHARLES HENRY. *A History of Transportation in the Ohio Valley.* Glendale, Cal.: Arthur H. Clark Co., 1932.

The American Railway: Its Construction, Development, Management and Appliances. New York: Scribner's Sons, 1892.

ANDERSON, OSCAR E. *Refrigeration in America: A History of the Technology and its Impact.* Princeton: Princeton University Press, 1953.

BAKER, IRA OSBORN. *A Treatise on Roads and Pavements.* 2nd ed., enl. New York: J. Wiley and Sons, 1913.

BARGER, HAROLD. *Distribution's Place in the American Economy Since 1869.* Princeton: Princeton University Press, 1955.

BELCHER, WYATT WINSTON. *The Economic Rivalry between St. Louis and Chicago 1850–1880.* New York: Columbia University Press, 1947.

BENSON, LEE. *Merchants, Farmers and Railroads: Railroad Regulation and New York Politics, 1850–1887.* Cambridge: Harvard University Press, 1955.

BERRY, THOMAS SENIOR. *Western Prices Before 1861.* (Harvard Economic Studies, Vol. LXXIV.) Cambridge: Harvard University Press, 1943.

BEZANSON, ANNE, GRAY, ROBERT D. and HUSSEY, MIRIAM. *Wholesale Prices in Philadelphia, 1784–1861.* 2 Vols. Philadelphia: University of Pennsylvania Press, 1937.

BIDWELL, PERCY WELLS and FALCONER, JOHN I. *History of Agriculture in the Northern United States, 1620–1860.* Washington, D. C.: Carnegie Institution of Washington, 1925.

BLACK, ROBERT C., III. *The Railroads of the Confederacy.* Chapel Hill: University of North Carolina Press, 1952.

BOLINO, AUGUST C. *The Development of the American Economy.* Columbus, Ohio: Charles E. Merrill Books, 1961.

BRAITHWAITE, RICHARD B. *Scientific Explanation: A Study of the Function of Theory, Probability and Law in Science.* Cambridge: Harvard University Press, 1953.

BROWNSON, HOWARD GRAY. *History of the Illinois Central Railroad to 1870.* Urbana, Ill.: University of Illinois, 1915.

CALLENDER, GUY STEVENS. *Selections from the Economic History of the United States, 1765–1860.* Boston: Ginn and Co., 1909.

CAREY, HENRY C. *Miscellaneous Works.* Philadelphia: Henry Carey Baird, 1872.

CLAPHAM, JOHN H. *An Economic History of Modern Britain.* 3 Vols. Cambridge: Harvard University Press, 1926–1938.

CLARK, VICTOR S. *History of Manufacturers in the United States.* 3 Vols. New York: McGraw-Hill, 1929.

CLEMEN, RUDOLF A. *The American Livestock and Meat Industry.* New York: Ronald Press, 1923.

CLEVELAND, FREDERICK A. and POWELL, FRED W. *Railroad Finance.* New York: Appleton, 1912.

————. *Railroad Promotion and Capitalization in the United States.* New York: Longmans, Green, 1909.

COCHRAN, THOMAS S. *Railroad Leaders, 1845–1890: The Business Mind in Action.* Cambridge: Harvard University Press, 1953.

COHEN, MORRIS RAPHAEL. *Reason and Nature: An Essay on the Meaning of Scientific Method.* 2nd ed. Glencoe, Ill.: Free Press, 1959.

COLBURN, ZERAH and HOLLY, ALEXANDER L. *The Permanent Way.* New York, 1858.

Cole, Arthur Harrison. *The American Wool Manufacture.* 2 Vols. Cambridge: Harvard University Press, 1926.

COLLINS, FRANCIS A. *Our Harbors and Inland Waters.* New York: The Century Company, 1924.

CONFERENCE ON RESEARCH IN INCOME AND WEALTH. *Trends in the American Economy in the Nineteenth Century.* (Vol. 24 of *Studies in Income and Wealth.*) Princeton: Princeton University Press, 1960.

CREAMER, DANIEL and OTHERS. *Capital in Manufacturing and Mining: Its Formation and Financing.* Princeton: Princeton University Press, 1960.

CUMMINGS, RICHARD OSBORN. *The American and His Food: A History of Food Habits in the United States.* Chicago: University of Chicago Press, 1940.

DADDOW, SAMUEL HARRIS and BANNON, BENJAMIN. *Coal, Iron and Oil.* Pottsville, Pa.: B. Bannon, 1866.

DAISH, JOHN B. *The Atlantic Port Differentials.* Washington, D. C.: W. H. Lowdermilk, 1918.

DEBow, J. D. B. *Industrial Resources of the Southern and Western States.* 3 Vols. New Orleans: DeBow's Review, 1852–53.

DEFEBAUGH, JAMES E. *History of the Lumber Industry of America.* 2 Vols. Chicago: The American Lumberman, 1906–7.

DRAY, WILLIAM. *Laws and Explanation in History.* London: Oxford University Press, 1957.

FELLER, WILLIAM. *An Introduction to Probability Theory and Its Applications.* Vol. I. 2nd ed. New York: J. Wiley and Sons, 1957.

FITE, GILBERT C. and REESE, JIM E. *An Economic History of the United States.* Cambridge: Houghton Mifflin, 1959.

FOGEL, ROBERT WILLIAM. *The Union Pacific Railroad: A Case in Premature Enterprise.* Baltimore: The Johns Hopkins Press, 1960.

FRANZIUS, OTTO. *Waterway Engineering.* Cambridge: Technology Press, 1936.

FRENCH, BENJAMIN F. *History of the Rise and Progress of the Iron Trade of the United States, from 1821 to 1857.* New York: Wiley and Halsted, 1858.

GARD, WAYNE. *The Chisholm Trail.* Norman: University of Oklahoma Press, 1954.

GARDINER, PATRICK (ed.). *Theories of History.* Glencoe, Ill.: Free Press, 1959.

GATES, PAUL W., *The Farmers' Age: Agriculture, 1815–1860.* Vol. III of *The Economic History of the United States.* Edited by Henry David and others. New York: Holt, Rinehart and Winston, 1960.

———. *The Illinois Central Railroad and Its Colonization Work.* Cambridge: Harvard University Press, 1934.

GAYER, ARTHUR D., ROSTOW, W. W. and SCHWARTZ, ANNA JACOBSON. *The Growth and Fluctuation of the British Economy, 1790–1850.* 2 vols. Oxford: Clarendon Press, 1953.

GEPHART, WILLIAM F. *Transportation and Industrial Development in the Middle West.* (Columbia University Studies in History, Economic and Public Law, Vol. XXXIV, No. 1.) New York: Columbia University Press, 1909.

GLOVER, JOHN G. and CORNELL, WILLIAM B. *The Development of American Industry.* Rev. ed. New York: Prentice-Hall, 1941.

GOODRICH, CARTER. *Government Promotion of American Canals and Railroads, 1800–1890.* New York: Columbia University Press, 1959.

——— and OTHERS. *Canals and American Economic Development.* New York: Columbia University Press, 1961.

GRAY, LEWIS C. *History of Agriculture in the Southern United States to 1860.* 2 Vols. Washington, D. C.: Carnegie Institution of Washington, 1933.

GROSVENOR, W. H. *Does Protection Protect?* New York: Appleton, 1871.

HABAKKUK, H. J. *American and British Technology in the Nineteenth Century.* Cambridge: At the University Press, 1962.

HADLEY, ARTHUR T. *Railroad Transportation: Its History and Laws.* New York: G. P. Putnam's Sons, 1899.

HANEY, LEWIS H. *A Congressional History of Railroads in the United States.* 2 Vols. Madison, Wisc.: Democrat Printing Co., 1908, 1910.

HARGRAVE, FRANK F. *A Pioneer Indiana Railroad.* Indianapolis: Burford Printing Co., 1932.

HAWLEY, EDITH. *Economics of Food Consumption.* New York: McGraw-Hill, 1932.

HEATH, MILTON S. *Constructive Liberalism: The Role of the State in Economic Development in Georgia to 1860.* Cambridge: Harvard University Press, 1954.

History of the Baldwin Locomotive Works, 1831–1923. N.p., n.d.

HOLMSTROM, JOHN EDWIN. *Railways and Roads in Pioneer Development Overseas.* London: P. S. King and Son, 1934.

HUNTER, LOUIS C. *Steamboats on the Western Rivers.* Cambridge: Harvard University Press, 1949.

ISARD, WALTER. *Methods of Regional Analysis: An Introduction to Regional Science.* Cambridge and New York: The Technology Press and J. Wiley and Sons, 1960.

JEANS, JAMES STEPHEN. *Waterways and Water Transportation.* London: E. and F. N. Spon, 1890.

JERVIS, JOHN B. *Railway Property.* New York: Phinney, Blakeman and Mason, 1861.

JOHNSON, EMORY R. *Ocean and Inland Water Transportation.* New York: Appleton, 1909.

———— and OTHERS. *History of Foreign and Domestic Commerce of the United States.* 2 Vols. Washington: Carnegie Institution of Washington, 1915.

KENDRICK, JOHN W., *Productivity Trends in the United States.* Princeton: Princeton University Press, 1861.

KIRKLAND, EDWARD C. *A History of American Economic Life.* 3rd. ed. New York: Appleton-Century-Crofts, 1951.

————. *Industry Comes of Age: Business, Labor, and Public Policy, 1860–1897.* Vol. VI of *The Economic History of the United States.* Edited by Henry David and Others. New York: Holt, Rinehart, and Winston, 1961.

————. *Men, Cities and Transportation: A Study in New England History, 1820–1900.* 2 Vols. Cambridge: Harvard University Press, 1948.

KROOSS, HERMAN E. *American Economic Development.* Englewood Cliffs, N.J.: Prentice-Hall, 1959.

KUHLMAN, CHARLES B. *The Development of the Flour Milling Industry in the United States.* Boston: Houghton Mifflin, 1929.

KUZNETS, SIMON. *Capital in the American Economy: Its Formation and Financing.* Princeton: Princeton University Press, 1961.

————. *Economic Change: Selected Essays in Business Cycles, National Income and Economic Growth.* New York: W. W. Norton, 1953.

————. *National Product Since 1869.* New York: National Bureau of Economic Research, 1946.

————. *Secular Movements in Production and Prices: Their Nature and Bearing upon Cyclical Fluctuations.* Boston and New York: Houghton Mifflin, 1930.

————. *Six Lectures on Economic Growth.* Glencoe, Ill.: Free Press, 1960.

————, and THOMAS, DOROTHY S. (eds.). *Population Redistribution and Economic Change in the United States, 1870–1950.* 2 Vols. Philadelphia: The American Philosophical Society, 1957–60.

LAMBIE, JOSEPH T. and CLEMENCE, RICHARD V. (eds.). *Economic Change in America: Readings in the Economic History of the United States.* Harrisburg, Pa.: Stackpole, 1954.

LANE, FREDERIC C. and RIEMERSMA, JELLE C. (eds.). *Enterprise and Secular Change: Readings in Economic History.* (Edited for the American Economic Association and the Economic History Association.) Homewood, Ill.: Richard D. Irwin, 1953.

LARRABEE, WILLIAM. *The Railroad Question.* Chicago: Schulte Publishing Co., 1893.

LARSON, HENRIETTA M. *The Wheat Market and the Farmer in Minnesota.* (Studies in History, Economics and Public Law, CXXII, No. 2.) New York: Columbia University Press, 1926.

LEACH, ALBERT E. *Food Inspection and Analysis.* 3rd ed., rev. and enl. by A. L. Winton. New York: J. Wiley and Sons, 1913.

LUCAS, WALTER ARNDT, (ed.). *100 Years of Steam Locomotives.* New York: Simmons-Boardman, 1957.

MACGILL, CAROLINE E. and OTHERS. *History of Transportation in the United States before 1860.* Washington: Carnegie Institution of Washington, 1917.

MARTIN, EDGAR W. *The Standard of Living in 1860.* Chicago: University of Chicago Press, 1942.

McPHERSON, LOGAN G. *Railway Freight Rates in Relation to the Industry and Commerce of the United States.* New York: H. Holt, 1909.

MEYER, JOHN R. and OTHERS. *The Economics of Competition in the Transportation Industries.* Cambridge: Harvard University Press, 1959.

MEYERHOFF, HANS. *The Philosophy of History in Our Time.* Garden City, N. Y.: Doubleday, 1959.

MOULTON, HAROLD G. *Waterways versus Railways.* Boston and New York: Houghton Mifflin, 1912.

MULHALL, MICHAEL G. *Dictionary of Statistics.* 4th ed. London: Routledge, 1899.

NAGEL, ERNEST. *The Structure of Science: Problems in the Logic of Scientific Explanation*. New York: Harcourt, Brace and World, 1961.

NORTH, DOUGLASS C. *The Economic Growth of the United States, 1790–1860*. Englewood Cliffs, N.J.: Prentice-Hall, 1961.

OLIVER, JOHN W. *History of American Technology*. New York: Ronald Press, 1956.

OVERMAN, FREDERIC. *The Manufacture of Iron*. Philadelphia: H. C. Baird, 1850.

OVERTON, RICHARD C. *Burlington West*. Cambridge: Harvard University Press, 1941.

PANSCHAR, WILLIAM G. and SLATER, CHARLES C. *Baking in America*. 2 Vols. Evanston: Northwestern University Press, 1956.

PEARSE, JOHN B. *A Concise History of the Iron Manufacture of the Colonies up to the Revolution and of Pennsylvania until the Present Time*. Philadelphia: Allen, Lane, and Scott, 1876.

PETO, SIR S. MORTON. *Resources and Prospects of America*. New York and Philadelphia, 1866.

PHILLIPS, ULRICH BONNELL. *A History of Transportation in the Eastern Cotton Belt to 1860*. New York: Columbia University Press, 1908.

PITKIN, TIMOTHY. *A Statistical View of the Commerce of the United States of America*. New Haven: Durrie and Peck, 1835.

POOR, HENRY V. *History of the Railroads and Canals of the United States of America*. New York: J. H. Schultz, 1860.

RASMUSSEN, WAYNE D. *Readings in the History of American Agriculture*. Urbana: University of Illinois Press, 1960.

RIEGEL, ROBERT EDGAR. *The Story of Western Railroads*. New York: Macmillan, 1926.

RINGWALT, JOHN L. *Development of Transportation Systems in the United States*. Philadelphia: By the Author, 1888.

RIPLEY, WILLIAM Z. *Railroads: Finance and Organization*. New York: Longmans, Green, 1915.

———. *Railroads: Rates and Regulation*. New York: Longmans, Green, 1912.

ROSTOW, WALT WHITMAN. *The Process of Economic Growth*. 2nd ed. Oxford: Clarendon, 1960.

———. *The Stages of Economic Growth*. Cambridge: At the University Press, 1960.

———, (ed.). *The Economics of Take-Off into Sustained Growth*. (Proceedings of a conference held by the International Economic Association.) New York: St. Martin's, 1963.

SAVAGE, CHRISTOPHER I. *An Economic History of Transport.* London: Hutchinson, 1959.

SCHMIDT, LOUIS B. and ROSS, EARLE D. *Readings in the Economic History of American Agriculture.* New York: Macmillan, 1925.

SCHUMPETER, JOSEPH A. *Business Cycles.* 2 Vols. New York: McGraw-Hill, 1939.

SHANNON, FRED A. *The Farmer's Last Frontier.* Vol. V of *The Economic History of the United States.* Edited by Henry David and Others. New York: Holt, Rinehart, and Winston, 1961.

SHERMAN, WELLS A. *Merchandising Fruits and Vegetables.* Chicago: A. W. Shaw, 1928.

SMITH, WALTER BUCKINGHAM and COLE, ARTHUR HARRISON. *Fluctuations in American Business 1790–1860.* Cambridge: Harvard University Press, 1935.

SOROKIN, PITIRIM and ZIMMERMAN, CARLE C. *Principles of Rural-Urban Sociology.* New York: H. Holt, 1929.

SOULE, GEORGE. *Economic Forces in American History.* New York: William Sloane, 1952.

STOVER, JOHN F. *The Railroads of the South, 1865–1900.* Chapel Hill: University of North Carolina Press, 1955.

SWANK, JAMES M. *History of the Manufacture of Iron in All Ages.* 2nd ed. Philadelphia: American Iron and Steel Association, 1892.

TANNER, HENRY S. *A Description of the Canals and Railroads of the United States.* New York: T. R. Tanner and J. Disturnell, 1840.

TAYLOR, GEORGE ROGERS. *The Transportation Revolution, 1815–1860.* Vol. IV of *The Economic History of the United States.* Edited by Henry David and Others. New York: Rinehart, 1958.

————, (ed.). *The Turner Thesis.* Rev. ed. Boston: Heath, 1956.

————, and NEU, IRENE D. *The American Railroad Network, 1861–1890.* Cambridge: Harvard University Press, 1956.

TOSTLEBE, ALVIN S. *Capital in Agriculture: Its Formation and Financing since 1870.* Princeton: Princeton University Press, 1957.

TRATMAN, E. E. RUSSEL. *Railway Track and Track Work.* 3rd ed. New York: McGraw-Hill, 1909.

TRYON, ROLLA MILTON. *Household Manufacturers in the United States, 1640–1860.* Chicago: University of Chicago Press, 1917.

ULMER, MELVILLE J. *Capital in Transportation, Communications, and Public Utilities: Its Formation and Financing.* Princeton: Princeton University Press, 1960.

USHER, ABBOTT PAYSON. *A History of Mechanical Inventions.* New York: McGraw-Hill, 1929.

VAN METRE, THURMAN WILLIAM. *Early Opposition to Steam Railroads.* New York: n.p., 1924.

WARE, CAROLINE F. *The Early New England Cotton Manufacture.* Boston: Houghton Mifflin, 1931.

WEBER, THOMAS. *The Northern Railroads in the Civil War, 1861–1865.* New York: Kings Crown Press, 1952.

WELCH, ASHBEL. *Comparative Economy of Iron and Steel Rails.* Philadelphia: DeArmond, 1870.

WELD, LOUIS D. H. *Studies in the Marketing of Farm Products.* (Studies in Social Science, No. 4.) Minneapolis: University of Minnesota, 1915.

WELLINGTON, ARTHUR MELLAN. *The Economic Theory of the Location of Railways.* 6th ed., corrected. New York: J. Wiley and Sons, and Engineering News, 1906.

WHITAKER, JOE R. and ACKERMAN EDWARD. *American Resources.* New York: Harcourt, 1951.

WILLIAMSON, HAROLD F. (ed). *The Growth of the American Economy.* New York: Prentice-Hall, 1944. (2nd ed., 1951.)

WOYTINSKY, WLADIMIR S. and WOYTINSKY, E. S. *World Commerce and Governments.* New York: Twentieth Century Fund, 1955.

———. *World Population and Production.* New York: Twentieth Century Fund, 1953.

WRIGHT, CARROLL D. *The Industrial Evolution of the United States.* New York: Scribner's Sons, 1902.

WRIGHT, CHESTER W. *Economic History of the United States.* 1st ed. New York: McGraw-Hill, 1941. (2nd. ed., 1949.)

ZIMMERMAN, CARLE C. *Consumption and Standards of Living.* New York: Van Nostrand, 1936.

ARTICLES AND JOURNALS

ABRAMOVITZ, MOSES. "Resource Output and Trends in the United States Since 1870," *American Economic Review,* Vol. 46 (May, 1956).

ALBION, ROBERT G. "The New York Port and Its Disappointed Rivals, 1815–1860," *Journal of Economic and Business History,* III (August, 1931).

Annals of the American Academy of Political and Social Science, Vols. I–XCLL. Philadelphia, 1890–1920.

BOGUE, ALLAN AND MARGARET B. "'Profits' and the Frontier Land Speculator," *Journal of Economic History,* XVII (March, 1957).

BURNETT, EDMUND C. "Hog Raising and Hog Driving in the Region of the French Broad River," *Agricultural History,* XX (April, 1946).

CALLENDER, GUY S. "The Position of American Economic History," *American Historical Review,* XIX (October, 1913).

CAULEY, TROY J. "The Cost of Marketing Texas Cattle in the Old Trail Days," *Journal of Farm Economics,* Vol. 9 (July, 1927).

CHILD, C. G. "The Iron Trade of Europe and the United States," *Merchants' Magazine and Commercial Review,* Vol. 16 (June, 1847).

CLEMEN, RUDOLPH A. "Cattle Trails as a Factor in the Development of Livestock Marketing," *Journal of Farm Economics,* Vol. 8 (October, 1926).

———. "Waterways in Livestock and Meat Trade," *American Economic Review,* XVI (December, 1926).

COCHRAN, THOMAS C. "Did the Civil War Retard Industrialization?," *Mississippi Valley Historical Review,* XLVIII (1961).

CONRAD, ALFRED H. AND MEYER, JOHN R. "The Economics of Slavery in the Ante Bellum South," *Journal of Political Economy,* LXVI (April, 1958).

CRANMER, H. JEROME. "Canal Investment, 1815-1860," Conference on Income and Wealth. *Trends in the American Economy in the Nineteenth Century.* (Vol. 24 of *Studies in Income and Wealth.*) Princeton: Princeton University Press, 1960.

CROMER, ORVILLE CHARLES. "Internal-Combustion Engines." *Encyclopaedia Britannica.* Vol. 12. Chicago: 1961.

DAUGHERTY, CARROLL R. "An Index of the Installation of Machinery in the United States Since 1850," *Harvard Business Review,* VI (April, 1928).

DAVIS, C. WOOD. "The Farmer, the Investor, and the Railway," *The Arena,* Vol. 3 (1891).

Dillon, Sidney. "The West and the Railroads," *North American Review,* CLII (1891).

EASTERLIN, RICHARD A. "Interregional Differences in Per Capita Income, Population, and Total Income, 1840–1950." Conference on Research in Income and Wealth, *Trends in the American Economy in the Nineteenth Century.* (Vol. 24 of *Studies in Income and Wealth.*) Princeton: Princeton University Press, 1960.

———. "Influences in European Overseas Emigration Before World War I," *Economic Development and Cultural Change,* IX (April, 1961).

ELY, RICHARD T. "Social Studies; I. The Nature of the Railway Problem," *Harper's Magazine,* Vol. 73 (1886).

———. "Social Studies; II. The Economic Evils in American Railway Methods," *Harper's Magazine,* Vol. 73 (1886).

FIELD, D. C. "Mechanical Road-Vehicles." *A History of Technology.* Edited by Charles Singer and Others. Vol. V. New York and London: Oxford University Press, 1958.

FISHLOW, ALBERT. "Antebellum Interregional Trade Reconsidered," *American Economic Review,* LIV (May, 1964).

――――. "Trends in the American Economy in the Nineteenth Century," *Journal of Economic History,* XXII (March, 1962).

FOGEL, ROBERT WILLIAM. "A Quantitative Approach to the Study of Railroads in American Economic Growth: A Report of Some Preliminary Findings," *Journal of Economic History,* XXII (June, 1962).

――――. ["A Provisional View of the 'New Economic History',"] *American Economic Review,* LIV (May, 1964).

FRANKLIN INSTITUTE. *The Journal.* Vols. 11–120. Philadelphia, 1831-85.

GALLMAN, ROBERT E. "Commodity Output in the United States." Conference on Income and Wealth, *Trends in the American Economy in the Nineteenth Century.* (Vol. 24 of *Studies in Income and Wealth.*) Princeton: Princeton University Press, 1960.

GOLDSMITH, RAYMOND. "The Growth of Reproducible Wealth of the United States of America from 1805 to 1950." International Association for Research in Income and Wealth. *Income and Wealth of the United States.* (Income and Wealth Series II.) Baltimore: The Johns Hopkins Press, 1952.

HEALY, KENT T. "American Transportation Before the War Between the States." *The Growth of the American Economy.* Edited by Harold F. Williamson. New York: Prentice-Hall, 1944.

――――. "Transportation as a Factor in Economic Growth," *Journal of Economic History,* VII (December, 1947).

HEMPEL, CARL G. "The Function of General Laws in History," *The Journal of Philosophy,* XXXIX (1942).

HENNING, GEORGE F. "The Influence of the Truck in Marketing Corn Belt Livestock," *Journal of Farm Economics,* Vol. 13 (July, 1931).

HIBBARD, BENJAMIN H. "The Effect of Freight Rates on Agricultural Geography," *Journal of Farm Economics,* Vol. 4 (July, 1922).

HULL, CHARLES H. "The Service of Statistics to History," *Journal of the American Statistical Association,* Vol. 75 (March, 1914).

HUNTER, LOUIS C. "Influence of the Market upon Technique in the Iron Industry in Western Pennsylvania Up to 1860," *Journal of Economic and Business History,* I (February, 1929).

ISARD, WALTER. "A Neglected Cycle: The Transport Building Cycle," *Review of Economic Statistics,* XXIV (November, 1924).

――――. "Some Locational Factors in the Iron and Steel Industry since the Early Nineteenth Century," *Journal of Political Economy,* LVI (June, 1948).

————. "Transport Development and Building Cycles," *Quarterly Journal of Economics,* LVII (November, 1942).

JENKS, LELAND H. "Railroads as an Economic Force in American Development," *Journal of Economic History,* IV (May, 1944).

JOYNT, CAREY B. and RESCHER, NICHOLAS. "The Problem of Uniqueness in History," *History and Theory,* I (1961).

KEMMERER, DONALD L. "The Pre-Civil War South's Leading Crop, Corn," *Agricultural History,* XXIII (October, 1949).

KLEIN, L. "Railroads in the United States," *Journal of the Franklin Institute,* Vol. 30 (1840).

KUZNETS, SIMON. "Long-Term Changes in the National Income of the United States of America since 1870." International Association for Research in Income and Wealth, *Income and Wealth of the United States.* (Income and Wealth Series II.) Baltimore: The Johns Hopkins Press, 1952.

————. "The Interrelation of Theory and History: Summary of Discussion and Postscript," *Journal of Economic History,* XVII (December, 1957).

————. "Measurement and Economic Growth," *Journal of Economic History,* VII (December, 1947).

————. "National Income Estimates for the United States Prior to 1870," *Journal of Economic History,* XII (1952).

————. "Notes on the Take-off," W. W. Rostow (ed.). *The Economics of Take-Off into Sustained Growth.* (Proceedings of a conference held by the International Economic Association.) New York: St. Martin's, 1963.

————. "Statistics and Economic History," *Journal of Economic History,* I (May, 1941).

————. "Toward a Theory of Economic Growth." Robert Lekachman (ed.). *National Policy for Economic Welfare at Home and Abroad.* Garden City, N. Y.: Doubleday, 1955.

LEAVITT, CHARLES T. "Transportation and the Livestock Industry of the Middle West to 1860," *Agricultural History,* VIII (January, 1934).

LEE, GUY A. "The Historical Significance of the Chicago Grain Elevator System," *"Agricultural History,* XI (January, 1937).

LIPPINCOTT, ISAAC. "A History of River Improvement," *Journal of Political Economy,* XXII (July, 1914).

MACHLUP, FRITZ. "Structure and Structural Change: Weaselwords and Jargon," *Zeitschrift Für Nationalökonomie,* XVIII (1958).

MANDELBAUM, MAURICE. "Historical Explanations: The Problem of 'Covering-Laws,'" *History and Theory,* I (1961).

MERCHANT, E. A. J. "The Iron Trade," *Merchants' Magazine and Commercial Review,* Vol. 12 (March, 1845).

MEYER, JOHN R. and CONRAD, ALFRED H. "Economic Theory, Statistical Inference and Economic History," *Journal of Economic History,* XVII (December, 1957).

NILES WEEKLY REGISTER. Vol. 54–75. Baltimore and Philadelphia, 1838–1849.

North American Review. Vols. 50–171. New York, 1840–1900.

PAINE, CHARLES. "History of Iron Rails on the Michigan Southern and Northern Indian Railway," *Transactions of the American Society of Civil Engineers* (1872).

PARKER, WILLIAM N. and WARTENBY, FRANKLEE. "The Growth of Output Before 1840." Conference on Research in Income and Wealth. *Trends in the American Economy in the Nineteenth Century.* (Vol. 24 of *Studies in Income and Wealth.*) Princeton: Princeton University Press, 1960.

PAXSON, FREDERIC L. "The Railroads of the 'Old Northwest' before the Civil War," *Transactions of the Wisconsin Academy of Science, Arts and Letters,* XVII (1914).

PRIMACK, MARTIN L. "Land Clearing Under Nineteenth-Century Techniques: Some Preliminary Calculations," *Journal of Economic History,* XXII (December, 1962).

"The Railroad System," *North American Review,* XIV (1867).

RANSDELL, JOSEPH E. "Legislative Program Congress Should Adopt for Improvement of American Waterways," *Annals of the American Academy of Political and Social Science,* XXXI (1908).

SAVETH, EDWARD M. "Scientific History in America; Eclipse of an Idea." Donald Sheehan and Harold C. Syrett (eds.). *Essays in American Historiography.* New York: Columbia University Press, 1960.

SCHMIDT, LOUIS BERNARD. "The Internal Grain Trade of the United States, 1850–1890," *Iowa Journal of History and Politics,* Vols. 18, 19, 20 (1920–22).

SCOTT, J. W. "A National System of Railways," *Merchants' Magazine and Commercial Review,* XVII (December, 1847).

SMITH, CHARLES E. "The Manufacture of Iron in Pennsylvania," *Merchants' Magazine and Commercial Review,* Vol. 25 (November, 1851).

TAUSSIG, F. W. "The Tariff, 1830–1860," *Quarterly Journal of Economics,* II (April, 1888).

THRONE, MILDRED. "Southern Iowa Agriculture, 1833–1890: The Progress from Subsistence to Commercial Corn-Belt Farming," *Agricultural History,* XXIII (April, 1949).

TUNELL, GEORGE G. "The Diversion of the Flour and Grain Traffic from the Great Lakes to the Railroads," *Journal of Political Economy,* V (June, 1897).

————. "The Growth and Character of the Commerce of the Great Lakes," *Journal of Political Economy,* IV (March, 1896).

————. "Transportation on the Great Lakes of North America," *Journal of Political Economy,* IV (June, 1896).

WICKER, E. R. "Railroad Investment Before the Civil War." Conference on Research in Income and Wealth. *Trends in the American Economy in the Nineteenth Century.* (Vol. 24 of *Studies in Income and Wealth.*) Princeton: Princeton University Press, 1960.

WORKING, HOLBROOK. "The Decline in Per Capita Consumption of Flour in the United States," *Wheat Studies,* II (July, 1926).

ZIMMERMAN, WILLIAM D. "Live Cattle Export Trade Between United States and Great Britain, 1868–1885," *Agricultural History,* XXXVI (January, 1962).

MAPS AND ATLASES

Asher and Adams' New Statistical and Topographical Atlas of the United States. New York: Asher and Adams, 1874.

BOWLES, R. C. M. *A Map Showing Railway Distances between Cities, Towns and Places of Interest in the British Possessions in North America, the United States, and Mexico.* Boston: R. C. M. Bowles, 1896.

Cram's Standard American Railway System Atlas, 1892. Chicago and New York: George F. Cram, 1892.

LORD, CLIFFORD L. and ELIZABETH L. *Historical Atlas of the United States.* New York: H. Holt, 1944.

PAULIN, CHARLES O. *Atlas of the Historical Geography of the United States.* Edited by John K. Wright. Washington, D.C. and New York: Carnegie Institution of Washington and American Geographical Society of New York, 1932.

RAND MCNALLY AND CO. *Rand McNally Commercial Atlas and Marketing Guide.* 88th ed. New York: Rand McNally, 1957.

————. *Rand McNally Company's Enlarged Business Atlas for 1891.* Chicago: 1891.

U.S. GEOLOGICAL SURVEY. *United States Quadrangle Maps.*

UNPUBLISHED MATERIAL

Unpublished records of the Bureau of Public Roads are described in: U.S. General Services Administration. NATIONAL ARCHIVES AND RECORDS SERVICE. *Preliminary Inventory of the Records of the Bureau of Public Roads.* No. 134. (Record Group 30.) 1952.

AMERICAN IRON AND STEEL ASSOCIATION, *Statistics, 1830–1867.* This volume is in the manuscript collection of the New York Public Library.

CONRAD, ALFRED H. "Statistical Inference and Historical Causation."

COOTNER, PAUL H. *Transportation Innovation and Economic Development.* Unpublished doctoral dissertation, Massachusetts Institute of Technology, 1953.

ENGERMAN, STANLEY L. and FOGEL, ROBERT W. *The Growth of the American Iron Industry, 1800–1860: A Statistical Reconstruction.* In progress.

FISHLOW, ALBERT. The *Economic Contribution of American Railroads Before the Civil War.* Unpublished doctoral dissertation, Harvard University, 1963.

——. "Productivity Change in the Railroad Sector, 1840–1910." Presented to the Conference on Research in Income and Wealth, Chapel Hill, September 4–5, 1963.

GALLMAN, ROBERT E. *Value Added by Agriculture, Mining and Manufacturing in the United States, 1840–1880.* Unpublished doctoral dissertation, University of Pennsylvania, 1956.

PARKER, WILLIAM N. "The Productivity of the American Farmer in the Nineteenth Century." Presented to the Mississippi Valley Historical Association Meeting, Omaha, May 3–4, 1963.

PRIMACK, MARTIN L. *Farm-formed Capital in American Agriculture, 1850–1910.* Unpublished doctoral dissertation, University of North Carolina, 1962.

RANSOM, ROGER LESLIE. *Government Investment in Canals: A Study of the Ohio Canal.* Unpublished doctoral dissertation, University of Washington, 1963.

TEMIN, PETER. *A History of the American Iron and Steel Industry from 1830 to 1900.* Unpublished doctoral dissertation, Massachusetts Institute of Technology, 1964.

——. "A Review of the Statistics of Pig-Iron Production." Appendix A of Temin's dissertation is a somewhat altered version of this paper.

Index

Aaron, Daniel, 230
Acre-weight: defined, 78
Adams, Henry, 239, 243*n*
Agricultural production: geographic pattern of, 17–18, 21–22; and self-sufficiency, 17, 26*n*; surplus and deficit regions of, 17–18; of various commodities, 76; decline in share of national product, 116. *See also* Distribution of agricultural surpluses
Agricultural regions. *See* Agricultural production
A.I.S.A. *See* American Iron and Steel Association
Aldrich Committee, 36
Alpha (α) estimate. *See* Social saving, intraregional
Alternative cost doctrine, 108–9
American Iron and Steel Association: surveys by, 162*n*, 176*n*, 178*n*; rail consumption as defined by, 166; data used to test model of rail consumption, 176–78, 181–88, 231; rail consumption series, 183; on rail inventories, 188; estimates of scrapped rails, 188–89*n*. *See also* Blast furnaces; Iron industry; Pig iron; Rails; Rolling mills
Arkansas River, 90
Arkwright, Richard, 235
Axiom of indispensability: evolution of, 1–9; suggested by statistical correlations, 5; deduced from economic theory, 5; invoked by disputants, 7–8; caveats against, 8–9; crucial aspect of, 10; applied to intraregional transportation, 50; and settlement of prairies, 80, 110, 219; relationship to primary and derived effects of railroads, 208

Baker, Ira O., 109
Baldwin Locomotive Works, 133
Baltimore and Ohio Railroad, 179, 261
Bean, Louis H., 36
Beef: required for local consumption, 17, 18*n*; supply of, 18*n*; requirements of secondary markets, 35–36; urban

and rural consumption compared, 35; freight rates on, 40, 42, 70; amount shipped interregionally, 40, 42. *See also* Conversion ratios; Distribution of agricultural surpluses; Inventories; Price(s)
Bessemer, Henry, 235
Beta (β) estimate. See Social saving, intraregional
Bigler, William, 184
Black River Canal, 100, 105
Blast furnaces: charcoal, 136, 155, 156, 157, 158; capacity of, 153–55, 156, 157, 158; bankruptcies of, 153, 157 and *n*, 160*n*, 161; number of, 153 and *n*; abandoned, 153*n*, 156, 157; capacity of, 154, 156, 157; coal, 156, 157, 160; level of operation, 158–60; effect of rails on, 199, 206, 232. *See also* Iron industry and references there
Bogue, Allan and Margaret, 238
Bolino, August C., 9
Boundary of feasible commercial agriculture: defined, 52, 212–13; method of estimating 53–55, 73, 75–84, 214–15; average distance from waterways, 79, 109, 216, 219; biases in location of, 79 and *n*; value of agricultural products within, 84; and proposed canals, 92, 218; adjusted for reduced wagon rates, 109–10, 219. *See also* Land; Rent theory; Social saving, intraregional
Budget studies: of urban workers, 32, 64; of farm families, 33 and *n*, 64; review of, 33*n*
Buffalo, Rochester, and Pittsburgh Railroad, 70
Buildings, farm: value of, 83

Callender, Guy S., 239–40
Canals: effect on transportation rates, 9; in operation and abandoned, 46, 250, 252–53; aborted in praires, 80; proposed system of, 92–107, 218–19; method of estimating construction cost of, 98; method of estimating water requirements of, 98, 106; ca-

pacity of, 98, 106; plan to operate during winter, 224. *See also* Water transportation; under names of various canals

Carey, Henry, 151–65 *passim,* 245

Cargo losses: frequency of, 24; method of estimating, 41; value of, 41, 43, 88, 214. *See also* Insurance; Water transportation

Carpets: production of, 126

Cast iron: in rail fastenings, 133; in locomotives, 133, 136*n*; in railroad cars, 133, 136*n*; value of, 256; pig iron consumed in, 256. *See also* Iron industry and references there

Champlain Canal, 100, 105

Chemung Canal, 100, 105

Chenango Canal, 100, 105

Chesapeake and Ohio Railroad, 3

Chicago Board of Trade, 49, 50

Clapham, John, 111

Clark, Victor S., 123*n*

Coal: consumed by locomotives, 135–36, 233; required for production of railroad iron, 136, 233; production of, 136, 233; share of railroad freight, 221; localization in production and consumption of, 221

Cohen, Morris Raphael, 17, 49

Colburn, Zerah, 180, 195

Cole, Arthur H., 129

Connecticut River, 70

Conrad, Alfred H., 238

Consumption of agricultural products: urban-rural differences in, 33 and *n,* 35, 64–66; regional differences in, 33 and *n,* 35, 62, 64–66; by animals, 35*n,* 66; meats, 36; dairy products, 62; method of estimating, 62–66. *See also* Distribution of agricultural surpluses

Conversion ratios: wheat into flour, 31, 34; corn into corn meal, 31, 35; wheat into bread, cake, and macaroni, 32*n*; live animals into dressed meats, 43; "airline" into road distances, 67 and *n,* 68 and *n*; pig iron into rails, 195

Corn: required for local consumption, 17; supply of, 18*n,* shipment from primary markets, 30, 31; in Southern diet, 33*n*; requirements of secondary markets, 35; consumption by various animals, 35*n*; amount shipped inter-

regionally, 40, 42. *See also* Conversion ratios; Distribution of agricultural surpluses; Inventories; Price(s)

Cost of time. *See* Inventories; Social saving

Cotton: shipped interregionally, 25; retained for consumption in counties, 77*n*; consumption in U.S. and Great Britain compared, 123–24

Cotton textiles: importance in British "take-off," 114, 124*n*; decline in home manufacture of, 121–22; rate of growth of, 122–24, 229; and manufacturing share of commodity production, 125–26; technology of, 128. *See also* Leading sector; Manufactured goods; "Take-off"

Coxe, Tench, 124

Cranmer, H. Jerome, 98

Crude iron: domestic consumption of, 131, 190–93, 232; used in production of rails, 131–34, 196; total consumed by railroads, 132, 133–34, 232; consumed as nails, 135; and imports of finished iron, 190*n*; effect of scrapped rails on supply of, 205, 206, 232. *See also* Iron industry; Pig iron; Rails

Dairy products: shipped interregionally, 25; per capita consumption of butter, 62; butter shipped from counties, 63; milk shipped by wagons, 75. *See also* Distribution of agricultural surpluses

David, Henry, 239

Deficit agricultural regions. *See* Agricultural production; Distribution of agricultural surpluses; S e c o n d a r y markets

Delaware River, 70

Diet studies. *See* Budget studies; Conversion ratios; under various foods

Dillon, Sidney, 5–6, 7–8, 80*n*

Distances: of interregional shipments, 40 and *n,* 42, 210; of wagon hauls, 46, 51, 57, 68, 77–78, 79; method of estimating average, 66–69; ratio of "airline" to road, 67 and *n,* 68 and *n,* 69, 79; estimates compared with U.S.D.A. survey, 68; intraregionally by rail and boat, 72–73, 84–85*n,* 88*n.* *See also* Railroads; Wagon transportation; Water transportation

Distribution of agricultural surpluses: pattern of, 18–19; inter- and intraregional defined, 19; cotton, 25; diary, 25–26; wool, 26; from primary markets, 29–31; interregionally, 40, 42; and number of interior shipping points, 51; from farms and counties, 58, 59–66, 78; exclusively by wagon, 61, 62, 75; bulkiness of shipments, 73; intraregionally by railroad, 74–75, 84, 85, 86, 87, 88n; from non-feasible region, 85, 87. *See also* Railroads; Social saving; Wagon transportation; Water transportation

Economic growth: implications for theory of, 234–37; a consequence of scientific revolution, 235; railroads not a condition for, 235; outcome of a broad supply of opportunity, 236; path affected by chance factors, 236; the effect of choice of solutions on, 237. *See also* Axiom of indispensability; Supply of alternative opportunity
Efficiency: of railroads, wagons, and boats compared, 10n, 110, 219; and equity issues confused, 12–13
Ely, Richard T., 5, 6
Embargo Act, 124
Engineering News, 108–9
Equity. *See* Efficiency
Erie Canal: as a possible bottleneck, 28n, 54n: secondary markets on, 51; rise and fall on, 100; profile of, 105; mentioned, 37, 49
Explanations. *See* Historical explanations

Feasible range. *See* Boundary of feasible commercial agriculture
Fences: amount and cost of, 83
Fishlow, Albert: on coal-burning locomotives, 135n; on statistical reconstructions, 149n; revision of track construction estimates by, 171n, 257–61; on amount of rail freight service, 172n, 178n; acknowledgments to, 179, 182; on amount of pig iron in rerolled rails, 195; estimates of social saving by, 223n; on gain from regional specialization, 225n; on domestic production of rails, 260–61, 260n

Fite, Gilbert C., 9
Frankel, Charles, 207
Freight rates. *See* Rates, freight
French, Benjamin F., 165 and n
Funk, W. C., 33n, 36n, 64

Galena and Chicago Union Railroad, 50, 180
Gallatin, Albert, 122
Gallman, Robert E., 23, 115–31 *passim*, 143, 228
Genesee Valley Canal, 100, 105
Gerstner, Francis Anthony Chevalier de, 179, 257, 258, 259, 260
Gerstner, Franz Anton von. *See* Gerstner, Francis Anthony Chevalier de
Glass: production of, 127
Goodrich, Carter, 9
Great Britain, Board of Trade, 32
Great Lakes, 37, 51
Grosvenor, W. H., 151–65 *passim,* 245

Hargreaves, James, 235
Harrisburg Convention, 153, 154n, 165n
Hay: consumption of, 66; shipments of, 73, 75, 76. *See also* Agricultural production; Distribution of agricultural surpluses
Healy, Kent T., 8–9, 225n
Heckscher, Eli F., 111
Hempel, Carl G., 1, 247, 248
Hepburn Committee, 6, 7
Hewitt, Abraham, 245
Historical explanations: criteria of soundness 1, 149; role of hypothetico-deductive systems in, 246, 247–48; applicability of economic models to, 246–47; and "explanation sketches," 248; and implicit models, 248–49. *See also* Mathematics, applicability to economic history; Measurement; Social saving; Statistical reconstructions
Historical reconstructions. *See* Statistical reconstructions
Historicism: tenets of, 238–39, 238n. *See also* Historical explanations; Measurement
Hofstadter, Richard, 230
Holly, Alexander L., 180, 195
Horseless carriage. *See* Motor vehicles

Hudson River, 70
Hull, Charles H., 238
Hypothetico-deductive systems. *See* Historical explanations

Illinois and Michigan Canal, 98
Illinois Central Railroad, 144*n*, 187 and *n*
Indexes of rails in iron market: bias in, 131*n*; movements in, 132, 134, 193–99, 199*n*, 200; problem of, 149–51; defined, 150, 151, 197, 199, 200, 201, 256; relationship among, 150–51, 157, 254–56; I_1 computed for 1856 and 1859, 255–56; I_7 computed for 1859, 257. *See also* Mathematics, applicability to economic history; Measurement; Statistical reconstructions
Industrial Commission of 1900, 49
Inland Waterways Commission, 91
Innovations: stiffled by railroads, 14–15; no one vital to economic growth, 234–35; and multiplicity of solutions, 235–36; conditionally indispensable, 237. *See also* Economic growth; Supply of opportunity; Technology
Insurance: rates, 39 and *n*, 43; as a measure of the cost of cargo losses, 41, 43, 88; included in cost of rails, 144*n*. *See also* Cargo losses; Social saving
Interest: charges on inventories, 46, 91*n*, 211; rates on mortgages, 79, 82–83; rates on bonds, 108, 187. *See also* Profits
Internal-combustion engine. *See* Motor vehicles
Internal navigation. *See* Canals; Water transportation
Interregional trade: defined, 19, 209; hypothesis stated, 19; conceptual basis for test of, 19–29; growth over time in, 22–23; volume of, 40–42. *See* Distribution of agricultural surpluses and references there
Intraregional trade: defined, 19, 50–51, 211–12; agricultural tonnage entering, 57–58; shipments in North Atlantic region, 59–66; agricultural shipments via rail, 74–75. *See also* Distribution of agricultural surpluses and references there

Inventories: on farms, 34, 90*n*; and time, 44–46, 88–89, 210–11, 214, 217; and limited season of navigation, 45–46, 89–91, 91*n*, 92, 210–11, 214, 217; and risk, 45; in primary markets, 88–90, 90*n*; in South, 90–91; of rails, 178, 184–85; cycle of rails in, 183–88; ratio of rail consmumption to, 183, 188 and *n*; cost of holding rails in, 187*n*; cost of holding minerals in, 222. *See also* Rails; Social saving
Iron industry: growth of, 124–25, 131–35, 159, 229; and manufacturing share of commodity production, 125–26; technology of, 125, 129; effect of railroads on growth of, 131–35, 232–33; qualitative statements on railroad purchases from, 147; boom in, 159–60; depression in, 160, 164–65; effect of rails on growth of, 199–206, 230, 233. *See also* Blast furnaces; Cast iron; Crude iron; Pig iron; Rails; Rolling mills
Iron ore: share in railroad freight tonnage, 221; localization of production and consumption of, 221–22

Jefferson, Thomas, 17*n*
Joint Traffic Committee, 70

Klein, L., 179
Krooss, Herman E., 9
Kuznets, Simon, 48, 128*n*, 147

Lake Champlain, 70
Lake George, 70
Land: effect of railroads on supply of, 53–55, 214–16; in farms, 78; value of, 78, 79, 80, 83; within feasible region, 79–83, 92, 99, 110, 216–17, 218, 219; effect of diminished supply on national income, 80, 82–83, 84, 86, 92, 99, 110, 217; distribution of, 80; cost of clearing, 83. *See also* Boundary of feasible commercial agriculture; Rent theory; Social saving, intraregional
Land grants. *See* Railroads
Larrabee, William, 6

Lead: production of, 127
Leading sector: concept of, 113; railroads as a, 114, 129; cotton textiles as a, 114; indirect effects of, 130; as a hero theory of history, 236. *See also* Structural change; "Take-off"
Lehigh Canal, 125
Lehigh Valley Railroad, 70
Lesley, J. P., 156, 158
Linear programming. *See* Mathematics, applicability to economic history
Locomotives: production of, 133, 139; average weight of, 133, pig iron in, 133; coal-burning, 133, 135*n*, value of, 144
Long-haul railroads. *See* Railroads
Long Island Sound, 70
Lumber: firewood distinct from, 136–37, 233; consumed by railroads, 137–38, 139, 233–34; production of, 138

Machinery: railroad share in production of, 139–40, 142, 234
Machlup, Fritz, 114
Manufactured goods: consumed by railroads, 13–14, 16, 140–46, 234; share in national income, 116–17, 121; share in commodity production, 117–21, 125–27, 129, 229; decline in household production of, 121–22, 229; production of various, 126–27; effect of railroads on growth of, 141 and *n*, 234
Martin, Robert F., 115–16, 121
Mathematics, applicability to economic history: and effect on data requirements, 26; of linear programming, 26–29, 28*n*, 29*n*, 37–38, 48, 244, 247; of sampling procedures, 40 and *n*, 59, 67*n*, 68 and *n*, 84–85*n*, 210, 239, 243*n*; equations for estimate α, 56, 57, 87, 213; relationship between $\overline{Z}^1$ and Z^1, 64–65; in estimation of average distances, 66–67; of regression analysis, 69–70, 84–85*n*, 90 and *n*, 98, 134, 143, 163 and *n*, 172*n*, 176, 178*n*, 199*n*, 204 and *n*, 255; of indexes, 72 and *n*, 131 and *n*, 134*n*, 149–51, 157, 193–99, 200–1, 242–43, 244, 254–57; equations for estimate β, 86; equation for water requirements, 98; in measuring structural change, 120–21*n*; of input-output analysis, 130–41; of simulation models, 168–89, 203–5, 230–32; of stochastic distributions, 171–73, 206, 231; of chi-square test, 206*n*; of general equilibrium models, 223*n*; and realm to which statistical procedures apply, 237–42; in proof that I_4 exceeds I_1, 254–55. *See also* Measurement; Statistical reconstructions
Measurement: in analysis of railroad impact, 147–48; opinions as a substitute for, 147–48, 242–46; recent applications in economic history, 238; historicist position on, 238–39; relationship to qualitative analysis, 239–42. *See also* Historical explanations; Mathematics, applicability to economic history; Statistical reconstructions
Merchant, E. A. J., 153*n*, 159, 165*n*
Meyer, John R., 238
Michigan Central Railroad, 180
Miller, William, 230
Mississippi River, 37, 53, 80, 90
Missouri River, 80
Motor vehicles: as an alternative to railroads, 14–15, 92, 224; and internal-combustion engines, 15, 92; conformed to existing trade patterns, 31–32; registrations of, 75*n*. *See also* Supply of alternative opportunity

Nails: production of, 135 and *n*, 233
New Albany and Salem Railroad, 180
New York, Lake Erie, and Western Railroad, 69–70
New York, New Haven, and Hartford Railroad, 69
New York Board of Trade, 7
New York Central Railroad, 3
New York Home League: surveys by, 153*n*, 155, 156, 157, 162, 164–65, 164*n*; formation of, 165*n*
New York State Barge Canal, 28*n*
North, Douglass C., 128*n*
North American Review: appraisal of railroads by, 3–4

Office of Public Roads. *See* U.S. Department of Agriculture
Overman, Frederic, 179

Paper: production of, 126; technology of, 129

Pennsylvania Railroad, 3, 6, 70

Philadelphia Commercial List: survey by, 163

Philadelphia Convention of Ironmasters: survey by, 152–65 *passim*

Philadelphia, Wilmington, and Baltimore Railroad, 180

Pickard, James, 236

Pig iron: production of, 124–25, 124n, 125n, 162n, 165n, 190–93, 229; imports of, 124 and n, 193, 194, 195; rise in demand for, 125; in U.S. and Great Britain compared, 125; series in *Historical Statistics*, 151; Taussig's criticism of Carey's series on, 152–55; production by type, 152, 156; production by region, 153–54, 162; ratio of national to Pennsylvania production of, 153, 162–63, 164; Grosvenor's production estimates of, 154, 155–58; Carey's production estimates of, 154, 158–60; revised production estimates of, 163–66; confusion between production and consumption of, 190–93; consumed in rails, 193, 194, 195, 232; required per ton of rails, 195; effect of changes in rail demand on, 201–3; rail share of value added in, 256–57, 257n. *See also* American Iron and Steel Association; Iron industry and references there; Philadelphia Convention of Ironmasters; Harrisburg convention

Pitkin, Timothy, 125, 127

Platte River, 160n

Poor, Henry V., 169–70, 171n, 257, 258

Population: growth correlated with railroad construction, 5; growth of 8, 122; urbanization of, 48, 122, 235; and inventories, 89–90, 90n; effect of social saving on, 225–26; effect of railroads on spatial distribution of, 227

Pork: required for local consumption, 18 and n; forms of, 29n; requirements of secondary markets, 35–36; urban and rural consumption compared, 35; freight rates on, 40, 42, 70; shipped interregionally, 40–42. *See also* Conversion ratios; Distribution of agricultural surpluses; Inventories; Price(s)

Potatoes; shipments of, 73, 76

Price(s): of grains, 25n, 43; of cattle, swine, and meats, 43; and wagon rates, 55–56, 72n, 84; index for canal construction, 98; of pig iron, 124 and n, 160, 161 and n, 165; changes in level of, 125, 160, 161n; of rails, 145n, 187n, 255 and n, 256, 261; of rolled iron other than rails, 255 and n; of various iron products, 256; of bar iron, 261

Primack, Martin, 83

Primary growth sector. *See* Leading sector

Primary markets: listed, 18–19; location with respect to waterways, 24, 209; shipments from, 29–30, 49, 209; receipts of, 50; defined for intraregional case, 51, 212n; inventories in, 89–90. *See also* Distribution of agricultural surpluses and references there

Production potential: effect of railroads on, 12, 208; and social saving, 21n, 47n, 208, 225n. *See also* Social saving

Profits: sensitivity to rate differentials, 12, 24–25; of railroads, 50; on the improvement of roads, 108; on proposed canals, 218n. *See also* Interest

Qualitative analysis. *See* Measurement

Quantitative analysis. *See* Mathematics, applicability to economic history; Measurement; Statistical reconstructions

Rail consumption, model of: discussed, 166–76, 230–32; equations for, 168–69, 231; tests of empirical validity of, 172n, 176–89, 206n, 231; estimates derived from, 174–76, 194, 204, 205; implications regarding decentralization of rolling mills, 203–6. *See also* Mathematics, applicability to economic history; Rails and references there

Rail fastenings: average weight of, 133

Railroad cars: average weight of, 133–34; production of, 133–34, 139; lumber in, 139; value of, 144 and n

Railroad network: size of 3, 4, 51; density of, 14, 77, 80. *See also* Railroad track

Railroads: conceptions of, 1–9; land grants to, 3; financial aid to, 3; technological development of, 3–4, 22; share in freight movements, 4–5, 39, 40n, 61, 62, 74–75, 88n; social and political aspects of, 4, 7–8, 227–28; psychological impact of, 10–11; unique effects of, 11; appurtenances of, 11, 236–37; and fallacy of composition, 11–12; effect on manufacturing share in commodity production, 12, 140–46; and growth of manufacturing, 13–14, 129–30; trunk lines of, 13, 50; effect on other innovations, 15; inter- and intraregional defined, 19; average distance of haul by, 40 and n, 42, 72, 84n, 88n; speed of trains, 44–45n, 89; inter- and intraregional compared, 50–51; and settlement of prairies, 80, 108, 219; average cost of constructing, 141 and n; distribution of construction expenditures on, 144n; role of quantitative analysis in study of, 147–48; average length of, 178n; cost of interruptions in construction of, 187 and n; primary and derived effects defined, 207–8; embodied and disembodied effects defined, 224; relationship between primary and derived effects of, 224–28; disembodied effects of, 224–26; embodied effects of, 226–37. *See also* Axiom of indispensability; Economic growth; under names of railroads

Railroad track: construction estimates, 169–71, 171n, 257–61; method of estimating extra, 171; average weight of rails on, 178–81, 189. *See also* Rails and references there

Rails: steel, 4, 130, 172n; share domestically produced, 135, 150, 193, 194, 260n; imports of, 135, 187, 193; value added by rolling mills attributable to, 143; value of, in new construction, 145; average life of, 171–72, 172n, 178n; replacements of, 171, 173–76, 203–6, 232, 257n, 258n; variability of life of, 172 and n, 206; intensity of utilization of, 172n; estimated consumption of, 174, 257n; ratio of track

mileage to consumption of, 176; consumption estimates of, compared, 176–78; weight of, 178–81, 178n, 182, 189, 257–58n; difficulty in rolling, 180; cycle in inventory of, 183–88; types produced, 184, 261; produced from imported pig iron, 193; rerolled, 193, 194, 195, 199, 232; pig iron consumed in, 193, 194, 232; effect on growth of iron industry, 199–206, 233. *See also* American Iron and Steel Association; Blast furnaces; Crude iron; Indexes of rails in iron market; Pig iron; Prices; Rail consumption, model of; Rail wear, model of; Rolling mills; Scrapped rails

Rail wear, model of: discussed, 171–73, 206n, 231; implies parameters of scrap equation, 188. *See also* Rails and references there

Rates, freight: compared, 9, 23, 24, 38, 39, 42, 72, 85n

—railroad: decline in, 4, 37 and n, 57; power of control of, 7; national average, 23; interregional, 36–37, 42; on wheat, 38–39; controlled by waterways, 49; intraregional, 69–70, 72, 85n

—wagon: in given years, 23, 56–57; upward biases in, 54–55, 71–72; U.S.D.A. estimates of, 71–72, 108, 109, 219; average in North Atlantic region, 71–72, 84; price index for, 72n, 84; national average, 84, 86; average in North Central region, 85n; effect of road improvements on, 107–9, 219; in rural areas, 109

—water: and marginal cost of service, 27–28, 54; source of, 37; on wheat and pork, 38, 39, 42; decline in, 57; intraregional, 70–71; average in North Atlantic region, 72; average in North Central region, 85n. *See also* Rebates; Social saving

Raymond, R. W., 165, 165n

Rebates: effect on grain trade, 6–7; extent of, 36–37, 69

Reconstructions. *See* Statistical reconstructions

Red River, 90

Reese, Jim E., 9

Reeves, Samuel, 160

Rent theory: and establishment of feasible boundary, 53–55, 78–79, 214–16;

and loss in income due to diminished supply of, 55, 216, 247. *See also* Boundary of feasible commercial agriculture; Land; Social saving

Replacements. *See* Rails and references listed there

Rerolling. *See* Rails and references listed there

Rivers. *See* Water transportation

Roads, wagon: improvement of, 56, 92, 107–9, 218, 219. *See also* Rates, freight; U.S. Department of Agriculture; Wagon transportation

Rolling mills: distribution of value added between rails and other products of, 143; not adapted for heavy rails, 180; scrap consumed by, 188*n*; and rerolled rails, 193, 195, 232; effect of rails on growth of, 199–206; geographic decentralization of, 203–6; growth correlated with replacements, 204 and *n*; distribution of value between rails and other products of, 255; growth in capacity of, 261. *See also* Rails and references there

Rostow, Walt W., 13, 16, 111–35 *passim*, 228–33 *passim*

Rural Post Roads Act, 107

Salt: production of, 127

Saveth, Edward M., 239

Schmidt, Louis B., 30, 33*n*

Schumpeter, Joseph, 13

Scientific methods. *See* Historical explanations and references there

Scott, J. W., 2–3

Scrapped rails: model of, 169, 188–89, 231; A.I.S.A. estimates of, 188–89*n*, 190; as a per cent of all scrap, 188*n*; model estimates of, 189, 190, 192; and other scrap, 192, 193; used for nonrail purposes, 194, 232; share rerolled, 195; and decentralization of rolling mills, 203–6. *See also* Rails and references there

Secondary markets: listed, 19; location with respect to waterways, 24, 51, 209; method of estimating requirements of, 30–36. *See also* Distribution of agricultural surpluses and references there

Ships: production of, 28, 127

Short-haul railroads. *See* Railroads

Shuman, Armin, 169–70, 171*n*, 257–60 *passim*

Siemens, Frederick and William, 236

Smith, Charles E., 160*n*, 161*n*, 164*n*

Social saving: "true," 20, 20–21*n*, 27 and *n*, 52, 208–9; per ton-mile, 22, 209; significance of, 47–48, 47*n*, 211; and balance of trade, 47*n*; defined, 208; extension to all commodities, 219–24; ton-miles a biased extrapolator of, 219–20, 221, 222–23; crucial components of, 220; on products of mines, 221–22; "pure" agricultural, 222–23; Fishlow's estimate of, 223*n*; subsumes disembodied effects, 224–26

—interregional: defined, 20–21; upward bias in, 20, 27, 28, 208–9; and locus of agricultural production, 21–22; if wagons only alternative, 23; data needed for estimation of, 29–37; 210; preliminary estimate of, 37–48, 211; first approximation of, 41, 42, 210; cost of limited season of navigation, 44–46, 210–11; cost of uncompensated capital, 46–47, 87–88, 214; summarized, 47*n*, 211; cost of slow transportation, 210–11; compared to cost of shipping, 211

—intraregional: crux of, 51; on substitution of railroads for boats, 51, 57, 84, 84–85*n*, 86, 87, 213; estimate α defined, 52, 212; upward biases in estimate α defined, 52, 212; upward biases in estimate α, 52, 106–7, 212; estimate β defined, 52–53, 212–13; method of extrapolating α estimate over time, 53–55; theoretical basis of β estimate, 53–55, 214–15; biases in estimate β, 54–55, 79, 80–84, 106–7, 215–16; interpretation of estimate β, 55, 216; equations for, 56, 86, 87, 213; on wagon transportation, 57, 86, 87, 213; in 1870, 57–58; non-agricultural components of, 72, 88*n*; preliminary estimates of, 73–91, 214, 217; first approximations of, 84–87, 85*n*, 213–14; for feasible region, 84, 85, 86, 87; for non-feasible region, 85, 87; adjusted for indirect components, 85–91, 214; and cost of slow transportation, 88–89, 214; and cost of limited season of navigation, 89–91, 214; adjusted for proposed canals, 92–100, 218; adjusted for reduced wagon rate, 110, 219

—North Atlantic region: discussed, 59–73; estimated from sample, 59; preliminary estimate of, 60–61; major features of, 72–73; on wagon transportation, 73; on substitution of railroads for boats, 73, 78, 79, 84, 84–85n. *See also* Boundary of feasible commercial agriculture; Cargo losses; Insurance; Land; Transshipping

Southern Railroad, 3

Standard Oil Company, 6

Statistical reconstructions: and analogy to palaeontology, 148–49; as theories, 148–49; criteria for, 149, 245–46; literature on, 149n; value of, 205. *See also* Historical explanations; Mathematics, applicability to economic history; Measurement

Steam engines: production of, 127

Sterne, Simon, 7

Storage: rates of, 46n, 91; factors affecting social cost of, 90n. *See also* Inventories

Strauss, Frederick, 36

Structural change: role in "take-off" thesis, 112–13; definition of, 114–15; measures of, 116–19, 120–21n, 228; rapid periods of, 120–21, 127, 128, 228–29; continuity of, 127–29, 229. *See also* "Take-off"

Substitution: between rail and water transportation, 4–5, 13, 22; elasticity of, 50, 223n

Sugar: production of, 127

Supply of alternative opportunity: concept of, 10–15, 207; not systematically examined in past, 10, 207; need for further study of, 224; and illusion of no alternatives, 236–37. *See also* Economic growth

Surplus agricultural regions: *See* Agricultural production

Swank, James M., 195

Syracuse and Utica Railroad, 179

"Take-off": and other stages identified, 111–12; characteristics of, 112 and n, 228; necessary conditions for, 113; dated, 114; rate of structural change during, 116–20, 228; uniqueness of, 128–29, 229; automaticity of, 128n; as a theory of embodied consequences, 228. *See also* Leading sector; Structural change

Tariff: on pig iron, 124; rebate on rails, 261

Taussig, F. W., 152, 153, 159n

Taylor, George Rogers, 50, 56, 169

Technology: changes in railroad, 3–4, 22; stiffled by railroads, 14–15; possibility of adapting, 20, 91–110, 218–19, 224; of iron production, 125; changes in various industries of, 128–29. *See also* Innovations

Temin, Peter, 124n, 125n, 151, 164n

Thurston, R. H., 224

Trading areas: method of determining, 31–32; consumption in, 32–33, 209–10; supply in, 33–34, 210

Transportation equipment, 138–39, 234

Transportation policy, 1, 7–8, 49

Transshipping: rates, 30 and n, 44; cost of, 44, 86–87, 214

Tratman, E. E. R., 137, 138–39

Trunk-lines. *See* Railroads

Tryon, Rolla Milton, 121

U.S. Bureau of Labor: budget study of, 35, 64

U.S. Corps of Engineers, 98

U.S. Department of Agriculture: estimates of wheat production, 33; on inventories, 34; method of computing disappearance estimates, 35, 62; study of wagon transportation, 56, 68, 71–72, 77–78, 107, 219; studies of country roads, 107, 108–9

U.S. Department of Commerce: reports on wholesale grocery territories, 31–32

U.S. Treasury Department, 32, 34, 36

Wages, 72, and n, 187n

Wagon transportation: importance of, 51, 75, 212; exaggerated by estimate α, 52; method of estimating average distance of, 57, 68, 73, 77–78, 84 and n, 85, 89; neglected by historians, 109. *See also* Distances; Rates, freight; Social saving

Water transportation: share in freight movements, 4–5, 49, 50; circuity of, 24, 40*n*; indirect costs of, 41–47, 85–92, 210–11, 214; speed of boats, 44–45*n*, 89; capital costs of, 46, 87–88, 92, 210, 214; influence on railroad rates. 49; length of navigable waterways, 51; and waterways in use, 79*n*, 250, 251–52; season of, 90–91; in South, 91; U.S. situation with respect to, 226. *See also* Canals; Distances; Rates, freight; Social saving; under names of waterways

Watt, James, 236
Wells, David A., 244, 245
Wheat: consumption of, 17–18, 32–35, 33*n*, 90*n*; exports of, 18–34; supply of, 18*n*, 33–34; products of, 29*n*; shipments of, 30, 31, 39, 40, 41; inventories of, 34, 35, 89–90, 90*n*. *See also* Conversion ratios; Distribution of agricultural surpluses; Inventories; Price(s); Rates, freight
Wicker, E. R., 169
Wool, 26, 126, 128–29
Wright, Chester W., 9